Religious Pluralism and Religious Education

Contributors

Norma H. Thompson

Gabriel Moran

James Michael Lee

David Ng

Grant S. Shockley

William Clemmons

Constance J. Tarasar

Sherry H. Blumberg

Eugene B. Borowitz

Abdullah Muhammad Khouj

Young Bong Oh

Sun Young Park

Swami Tathagatananda

Religious Pluralism and Religious Education

Edited by

Norma H. Thompson

Religious Education Press
Birmingham, Alabama

Library of Congress Cataloging-in-Publication Data

Religious pluralism and religious education/edited by Norma H. Thompson

  ISBN 0-89135-061-6
  1. Religious education. 2. Religious pluralism. I. Thompson, Norma H.
BL42.R45 1988
291.7—dc19   88-5394
                                                  CIP

Religious Education Press, Inc.
5316 Meadow Brook Road
Birmingham, Alabama 35243
10 9 8 7 6 5 4 3 2

Religious Education Press publishes books exclusively in religious education and in areas closely related to religious education. It is committed to enhancing and professionalizing religious education through the publication of serious, significant, and scholarly works.

PUBLISHER TO THE PROFESSION

Contents

Preface

Most of my professional life has been spent in situations involving more than one denomination or religion. I began my work in religious education supervising weekday and vacation church schools for the Federation of Churches of Greater New York (the forerunner of the Protestant Council of the City of New York and now the Council of Churches of the City of New York). Traveling to churches throughout the boroughs of Manhattan, Bronx, and Staten Island—churches of many denominations, several ethnic backgrounds, and diverse social and economic conditions—I found my life enriched by these contacts and my mind expanded by the traditions which each represented.

Union Theological Seminary in New York, which I attended in those days, was also interdenominational, and international as well. For one year I worked in a local congregation, Fifth Avenue Presbyterian Church, hardly a typical congregation but it introduced me to a different membership from any previous experience and helped me to begin to understand the problems of ministering to the affluent.

Seven years as the executive for the Bronx Division of the Protestant Council of the City of New York enabled me to become rather deeply involved with a wide variety of churches and members of those churches. Then I joined the faculty of the Department of Religious Education at New York University, where I spent the last twenty-nine years of my career as a professor of religious education. At New York University my horizons were expanded beyond the Christian circle, and

1

particularly beyond Protestant Christian circles. In my undergraduate classes were Christians of many persuasions—Protestants, Roman Catholics, Christian Scientists, Mormons, Jehovah's Witnesses, among others. There were Jews, and an occasional Hindu, or Buddhist, and there were agnostics and atheists.

All of these students stretched my mind even further, and working with graduate students on an individual basis as they have pursued doctoral degrees has taught me more than can ever be expressed. Among these students were Japanese Christians and Buddhists, Thai Buddhists, Korean Christians and Buddhists, Taiwanese Christians, a Hindu from India, Christians from several African nations (Kenya, Nigeria, Zimbabwe, and Tanzania, at least). There were Orthodox, Conservative, and Reform Jews; Protestants from many denominations from conservative to liberal; Orthodox Church of America leaders; and after Vatican II a good many Roman Catholic priests, sisters, and brothers. I think I have not begun to portray the diversity of these students. They were clergy, religious, workers in diocesan, denominational, and interdenominational offices, curriculum writers, high-school, college, university, and seminary teachers, missionaries, public and private school teachers, directors of religious education in local parishes, and almost any position which a person trained in or training for a vocation in the field of religion might hold.

This personal background has been presented to show that the subject of religious pluralism is a concern of long-standing. For years I have wondered what the commonalities in religious education are which would form a framework on which all of these groups could build. Is there a religious education theory and practice that might be applicable to Jewish education, Muslim education, Buddhist education, Hindu education, Christian education, and all the others? If so, what are the distinctive elements which make it "religious" education? In order to pursue some discussion and thinking on the part of religious educators, this book was designed. Fortunately, it is a concern of the publisher, James Michael Lee, as well. In order to attain a wide spread of approaches and perspectives, representatives from many of the religious groups mentioned above were needed, but still many religions are not represented here. Within religions, only one or two viewpoints could be presented, or the book would have become voluminous. I extend my apologies to those groups and sub-groups which do not have adequate representation here, but I sincerely hope this book will be only a beginning of interchange of many perspectives on religious pluralism and religious education.

Although the writers of these chapters represent some of the major religions or denominations in our culture, they were told they might write from their own perspective or they might present the approach of their group, as a representative of that group in a sense. Some writers have pursued this latter course (in particular, Abdullah Muhammad Khouj for Muslim education and Young Bong Oh and Sun Young Park for Buddhist education), though these perspectives represent their own views as well. Chapter 1 introduces some of the issues involved in relating religious education to religious pluralism. Chapters 2 and 3 present two approaches to the subject by Roman Catholic religious educators. Gabriel Moran examines historically pluralism and Catholicism and pluralism in the United States; then he discusses the British experience of religious pluralism and religious education, compares that experience with that of the U.S.A., and makes some suggestions of direction for the future. As would be expected he grapples with the language used in all of these experiences. James Michael Lee looks at religious pluralism and religious education from the social-science approach and in this chapter fills another gap in his theoretical structure of a social-science approach to religious instruction. As background he also examines terminology and the necessity for religious pluralism and basic principles involved.

Chapters 4, 5, and 6 present three Protestant perspectives: David Ng from the perspective of a mainline Protestant denomination, the Presbyterian Church in the U.S.A., but also as an Asian American and a person who has spent several years as an executive in an interdenominational organization; Grant S. Shockley from the perspective of the black experience, but again as a Methodist and as a religious educator who has been president of an interdenominational theological seminary; and William Clemmons, a Southern Baptist, a professor in one of the theological seminaries of that denomination at the present time and a person who is struggling with the pluralism within that communion, a pluralism which erupts from time to time in such an intense fashion that the media give it wide coverage. David Ng writes out of his own experiences and then discusses the tasks of religious education in a pluralistic society. Grant Shockley discusses two basic issues: 1) The significance of pluralism for religion, theology, and religious education in Protestantism as it faces a religiously, culturally, and racially diverse society. 2) The significance of pluralism for the black experience, black theology, and religious education in the black church, community, nation, and world. William Clemmons traces the history of Southern Baptists from its beginnings through the challenges of pluralism within its ranks, as well as outside, and relates these to the effects of pluralism on Christian education—racial pluralism, cultural pluralism, and theological pluralism.

In chapter 7, Constance Tarasar writes as a person who has been deeply involved in the Orthodox Church in America, both as a member and as an administrator and theological professor. She looks at the subject of religious education and religious pluralism from the perspective of a minority group among the Christian majority in our pluralistic society and discusses the tasks for Christian education in that context.

For chapter 8, Sherry Blumberg and Eugene Borowitz cooperated to present a chapter on Judaism from the perspective of Reform Jews. Unfortunately, the parameters of this volume allowed for representation by only one Jewish group. Approaches of Orthodox, Conservative, and Reconstructionist Jewish educators are very much needed. Blumberg and Borowitz are conscious that they do not speak for all of Judaism and also see themselves as members of a minority group. They discuss the particular Jewish context of the problems of pluralism, which is not at all a modern phenomenon. Then they turn to relating this particular context to such practical problems of Jewish education as content, the learner, the teacher, and the school.

Abdullah Muhammad Khouj, an educational psychologist and the director of the Islamic Center in Washington, D.C., presents in chapter 9 an overall picture of Islamic education. To my knowledge this is the first time such a description in English has been made available to the religious education community in the Western world. He states that the educational system of Islam derives from the Qur'an, the Muslim's revealed scripture, and proceeds to set forth the objectives, including the relationships of human beings with Allah, themselves, other persons, society, and the environment; the knowledge that is beneficial to human beings; the characteristics of the educational system in Islam; and the methods by which that system can be implemented. The relation of Islamic education to religious pluralism is integrated throughout the discussion and explanation of these aspects.

In chapter 10, Young Bong Oh and Sun Young Park coordinated their writing across the Pacific Ocean (Oh in New York and Park in Seoul, Korea) to describe Buddhist education. As with Islamic education, I believe this is the first such description in English published in a form in which it can be widely available to leaders in religion and religious education. It covers the goals of Buddhist education, the ideals, and the possibility for realizing these ideals. The chapter concludes by relating Buddhism and Buddhist education to religious pluralism as it is known in the world today.

Chapter 11 presents a Hindu perspective on religious education and religious pluralism. Swami Tathagatananda explains the philosophy and concepts of Hinduism and how it is transmitted from one generation to the next. Since Hinduism, like Buddhism, believes in prenatal learning, emphasis is placed on the mother and the family, but the Swami also develops the model of illumined saints and sages, both in the history of Hinduism and in modern times. Shri Ramakrishna, Swami Vivekananda, and Gandhi are selected among modern examples of leaders whose lives and teachings articulated a "message of peace, goodwill, and the spirit of accommodation."

Finally, chapter 12 attempts to pull together some of these strands and suggest some directions for the future. What implications can be drawn from the various discussions of the meaning of pluralism? What commonalities exist among the minority groups, if any? Are the experiences of ethnic minorities, of blacks, of women, of Jews, of the religions which we call "others," of such a group as the Orthodox Christian different enough that no overall patterns can be discerned? If a denomination is torn by pluralism within its own ranks, is it still possible, and perhaps necessary, for the members of that denomination to relate to religions outside that group? What model for religious education theory and practice begins to emerge from these essays, or do we find no model emerging as satisfactory for many of these groups? It would be presumptuous, of course, to believe that answers to all of these questions can be found in such a preliminary set of essays, so what the final chapter actually does is to discuss the problems and issues from the stance of examining the entire set, in the hope that the volume will provide a foundation for discussion and classroom teaching that may move the field of religious education forward in respect to religious pluralism.

NORMA H. THOMPSON
Professor Emerita
New York University

1

The Challenge of Religious Pluralism

Norma II. Thompson

"Muslims constitute a major group of 'the new Americans' whose growing numbers are altering the patterns of the American ethnic and religious mosaic."[1] These words, taken from a letter from the National Conference of Christians and Jews in New York, inviting people of various religions to a meeting on "Our Neighbors: the Muslims," exhibit graphically the increasing religious pluralism in the United States of America. The letter further notes that in September, 1986, on Lexington Avenue, New York, there took place the first United American Muslim's Day Parade; the Ecumenical Commission of the Roman Catholic Archdiocese of New York had a dialogue program with Muslims; and the Islamic Society of North America was unanimously granted "observer status by the Governing Board of the National Council of Churches." It is reported that there are eight million Muslims in the United States, with about 250,000 in the New York area[2] and approximately 250,000 in the Chicago area.

Although the Muslims are among the newest groups of people representing less common religions in the U.S.A., they are not by any means

---

1. From a letter from Margaret Gilmore, executive director, Greater New York Region, National Conference of Christians and Jews and Jack Price, director, Manhattan Chapter, to Intergroup Relations Agency Executives, undated, announcing a Breakfast Meeting for Thursday, December 11, 1986.

2. Charles W. Bell, "Moslem Bid Is Plea for Recognition," *Daily News,* Religion Section (August 31, 1985).

the only such group. For example, the population in the borough of
Queens in New York City has radically changed in the past twenty-five
years. At the present time there are substantial numbers of Hindus and
Sikhs[3] from India, and Buddhists from Korea, Japan, China, Vietnam,
Hong Kong, Taiwan, and Thailand; in addition, there are persons from
many nations and cultures, including Egyptians, Ethiopians, Ruma-
nians, Pakistanis, and Iranians, as well as Hispanics, West Indian and
American blacks, and Asians from other countries not mentioned
above. As one travels across the United States, it is common to find
families from other cultures in many small towns, to say nothing of the
numbers who live in the cities, small cities as well as large. A good
example of the cultural pluralism in the U.S.A. can be found in a
kindergarten class at the First Baptist Church of Los Angeles, the members of which currently include children from Korea, Mexico, El Salva-
dor, the Philippines, and the U.S.A.,[4] and it is probable that this mix of
peoples will become more common. "Demographers predict that by
2010 immigrants and ethnic minorities will make up a large portion of
the total population of the U.S.," says Ernestine Galloway of the Board
of National Ministries of the American Baptist Churches.[5]

Of course, the greatest mixtures of cultures are in the major cities,
such as San Francisco, Los Angeles, Chicago, New York, Miami, and
Houston, but the impact of recent immigration is to be felt in almost
every residential area in the country. *The New York Times* reported in
May of this year that there are "about 29 million blacks, 17 million
Hispanic Americans, 6 million Jews, and 2.5 million people of Arab
descent in the United States population of 239 million as of 1985."[6]
These figures do not include Asians, Africans, and many others.
Though they deal with cultures rather than religions, one recognizes
that each culture represents several, and sometimes many religions,
even though one religion may be the dominant one.

There is some evidence that religious leaders in the U.S.A. are beginning to take seriously this influx of immigrants and the impact of many

---

3. In an article in *The New York Times* (May 15, 1987, p. B6) it was stated
that "about 5,000 Sikhs, who are readily identifiable by their turbans and whose
stronghold is in the Punjab in India, live in the New York area, at least half of
them in Queens."

4. H. James Hopkins, "An Intercultural Adventure," *APCE Advocate* (May,
1987), p. 3.

5. Ernestine R. Galloway, "A Conversation: In Search of Leadership," *The
Baptist Leader* (July/August, 1987), p. 47.

6. *The New York Times*, "High Court Holds 1866 Race-Bias Law Is a Broader
Tool" (May 19, 1987).

cultures on society; it is only a beginning. The British have taken measures to include Hindus, Buddhists, and Jews, as well as Christians in their system of teaching religion in the schools, but there appears to be little indication that the churches, synagogues, and temples see a responsibility to participate in this educational process. For the most part, education in religion is seen as a function of the schools.

The significance of this movement of peoples is often lost on the ordinary individual in the Western world as he or she goes about the daily affairs of living. Persons involved in international affairs seem usually more aware of the issues which arise from such immigration. One sees this awareness in the missionary journals, for instance. Wilbert R. Shenk, in commenting in the *International Bulletin of Missionary Research,* calls attention to this movement and points up something of its importance for our day.

> With unceasing restlessness the peoples of the world continue to move from ancestral homes to take up residence in alien climes and cultures. They migrate with their traditions and cultures largely intact. Particularly in the West an intermingling of cultures and religions is occurring on a scale no one could have foreseen a generation ago. Western societies that traditionally thought of themselves as Christian, with possibly a Jewish minority, today have become pluralistic. This is affecting how we carry on public discourse, interpret laws, teach religious and moral issues in public schools, and so forth.[7]

He believes that for Christians this is the central theological issue today and asks the question: "What impact should this new fact have on how Christians understand and speak about Jesus Christ?"

Not only for Christians is the fact of religious pluralism raising both theoretical and practical questions, but for other faiths as well. Hardly any other experience causes persons to examine their presuppositions and beliefs, as well as their ways of worship, as does living with persons of other faiths as neighbors and attempting to communicate with them over the matters of daily life. One culture facing the theological and practical issues related to a religiously pluralistic society is the Muslims in Indonesia, where they are being forced to rethink fundamental Islamic concepts of church and state because of new laws which prohibit sectarian political parties. "Some of the most modern Islamic thinking is being done in Indonesia," Abdurrahman Wahid is reported to have

---

7. Wilbert R. Shenk in a review of S. Mark Heim, *Is Christ the Only Way? Christian Faith in a Pluralistic World* (Valley Forge, Pa.: Judson Press, 1985), in *International Bulletin of Missionary Research* 11:2 (April, 1987).

said. He serves as chair for the Nahdlatul Ulama, which functions as a national council of scholars and religious leaders. Islamic intellectuals in Indonesia are debating "not only the Islamic tenet that there can be no division between religious and civil authority, but also cultural, social, and economic issues and attitudes toward ecumenism and 'interfaith activities.' " Wahid is said to have added: "Our mullahs are preparing people to accept change, to give citizens the theological basis for change."[8]

THE MEANING OF RELIGIOUS PLURALISM

Perhaps a look at what is meant by religious pluralism is in order at this point. The term, pluralism, is used to cover many aspects of a society—ethnic groupings, political ideologies, economic theories, sexes, religious groups, and even, as found in some books and articles in religious educational literature, a variety of methodological techniques, teachers, students, and philosophies of education. John Westerhoff editorializes that "pluralism, a social order founded upon the principle of harmonious interaction, for common ends, among various distinct communities, each of which possesses both identity and openness, has plagued the history of education on this continent."[9] He believes that "true pluralism is a utopian vision frustrated by continual threat." It calls for both identity and openness.

In the religious arena there has rarely been openness, and there has usually been great concern for identity, but this identity has been sought under threat. The question is whether religious groups can come to a joining of these two characteristics into a true pluralism. If so, what is involved in this joining?

Martin Marty suggests that pluralism can mean three things: 1) "It can grow simply out of the empirical reality, the given situation, the morning news." By this he means that when we look at Western culture there are many groups of various kinds, and he illustrates with religious groups—at least 440—to which must be added the number of sects, cults, causes, and cells; "And you look out on a nation in which there are a great number of religious realities." 2) Pluralism can mean "political resolution, the polity which allows a people to have civic peace." For

---

8. *The New York Times,* "In Indonesia, The Moslems Are Changing" (February 5, 1987, p. A13).

9. John H. Westerhoff III, editorial, *Religious Education* 74:4 (July-August, 1979), p. 338.

example, in the U.S.A. we "have agreed that any and all religious groups, as long as they keep to certain general norms and standards of the society—a society that has the broadest norms ever known—are fully welcome; there is not to be a privileged group; there are not to be liabilities against those who keep the civic peace." 3) Pluralism can mean "philosophical pluralism." Here Marty is talking about whether people view reality as cohesive with a single center, or it is in some way plural. He cites William James' division between pluralists and monists; that is:

> For many people, and for most religious people, in the end the universe coheres; it comes out of a single center. God, the Unum, the One, the All, the Center. But James in his work on a pluralistic universe was pointing to the fact that there is another philosophical tradition, and a strong one, which says that in the end, reality is plural, and we should come to terms with it and relish it.

For Marty, the third form of pluralism is not usually found among religious educators, so what we are dealing with is the fact that there are "many groups educating, and we recognize that many groups doing education have to find ways to learn to live with each other." For them, he says, "We need to renew a pluralistic vision."[10]

Another term often used in connection with efforts to cooperate as religious groups is *ecumenism*. In his report on the World Institute on Christian Education at Nairobi, Kenya, in July, 1967, C. Ellis Nelson included the question, "Is total ecumenism possible?" as one of the issues which was discussed at the conference. He noted that "in the present climate of opinion there is a demand for expanding the word 'ecumenical' to include secular agencies; and, indeed, officials of the UN and other nonreligious groups have become important sources of help to the churches in their educational work. Such 'world' ecumenism is on the increase."[11] Not only have nonreligious groups begun to identify with the word *ecumenical,* but the term is being used to relate to non-Christian groups where there is a cooperative effort across Christian and Jewish lines, or in Muslim-Jewish-Christian relations.

When Mohammed Mehdi, Secretary-General of the National Council on Islamic Affairs, recently requested that the National Conference

---

10. Martin Marty, "This We Can Believe: A Pluralistic Vision" *Religious Education* 75:1 (January-February, 1980), pp. 37-38.

11. C. Ellis Nelson, *Issues in Christian Education* (Geneva, Switzerland: World Council of Christian Education, 1968), p. 6.

of Christians and Jews change its name to the National Conference of Christians, Jews, and Muslims, he said, among other statements, "Our concern is purely religious, dealing with spiritual questions that affect the human race. We want to play our part in the ecumenical growth of the United States."[12] Such statements give the impression that the term ecumenical is gradually being used by leaders of other religions than Christianity. In his book, *Design for Religion,* Gabriel Moran proposed an "ecumenical curriculum," a course for education in religion from birth to grave. Although his diagram for and discussion of this curriculum showed how Christianity fit into a broader framework of education in religion, he recognized that a Christian was constructing the curriculum and that he had certain presuppositions. However, he believed that it could become a basis for discussion at least for leaders of other religious groups, even though it might not be accepted as being "ecumenically perfect."[13]

Still, the history of this term has been so involved with the Christian religion, and in modern times with the Protestant drawing together of groups across denominational lines (as in the National Council of the Churches of Christ in the U.S.A.) and from various nations of the world (especially in the World Council of Churches), that one wonders whether or not it is possible for it to become a useful term to describe what is needed when not only Jews, Christians, and Muslims face each other in cooperation and dialogue but also Hindus, Buddhists, Confucians, Taoists, Sikhs, and many others. Will it be adequate when these people live in the same neighborhood, go to work daily on the same transportation systems, work together in offices and factories, and find recreation in the same facilities? It seems, then, that *pluralism* is perhaps a better term for designating this phenomenon, and indeed current literature and the media seem to be making the term a common one.

However, the concern demonstrated thus far in the literature and the media is for cultural pluralism, a broader term involving ethnic diversity, social, economic, and political pluralism, as well as religious pluralism. It is the diversity of religions about which this book is concerned, realizing that there are usually one or a few religions within any culture which stand numerically in the majority, while all the others have minority status with its attendant problems. Some religions will be new in a culture, having been recently formed, either as a reformation of an

---

12. Charles W. Bell, "Moslem Bid Is Plea for Recognition," *Daily News,* Religion Section (August 31, 1986).

13. Gabriel Moran, *Design for Religion* (New York: Herder and Herder, 1971). See chapter 4, "An Ecumenical Framework," particularly pp. 90-95.

existing religion or as a new religion not readily associated with any existing group. These new religions find different problems as they attempt to survive and grow in a religiously pluralistic society. There will be religions which have moved from what sociologists of religion have called "sects" to "churches,"[14] in many instances persecuted as new fledgling religious groups and moving slowly to an accepted state in the social situation and sometimes becoming the status denomination in the society. All of these religious groups are embodied in the term, religious pluralism.

THE CONCERN OF EDUCATORS FOR RELIGIOUS PLURALISM

By and large, religious educators, though becoming aware of cultural pluralism, have not faced the issues and problems of that pluralism as it pertains to the varied religious backgrounds of the ethnic and national groups which have immigrated to the Western world. Usually discussions in the literature center around the broader considerations of ethnic and cultural differences rather than the problems related to religious pluralism. However, the scholars and leaders who have addressed the subject of cultural pluralism and religious education, and those who are exploring the possible broadening of the term *ecumenism,* have provided a foundation on which theoretical and practical issues can be explored.

Some of these foundational statements were developed by the Joint Educational Development, a consortium of Protestant denominations cooperating for religious educational purposes, among which was the development of curriculum resources, especially "Christian Education: Shared Approaches." One paper prepared by the Task Force on Guidelines to Alleviate Stereotyping is entitled, "Liberating Words, Images, and Actions."[15] The thrust of this paper is to reaffirm commitment to religious education as "a means of helping persons achieve full humanness." To do this, stereotypes of age, race, sex, and ethnic background must be avoided. While this paper specifically discusses anti-Semitism

---

14. See Ernst Troeltsch, *The Social Teaching of the Christian Churches,* trans. Olive Wyon (London: Allen & Unwin, 1931, 2 Vols.); H. Richard Niebuhr, *The Social Sources of Denominationalism* (Hamden, Conn.: The Shoe String Press, 1954).

15. Edward A. Powers, chairperson, Task Force on Guidelines to Alleviate Stereotyping, Joint Educational Development (JED), "Liberating Words, Images, and Actions."

and the stereotypes which accompany it, the principles developed are useful for any religion. Unfortunately, the trend in the United States toward the use of stereotypes for Arabs, most of whom are Muslims, seems to be growing. The "Guidelines" state: "The approach to life and people requires authentic portrayal of human beings, and of the human situation in its cultural settings. Thus, cultural accuracy and full-blown humanity must be sought in such portrayal."[16]

Further, some denominations have recently passed resolutions or developed statements committing themselves to multicultural education. The General Assembly of the Christian Church (Disciples of Christ) is an example of this trend. In 1985 it passed a resolution that stated that "the human family is a multicultural, multiethnic people created in the image of God—forming a pluralistic world through which to proclaim and demonstrate the divine will," and, therefore, the Assembly affirmed a "multicultural educational ministry."[17]

At the General Assembly of the Presbyterian Church (U.S.A.) held in June, 1987, the delegates voted to adopt two papers setting out guidelines for relations with other religious groups: one on relations between Christians and Jews, and one on relations between Christians and Muslims. The paper on Islam noted the vigorous revival, "a significant fact in our world today," and stressed that Christian perceptions of this revival are often "distorted by ignorance and prejudice."[18] These statements by the governing body of this denomination will no doubt be influential among the members of the educational staff and by many of the leaders in the churches. A "Study Guide" is being developed for the use of educators as they deal with the misconceptions and stereotypes both in the literature of the denomination and in the minds of its members.

The National Catechetical Directory for Catholics of the United States, *Sharing the Light of Faith,*[19] included a section on relating the educational work to other religions; The Association of Presbyterian Church Educators devoted the May, 1987, issue of the *APCE Advocate* to "Christian Education in a Multi-Cultural Society";[20] and the *Baptist*

16. Ibid., "Guidelines to Avoid Ageism, Anti-Semitism, Racism, and Sexism in CE:SA and other JED Projects."

17. Christian Board of Publication, Division of Homeland Ministries, General Assembly of the Christian Church (Disciples of Christ) meeting in Des Moines, Iowa, August 27, 1985.

18. *The New York Times,* "Presbyterians Denounce Anti-Moslem Views" (June 18, 1987).

19. United States Catholic Conference, *Sharing the Light of Faith: National Catechetical Directory for Catholics of the United States* (1979), pp. 42-46.

20. The Association of Presbyterian Church Educators, *APCE Advocate,* (May, 1987).

Leader, magazine of the American Baptist Churches, USA, has carried articles on multicultural education.

A Multicultural Resources Center has been developed at Scarritt Graduate School under the direction of Charles R. Foster. In 1985, a consultation was sponsored by Scarritt with the intent "to make more visible the variety of cultural assumptions at work in the church's religious education."[21] This consultation resulted in a book edited by Foster entitled, *Ethnicity in the Education of the Church.*[22] Contributions describe the religious experience of Pacific Asian Americans, blacks in the U.S.A., Anglos, and Mexican Americans. The problems in intercultural education, even when limited to the Christian setting, surfaced immediately.

It is obvious from these resources and research efforts that cultural pluralism is used as a point of entry into the relation with religious education. Very little journal literature deals with religious pluralism as only one aspect of this larger picture.

A full historical overview of the relation of cultural pluralism and religious education as revealed in the literature over the past eighty-five years (essentially from the time of the founding of the Religious Education Association in 1903 to the present time) would be most helpful; however, such a history is not possible in a work with the purpose of this volume. Nevertheless, a brief survey of a few writers and the problems and issues which they discuss may prove valuable.

In 1979, Kendig B. Cully edited a book entitled, *Does the Church Know How to Teach? An Ecumenical Inquiry.*[23] It is easy to overlook the significance of this work when one notices only the first part of the title. But when one examines the second section of the title, "An Ecumenical Inquiry," one realizes that the entire work is intended as a thrust into the nature of religious education from the perspectives of more than one religion. In this book, though, the inquiry appears to cover the mainline Protestant denominations and the Roman Catholic Church only. Nevertheless, it represents a movement and a recognition of issues and concerns that the two groups have in common. The religious education leaders explored the educational implications of the Catholic-Protestant dialogue and, according to Cully, "the advent of the ecumenical age calls for an educational approach that will condition church people to react ecumenically, just as in earlier days they were conditioned to react

---

21. See Charles R. Foster, *Ethnicity in the Education of the Church* (Nashville: Scarritt Press, 1987), p. 2.

22. Ibid.

23. Kendig B. Cully, ed., *Does the Church Know How to Teach? An Ecumenical Inquiry* (London: Macmillan, 1970).

confessionally."[24] Cully included in his presentation the "Dialogue with Non-believers" issued by the Vatican Secretariat for Non-believers in October, 1968. This document briefly addresses persons of atheistic orientation, as well as those who belong to the non-Christian religions, especially Jews and Muslims, but the thrust of the dialogue is with other Christians.

As early as 1964 Solomon Bernards recognized the increasing presence of non-Christians in American society. At a conference on theological education for a pluralistic society sponsored by the National Conference of Christians and Jews and the Indiana School of Religion, he stated:

> America of 1964 is quite different from that of the eighteenth and nineteenth centuries. From a predominantly Protestant, white Anglo-Saxon community, we have changed into a country with a many-hued religious, ethnic, and cultural background. There is a strong, articulate Catholic group; there is a substantial Jewish community; there are numbers of groups who adhere to Buddhism, Confucianism, and other oriental faiths, and there are many shadings of non-belief from agnosticism to atheism.[25]

Bernards called for a beginning effort to address the pluralism in our midst, to "begin to understand our problems of living with each other's faiths, preconceptions, positions and interpretations in a new light." He beseeched: "Let us stop pushing each other around; let us cease the name-calling; let us call a halt to the setting up of straw men which we can knock down." But he applied his comments specifically to political rather than to educational issues, though these are inherent in his broader statements:

> Holding to our principles and beliefs, adhering to our own perspectives, let us think through together our common problems—in the area of church and state, for an example—at the same time that we recognize, accept, and support our respective rights and responsibilities under our Constitution, as the United States Supreme Court

---

24. Ibid., p. 344.
25. Lecture presented at a conference on theological education for a pluralistic society sponsored by the National Conference of Christians and Jews and the Indiana School of Religion, February 28-29, 1964. Reprinted from *Encounter,* (1964), p. 1.

interprets it, and as our executive and legislative arms of government try to conform to those interpretations.[26]

A review of the journal *Religious Education* over the past ten years reveals some articles dealing with religious education and religious pluralism. One noticeable concern is the importance of including articles by Jewish, Roman Catholic, and Protestant religious educators addressing the issues of education in their own religious groups, as well as their attitudes toward and practical approaches to problems within the society and common to all faiths—matters of prejudice, discrimination, social justice, and inclusive language. Some examples of these concerns can be seen in such articles as the following.

The September/October 1979 issue, devoted to the theme, "Unheard Voices and Justice," examined the issue from the perspectives of Jews, the Hispanics in the U.S.A., women, black Americans, evangelicals, the Third World, and China, among others. These perspectives represent a mixture of ethnic and religious experiences, and they show a need to look at the issues of interest to religious education from the pluralistic standpoints of the world.[27]

In a symposium on "Curriculum in Religious Education," the writers discussed curriculum from the view of Roman Catholicism, Protestantism (mainline and evangelical Protestantism), Judaism, a Caribbean culture, and Appalachia, while an article on generative words (according to Paulo Freire, the words people use to name their world) covered six diverse cultures.[28]

Themes developed in issues of the journal have included "Jewish-Christian Dialogue"; "Women and Religious Education"; "Inclusive Language"; and "Issues in Jewish and Christian Education." It is evident from a perusal of these articles that the major concern with respect to religious pluralism is the relation between Christians and Jews, a natural first effort in light of the visibility of the Jewish population in the United States, the common history of the two groups, and the tensions and persecutions which have existed over the centuries.

One entire issue of the journal was devoted to "Religious Education in a Pluralistic Society."[29] Again, in this issue the approach is for the most part cross-cultural in the broad sense, rather than focusing on the

---

26. Ibid.

27. See *Religious Education* 74:5 (September-October, 1979).

28. Symposium, "Curriculum in Religious Education," *Religious Education,* 75:5 (September-October, 1980).

29. Gabriel Moran, "The American Experience," in *Religious Education* 76:3 (May-June, 1981), pp. 243-257.

diverse religious groups that make up our society. In the lead article, Moran calls attention to our use of the term "America" to refer to the United States of America, whereas the U.S.A. is only one part of the Americas. "The two American continents are four and a half times the size of the United States."[30] He goes on to contrast this usage to the frequent use of the word to refer to the idea or the dream called "America."

Other articles in this same issue are concerned with a bicultural approach (Hispanic-Americans, in particular Mexican-Americans) to religious education; families in a cross-cultural setting (native Americans—Pueblos, Spanish-descent Americans, and Anglo-Americans); the challenge of rational dialogue for religious education in relation to "the plight of the poor, the oppressed, and the alienated among the peoples of the world"; pluralism in five areas of the Christian school (teacher training, students, the curriculum, finances, and philosophy of education); the role of faith in the schools of a pluralistic society; and "an examination of teacher commitment, that is, given our multicultural world, whether pupils should even be exposed to the teacher's own ideological stance."[31]

As one peruses this journal, one occasionally discovers an article on pluralism related to a different theme. Such an article is Martin Marty's discussion of "This We Can Believe: A Pluralistic Vision,"[32] in which he tackles the question of content in religious education. Is content one of the aspects where pluralism can operate? Marty says that, "As far as substance or content of religious education and the method which is integrally connected with the substance or content are concerned, we *do* agree and probably *will* agree on far too little to make it the constitutive basis of the enterprise, the vocation, or the profession."[33] Yet he goes on to explore levels of consensus or convergence in historical groups and periods—the founding of the Religious Education Association, for example.

These articles in the major interfaith professional journal in the field of religious education are indicative of the growing literature in cultural pluralism and the lack of literature on religious pluralism. Because this journal is intentionally interfaith, it carries more articles with a broad perspective than do most of the journals and magazines which are issued by denominations or other religious groups. However, recent denominational magazines are showing this same trend.

---

30. Ibid., p. 243.
31. *Religious Education* 76:3 (May-June, 1981).
32. *Religious Education* 75:1 (January-February, 1980), pp. 37-49.
33. Ibid., p. 41.

THE ISSUES PLURALISM RAISES FOR
RELIGIOUS EDUCATION

Given the complexities of religious pluralism in the Western world, and given the need to find ways to live together in peace, to say nothing of cooperating in special projects or in building a just government, what are the problems which must be faced? What issues must be resolved in seeking the pluralistic vision which Marty dreams of? The limitations of time and space mean that we can examine only the role of religious education in this vision, as needful as other dimensions such as the political, the economic, the military, and the philosophical/ideological may be.

Questions that come readily to mind include the relation of religious pluralism to such aspects of religious education as: 1) Objectives, or purposes; 2) Theology, philosophy, or ideology; 3) Context; 4) Content; 5) Methodology; 6) Curriculum theory; and 7) Worship, or liturgy. Each of these aspects is worthy of lengthy consideration, but it is impossible to cover them all even briefly in this chapter. Therefore, only the first four aspects will be discussed here, with the hope that the questions and insights presented may stimulate thinking on both these aspects and the ones not discussed. There is some overlapping, of course, because one cannot deal with these factors in isolation.

OBJECTIVES AND RELIGIOUS PLURALISM

A crucial question for religious education is: "What is it all about?" In fact, much of the failure of religious education arises from the confusion in the minds of most of the practitioners in this field about what they are doing, and why they are doing it. They have a lot of commitment and want to help in the educational task, but their objectives are rarely clear. Neither are the objectives of the leaders in local churches and temples clear, even when the focus is upon transmitting the heritage of the particular religion. How much more confusing and complicated must the objectives become when these persons are faced with relating what they are doing in one religious group to what is being done by their counterparts in many other religious groups. Add to this the conviction that education is more than transmitting a heritage; it is learning, living, and growing within a community which must relate to larger and larger communities until it encompasses the entire world. It is little wonder that the broader task of educating in religion is neglected or left primarily for the colleges, seminaries, and universities, while the local parishes, congregations, and temples are content to focus upon their own scriptures, liturgies, and values.

The question for this volume, then, is whether or not the purposes of a local religious group, a denomination, or a faith group are affected by attempts to come to grips with the existence within a culture of other religious groups beside their own. If affected, is the purpose to create respect, some knowledge and understanding, and cooperation? Is it to maintain a peaceful community where religious groups live together in some harmony? Is it to teach and act in such a way that members of other groups will see the superiority of one's own religion and be converted? Surely respect, understanding, and mutual cooperation are vital concerns for any religious grouping, but understanding, in particular, often calls for a deeper knowledge and probing of one's own religious concepts than is commonly thought. One does not long continue as a member of a Jewish-Christian dialogue group without realizing that the issues are more profound and agonizing than respecting one another and working together. Some of these issues which arise almost immediately for Christians include: What is the status of Judaism since the beginning of Christianity? How does one regard the covenant, or covenants? What are the roles of love and the law in Judaism and in Christianity? Is it necessary to reexamine the New Testament scriptures to arrive at an adequate understanding of Judaism? Is it necessary to take a fresh look at one's Christology?

For Jews in such a dialogue some of the issues include: How should Jews regard Christians in the light of centuries of persecution? How does one show Judaism as a religion of love and not solely of law? What attitude should Jews take to the Christian scriptures (New Testament)? Toward Jesus?

Although the fact that Jews and Christians share the Hebrew scriptures in common (thus having a common history during that period) makes these questions more obvious for religious education between Jews and Christians than with some other religions, still equally important issues will be found as one studies in depth any religion. The matter of a personal God, for instance, raises the question of what sort of God language can be used in dialogue with members of religious groups who do not hold to such a God. The tendency is to lump together the God of Judaism, Christianity, and Islam with the Ultimate (Brahma) of Hinduism and to fuse into Buddhism something similar. Although philosophically there is no personal God in some of these religions, still there are images of gods and goddesses in the local temples, which are symbols of aspects of the Ultimate, or the One. How should Jews, Muslims, and Christians interpret those images, then, and how should members of those religions interpret references to the Trinity, or the Holy Spirit, in Christianity? What is the difference between the Holy Spirit and the spirits of the river, the trees, the mountains, and other natural phenomena in many traditional religions? In some countries these spirits have assumed important positions in the dominant religions, as well as forming the basis for the traditional religions of the people.

As noted above, the fact is that most religious educators, clergy and lay, have conceived their objective to be transmitting of a particular religious heritage, often including a conversion experience. This has meant that the emphasis has been upon the scriptural and liturgical materials, and upon the lifestyle approved by the group. Often it has led to persecutions, discriminations, or at the very best avoidance. Educating in religion should not devalue the process of growing up in a faith community, coming to know the concepts and practices of that community, and developing a faith of one's own. But it must also have as an important objective the relating of one religion to another and the knowledge that allows for dialogue, and more than dialogue to the discussion of the issues and problems which separate human beings. It must truly educate in religion—of which Jewish education, Muslim education, Christian education, Buddhist education, and Hindu education are only parts. Religious educators must also recognize that education in religion is a lifelong process and cannot be handled in classes or courses only; that the school (public or private) may handle part of the task, and the college, university, and theological seminary may add further experiences; that family and community are important participants in this educational work; but the religious groups (including the local congregations, parishes, synagogues, and temples) must themselves share responsibility in this broad area of "religious education."

THEOLOGY, RELIGIOUS PLURALISM, AND RELIGIOUS EDUCATION

Although theology is a term which is used by only a few of the world's religions, it is used here to cover the basic concepts of any religion. It is a term which has developed in Christianity, for the most part, although it is now being used by some Jewish and Muslim scholars. Since its root meaning is "the study of God," it seems appropriate for many religions, and even those religions built upon a philosophical system without an entity which might be called God often have symbolic forms in the working out of the religion which are popularly referred to as gods and goddesses. Whether or not we call it "theology," it is the basic concepts of a religious group in the process of religious education as it relates to religious pluralism that is of concern in this chapter.

The Impact of the Study of the History of Religions

The study of religion, or religions, must necessarily involve becoming acquainted with the ideas which form and motivate those religions, regardless of methodology—dialogue, lecture, visiting other houses of worship, participant observation, intensive reading, or something else. One's own ideas are challenged and affected by such education. Even theologians are influenced by such religious educational experiences. In a lecture on the significance of the study of the history of religions for the systematic theologian, Paul Tillich claimed that any systematic theologian who takes seriously such study has made two decisions. "On the one hand he has separated himself from a theology which rejects all religions other than that of which he is a theologian. On the other hand if one accepts the subject affirmatively and seriously, he has rejected the paradox of a religion of nonreligion, or a theology without theos, also called a theology of the secular."[34]

Tillich asserted that, as theologians, they must "break through two barriers against a free approach to the history of religions: the orthodox-exclusive one and the secular-rejective one." Even the term, "religion," presents the theologian with a flood of problems, and these two opposing views form an alliance which is reductionistic and which must be broken through in order to come to an understanding of the significance of the history of religions. What is needed is "a theology of the history of religions in which the positive valuation of universal revelation balances the critical one. . . . This theology of the history of religions can help systematic theologians to understand the present moment and the nature of our own historical place."[35]

I am still grateful, looking back to my own formative period of study and the time after it, to what in German is called the *religionsgeschichtliche Schule,* to School of History of Religions in biblical and church historical studies. These studies opened our eyes and demonstrated the degree to which the biblical tradition participates in the Asia Minor and Mediterranean traditions. I remember the liberating effect of the understanding of universal, human motives

---

34. Paul Tillich, "The Significance of the History of Religions for the Systematic Theologian," in *The Future of Religions,* ed. Jerald C. Brauer (New York: Harper & Row, 1966), p. 80.
35. Ibid., p. 84.

in the stories of Genesis, or in Hellenistic existentialism and in Persian eschatology as they appeared in the late periods of the Old and New Testament.

From this point of view, all the history of religions produced symbols for savior figures which then supplied the framework for the New Testament understanding of Jesus and his work. This was liberating. . . . Later on, in my own development, as in that of many other theologians, the significance was made clear both of the religions which surrounded the Old and New Testament situation, and the importance of religions further removed from biblical history.[36]

This experience from Tillich's personal and professional life exemplifies the broadening and liberating features of the study of world religions, not only the history as such, but also the concepts, rituals, practices, and attitudes toward societal concerns—human beings, the natural world, and the political and social constructs of society. These are the values which students in high-school and college courses on world religions, on the psychology and sociology of religion, the philosophy of religion, and the history and literature of religions have found as they relate their learnings to their understandings of their own religious groups in the Western world. I am less familiar with the results of such courses in the Far East and other parts of the world, but I understand that such courses are increasingly included in the curricula in Thailand, Korea, and Nigeria, and in all probability this is true for other countries.

The Reconstructive Role of Religious Education in Theology

Since the days of George Albert Coe and Harrison Elliott, some religious educators have seen a reconstructive role for religious education in relation to theology.[37] In the face of a long history of the relation of Christian theology to religious education as communicating the "true interpretation of the Christian religion which has the authority of divine revelation,"[38] Elliott emphasized a concept of theology and the educational process as interacting in such a fashion that each is retesting, reinterpreting, and restructuring the other. His idea was based upon and not dissimilar to Coe's "creative" education, in which those things transmitted from the past are actually changed in the process of adapt-

---

36. Ibid., pp. 84-85.
37. Harrison S. Elliott, *Can Religious Education Be Christian?* (New York: Macmillan, 1949).
38. Ibid., p. 79.

ing them to the present situation. Coe stated regarding creative education, looked at from the standpoint of the pupil, that "learning to be a Christian should be, essentially and primarily, an experience of free creativity. Looked at from the standpoint of the teacher, it means fellowship of teacher and pupil in forming and executing purposes that are unprecedented as well as those that follow precedent. From the standpoint of the church, it means ecclesiastical self-reconstruction in and through fresh approaches to the surrounding world."[39]

Many Christian theologians and denominational leaders have not accepted the notion that religious education has such a reconstructive and creative role, but others have, and perhaps the eagerness with which the field of religious education has embraced liberation theology is testimony to this fact. This theology, which in general relates the experience of a people through a reconstructed theology and view of the church to the problems of living seems very near to Coe's "ecclesiastical self-reconstruction in and through fresh approaches to the surrounding world." As a result, for example, there is a growing literature on black Christian education. Although there is not to my knowledge as yet a "women's Christian education," there is a great deal of thinking and writing on women's theology, and these works are important resources for Christian educators, especially women educators who can identify with the experiences discussed in the literature. A rapidly growing list of books and articles on women and religious education is developing. The liberation theologies of the Third World have been the force behind much of this movement, popularized in religious educational circles by scholars like Paulo Freire *(Pedagogy of the Oppressed)* and Ivan Illich *(Deschooling Society)* and developed into an approach to Christian religious education by Thomas Groome in his book, *Christian Religious Education.*[40]

It does not appear that other religions have been as touched by liberation theologies as have the Christian groups, particularly Roman Catholicism and mainline Protestant denominations. However, since the world Christian organization, the World Council of Churches, and the world organization of the Roman Catholic Church are so involved in it (often controversially), it seems quite possible that the reconstruction and creativity which liberation theology brings will affect the basic concepts of other religions in the world community as well. Seeking for a relevant

39. George Albert Coe, *What Is Christian Education?* (New York: Charles Scribner's Sons, 1930).

40. Thomas H. Groome, *Christian Religious Education* (San Francisco: Harper & Row, 1980).

theology is exemplified in a statement made by S. Wesley Ariarajah, minister from Sri Lanka and director of the Dialogue Sub-unit of the World Council of Churches. As a result of the educational method of dialogue he stated that "religious pluralism is here to stay, and we will need to find theological bases and spiritual resources to accept and affirm the whole realm of human life as the arena of God's love and activity."[41] He went on to quote Stanley Samartha from his book, *Courage for Dialogue,* to the effect that the theology we need is one

> that is not less but more true to God by being generous and open, a theology not less but more loving toward the neighbor by being friendly and willing to listen, a theology that does not separate us from our fellow human beings but supports us in our common struggles and hopes. As we live together with our neighbors, what we need today is a theology that refuses to be impregnable but which, in the spirit of Christ, is both ready and willing to be vulnerable.[42]

Theology Behind-the-Curriculum, or a Determinant of Curriculum

Using the terminology of Randolph Crump Miller, "theology-behind-the-curriculum,"[43] as a springboard for discussion of all those approaches to religious education which consider that theology or the basic concepts of a religion have the major role in forming the content and methodology of curriculum, one asks what this means for the approach of religious education to religious pluralism. Miller has said: "My own position . . . is that theology stands behind the curriculum but also that theology and educational theory must be in conversation, with both elements having equal status."[44] He believes that a "particular theology stands in the background for every educator. . . . What one assumes about the nature of God or the value of human beings becomes evident as various educational problems are faced." But the human response to God and God's response to human beings must be in the foreground, so Miller concludes that "faith and grace (or grace and

---

41. S. Wesley Ariarajah, *Is Jesus the Only Way? The International Christian Digest* 1:4 (May, 1987), p. 33, from World Council of Churches, *The Bible and People of Other Faiths.*

42. Ibid.

43. Randolph Crump Miller, *The Clue to Christian Education* (New York: Charles Scribner & Son, 1950).

44. Randolph Crump Miller, "Theology in the Background," in *Religious Education and Theology,* ed. Norma H. Thompson (Birmingham, Ala.: Religious Education Press, 1982), p. 31.

faith) [are] in the foreground."[45] He noted that Sara Little, in *The Role of the Bible in Contemporary Christian Education,* "develops the thesis that the theory of revelation is the key to theology and its impact on educational theory and practice."[46] Miller developed his own position from a perspective of process theology, and he believed that all educators should be aware of "their own theological assumptions and be capable of expressing their beliefs as they relate to educational practice."[47]

Does theology, then, provide the "clue" to religious educational theory and practice respecting religious pluralism? Within theology, does "revelation" serve as the key to the impact of theology on education? Does how the educator interprets revelation lead to the openness and humanness which the JED group calls for in its Guidelines regarding stereotypes and which seems to open the way for understanding, respecting, and appreciating persons belonging to other religions? Or may it lead to dogmatism in both theology and education which closes the mind and alienates human beings? For Miller, process theology offers what he calls a "right theology" which is open-ended, in which "the learner's sense of worth will be underscored and the teacher-pupil relations will operate on an I-thou level within the broader community of the church."[48]

The question remains, though, as to what will be the result of experiences with and study of other religions for students with theologies of a very orthodox nature whose doctrines, or basic concepts, are conceived never to change. Will greater understanding and personal contact lead to respect and cooperation? If so, will that respect and cooperation be enough? Is there something more required in a religiously pluralistic society?

THE CONTEXT FOR EDUCATION IN
RELIGIOUS PLURALISM

Bishop G. Emmett Carter of London, Ontario, Canada, described the context of religious education, and education in general, by saying that "education now takes place in a total cultural milieu, a world milieu made possible by electronic communication, a milieu that is swept by all ideologies and interests."[49] The point of this statement appears to be

---

45. Ibid., p. 32.
46. Ibid., p. 24.
47. Ibid., p. 41.
48. Ibid., p. 40.
49. G. Emmett Carter, "Religious Education in a Complicated World," *Living Light* 15:1 (Spring, 1978), p. 41.

that religious education cannot escape the setting of a complicated world. It must accept the fact that there are many competing philosophies and ideologies, religious among others; that even in remote parts of the world new ethnic groups or people from other cultures are moving in; that electronic communications have also penetrated many of these areas, so few peoples are truly isolated from the rest of the world. The sight of a young boy on a water buffalo with a transistor radio blaring in the countryside in Thailand twenty years ago has left an indelible impression on my mind. The "global village" of Marshall McLuhan[50] has become a reality.

How does this world situation in which religious education takes place affect various religious groups? What are their attitudes toward one another? Are those attitudes changing, as the Vatican II document *Nostra Aetate* [51] indicates is true of the Roman Catholic Church, a document which describes a new approach to the Jewish community? What are the attitudes of religious groups as seen in members and leaders of local congregations, parishes, synagogues, and temples; as found not only in their rituals and practices but also in their lifestyles within the community? What are their approaches to society—to the local area, to the nation, to the world? Do they work together on local issues and problems, or do they each "do their own thing," so to speak?

Other questions of context center on the religious educational facilities and agencies themselves. Where do religious experiences for understanding other religions take place? Are schools with classes the most effective contexts? Are informal experiences in the community and in the houses of worship of religious groups more effective in achieving goals than formal sessions? How do the customs and traditions of a society affect education in religion?

The literature on Christian missions often utilizes the term *contextualization*[52] to denote the relating of one's teaching and preaching to the cultures in which education takes place. One example of failure to take the culture into consideration is presented by Yasuko Morihara Grosjean, Assistant Dean of the Graduate School of Drew University, in discussing the reasons why Christianity has never grown rapidly among the Japanese. Although Christian missionaries arrived

---

50. See Marshall McLuhan's *Understanding Media: The Extensions of Man* (New York: McGraw-Hill, 1964); Marshall McLuhan & Quentin Fiore, *The Medium Is the Massage* (New York: Bantam Books, 1967).

51. Sacred Synod, *Documents of Vatican II*, ed. Walter M. Abbott S.J. (New York: Guild Press, 1966).

52. Paul G. Hiebert, "Critical Contextualization," *International Bulletin of Missionary Research* 2:3 (July, 1987), pp. 104-111.

there over 130 years ago, the membership in all Christian churches is still less than 1 percent of the population. He mentions the fact that the Japanese "put their religious devotion and trust in great religious personalities rather than principles, abstract doctrines, or even transcendent deities." The *sensei,* a title applied to teachers, doctors, ministers, and missionaries, invokes a very powerful relationship in the lives of the Japanese—a relationship almost of awe. A second aspect of culture which Westerners do not easily understand is the closeness of humans, gods, and nature. There is a unity which allows the Japanese to participate in many religions at the same time—Shintoism, Buddhism, Confucianism, Taoism, and even Christianity. Shinto shrines and Buddhist temples "are intended to appeal to the Japanese love of nature and aesthetic sense, drawing upon art, architecture, and beautiful settings with a view." They are often set on top of a hill, giving "an infinite sense of transcendence from this world." A third cultural aspect is the extended family system and hierarchical society, which does not allow for the individual decision making which is common in the Western world. A fourth aspect of culture for the Japanese is the prominence of festivals and individual cults. At some shrine or temple there is a festival going on at nearly any time. Finally, the close tie between Japanese religion and the Japanese nation makes it seem to the individual person as if he or she is forsaking the nation if they convert; that the choice is between accepting a foreign religion with allegiance to a foreign church in a foreign land and remaining Japanese.[53]

It is necessary, then, to see the context as this "complicated world" in which the local unit is one microcosm reflecting many of the aspects of the world macrocosm.

THE CONTENT OF RELIGIOUS EDUCATION IN A RELIGIOUSLY PLURALISTIC SOCIETY

Earlier in this chapter Martin Marty was quoted as saying that religious groups agree on so little of the substance of religious education that it cannot become "the constitutive basis" of the profession. He does, however, explore those times and places where there has been convergence or some form of consensus among religious groups. Are there not, then, some important issues to be raised regarding content in

---

53. Yasuko Morihara Grosjean, "Understanding Japanese Christianity," *International Christian Digest* 1:6 (July-August, 1987), pp. 37-39.

religious education and religious pluralism even though many efforts to develop a common content have proven frustrating and unfruitful—perhaps even impossible? Attempts to develop a common prayer for use in public schools in the United States have raised many objections and ultimately were doomed to a judgment of unconstitutionality by the United States Supreme Court. Efforts to select a common core curriculum for public education where only Jews and Christians were involved became equally controversial as not satisfactory for either Jews or Christians because the common core (drawn from the Hebrew scriptures, or Old Testament) could not adequately reflect the essence of Judaism and could not include even a hint of Christology. Clearly, insofar as basic concepts are concerned, content must be broader than transmission of the particular heritage of which the learners are a part if it is to educate with respect to the religions which make up the community, or to broaden the insights of persons to the rich variety of religions in the world.

Education has been so much associated with schooling that the first inclination is to think of content as intellectual in nature. Thus, the emphasis has been placed upon concepts, history, stories, and literature, and religious education has tended to follow the practice of general education in setting up educational experiences as classes structured around a discipline, or a subject. At the same time, educators acknowledge that learning is not only cognitive, but affective and behavioral as well. James Michael Lee follows this threefold pattern for content in his voluminous book, *The Content of Religious Instruction*,[54] but tends to use the term "lifestyle content" rather than behavioral.

Much thought has been given and work has been done on the cognitive aspects of content in religious education. The work of the Cooperative Curriculum Project of the National Council of Churches, comprised of representatives from Protestant denominations, resulting in publication in 1966 of *The Church's Educational Ministry: A Curriculum Plan*,[55] provides an excellent example of such an effort to delineate the scope of content. Although the scope as outlined in this plan includes relationships with others and with nature, among a number of affective areas of curriculum, these areas are expressed in cognitive terms, probably evoking intellectual aspects of such relationships when developed into actual curricular materials by the denominations in-

54. James Michael Lee, *The Content of Religious Instruction* (Birmingham, Ala.: Religious Education Press, 1985).

55. National Council of the Churches of Christ in the U.S.A., *The Church's Educational Ministry: A Curriculum Plan* (St. Louis, Mo.: Bethany Press, 1986).

volved and, in turn, implemented by local congregations. In fact, utter dependence upon words to express so much of what is included in the content of curriculum makes it extremely difficult to move away from the cognitive in religious education. Buddhism and Hinduism with their emphasis upon meditation and rich pageantry are probably much more effective in the affective areas of content than most of the religions of the Western world. The Zen "koan" also appears to provide an experience in which the person grapples with what seems to be an intellectual statement, but when the sense of understanding comes it is not something that one can put into words but rather one has the "feeling" or "sense of the thing"—a meaning that is not cognitive.

As for the cognitive, however, granted that each religion has its own distinctive concepts, history, and liturgy, several questions arise with respect to other religions. Are there facts about the various religions in a society, or in the world, which a person should know to be educated? To understand the literature, theater, art, and music of the culture? To function as a member of the society? To sort out the moral and ethical issues of that society? To understand and appreciate one's own religious heritage? If we answer any of these questions in the affirmative, then further questions arise: When should such education begin? With very small children as they interact on the playground? With elementary school children who can become acquainted with the houses of worship and the clergy in the neighborhood and with the festivals and holy days of their classmates? With older children who are already picking up the prejudices of the society? With high-school students in some more structured course of study on the world's religions, perhaps especially the religions of their own communities? With adults who tend to set the values and priorities of a society? With all of these in diverse ways?

Having arrived at some conclusions as to the persons one is educating, what facts about the various religions should be included in the cognitive content for the indicated stages? Because of the numbers of religions in the world, how does one select which religions to include? Perhaps the local community provides a starting point, but even in the surrounding area there are often several forms of some of the religions. How much of the history of these religions with its schisms, reforms, and protests is important?

Since cognitive content centers primarily on the facts about the religions studied, one wonders if facts are the most important things for persons to know. Does one pick up the attitudes toward life, nature, and the mysteries of the universe from the facts? What role does the knowledge of facts play in respect and cooperation? Certainly without some knowledge of facts, the way is open for indifference, fear, suspicion, prejudice, and even hate.

The power of the affective component of content is being recognized in religious education to a much greater extent than in previous periods.[56] The Eastern religions, Roman Catholicism, and the Orthodox Churches have depended greatly upon the affective element, with ornate temples and churches, softly glowing lights, flowers and incense, elaborate altars with statues, icons, and candles. One stands in awe before a golden Buddha, even though one knows the Buddha is not a god in the Christian, Jewish, and Muslim sense, but rather he is the Enlightened One. Jews and Muslims, though they have created beautiful mosques, synagogues, and temples, have avoided the statues, icons, and altars, but even these buildings tend to raise powerful feelings of awe in their simplicity. Protestant Christians, on the whole, have rejected the art objects of the Roman Catholic and Orthodox Churches, but still their churches range from very ornate to completely bare, stark houses of worship.

Though there have been such rejections, religion has historically been tied closely to some of the riches of cultural and artistic expressions—music, art, literature, and dance. What kinds of experiences, then, can religious educators include in the content which evoke deep feelings of beauty, awe, or reverence with respect to other religions and yet retain the integrity of the persons and their commitment to their particular religious traditions? What experiences can help to promote feelings of friendship, understanding, respect for differences, and desire for cooperation? Is it important to separate out what is religious from what is purely cultural? Is it possible? If we attempt to separate the cultural from the religious in such aspects as music, dance, and art, are we doing violence to both? Recognizing the importance of the affective in education in religion, one must also realize the delicacy involved in planning such experiences as well as the possibility for controversy and misunderstanding.

Finally, the behavioral component of content with respect to other religions raises a number of issues. What behaviors are desirable from the perspective of religion? Is the religious perspective what we seek, or do the behaviors have their focus in the community? Are we seeking for friendliness and a peaceful society? For inclusiveness? For enrichment of life? How does the prophetic in religion fit with these goals? How we answer these questions will help to determine the kinds of experiences we design both to include behaviors that move in that direction and the hope that the actions of the students will be influenced by these experiences. There is a theological question here as well. Do the hoped-for

---

56. Gloria Durka and Joanmarie Smith, eds., *Aesthetic Dimensions of Religious Education* (New York: Paulist Press, 1979).

actions fit the theology of the learners? This is particularly a problem when the religion is a converting religion. Members of other religions are usually suspicious that the ultimate purpose of the expressed friendship, the visit to the house of worship, the intensive study, or working together in a community project is conversion. Thus a barrier exists which is difficult to eliminate, even when the desire to do so is great.

Having briefly explored these three components of content, we must not ignore what has often been called the "hidden curriculum." Here is content that has not been planned, often very negative content. Our choice of experiences for the programs we conduct, the way we set up rooms and other spaces, the language we use, the selections from scriptures and sacred writings, hymns, and liturgical materials, the attitude of the teacher or leader, and the emphasis we place on formal and informal activities—all of these speak volumes to the participants. This curriculum, which is not usually considered in the planning process, seems related to what Maria Harris calls the "null curriculum," which she has defined as "what is not present—areas of study left out of the curriculum; bodies of knowledge not addressed; processes not included."[57] By selecting certain experiences and not others we bias the curriculum in all three elements of content (cognitive, affective, and behavioral); the inclusion or omission of certain processes, techniques, or methodologies influences the knowledge, attitudes, and actions of the learners.

An illustration of the hidden curriculum is the anti-Jewish statements and overtones in the curricula used in most Christian churches for the education of their children and youth. The curriculum writers did not intentionally include anti-Jewish statements, but the selections and the way the material is presented leave this impression. As part of a series of projects initiated by the American Jewish Committee in the 1950s, intended to evaluate the way intergroup relations were treated in teaching materials produced by Protestant, Catholic, and Jewish educators, Bernhard Olson of Yale University studied approximately 120,000 lesson units in Protestant materials. He found "a disturbingly high percentage of anti-Jewish statements."[58] Gerald Strober conducted a similar study of Protestant texts in 1972,[59] and found almost no improve-

---

57. Definition used at an "Institute on Teaching the Holocaust" sponsored by the Program in Religious Education, New York University, on April 1, 1987.

58. Bernhard E. Olson, *Faith and Prejudice* (New Haven, Conn.: Yale University Press, 1963).

59. As reported by Eugene Fisher, "Future Agenda for Catholic-Jewish Relations," *Origins* 7:47 (May 11, 1978). Reprinted in *The Future of Jewish-Christian Relations*, ed. Norma H. Thompson (Schenectady, N.Y.: Character Research Press, 1982), p. 143.

ment over the results of the earlier study. Eugene Fisher, executive secretary for Catholic-Jewish Relations, National Conference of Catholic Bishops, reported that in Olson's research such anti-Jewish statements as these were found:

> Judaism at the time of Jesus and thereafter was portrayed as degenerate and legalistic. Jesus and the disciples were shown as "somehow not Jews," while Judas and the enemies of Jesus among the Saducces and the temple priesthood were clearly identified as Jewish. The collective responsibility and divine retribution canards predominated in the portrayal of the Passion. The Holocaust and the State of Israel, the two central events of modern Jewish history, received virtually no attention and the history and nature of postbiblical Judaism were virtually ignored.[60]

A similar study of Catholic teaching materials was conducted by Father Trafford Maher S.J., of St. Louis University.[61] That study found the Catholic texts presented as stereotyped and negative treatment of Jews and Judaism as did the Protestant texts. In 1976 Fisher carried out a follow-up study to ascertain if any changes had occurred in the intervening period, especially since during that time the *Nostra Aetate* had been promulgated in 1965 and the "Guidelines for Catholic-Jewish Relations" had been issued in 1976 by the Secretariat for Catholic-Jewish Relations. He analyzed each lesson of sixteen major and representative religion series in use in the United States for grades 1-12. In general, he found there had been improvement, and "American Catholic textbooks are clearly more positive toward Judaism and historically more accurate than before the Second Vatican Council," but he noted "many subtle negative dynamics remain."[62]

Further, scholars who work in Jewish-Christian relations report that passages of scripture, particularly the New Testament, as they are read in the liturgy or studied in classes, clearly point to negative attitudes of Christians toward Jews when they are used without explanation or comment. Paul Kirsch reviewed the gospels for such passages in a chapter entitled, "The Gospel Passion Narratives and Jews," in *The Future of Jewish-Christian Relations*. He noted that there had been a major revision of the church lectionary, starting with the Roman Catho-

---

60. Gerald S. Strober, *Portrait of the Elder Brother: Jews and Judaism in Protestant Teaching Materials* (New York: National Conference of Christians and Jews—American Jewish Committee, 1972).

61. Fisher, "Future Agenda," p. 143.

62. Ibid., pp. 143-147.

lic Church after Vatican II (1962-65) and continuing with the Episcopal, Lutheran, Presbyterian, and United Methodist Churches, as well as the United Church of Christ. The problems in Christian relations with Jews was no doubt at least partially responsible for these revisions. But, Kirsch added, "a problem remains with those lessons that reflects what has been called the 'anti-Judaism of the New Testament.' The problem is especially evident in the lessons for Holy Week."[63] He then examined the passion narratives of each of the four gospels, pointing out those sections which allowed for negative interpretations by worshipers and learners.

To my knowledge no similar studies of the curriculum materials of Muslims, Hindus, Buddhists, Mormons, Christian Scientists, Jehovah's Witnesses, the Unification Church, and other religions have been conducted, but in all likelihood such studies would reveal a great deal of utter neglect of dealing with other religions, almost as if they do not exist, and where references to other religions are found the probability of misinformation and stereotyping is great.

The stereotypes which tend to pervade the literature of religious education relate not only to religion, but also to several other types of stereotypes—sex, race, age, physical and mental handicaps, nationality, and ethnic background. All of these help to provide the bases for the hidden curriculum.

Although religious educators have little direct control over the experiences of students in their homes, at school, at play, watching television, and other activities, they must be aware of the content (cognitive, affective, and behavioral) which is being experienced, absorbed, or rejected in the process of living. William Fore, in his book *Television and Religion,* claims that there is a hidden role of television, for instance, and "that primary, but hidden, role of television is to tell what our world is like, how it works, and what it means."[64] As we watch television, we are being changed. "This developmental process, this slow change, takes place constantly as we watch the television images. The process goes on regardless of what program is viewed at a given moment. It is present in every sitcom, every soap-opera, every movie, every newscast and commercial—regardless of whether the particular program is in good taste or bad, high art or kitsch, pandering or profound."[65]

---

63. Paul Kirsch, "The Gospel Passion Narratives and Jews," in *The Future of Jewish-Christian Relations,* pp. 185-204.

64. William F. Fore, *Television and Religion: The Shaping of Faith, Values, and Culture* (Minneapolis: Augsburg Publishing House, 1987)

65. Ibid., p. 21.

Fore believes that "the whole medium reflects and expresses the myths by which we live. . . . The whole process of television is providing us with a worldview which not only determines what we think but also how we think and who we are."[66]

In spite of the problems of the contemporary home, the changing patterns of families, and the diffusion of the members of the household into all sorts of activities, there is considerable evidence that the home is still the most formative influence on younger children and perhaps a more powerful influence on adolescents than has been commonly thought. There the attitudes of the adults are picked up by the children and youth. There they are taught the values, attitudes, and actions which form the basis of the lifestyle and the behaviors of that family group. There is profundity in the line from the musical, "South Pacific," with respect to racism: "You have to be carefully taught."

CONCLUSION

In this chapter I have attempted to outline a few of the issues involved in religious pluralism and religious education. There are no doubt other issues of equal importance in the chapters which follow, and still others which time and space will not allow to be dealt with in this volume. Nor have I done justice to some of those issues discussed here. What I hope has been accomplished is to open up the questions for thought and discussion. The writers who follow will discuss some of these issues from their own particular perspectives. They have contributed to what may eventuate in greater communication among religious educators of diverse religions. For want of a better word, this process is often called "dialogue," but since dialogue connotes only two entities in communication, perhaps we must seek for a better word. Irrespective of what we call it, the process denoted has been lauded by many persons as opening the mind and changing lives. Diana Eck and Devaki Jain, after experiencing such an interchange at an international, interreligious conference on "Women, Religion, and Social Change," with women from various cultures throughout the world, commented that "perhaps the most important outcome of the conference was not only its contribution to the understanding of particular issues but our affirmation and consensus that the process of dialogue is itself illumining and crucially important—important enough to elicit the continued commitment of

---

66. Ibid., pp. 21-22.

the participants to ongoing relationship and dialogue."[67]

Once again, the question arises: What are we seeking in religious education as we attempt to deal with religious pluralism? Knowledge and understanding? Cooperation and justice? The wholeness of human beings? A way of dealing with the religious in life that rises above our individual heritages and commitments? Perhaps Gabriel Moran is pointing a direction when he says: "The existence of a concept called religious education challenges and transforms the Jewish way, the Protestant way, the Muslim way, or the Orthodox Christian way. Religious education is the name for the needed response in a radically and obviously pluralistic world."[68]

---

67. Diana L. Eck and Devaki Jain, eds., *Speaking of Faith: Global Perspectives on Women, Religion, and Social Change* (Philadelphia: New Society Publishers, 1986), p. 15.

68. Gabriel Moran, *Religious Education Development: Images for the Future* (Minneapolis: Winston Press, 1983), pp. 12-13.

2

Religious Pluralism:
A U.S. and Roman Catholic View

Gabriel Moran

The two elements in the title of this book, religious education and religious pluralism, imply each other. A religious education that lacked all religious pluralism would come close to being self-contradictory; at the least it would be unnecessary. Religious education, as distinct from Jewish education, Muslim education, and so forth, arises when plurality and comparison are part of community, nation, or world. The connection in the opposite direction, that is, religious pluralism implying religious education, is less obvious. And indeed a diversity of religion can lead to bloodshed rather than education. That seems to have been the typical pattern of the past. Nevertheless, a true and lasting religious pluralism does imply a religious education. Violence tends to undermine pluralism and to place one group on top; thus there is no way to sustain a pluralistic situation without an educational approach to the differences. Our world as a whole is still at an early stage of deciding whether the path to be chosen is education or violence.

The inherently pluralistic nature of religious education has been obscured in the United States by the most common uses of the term. The adjective "religious" and the noun "education" can occasionally be found next to one another as far back as the Puritan literature of the North American colonies. But the single term, "religious education," with its implied referent of a theory and a set of practices is a child of the twentieth century. The Religious Education Association, founded in 1903, gave the main stamp to the term in the United States. Although the founders of this organization wished to include Catholics, Protestants, and Jews of the United States and Canada, the organization tended to be strongly Protestant; in fact, not only Protestant but white, male, and liberal Protestant. No conspiracy theories are necessary to explain that fact; the REA tended to reflect the composition of the United Sates. But in doing so, the REA conveyed a meaning of religious education that was more religiously monolithic than one might logically expect.

A comparison to the United Kingdom will be helpful in this essay. In the first half of the twentieth century, England had a greater unity of religion than did the United States. The term "religious education" came to prominence in England forty years later than it did in the United States. Until the beginning of the 1960s, religious education in England suggested very little pluralism of religion. But with the arrival of new populations from the East and Middle East, England was confronted with some real religious diversity. The religious education mandated in the state schools had to learn quickly how to be religiously pluralistic. I return below to what educators in the United States might learn from the English/Welsh experience of religious education in their schools.

Religion, as we now use the term, is largely an invention of Western Enlightenment. For many of the eighteenth-century philosophers, religion was a term synonymous with superstition. The choice was between reason and religion (superstition, magic, irrationality) and, while the masses insisted on retaining their ancient rituals, any educated person would escape from the shackles of religion. For the most part, the word religion referred to the external practices of Christianity.

Christian writers from the earliest era to the modern era had provided the backdrop for this meaning of religion. The church fathers saw themselves as offering true philosophy to the Greeks and true religion to the Romans. For the speculative thinkers influenced by Hellenistic thought, Christianity provided the real *theos-logos,* God's word itself. For the less speculative minded, the Christian religion was a set of practices that tied the believer to a people and to eternity. As one historian of that period puts it, Christianity triumphed on the basis of its social security. The true religion is what proves itself in practice.[1]

The pluralism in this meaning of religion lies in the contrast between false religion and true religion. There was, of course, some recognition that people belonged to "other religions," but all variety was submerged in categories like pagan or idolater. The conflict was simply between

---

1. A. D. Nock, *Conversion* (London: Oxford, 1933), p. 135.

Christianity and the forces of false worship. Augustine's treatise "On True Religion" is not about belonging to Christianity as opposed to Buddhism or Judaism. True religion is the practice of the only real religion there is. Thus Augustine writes: "That which today is called the Christian religion existed among the Ancients and has never ceased to exist from the origin of the human race until the time when Christ Himself came and men began to call Christian the true religion which already existed beforehand."[2]

Throughout the Christian Middle Ages and even into the Reformation period religion retains this stamp of the early church. For Thomas Aquinas, religion as a topic shows up under the virtue of justice. Religion is the set of practices that we are bound in justice to render to God. Aquinas, like Augustine, would have known of a multiplicity of "religion." Judaism and Islam were visible and active in his world, but they were not really accepted as genuine alternatives to Christendom. Similar comments can be made about the Reformation period. The title of John Calvin's great work, *The Institutes of the Christian Religion,* might as appropriately be translated as "the practice of the one, true religion." Religious pluralism was hardly the ideal of either Protestant or Catholic reformers. Even the English settlers who fled their homeland for the strands of North America did not come to establish a pluralistic plantation. As the Quakers and Baptists quickly discovered in Massachusetts, the freedom to practice religion did not extend as far as heretics. A religious "tolerance" did find some footing in Rhode Island, Pennsylvania, and Maryland, but tolerating differences is only a first step toward embracing diversity.[3]

The Protestant Reformation, especially on the Lutheran side, cast a suspicious eye on religion as a set of practices. The religion of the "inward man," the standing in faith before God, was sharply contrasted to the mere repetition of external rituals. For Luther, medieval Catholicism had become Judaized, entangled in superstition and lacking in faith. "Every man must do his own believing," said Luther; it is faith and only faith that opens a "man's" life to God's saving action. In Protestant Christianity, the sharp opposition between faith and religion has continued to the present day. In this usage, there is still very little pluralism of meaning beyond the dichotomy of true and false. The true religion is the inwardness of faith; the false religion is any rituals that are not "expressions of faith."

---

2. Retract. I, 13, 3 as quoted in Frithjof Schuon, *The Transcendental Unity of Religions* (New York: Harper, 1975), p. 120.

3. Perry Miller, *Errand into the Wilderness* (New York: Harper, 1964).

The rise of religious pluralism must largely be credited to the budding sciences of the eighteenth and nineteenth centuries. As students of history, anthropology, and archeology confronted the human record, they came to see that there were internally consistent patterns of religious practice in different parts of the world. These patterns could be compared across cultural barriers with some resulting illumination. The word available for this description and comparison was "religion." Drawing upon the Christian usage of that word, scientists tried to create a neutral term, although complete neutrality in this area seems to be impossible. To much of the world the word religion carries a Western and Christian bias. To many Christians the scientific study of religion(s) is a direct threat because it places the Christian faith and its expressions on the same plane as mere religions of the world. (To this day when people say "world religions" they often mean religions other than Christianity.)

A "scientific study of religion" has not had an easy time finding an accepting public. The rest of the scientific world is skeptical about religion. Christian theologians assume that *they* are the real experts in this domain. And many people who really would like a religious pluralism prefer to have an "artistic study of religion" as the way to understand convictions and practices. Nevertheless, the scientists of religion have managed to use the idea of religion as an external phenomenon, the varieties of which can be studied, compared, and understood. Thus, religion is probably as "nonjudgmental" a term as we are likely to get, at least in a Western language. It allows us to classify groups and to understand the group's relation to individuals. It allows us to follow themes and symbols through various literatures while witholding judgments of truth or falsity. If something resembling a "Christ figure" shows up in many religions, that fact neither confirms nor denies the truth of the gospels. The scientific emphasis remains on the externals. Religion may be superstitious magic or expressions of the true faith. The student of religion prefers not to judge.

Roman Catholicism has generally been more comfortable with the idea of religion than has Protestantism. Catholic intellectuals may wince at some of the practices of their church, but they tend to accept a bit of superstition as part of human nature. If a religion is to be catholic or universal, it is going to have some of the best and the worst of humanity. As William James noted, much of what Protestants call childish in religion is what Roman Catholics call childlike.[4] At least until the Sec-

---

4. William James, *The Varieties of Religious Experience* (New York: New American Library, 1958), p. 350.

ond Vatican Council, Roman Catholicism was something to be practiced. You began by observing Friday abstinence, Sunday Mass obligation, Lenten fast, rosary, benediction, scapulars, novenas, and dozens of similar activities. The theological, biblical, or ecclesiastical explanation of these things came later if at all.

The Catholic religion was thereby rooted in the body and in community. And for the very same reasons, it had elements of superstition and magic. The anthropologist Mary Douglas, referring to the seemingly irrational practices of Catholicism and other religions, notes: "Pork avoidance and Friday abstinence gain significance as symbols of allegiance simply by their *lack of meaning* for other cultures."[5] Douglas is concerned that the contemporary reformers of the Roman Catholic church are oblivious of this principle. In making the church "up to date," that is, more reasonable and less demanding, reform threatens to dissolve the religious relation to history, body, and community.

The distinctiveness of Roman Catholic practice may be slowly disappearing and in thirty or fifty years it may be barely recognizable. For the present, however, many of the ancient practices and attitudes continue. The mix of legal, contemplative, and sacramental is still very much evident. This legal structure allows Catholics to understand at least some aspects of Judaism and Islam. The contemplative side of Catholicism has surprising parallels with Buddhism despite the vast differences between the two groups in interpretive framework. The sacramental side of the Catholic church, including its devotion to Mary and the saints, gives it similarity in practice to some of Hinduism.

I doubt that any Roman Catholics believe that "one religion is as good as another." They have been brought up to believe that there is one true religion. In that sense, the medieval meaning of religion lives on in Roman Catholicism. Today that can be a very intolerant position which recognizes no other religion than one's own. But if the scalpel of true and false religion is applied to one's own church, then the modern pluralism of religion can quickly surface. That is, for those who have been brought up to embrace the Catholic religion, the task is to recognize that the Roman Catholic church is only a partial realization of that religion. This small but not so easy maneuver leads into curiosity about other embodiments of the catholic or universal religion.

Implied in such a religious change is the need for education. Certainly in the past and to some extent today, the youngster growing up in a Roman Catholic family believed that church equaled Roman Catholic church, that the catholic religion meant Roman Catholicism, and that

---

5. Mary Douglas, *Natural Symbols* (New York: Vintage, 1973), p. 62.

church teaching is what has been held at all times and in all places. Even when education concentrated on Roman Catholic documents, it could when pursued far enough open a plurality of religion. As historical studies have improved throughout the past century, the chances of recognizing a pluralism within the same church also improved. "The great advantage of tradition when it is as long as that of any of the historic religions is that it gives the chance to appeal to more than one strand in it; it may at times be the reformer's strongest ally."[6] The Second Vatican Council can be seen as an inevitable result of the pent-up historical material that a preceding century had produced. The subsequent attempt to put the genie of pluralism back into the bottle could have been predicted. A little cautious restraint might actually be helpful these days, but the attempts to reinvent a monolithic church are painful to behold.

As an example of this emerged and still emerging pluralism, take the case of homosexuality. The Roman Catholic church is by no means the only institution confused and struggling with this issue. But this church tends to insist on the consistency and catholicity of its view on the subject. Then there appears a work like John Boswell's *Christianity, Social Tolerance and Homosexuality* which digs deeper into the first twelve centuries of Christian history than did any seminary manual.[7] The diversity Boswell unearths within church history calls for careful rethinking and further study. But once the change begins in earnest, it may well be confused and incoherent. While church officials worry about a moral theologian saying that "homosexual behavior may not always be intrinsically immoral," the rest of the world, including many Roman Catholics, consider such a framing of the question to be irrelevant to contemporary discussion. Unless a better dialogue can be opened within the Roman Catholic church, the pluralism could turn into schism and disarray, a condition that is probably not helpful to anyone interested in dialogue between religions. The U.S. Catholic Bishops to their credit have tried to initiate real dialogue and on most issues (abortion being the main exception) they have shown flexibility and tolerance for disagreement.

The Roman Catholic church in the United States has a long history of commitment to educational institutions. The Catholic immigrant groups of the nineteenth century often built schools before they put up a church. The first Roman Catholic school in 1791, Georgetown, required that students observe a moral code; religion was taught in the

---

6. Kathleen Bliss, *The Future of Religion* (Baltimore: Pelican, 1972), p. 43.
7. John Boswell, *Christianity, Social Tolerance and Homosexuality* (Chicago: University of Chicago Press, 1980).

school but a student's parents could request an exemption.[8] Generations of young Roman Catholics were exposed to a strict moral discipline and to a teaching of religion. One should note that this was the standard phrase: "the teaching of religion." Not bible, catechism, or doctrine, but religion. At least beyond the early primary grades, the name of the subject was religion. Usually it was the first subject of the day; often it was boring because the answers were already obvious. Nonetheless, it provided some interpretive unity to the school's work and to the young person's life.

I have no inclination to ridicule this whole tradition despite the severe limitations in the preparation of those who did the teaching. I am somewhat bemused by the fact that "teaching religion" has been a continuous work in my own life for over a quarter of a century. In 1960 I was "teaching religion" in a Catholic secondary school; in the 1980s I find myself "teaching religion" in a private university. The activity has radically changed, and yet there is enough similarity that the term is not equivocal. If I had a videotape of my high-school teaching, I would likely find it appalling. I would still like to think, however, that I was doing what I could to make sense of both religion and the students' lives. Today, I understand better the pluralism of religion and religious interpretations. But I am not so confident that I or anyone else is beyond being a novice in the world of religious pluralism.

THE RELIGION OF THE UNITED STATES

Has there been any radical shift recently in the religious pluralism of the United States? One can answer that question with statistics or with personal impressions. The second way counts for more than it usually does because religious pluralism requires recognition, tolerance, and then acceptance of diversity. The United States has always gloried in its pluralism although one might wish that instead of *E pluribus unum,* its motto were *In pluribus unum.* Certainly, no one can doubt the multiplicity of nationalities that make up the United States. The most obvious thing that binds all these peoples into a unity is the English language, a prerequisite for getting ahead in this highly competitive country.

People in the United States like to think of their country as religiously tolerant, and up to a point it is. But its tolerance for real religious diversity has always been quite limited and that remains true today.

---

8. Jay Dolan, *The American Catholic Experience* (Garden City, N.Y.: Doubleday, 1986).

There was a brief period at the end of the 1960s when it appeared that something religiously new was occurring. The statistics of the Gallup Poll indicated a sharp increase in Eastern religions. But by the mid-1970s that statistical bump had passed and the country settled back into its traditional pattern. More than 90 percent of the population professes to be Christian (the Roman Catholic part has increased and the Protestant part has decreased since World War II). While the Jewish population of the U.S. is less than 3 percent, it exercises considerable influence on many aspects of national life. Hindu, Buddhist, Eastern Orthodox, and other religions have difficulty getting visibility on the national scene.[9]

The religion that has seemed most likely to shake up the historic pattern has been Islam. It is quite possible that Muslim leaders are not interested in getting national attention. There have been prominent black leaders during the last two decades who have identified with a form of Islam. For the most part, however, the growth of Islam in the United States proceeds slowly and quietly. It is estimated that there are about 3 million Muslims in the United States, a number almost certain to grow in the next few decades. And Islam is likely to offer the best test of whether a wider tolerance for differences and an acceptance of religious pluralism has finally arrived in the United States.[10]

The reason why it is difficult to have significant religious change in the United States is because the country is unified under a single religious ideal. But whereas the linguistic unity of English is obvious, the religious unity is buried by the way people in the United States speak about themselves. What religiously unites the United States is the vision, dream, or belief that is called America. When people call themselves "Americans" they are stating their religion rather than their citizenship. Correspondingly, to be un-American is to be a religious heretic. "America" is the name Europe gave to its dream of paradise and eschatological fulfillment. Three centuries after America was invented, the United States blended itself into that religious dream (and with the same step made claim to the Western hemisphere). The origin and history of the country are almost impossible to decipher, so covered are they in myth and liturgy. The country celebrated its two hundredth anniversary in 1976 although the nation did not emerge until the late 1780s. Yearly, July fourth functions as the liturgical celebration of the idea of America. If future generations watch videotapes of the Miss

---

9. Princeton Religious Research Center, *Emerging Trends II* (April, 1980), p. 1.
10. Yvonne Haddad, *Contemporary Islam* (Albany: State University of New York Press, 1982).

Liberty weekend of 1986, their anthropologists will be puzzled at a people that seemed to worship a statue and kept saying "Happy Birthday, America."

My comments may seem like the standard academic condescension toward popular religion and patriotism. Actually, I am not opposed to the religious dream called "America." It has not been a bad idea, but as with most religious dreams it is extremely dangerous to collapse the difference between a finite reality (for example, a modern nation state) and a religious dream. For the sake of the dream itself, one has to offer resistance to its lure with finitude and diversity. America was a Spanish, French, Dutch, and Portuguese dream before it took its dominant form as an English dream. Other variations did continue to exist, and throughout Latin America today there is a long-delayed demand to get some small part of the dream. The United States cannot discuss the issue with any nation to the south because it has no language in which to even formulate the question. The passion with which the United States government tries to control countries in Central America is not explainable in economic or military terms; fundamentally, it is an ideological and religious issue. And the difficulty in getting at that ideology is well put by Richard Hofstadter: "It has been our fate as a nation not to have an ideology but to be one."[11]

The topic of "American religion" may seem to have been widely discussed in recent decades, going back to Will Herberg's studies in the 1950s and Robert Bellah's essay on "civil religion" in the 1960s.[12] I would claim, however, that we still lack the language to even ask the question let alone reach a clear understanding. So long as the people of the United States call themselves "the Americans," and so long as the United States identifies itself with America, it is a near impossibility to distinguish the political and the religious. The United States is enveloped in religiosity, a fact that is obvious to almost any outside visitor. Within the United States, what is called left-wing criticism or secular thinking practically never gets free of the religion that is America.

The discussion initiated by Bellah's essay has been particularly misleading. He brought in the artificial construct of "civil religion," which like many other European-based religious categories obscures what it is trying to explain in the United States. To ask about "America's civil

---

11. Richard Hofstadter, *Anti-Intellectualism in America* (New York: Vintage, 1963), p. 235.

12. Will Herberg, *Protestant, Catholic, Jew* (Garden City, N.Y.: Doubleday, 1955); Robert Bellah, "Civil Religion in America," in *Religion in America,* ed. William McLoughlin and Robert Bellah (Boston: Beacon, 1968), pp. 3-23.

religion" is already to have buried the answer in the question; it is not to get free of the religious use of "America" as the name for the United States. The religious question ought to be about the United States' religion and the answer to that question is America. Rousseau's conception of a "civil religion" in which the nation would take the place of God is intelligible enough, and it is of some relevance in the modern world. But it does not begin to explain the peculiar religiosity of the United States where people do not worship the country but rather "the sacred cause of liberty." People love an *idea* about the country and there is an extraordinary liturgy celebrating "America" as a universal hope. Every third or fourth sentence spoken in this country reinforces the confusion between the finite nation state and the eschatological dream.

A national government which tries to get the religious devotion of its people poses dangers to international peace; such governments are likely to be harsh, conniving, and brutally realistic. But a nation which worships the universal dream of liberty ("America") and calls itself by that name is terrifying to much of the world. No one knows what kind of unrealistic stunts it may try to pull off, done in all innocence and with good intentions.

Most people in the United States find it impossible to believe opinion polls from around the world which indicate that the United States is feared more than is the Soviet Union. The United States, of course, is also admired more. The people of the United States try to explain away the fear as based on misinformation or envy, but neither of those two is an adequate explanation. Envy would not lead to fear of the United States starting a war. As for lacking correct information, Europeans, Australians, and even the Soviet people know the United States better than United States people know anywhere else. Even with this country's massive technology for gathering information, only a trickle of information from other countries reaches the press and television. Censorship is not the problem. Rather, it is an underlying assumption based on religious belief. If all the world is on the way to becoming America, then it is unnecessary to investigate what is going on elsewhere when one is already in America.

I said above that America is not of itself a bad idea, and insofar as the United States has partially embodied that dream it has been a place of religious liberty. That has been dramatically true for the Jewish people. The United States is one of the few places on earth where real dialogue is possible between Christians and Jews. So great was the relief of Jews arriving on these shores that Judaism threatened to be swallowed by the idea of liberty. The nineteenth-century saying that "America is our

Zion" represented a threat to historic Judaism. The twentieth century has seen a righting of the balance and some religious transcending of America. At the same time, the presence of Jews in the United States as a small but articulate minority is a healthy resistance to the interpretation of "America" as a Christian ideology.

The term that is used to reabsorb everything religious into a unity is "Judeo-Christian tradition." That is a favorite phrase of people who want the American religion left undisturbed in the schools and in government. It may sound like a broad-minded and ecumenical phrase, but it undercuts the exploration of pluralism before we have begun. There is probably a reality that can be called "Christian tradition," despite all of the Catholic-Protestant conflict in U.S. history. There certainly is a "Jewish tradition" that can encompass all the debating voices within Judaism. Sometimes the Jewish and the Christian traditions have been together; sometimes they have been divergent; and sometimes they have been in direct opposition to each other. The nineteenth-century invention of "Judeo-Christian" is not an adequate way to talk about the complex relation of Christian and Jewish.[13]

Jews and Christians have lived with a relatively high degree of harmony in the United States. Unfortunately, however, there was little conversation between the religions until after World War II. Even today one would have to say that we are just at a beginning stage. It seems a shame that given a context of free speech and a generally peaceful environment there is not far more actual exchange at both scholarly and popular levels. My own suspicion is that Jewish-Christian conversation here will not become fully engaged until Islam comes in as a full partner. As I indicated above, Islam is almost invisible. Or what is worse, the Arab world is portrayed in the most bigoted stereotypes on U.S. television and in the press. Very likely, in a few decades people will not believe how oblivious the population of today was to the bigotry toward Arab people and Muslim religion.

The United States contribution to religious pluralism in the present and the near future is a narrow one but it can nonetheless be important. A genuine conversation between Christians and Jews (and Islam as soon as possible) is a necessary step in East-West relations. A restraint on the dangers of America as a religion depends on the older traditions of Judaism, Christianity, and Islam coming to bear on the country. Whether any Eastern religion can ever reach prominence under the umbrella

---

13. Arthur Cohen, *The Myth of the Judeo-Christian Tradition* (New York: Schocken, 1971); Martin Marty, "A Judeo-Christian Looks at the Judeo-Christian Tradition," *Christian Century,* Oct. 8, 1986, pp. 858-60.

of "America" remains doubtful. But genuine tolerance and respect are possible, along with a growing appreciation and understanding of the major religions of the East.

THE BRITISH EXPERIENCE

The British experience of religious education, which suddenly was confronted with religious pluralism, might offer some instruction to the United States. Few people in this country, even few religious educators, are familiar with religious education in the United Kingdom. Over the past twenty years I have often felt closer to the concerns of British writers than to the way religious education exists in the United States. However, I do strongly disagree with one linguistic turn in the United Kingdom that in my view presents an obstacle to dealing with the pluralism of religious life.

The Education Act of 1944 stipulated that religious education should be provided in the schools of England and Wales. This religious education was described as having two parts: a worship service and classroom instruction. Until the 1960s, this responsibility was carried out dutifully. The worship service was perhaps never a great attraction (although school assemblies can be entertaining if not always educational). The instruction in the classroom was the standard bible lesson and early church history. Adults tend to think that that kind of exposure is good for the children.

Starting in the mid-1960s and culminating perhaps in 1971, a new way of teaching religion in the schools was discussed.[14] This approach was variously called "nonconfessional," "objective," and "phenomenological." Ninian Smart played a major role in providing a theory of religion. In contrast to many scholars of religion who dwell in esoteric heights, Smart tried to relate his work to people in the schools responsible for religious education.[15] The assumption that the children were coming from Christian homes and were to be provided with Church of England history could no longer be sustained. Both parts of the 1944 Act's provision on religious education faced a crisis. Worship suffered the larger blow and could not really recover. The classroom, on the other hand, could benefit from the new religious diversity affecting

---

14. School Council, Working Paper 36, *Religious Education in Secondary Schools* (London: Evans/Methuen, 1971).

15. Ninian Smart, *Secular Education and the Logic of Religion* (London: Faber and Faber, 1968).

the country. That would happen if the schoolteachers could meet the challenge of doing what schools are set up to do, namely, put the mind to understanding complex phenomena of human life.

The Birmingham Syllabus of 1975 represents a breakthrough in that direction. Under the guiding hand of John Hull, this agreed syllabus was much shorter than its predecessors but provided a detailed teacher's handbook on teaching the religions of the world.[16] One has only to get off the train in Birmingham, England, and walk about the city to see why the school had to provide study of all the major religions of the world. The world's religions showed up in England, and the religious educators to their credit tried to confront the issue.

My one reservation concerns what may seem a minor point of language, but it interferes with getting a comprehensive meaning of religious education. As the worship element was criticized or abandoned, the term "religious education" came more and more to be equated with the classroom subject. What is easily forgotten is that worship as well as many other things (for example, family nurture) which do not belong in the classroom are nonetheless part of religious education. In England and Wales the name of the classroom subject became religious education. Instead of teaching religion to a child, one teaches religious education. The obvious illogicality of the statement is covered over by usually referring to "R.E." instead of religious education; one forgets after a while exactly what the letters stand for.

The problem with this convolution of language is that people keep raising questions about issues that do belong to religious education but are not best discussed as a classroom matter. As an example, Edward Hulmes, in a book entitled *Commitment and Neutrality in Religious Education,* writes that "commitment is both the point of departure and the final goal of religious education."[17] This strong emphasis on "commitment" is an overreaction to the exclusion of commitment in the theorizing of the early 1970s. There no doubt should be a place for discussing commitment in religious education, but the classroom setting is not the main referent for the discussion. However, instead of criticizing the equating of religious education with the subject taught in the classroom, Hulmes himself assumes that language throughout the book. Other writers, particularly Michael Grimmit, have given nuanced reac-

---

16. *Agreed Syllabus of Religious Instruction* and *Living Together: A Teacher's Handbook of Suggestions for Religious Education* (Birmingham: City of Birmingham Education Committee, 1975).

17. Edward Hulmes, *Commitment and Neutrality in Religious Education* (New York: Macmillan, 1979), p. 87.

tions to this appeal for commitment; the discussion is still forced to take place in too narrow a realm.[18]

In the later 1970s and 1980s, a number of writers have tried to bring in more of the student's personal life into the meaning of religious education. That leads predictably to cries of "neo-confessionalism" and "hidden confessionalism." But if religious pluralism has become a genuine reality, then to ask what the students are learning "from religion" as well as "about religion" is not to return to the bad old days of proselytizing and indoctrinating. Once again, however, if the name of the subject were "religion," then the religion teacher would not have to bear the whole burden of the religious education of the child. Other teachers in the school could be seen as contributing to the understanding of religion as personal questions arise in other parts of the school curriculum. Likewise, the parents and the ministers of religion could also be seen to have an appropriate place in religious education.

One other thing that happens when religious education is spoken of as equivalent to a school subject is that religious education is assumed to be something provided for children. Religious pluralism is difficult to grasp for any human being. Without education continuing throughout all of life, it is hopeless to expect a comprehensive understanding of religion. Religious education in England and Wales is ambitiously described as confronting the whole world of religion. But why then would anyone specify *children* within such descriptions, as in this typical statement by Raymond Holley: "Religious education is concerned with enabling children so to surrender themselves to any particular pattern of religious faith if they so wish, rather than directing them to one pattern of objective self-integration."[19]

Granted that the exploring should be begun by children, why exclude adults? Of course, one answer is that England, perhaps even more than the United States, lacks well-developed programs for continuing education beyond childhood. Nonetheless, a necessary step in the right direction is to stop talking as if education could be completed in childhood. A writer is just preparing herself or himself for a big disappointment and unnecessary criticism by stating that "the aim of religious education is therefore something to be completely achieved only in the later years of secondary school."[20] I doubt that the aim can be completely achieved

---

18. Michael Grimmitt, "When Is 'Commitment' a Problem in R.E.?" *British Journal of Educational Studies* 29 (1981), pp. 42-53.

19. Raymond Holley, *Religious Education and Religious Understanding* (Boston: Routledge and Kegan Paul, 1978), p. 141.

20. Jean Holm, *Teaching Religion in School* (London: Oxford, 1975), p. 10.

in this life, but at least one should have fifty years beyond the secondary school to try. In talking about the religious education of adults, I am not raising some strange new issue. One of the great British writers on the education of adults, Basil Yeaxlee, noted a half century ago that older people who came to adult education programs were particularly interested in religious issues.[21] Unfortunately, neither in England nor the United States is the response to that interest much improved from what it was fifty or a hundred years ago. And even the step of describing the meaning of religious education in such a way that this interest could conceivably be included has not been taken. Surely we could immediately stop explicitly excluding adults from descriptions of education.

The British narrowing of the term "religious education" is in part a result of a clearer focus and a greater professionalism. The British have recognized that religion has to be addressed in an academic way by all young people. And they are clear that the adjective in the term is "religious" not "Christian." Of course, Christians have every right to form their own members by various means and they have a right to protest against the word "religious" becoming a dry abstraction for rationalistic philosophers. But Christians do not have a right to assume that "Christian education" is simply a more concrete and realistic way to say "religious education." All or most of Christian education can fit within religious education; the reverse is not the case. That linguistic point has been made quite well in England; it remains to be accomplished in the United States.

THE UNITED STATES EXPERIENCE

With this brief excursus to England as background, what conclusions can be drawn for the United States? We have a massive deficiency in the understanding of religion because our state schools avoid the subject. More precisely, they avoid serious discussion of the teaching and study of religion. Instead, we have endless debate about prayer in the school and cries to "put God back into the classroom." Part of the problem we have in stating the question is that the word "religion" shows up for two very different purposes. Religion is used to designate the set of Catholic, Jewish, Muslim, and other practices. Religion is also the name of a school subject. Most of the time we know which meaning is intended, but things would be clearer if we had a word like "religiology" to refer

---

21. Basil Yeaxlee, *Lifelong Education: A Sketch of the Range and Significance of the Adult Education Movement* (London: Cassell, 1929), p. 60.

to the academic meaning. Of course, this lack of a term is part of the reason for the peculiar British use of "R.E.", a solution which has more drawbacks than advantages.

Right-wing groups in the United States are always demanding that religion be put into the school, by which they usually mean prayer and bible reading. Secular writers then reply that we must keep "the wall of separation between church and state"—a thoroughly inappropriate metaphor for discussing the relation of religion and education. While secular writers guard the schoolhouse door against books that might intelligently examine religion, they fail to notice that the school, like much of our political life, is bathed in religiosity which if not critically examined is likely to be mindless. And if the schools—the schools called "public"—cannot examine this feature of our public life, where is religion to be dealt with critically? One would never guess from reading the editorial pages of the *New York Times* that the study of religion in the public school is not only constitutional but was encouraged by the Supreme Court precisely at the time when the Court declared that the state has no business requiring prayer of children in school.

People who write about "public education religion studies" generally keep as much distance as they can from the term "religious education."[22] One can understand the historical reasons for fearing that the term "religious education" might be thought to connote some control by Christian or Jewish bodies. However, that is not sufficient reason for simply abandoning the term. Religious education is the poorer and the language of "public education religion studies" is never going to get very far with the general public. As the British use illustrates, religious education can and should include what goes on in the state school. At present we have two deficiencies: religious education in England that is nothing but a subject in state schools and religious education in the United States that, whatever else it may be, is *not* a subject in state schools.

The movement to bring religion into the curriculum of the public school has been a slow one since the Court decisions of over twenty years ago. Many high schools do have units on religion within the context of literature or social science. That may be the best we can do in this era and leave the formation of religion departments until later. The issue, in any case, is not so much the introduction of awkward, new material called "religion." Instead, the issue ought to be about the strange and artificial exclusion of religion from textbooks of the past

---

22. Nicholas Piediscalzi and William Collie, eds., *Teaching About Religion in Public Schools* (Niles, Ill.: Argus, 1977).

and present. To teach the history of the Reformation period without some "teaching of religion" is what requires noneducational convolutions. How many textbooks today on World War II provide any substantial treatment of the Holocaust? The flight from religion blinds us to events in which religion plays a major part. Allowing religion as a topic for discussion and analysis leads to more realistic treatment of social issues, literature, morality, and history.

The British are surely right to hold that religious education, in the form of the teaching of religion, entails comparison between religions. That does not necessarily mean a smorgasbord approach of trying to explain each of the complex systems in the world called "a religion." Schoolteachers are not prepared for that, and I doubt that they ever will be. "Explaining Buddhism" in a few pages or a lesson to adolescents in the United States may be deleterious to their religious understanding. Nevertheless, a student of any age can grasp some comparisons; for example, the comparison of Buddhist meditation practices to forms of prayer in Christianity that the student may be familiar with. Students are particularly open to comparisons in the form of living examples. Simply meeting a Buddhist or visiting a Buddhist temple, if there is one accessible, can have profound educational impact. Where such things are not possible, videotape can be used today to great advantage. Some limited study of texts might then be fruitful.

The result of such encounters is almost invariably positive. That is, people (children and adults) react with reverence, appreciation, and some degree of understanding. (Education is not fail-safe and one also has to expect the occasional dud or disaster.) Some people brought up on a brand of ethnocentrism seem to think that if their children appreciate other people more, they will appreciate their own tradition less. Intellectual appreciation is not a zero-sum game; the movement to understand the other generally leads to an understanding of oneself and one's upbringing. There are Christian and Jewish teenagers who run off to join strange religious sects. But such flights are seldom the consequence of a serious study of religion; it most often happens with students who have never seriously studied religion.

The language of confessional/nonconfessional is not an adequate way to discuss the teaching of religion in this country. The negation of a parochial term does not necessarily free oneself from parochialism. "Nonconfessional" is a confessional term; it makes sense only to people trying to get free from the form of religion which they call confessional. For most of the world, religion is neither confessional nor nonconfessional. Religion is a set of practices which people—billions of people—perform. A person who engages in such activity presumably has some understanding of what she or he is doing. The understanding may be minimal, and to the outsider the logic that is apparently at work may seem bizarre. Still, if they are human beings performing, and especially if the religious practice has existed for thousands of years, their activity can probably be understood by a patient and thoughtful observer.

Inside/outside is a dichotomy often used in this context and obviously there is some legitimacy to the contrast. It certainly has more universality than confessional/nonconfessional. However, understanding can also be envisioned as a thing of degrees. A Roman Catholic may never be able to understand Judaism in a way that a Jew brought up on the Hebrew Bible and Talmud can. More important, to be a Jew is to be provided an experience for understanding that is simply not available to a Roman Catholic. Still, the outsider can move by degrees to deeper understanding and appreciation of Judaism. The Roman Catholic who becomes sympathetic to Judaism for the purpose of study is doing something artificial in a complementary way to the distancing from one's own religious tradition for an academic examination which is also artificial. There is nothing wrong with artificiality; the human being is the animal of artifice. Education creates the fiction of being a Jew (Muslim, Catholic, and so forth) for fifty or a hundred minutes in a classroom. One may not be able to get further than "honorary Jew" or "adopted Jew," but that is a world removed from a hater of Jews. Although education is only a part of the political, economic, and cultural solutions to world problems, there is no hope at all without educational improvement.

All of these hopes for religious education cannot be placed exclusively on the shoulders of children. As in England, the United States needs a meaning of education that is inclusive of adults. While the "adult education movement" is more extensive in the United States, it has not succeeded in denting the operative meaning of education as the schooling of the young. The problems of a "lifelong education" and a religious education are more intimately related than is usually supposed. One can be a mathematical genius by age seventeen; one can learn to speak several languages before age seven. One can learn all sorts of things about literature, history, and sociology before twenty-one. But one cannot be a religious or philosophical expert until much later in life. The deepest things in life take at least a lifetime to learn. We cannot solve the problem of religious education outside of a "continuing education" that continues throughout all of life.

In the other direction, we are not likely to change our notions of education to include adults so long as religion is excluded in principle.

The adult education movement in the United States generally empha-sizes problem-solving courses and workshops (how to do your taxes, how to fix your car, how to fix your marriage) and presumes that grown-ups will not sit still for an hour with a teacher who can explore philo-sophical or religious themes. A course on religion may not be an imme-diate best seller in the marketplace of "adult education." Nonetheless, the lifelong education of a person has to seriously engage the mystery and meaning of life. If that does not happen in young adulthood the time may be ripe during midlife crisis or in a hospice. For most people, algebra, the names of the state capitals, and Cicero's orations recede in importance as they get older; philosophical and religious matters in one form or another keep recurring. The determined neglect of this fact by the adult education movement almost guarantees that education will remain *something* one gets in childhood instead of a process that begins at birth and continues until death.

Here is where the religious institution has its greatest educational opportunity. Instead of trying to duplicate the schools of the state sys-tem, a church could demonstrate a modest but real structure of lifelong education. Catholic tradition has always had the sacramental system as a kind of birth-to-death skeleton of educational structure. Although much of that system is in disarray today, there is enough that remains to work with. The particularities in other churches/synagogues/temples/mosques would be different, but each religion has a historical realization that full participation requires many years of maturing be-yond childhood.

In the churches of the United States, we seem destined to have each generation discover the education of adults as if it were a new discovery. There has been much talk in the last decade about adult education, often without any realization that such talk has been around in almost every decade of this century. Norman Richardson in 1931 wrote: "One of the newer aspects of the movement is the emphasis upon the religious education of adults."[23] Ten years later, Harrison Elliott was writing: "It would seem as if the religious education of adults were the strategic educational problem."[24] And a few years after that, Paul Vieth could say: "The conviction is growing that the most important emphasis in Christian education today is at the adult level. . . . At a time when society in general is stressing adult education the church must not lag

---

23. Norman Richardson, *The Christ of the Classroom* (New York: Macmil-lan, 1931), p. 325n.

24. Harrison Elliott, *Can Religious Education Be Christian?* (New York: Macmillan, 1940), p. 226.

behind."[25] The rationale given in this last statement is indicative, I think, of why this talk has not gone very far in the past. Catching up to society's supposed emphasis on adult education is not what the churches should be doing. Neither in the 1940s nor in the 1980s does society and its educational system offer a model for the religious groups to follow. The churches have to go into their own depths to offer some challenge to society in the meaning of lifelong education. Few religious bodies are prepared to build multimillion dollar schools with the latest technology. What many religious bodies do have are devoted people, long histories, and an effective set of symbols. Without extravagant expense, a birth-to-death educational pattern can be devised in a religious body. There is no plan that has to be followed, and there are no experts that have all the answers beforehand. Obviously, it does help to talk with similar groups who have been trying to accomplish similar goals.

The real change in religious education, therefore, is not the talk of adult education but the new pluralism that is on the horizon. This pluralism could be a help to concretizing birth-to-death education within churches and other religious bodies. Those who are going to learn from other religions do need a deep rooting in their own tradition. And while the roots are best established before age six, the plant will bear its best fruit only after age twenty-one. A deep appreciation of, for example, baptism and eucharist, poses no threat to interreligious understanding. Real love for our own religious group should lead us to appreciative understanding of other religions.

---

25. Paul Vieth, *The Church and Christian Education* (St. Louis: Bethany, 1947), p. 122.

3

The Blessings of Religious Pluralism

James Michael Lee

"The shell must break before the bird can fly."[1]
—Alfred Tennyson

INTRODUCTION

Religious pluralism is a salvific blessing of the Spirit in that it enables persons to vastly expand their vision and their contact with the God whom no human endeavor can ever adequately contain.

Religious pluralism is an emancipatory blessing of the Spirit in that it enables religious instruction to burst free from those parameters and contents which have so often crippled its primary task of helping learners to touch the God in all and of all.

Religious pluralism is an enriching blessing of the Spirit in that it constitutes an extraordinarily rich and privileged way in which the triune God is operatively and ontically present in the modern world.

Some Key Terms

Religious ecumenism refers to institutional or individual efforts to attain unity among currently divided corporate church groups. On the contemporary world scene, the term religious ecumenism denotes any

---

1. Alfred Tennyson, *The Ancient Sage.*

official or unofficial attempt to successfully promote unity among all
currently divided Christian confessions.[2] Christian unity is a technical
term. It does not mean a confederation of separate and autonomous
Christian denominations. Rather, Christian unity means the merging of
distinct denominations into one and only one completely unified Christian church. In such an amalgamation, only the essentials in all the
previously separated church bodies need to be unified. Depending on
diverse traditions, different cultures, and varied forms of personal religious orientation, there will always exist within the new unified Christian church a considerable assortment of modes of personal and corporate spiritual life, kinds of liturgical rites, and even differing theological
and religious interpretations of revealed truths.[3] While the newly formed
ecumenical Christian church must perforce hold fast to unity in essentials, it nonetheless will always allow and indeed will ever encourage a
productive variety of nonessential elements so that in all things the love
and service of God might prevail.

The primary motive of Christian ecumenism is to restore that unity
of thought, feeling, conduct, and worship which Jesus wished to be a
cardinal characteristic of his church on earth.[4] A divided Christianity is
thus not only a direct countervention of the will of God; it is also a
scandal to the entire world both Christian and non-Christian. Many
Christian bodies, notably Roman Catholicism, officially affirm that the
current efforts at Christian ecumenism are directly fostered by the Holy
Spirit in accordance with the providential and patient plan of God's
grace.[5]

The overarching task of all Christian ecumenical instruction, then, is
the facilitation of visible Christian unity and a common Christian witness.[6]

Religious pluralism refers to that condition in which individuals or
institutions coming from anywhere in the entire spectrum of sacral
orientations interact with each other autonomously but relatedly within

---

2. Sacrosanctum Concilium Oecumenicum Vaticanum II "Unitatis
Redinegratio" (21 Novembris 1964), *Acta Apostolicae Sedis* 57 (30 Januarii
1965), #4 (p. 94). See also August B. Hasler, "Ecumenism: I. The Ecumenical
Movement," in Karl Rahner et al., *Sacramentum Mundi*, vol. II (New York:
Herder and Herder, 1968), p. 192.

3. The situation described in this sentence has for centuries existed to a
remarkable and healthy degree in the Roman Catholic church.

4. John 17: 21-23; see also 1 Corinthians 1:10-13.

5. Sacrosanctum Concilium Oecumenicum Vaticanum II, "Unitatis
Redinegratio," #1 (p. 90).

6. For a further development of this point, see Ulrich Becker, "Ecumenical
Education," in *A Dictionary of Religious Education*, ed. John M. Sutcliffe
(London: SCM Press, 1984), pp. 119-120.

the boundaries of a common allegiance to the Holy. Religious pluralism is not the same as religious plurality. Religious pluralism means that members and institutions of various religious orientations not only intermingle with one another and respect each other's faith, but also actively cooperate with each other in order to broaden their own personal and corporate religious existence so as to infuse all reality with the full actuality of the Holy. *Religious plurality,* on the other hand, is merely the coexistence of the whole range of religious worldviews without any denotation or connotation of intermingling, cooperation, or joint activities among the persons or institutions embracing various orientations toward the Holy.

Unlike religious ecumenism, religious pluralism precludes any attempt at developing a super-system or a master sacral perspective which would incorporate all other orientations. Unlike religious ecumenism, then, religious pluralism does not seek the unity of religions as its near-term or long-term goal.

The profound respect and openness which one has for individuals and institutions of other religious orientations does not imply religious indifferentism.[7] This fact holds true for persons and institutions that incorporate to some extent the cognitions, affects, lifestyles, and liturgical practices of other religious groups. In other words, persons can be genuine religious pluralists and at the same time be firmly convinced that their particular form of religion is the fullest and finest available. To be a religious pluralist is to affirm that "no religion, ideology, culture, or tradition can reasonably claim to exhaust the universal range or even the total manifestation of the Sacred."[8]

THE NECESSITY OF RELIGIOUS PLURALISM

Religious pluralism is not a luxury for any and every particular religious group; it is a necessity. Religious pluralism is a necessity for at least four major reasons.

First, other religions are there. They are all around us in their resplendent richness and dazzling diversity. No one religion stands alone; it is just one among many. As Donald Dawe puts it, "Religious pluralism has

---

7. In this context, religious indifferentism is a principle which holds that all religions are of equal objective value and that no one religion is intrinsically superior to any other. Thus in terms both of being pleasing to God and of attaining personal salvation, it does not ultimately matter what religious body or orientation a person embraces.

8. Raimundo Panikkar, "Editorial," *Journal of Ecumenical Studies* 19 (Fall, 1982), p. 783.

become an intellectual and spiritual fact for contemporary life."[9] If we are to teach persons religiously, we must teach them for life in a religiously pluralistic society. Such religious instruction aims at empowering learners to actively work together with members of other religious groups in order to enrich the spiritual lives of all those involved and also to bring the religious dimension of life more potently into society. Religious instruction imbued with a pluralistic perspective does not primarily seek to teach learners either to look down on or to convert persons or institutions from other religious persuasions.[10] Religious pluralism should not be viewed by religious educators and church officials as the divisive and pernicious work of the devil but rather in some way as the permissive design of God. Avery Dulles expresses this point very well: "As a Roman Catholic, I gladly acknowledge that the existence of multiple autonomous traditions has been, providentially, a means of preserving pluralism at a time when there might have been too little tolerance for differences in any one organizational church."[11] Genuine religious pluralism is not a melting pot in which all diverse religions are liquefied into sameness. On the contrary, genuine religious pluralism is a mosaic in which all religions occupy privileged, autonomous, and interactive positions, thus revealing a picture which displays the full reality of God less inadequately than any single religion, however objectively great, is able to do by itself.

Second, religious pluralism is necessary because it enables us to more profoundly appreciate and to more deeply live our own particular form of religion. It is probably difficult if not impossible for religionists of any confession to truly fulfill their total religious existence if they have a parochial religious outlook, a parochial religious conscience, a parochial set of religious attitudes, and a parochial religious lifestyle. This is especially true in the modern, religiously pluralistic world. It is also eminently true for Catholicism and indeed for all Christianity. After all,

---

9. Donald G. Dawe, "Religious Pluralism and the Church," *Journal of Ecumenical Studies* 18 (Fall, 1981), p. 604. Most of this issue of the *Journal of Ecumenical Studies* is devoted to the topic "Can Religious Education be Ecumenical?"

10. I am in no way opposed to the efforts of persons or institutions to convert others to their own religious group. From the distinct perspective of religious pluralism, however, such conversion efforts must never be primary, though of course conversion endeavors might well result indirectly and unintentionally from religious instruction activities of a religiously pluralistic nature. The point I wish to emphasize in the body of the text is that authentic religious pluralism can never legitimately serve as a front or a disguise for primary conversion efforts.

11. Avery Dulles, *The Resilient Church* (Garden City, N.Y.: Doubleday, 1977), p. 182.

Christianity is only one religion and thus bears the inevitable limitations of anything that is one and not the whole. Though I believe that Christianity (and most especially Catholicism) is the best religion, it is still only the best one and not the totality of all that is religious.[12] I myself believe that Catholicism has been called by God to be the perfect religion. Though it can never attain perfection in an imperfect world of imperfect human beings, it nonetheless will not make any significant progress along the path to perfection unless it expands beyond its present confines to further amplification. Such an amplification must perforce be ongoing and not just intermittent, molar and not just minor. A prime and indeed an indispensable way that Catholicism and Catholics can successfully proceed along the path toward perfection is through continuous and continual contact, cooperation, and collaboration with other religions in all their human and institutional dimensionalities. Only by working first-hand with other religions and religionists in an equal and not in a superior fashion can Catholicism be pushed forward beyond its present truth and present existence to that continuingly fuller truth and fuller existence to which it has been divinely called. Catholicism like many other forms of Christianity has historically had to pay a heavy price for cutting itself off from the revelation of God as made to and through other religious groups. Let me use Judaism as an example of this point. For many centuries the Catholic church ghettoized Judaism politically, culturally, socially, and religiously. In so doing, the church severed itself, not only from its vitally important contextual Jewish roots, but also from the uniquely covenanted ongoing Jewish vision and living embodiment of God's revelation. In the process, Catholicism necessarily shrank in vision and became distorted in practice because it removed itself from the prophetic correction of Judaism past and present.[13] Mary Boys puts it well when she writes: "Today, as in the past, Judaism exists as a light to the Gentiles."[14]

Third, religious pluralism is necessary in order to correct, modify, and

---

12. For a nicely nuanced discussion of this point, see Gabriel Moran, *Design for Religion* (New York: Herder and Herder, 1970), p. 37.

13. John S. Spong, "The Continuing Christian Need for Judaism," *Religious Education* 76 (November-December, 1961), p. 632. Spong also states that the Christian severance from Judaism caused Christians to interpret the bible with less than full meaning and import because Christians failed to look at the scriptures in their original Jewish context.

14. Isaiah 60:3. Mary C. Boys, "Questions 'Which Touch the Heart of Our Faith,' " *Religious Education* 76 (November-December, 1981), p. 656. Boys also makes a statement (p. 650) which is relevant to the major thesis of this chapter: "Because the Word of God is expressed in human language and history, scripture reflects the limitations of the human condition even as it manifests divine revelation."

transform our own particular religion and to move it into the future. Thus religious pluralism helps each religion attain that fullness which would not be possible in the absence of yeasting contact with other religious traditions and orientations. Religion is essentially a human affair, and like all other human endeavors is necessarily in the process of continuous becoming. Today's religion is unfinished and will never be finished until the end of time. Every religion is eschatological in nature. It exists in a here-and-now temporality whose thrust is toward the future yet to come. Religion is always striving to achieve itself. Each religion desperately needs the enriching influence of other religious theories and practices if it is to fulfill its ongoing eschatological destiny. The same holds true for revelation, including Christian revelation. Though of divine origin, Christian revelation is also fully human because it is received, interpreted, felt, and lived in human beings. Because revelation in this authentic sense is totally human, it perforce requires correction, modification, and expansion if it is to grow in fullness and if it is to avoid being hopelessly trapped in a solipsism of its own making. Social-scientific research has conclusively shown that human beings will soon become deviant and often will die if they are deprived of outside stimuli.[15] Furthermore, social-scientific research has definitively shown that the less contact which human societies have with outside influences, the more withered, atrophied, and lacking in growth-orientation they become.[16] Revelation-based Catholic theories such as redemption, sacrament, grace, church, salvation, and even revelation have been altered and amplified over the centuries due in no small measure to the existential contact which Catholics have had with Protestants and Orthodox and more recently with Jews, Muslims, and Buddhists. Also, Catholic practices on mixed marriages, valid marriages, attendance at non-Catholic religious services, and a host of others have been modified significantly as a result of first-hand contact with other religionists in their holistic existential situation—psychomotor, cognitive, affective, and lifestyle. Religious pluralism is really a blessing and not a threat to authentic religion.[17] Religious pluralism might well constitute a threat to those church officials who wish to have a closed comfortable religion

---

15. This scientific finding is not only true for psychological stimulation but even for something as rudimentary as physiological stimulation as well. A classic and still valid review of the research on this point is Bernard Berelson and Gary A. Steiner, *Human Behavior: An Inventory of Scientific Findings* (New York: Harcourt, Brace, & World, 1964), pp. 87-100.

16. Ibid., pp. 604-640.

17. One sometimes gets the distinct impression that some ecclesiastical officials are afraid of religious pluralism because they fear that first-hand contact and collaboration with members of other religions can cause their own members

in which the security and the power that they have attained in that religious institution will not be threatened by the winds of growth.[18] There is a sense in which all religions and their leaders are prone to diminish God, to trap him in their doctrines, to tame him in their liturgies. But God is not inextricably bound by the confines of dogma and liturgy or in any religious tradition however exalted. God can never be adequately captured by any one religion or by all of them put together. God is an all-transcending reality, and this paramount fact makes religious pluralism necessary for each and every religion.[19]

Fourth, religious pluralism is necessary to bring the fruits of our religious tradition to persons and institutions representing different traditions. Each religion exists not only for its members but for the enrichment of others outside its direct ambit. Christianity especially cannot afford to remain wholly inner-directed because Jesus explicitly commanded his followers to teach all people his salvific message.[20] To bring the living fruits of our religious tradition to others means at least two reciprocal processes. We must not simply tolerate but rather actively encourage other religious orientations to bring the fruits of their traditions to our religion so that we can expand our own Christian glimpse of God and live more fully in his ways. And we must be firmly convinced that our success in making the Christian message available to others cannot be accurately measured by the number of converts we make to Christianity. From the specific standpoint of religious pluralism, the main thing is to assist persons of other traditions enhance their own personal and corporate religious living by enriching them with the Christian perspective. If converts are gained in this process, this is all to the good—not from the specific standpoint of religious pluralism but from the standpoint of the essential fecundity of Christianity. Religious pluralism ought never to be primarily an exercise in proof-thrusted apologetics or as a masquerade for a direct quest to make converts.

---

to fall away from their own religion or even convert to another religion. But it seems legitimate to ask whether a religion which is truly authentic should be a sealed enclosure or an expansive way of life? It appears to me that ecclesiastical officials ought to see to it that the members of their own faith communities are taught to have a firmer hand on the wheel rather than a stronger foot on the brake.

18. For a fine treatment of how institutions, especially in their bureaucratic manifestations, tend to muzzle human endeavors, see Gabriel Moran, *Religious Body* (New York: Seabury, 1974), pp. 31-67. Moran's insights are speculative rather than scientific.

19. Paul Avis, *Ecumenical Theology and the Elusiveness of Doctrine* (London: SPCK, 1986), p. 2.

20. Matthew 28: 19-20

BASIC PRINCIPLES OF RELIGIOUS PLURALISM

If religious instruction for genuine pluralism is to be successful, it must be guided all along the line by a set of basic underlying principles of existence, presence, and action. This section will deal very briefly with eight of the most important of these basic principles.

First, we must truly and sincerely recognize that throughout the millenia and continuing into the contemporary era, God seems to have used various religions and diverse revelations as authentic vehicles by which human beings can know, love, and walk with God. Whether one argues that the infinite nature of God almost requires a diversity of religious forms and revelations, or whether one argues that the divine and salvific character of different religions is a mystery known only to God,[21] the fundamental principle remains the same, namely that various religions actually do constitute in their own way true paths to present and future union with God. In this vein Bede Griffiths, a Benedictine monk living in India as a *sannyāsi*[22] forthrightly affirms that God's revelation is truly polyformic when he writes: "The Buddha, Krishna, Christ—each is a unique revelation of the divine mystery."[23] He goes on to write: "We have to learn to recognize the voice of the Spirit in every scripture and discover the hidden Source from which all scriptures come."[24] Seyyed Hossein Nasr, the renowned Islamic scholar, expresses this same point when he touchingly observes that every orthodox religion is the choice of heaven.[25] In our instructional efforts in religious pluralism, it is incumbent upon all of us, not simply to respect other religions, but to affirm that these other religions do indeed represent legitimate human responses to God.

---

21. The Second Vatican Council expressed this last point with moving accuracy: "Because Christ died for everyone, and because all persons are indeed called to one and the same divine destiny, we must hold that the Holy Spirit offers to all people the possibility of being made partners in the Paschal mystery, in a way known to God." Sacrosanctum Concilium Oecumenicum Vaticanum II, "Gaudium et Spes," (7 Decembris 1965), in *Acta Apostolicae Sedis* 58 (7 Decembris 1966), #22 (p. 1043), translation mine. This document is the Pastoral Constitution on the Church in the Modern World.

22. In Hinduism, the last and highest stage attainable in a person's life is that of total renunciation. In this stage a person breaks all attachments to the world and lives as a wanderer and a begger.

23. Bede Griffiths, *Return to the Center* (Springfield, Ill.: Templegate, 1977), pp. 86-87.

24. Ibid., p. 106.

25. Seyyed Hossein Nasr, *Ideals and Realities of Islam* (Boston: Beacon, 1972), p. 16.

Second, we must come to appreciate that each and every religion represents a distinct sociocultural[26] response to divine revelation. Social-scientific research evidence confirms the commonsense view that socioculture is a very powerful force in forming human behavior.[27] There is a very large sense in which a specific socioculture constructs the reality in which persons live. All human experience—and this includes the human experience of divine revelation—occurs within the filtered existential context of one's particular socioculture. While the whole of God's revelation is objectively one, nonetheless different cultures, because of their own distinctive natures and axes, necessarily filter and interpret this revelation differently, highlighting one aspect of revelation over another, glossing over a dimension of revelation not adequately encompassed in the specific socioculture, and so on. No one socioculture can ever begin to exhaust the inexhaustible richness of God's revelation. Therefore Christians should become aware that our revelation is received not directly from God but is always received in a distinct sociocultural framework, namely by a person-in-socioculture. This sociocultural framework intrinsically limits the capacity of any and all Christians to receive all of God's revelation or to interpret fully and wholly what revelation they did receive. Consequently, there is no way that Christianity can claim to have received the whole or anything approximating the whole of God's revelation, even though Christianity might justifiably claim to have received the clearest and fullest available form of that revelation. Christianity not only was born and now lives in one or another socioculture; Christianity is itself its own socioculture.[28]

---

26. Many social scientists working in the area of society and culture prefer to speak of three distinct but heavily interactive forces strongly influencing human behavior: the individual, the social, and the cultural. For purposes of understanding more potently the point I am making in the body of the text, I am combining social and cultural. For a famous elaboration of individual, social, and cultural, see Pitirim A. Sorokin, *Society, Culture, and Personality: Their Structure and Dynamics* (New York: Cooper Square, 1947), pp. 63-65; 342-364.

27. Peter Berger observes that the fundamental coerciveness of a socioculture lies not so much in its mechanisms of social control but in its power to constitute and to impose itself as a reality. Peter Berger, *The Sacred Canopy* (Garden City, N.Y.: Doubleday, 1967), p. 12.

28. In this connection I am reminded of an insightful comment made by H. Richard Niebuhr: "On the one hand [Christians] interpret culture through Christ, regarding those elements in it as most important which are most accordant with his work and person; on the other hand they understand Christ through culture, selecting from his teaching and action as well as from the Christian doctrine about him such points as seem to agree with what is best in civilization. (H. Richard Niebuhr, *Christ and Culture* [New York: Harper & Row, 1951], p. 83.)

Hence Christianity suffers doubly from the limitations of any socioculture, limitations which restrict the breadth and depth of its possible responses to the totality of divine revelation. "The Christian religion emerged as a human response to God's revelation in Jesus Christ but is not equivalent to that revelation."[29]

Third, we ought to realize that each and every human being grows and learns and encounters revelation in a somewhat different manner than other human beings. This fact holds true regardless of the sociocultural milieu in which the person lives. Social scientists refer to dissimilarities among human beings as "the psychology of individual differences."[30] From the philosophical perspective, Bernard Lonergan terms it "polymorphic consciousness."[31] Theologians call it "the differentiated movement of grace in persons."[32] The considerable variety of learning and experience resulting from the vast array of human personalities indicates that religious pluralism is in all probability endemic to the human condition. Thus, in education for religious pluralism each of us must realize that no one person or group of persons is the repository of all or even of most of God's revelation but that the other individual's religion is authentic both for that other person and for us as well. As Paul Tillich observes, each person's religious commitment is both objectively and subjectively valuable.[33] In a somewhat similar vein, Raimundo Panikkar writes that "no one individual or collectivity has universal awareness. . . . Human awareness can be stillborn unless it begins to assimilate this fundamental polarity."[34] *If each person in the world is going to be as fully religious as possible, then it seems necessary for each person to have a pluriform experience of God.* This pluriform experience, in turn, almost demands the necessity of different religions[35]—and therefore the necessity of religious instruction for religious pluralism.

---

29. Dawe, "Religious Pluralism and the Church," p. 613.

30. A good summary of the psychological and sociological bases for individual differences, together with appropriate biological foundations, can be found in National Society for the Study of Education, *Individual Differences and the Common Curriculum* Eighty-second Yearbook of the National Society for the Study of Education (Chicago: The Society, 1983), pp. 9-120.

31. Bernard J. F. Lonergan, *Insight: A Study in Human Understanding* (San Francisco: Harper & Row, 1978), pp. 385-386.

32. Jean L. Jadot, "The Growth in Roman Catholic Commitment to Interreligious Dialogue Since Vatican II," *Journal of Ecumenical Studies* 20 (Summer, 1983), p. 371.

33. Paul Tillich, *Christianity and the Encounter of World Religions* (New York: Columbia University Press, 1964), p. 62.

34. Panikkar, "Editorial," p. 782.

35. This statement holds true in terms of how religions are currently set up and institutionalized.

Fourth, genuine religious pluralism requires humility on the part of all its individual and institutional participants. Persons and groups involved in religious pluralism should treat each other as equals.[36] This equality should not be accorded simply for reasons of courtesy but because all participants arc wholly committed to living God's revelation to the fullest and because all participants are deeply aware that every religion authentically refracts a further dimension of that revelation. Each Christian church teaches and witnesses to the reign of God. But no Christian church is itself this reign. It is the height of triumphalism for any Christian church, including the Catholic church, to identify itself totally with God's reign. In the final analysis, God's once and future revelation is the ultimate judge and the ultimate axis of any church. Owing to God's fullness without end and God's dynamism without ceasing, revelation is both polyform and ongoing.[37] In the eyes of God, each religion has lived some aspects of the totality of God's revelation and has failed to live other aspects of that total revelation. In this and in many other religious dimensions of commission and omission, all of us are in many ways equal. To treat persons and groups from other religious orientations as equals does not in any way imply that all religions are in fact equal or that all religions do indeed encapsulate with equal fullness the totality of God's inexhaustible revelation. Rather, to treat persons and groups from other religious orientations as equals is to accord them that respect due to all individuals and institutions who have received God's revelation and who have striven to live that revelation to the best of their ability. We are all sons and daughters of God. We are all brothers and sisters of Jesus. Thus we should treat persons from all religious orientations as we should treat members of God's family on earth and on pilgrimage.

Fifth, openness to the insights and revelatory authenticity of other persons and institutions is a necessary characteristic of fruitful religious pluralism.[38] This openness is two-sided. It requires our recognition of

---

36. The Vatican's Secretariat for the Promotion of Christian Unity similarly states that a major condition for *ecumenical* dialogue is that it be conducted among the participants as among equals. Secretariat for the Promotion of Christian Unity, "Reflections and Suggestions Concerning Ecumenical Dialogue", August 15, 1970, IV. 2, in *Vatican Council II: The Conciliar and Post-Conciliar Documents,* ed. Austin Flannery (Northport, N.Y.: Costello, 1975), p. 542, translated by S.P.C.U.

37. Somewhat apropos of this point, Gampopa writes: "A mere glimpse of Reality may be wrongly taken for a complete realization." (Gampopa, "Tibetian Texts," *Studies in Comparative Religion* 16 [Summer/Autumn, 1986], p. 137.) Gampopa, a guru, is of the Kadjupa Order in the Spiritual Line of Milarepa.

38. S. J. Samartha, "The Progress and Promise of Inter-Religious Dialogue," *Journal of Ecumenical Studies* 9 (Summer, 1972), p. 473.

the legitimacy and genuineness of other religions.[39] It also requires a definite willingness to have our entire Christian life, traditions, and doctrines questioned, and questioned intensely. Such no-holds-barred questioning can have a decidedly salutary and purifying effect on each participating person and institution. Every religion, including Catholicism, has to some extent failed God's revelation, not only with respect to those dimensions of total revelation which it has not encountered, but also to those dimensions of revelation which it has experienced. Sometimes this failure is culpable due to personal and institutional weakness. At other times, this failure is not culpable because that which we think is our authentic response to revelation is not in fact as fully authentic as it should be. One cause of this last-mentioned failure is an excessive reliance on cognition, notably a misguided belief that one or another cognitive doctrinal formulation somehow captures the heart and soul of revelation. For example, there are differences between the truths of faith and the doctrinal formulae in which these truths are couched. To illustrate: There are numerous differing authentic definitions, and numerous differing authentic approaches, to that reality we call a sacrament. These differences arose because of varying personal/cultural background factors, varying existential points of departure, and varying resources. "One can express authentic christological faith without using the Chalcedonian definition."[40] We ought to remember that truth on earth is not only cognitive but even more importantly affective and also lifestyle—in a word, holistically existential. Hence cognitive formulae cannot wholly (and some would argue, adequately) capture existential truth. Religious educators should help learners to become aware of the parameters and limitations of the cognitive doctrinal formulae of their own religions as well as those of other religions. For example, learners should be taught the difference between revealed truths and nonrevealed

---

39. In its document entitled, "Declaration on the Relations of the Church to Non-Christian Religions," the Second Vatican Council expresses this point with beauty and clarity: "The Catholic Church rejects nothing that is true and holy in [non-Christian] religions. She has high regard for the lifestyle and conduct, the precepts and cognitive doctrines which, though differing in many respects from her own teaching, still reflect a ray of that [divine] truth which enlightens all persons. . . . Let Christians, while witnessing to their own faith and lifestyle, acknowledge, preserve, and encourage the spiritual and moral truths found among non-Christians, including their social life and culture." Sacrosanctum Concilium Oecumenicum Vaticanum II, "Nostra Aetate" (28 Octobris 1965), *Acta Apostolicae Sedis* 58 (8 Octobris 1966), #2 (p. 741), translation mine. This document is the Declaration on the Relation of the Church to Non-Christian Religions.

40. Yves Congar, *Diversity and Communion*, trans. John Bowden (London: SCM, 1984), p. 169.

truths. They should also be taught that the standard theological formulae are not necessarily the best, the most authentic, or even genuinely valid expressions of one or another dimension of revelation. In activities of a religiously pluralistic nature, learners should be taught that the doctrines and official documents of their particular religious group are not to be used as tests of correctness by which to judge other religions but rather as points of departure to come to a fuller encounter with the inexhaustibly polyform manifestation of God in our world. All this requires openness on the part of both the religious educator and the learners.

Sixth, religious pluralism implies that each religion has a right to be experienced in the light of its own particular mode of existence. Thus each participant in religiously pluralistic activity ought not to experience other persons or traditions primarily from the standpoint of his or her own individual religious tradition but from the vantage point of the other tradition.[41] If such an empathic encounter with other religions is to be genuinely rather than obliquely existential, then this encounter must be holistic. Consequently instruction for religious pluralism should seek to have us know the other religious tradition as that tradition knows itself rather than as we know that tradition (cognitive domain). Instruction for religious pluralism should seek to have us feel and love and value the other religious tradition as that tradition feels and loves and values itself rather than simply as we feel and love and value that tradition (affective domain). And again, instruction for religious pluralism should seek to have us live the other religious tradition as that tradition lives itself rather than how we imagine that other tradition is lived (lifestyle domain). Learners cannot acquire a holistic experience of other religious traditions just by reading about them or by entering into a cognitive dialogue with them. Learners can only acquire a holistic experience of other religions by participating in their worship services, working together with them in their outreach programs and community service activities, and even if possible living for a while in their communities.

---

41. I use the word, "primarily" here. It is manifestly impossible to totally abandon consciousness on one's own religious stance. In this regard, Donald Dawe's advice is sage: "When talking about another religion, do not compare your theory with the practice of others. When interpreting other religions, the normative ethical, theological, and philosophical ideas of your own tradition should be compared to their counterparts in the other traditions and not to the fragmentary and contradictory expression given these ideas in particular religious communities." (Dawe, "Religious Pluralism in the Church," p. 612.) Further, when comparing our religion with that of others, we should compare theory to theory and practice to practice.

Seventh, religious pluralism necessitates an encounter with the entire lived religion of the participants from other traditions. All too often persons stop with the institutional form of other religions rather than meet and greet the entire terminology. It not infrequently happens that the ecclesia is far more dynamic, far more filled with love, and far more religious than the ecclesiasticum. In many ways the future of religious pluralism lies more with the ecclesia than with the ecclesiasticum. The ecclesiasticum is inherently political, and politics in any shape is concerned primarily with power and self-preservation. In dealing with the ecclesiasticum of any religious tradition we should realize that there lurks within its being a streak and even to some extent a pervasive tint of evil. Religious pluralism is furthered when we recognize this streak and tint of evil, deal with it, but also go beyond it to the grace-touched ecclesia which the ecclesiasticum purports to lead and manage.

Eighth, our activities should be thoroughly imbued with the goal of religious pluralism, namely, the enlargement of the religious cognition/affect/lifestyle of each individual and each institutional participant so that every person and every group can fill up what is lacking in their own response to the totality of God's revelation. The goal of religious pluralism is the enhancement of the religious life of all participants.[42] If some consensus or even some mergers among religious institutions eventually occur, well and good in terms of religious pluralism. Unlike religious ecumenism, unity is not the goal of religious pluralism. The goal of religious pluralism is always to a deeper loyalty and commitment to God's revelation as each of us experiences it. Correlative to this, the goal is also profound openness to accepting new and different revelation. A "harmony of enlightened hearts" is an important aspect of the goal of religious pluralism.[43] Love plays a far more important role than cognition in productive religious pluralism. In this vein Bernard Lonergan writes that it is love, the grace of God's flooding love, which replaces cognitive doctrine as the *unum necessarium* in religions generally.[44] Cognition often blocks the path to religious pluralism, while love

---

42. What Heinrich Fries and Karl Rahner hold to be a basic principle of religious ecumenism applies even more forcefully to religious pluralism: "The particular churches live in mutual fraternal exchange of all aspects of their life, so that the previous history and experiences of the churches separated earlier can become effective in the life of the other partner churches." (Heinrich Fries and Karl Rahner, *Unity of the Churches*, trans. Ruth C. L. Gritsch and Eric W. Gritsch [Philadelphia: Fortress, and New York: Paulist, 1985], p. 8.)

43. Panikkar, "Editorial," p. 781.

44. Bernard Lonergan, *Doctrinal Pluralism* (Milwaukee: Marquette University Press, 1971), p. 27.

tends to open up these paths. If we are to teach learners to engage in religiously pluralistic activities, we should teach them how to love other religious traditions and their adherents rather than simply to know them. There is a sense in which persons of all religious traditions share the same common religious patrimony, namely, the patrimony of pluriform revelation from the same God. This patrimony comes from God and leads to God. Religious educators, therefore, should structure the pedagogical situation in such a way that at appropriate times learners share spiritual activities and spiritual resources, *communicatio in spiritualibus*,[45] as well as active participation in activities sponsored by individuals or official groups from other religions. This combination of *communicatio in spiritualibus* and participation in other endeavors undertaken by persons and groups from other religions is surely the soul of religious pluralism, for it leads to a change of heart and increased holiness of life.[46]

FALSE IRENICISM

False irenicism is the attempt to achieve harmony and if possible ontic unity among diverse religions by excessively minimizing or even at times obliterating those major irreconcilable differences which do in fact separate these religions. False irenicism must be distinguished from genuine irenicism which seeks to promote peace, respect, joint activi-

---

45. The Vatican's Secretariat for the Promotion of Christian Unity defines *communicatio in spiritualibus* as that sharing of spiritual activity and resources which includes prayer offered in common, joint use of sacred places and objects, as well as all sharing in liturgical worship (*communicatio in sacris*) in the strict sense of this last-mentioned term. *Communicatio in sacris* is defined as "participating in the liturgical worship or sacramental activity of another church or ecclesial community." Liturgical worship is defined as "worship carried out in accordance with the books, prescriptions, or customs of a church or ecclesial community, celebrated by a duly-authorized minister or delegate of that church or ecclesial community in that person's formal capacity as a duly-authorized minister." Secretariatus Ad Christianorum Unitatem Fovendam, "Ad Totam Ecclesiam" (14 Maii 1967), *Acta Apostolicae Sedis*, 59 (5 Julii 1967), #a 30-31 (p. 584), translation mine. Most regretfully, in my view, the official Catholic church places considerable restrictions on *communicatio in sacris*, a fact which surely diminishes the limitless possible advantages of *communicatio in spiritualibus*.

46. Secretariat for the Promotion of Christian Unity cites *De Oecumensismo* to the effect that this change of heart and increased holiness of life, along with public and private prayer for Christian unity, constitute the soul of the ecumenical movement as well. Ibid., #21 (p. 581).

ties, and open explorations of zones of commonality among various religious groups without compromising the integrity or uniqueness of any of the diverse religions.

Instruction for religious pluralism should endeavor to embrace authentic irenicism and eschew false irenicism. There are at least three kinds of false irenicism against which religious educators should be on guard.

The first form of false irenicism is that of being deliberately blind to the major irreconcilable differences which do indeed separate religions. A prime result of religious pluralism might well be that minor nonessential differences among religions will be deemphasized and possibly eliminated. But there are some major irreconcilable differences among world religions, such as the divinity of Jesus for example. If it is to be productive, instruction in and for religious pluralism must honestly deal with these differences rather than paper them over.[47] The ideal of productive religious pluralism is ill served by attempting to conceal either the major or the minor differences in the content, development, or expression of the various religions. After all, the source of strength and fecundity of religious pluralism directly flows from the diversity by which various religions refract in their own special way the inexhaustible revelation of God. While the structural goal of religious ecumenism is the unity of Christian religions, the structural goal of religious pluralism might well be a loose confederation of world religions held together by a common bond of love of God, the desire to become more individually and corporately holy through expanding one's own response to revelation, and the willingness to offer the living fruits of one's own religious orientation to other religious groups.[48] I should note that religious ecumenism has a strong inbuilt pressure, namely, the pressure to achieve unity. This pressure can possibly cause the ecumenical move-

---

47. Stephen A. Schmidt, "Response," *Journal of Ecumenical Studies* 17 (Fall, 1981), p. 389.

48. In making this statement I am not in any way minimizing the absolutely crucial importance of religious ecumenism. I am a confirmed and indeed a fervent ecumenist. I fully agree with Geoffrey Wainright when he writes: "An ecclesiology which denies the existence of [Christian] disunity is docetist: 'institutional unity is not important because true Christians are known to the Lord and are inwardly one in him.' A more satisfactory ecclesiology recognizes the tension between history and eschatology, recognizes the imperfection of present human response to the divine vocation. . . . The church is becoming what it will be. In this perspective, we can both admit that some disunity still exists among Christians and see the need to overcome such disunity." (Geoffrey Wainright, *The Ecumenical Moment* [Grand Rapids, Mich.: Eerdmans, 1983], p. 89, italics deleted.)

ment to be tempted by the siren song of false irenicism far more readily than is the case with religious pluralism which does not have to live with inbuilt pressures of this sort.

The second kind of false irenicism is that of being superficial in our encounter with other religions. This superficiality assumes different forms, as, for example, trendiness and tokenism. *Trendiness* is the collaboration with persons and groups from various religious orientations in order to be socially fashionable. (Trendiness is typically a temptation of ultraliberals, religious and otherwise.) Trendiness is thrusted toward faddishness and novelty for its own sake rather than for the sake of some benefit external to it. Thus trendiness in religious pluralism gives the person a certain feeling of intellectual chic and a sheer delight of perceiving oneself as "in." By contrast, authentic religious pluralism is thrusted away from itself. It is thrusted toward the growth of all persons and groups as these persons and groups encounter different religious orientations at progressively deeper levels.

Another kind of superficiality is that of *tokenism* in which persons representing various religious orientations are invited by some sponsor group "to do their thing." This "thing" almost always is nonthreatening, irrelevant, and devoid of any possible fundamental impact on the religious life of the sponsor group. Tokenism is thrusted either toward the amusement of the sponsor group or toward relieving any guilt feelings on the part of the sponsor group that its members singly or corporately are not sufficiently mixing with persons from other religious orientations. Liturgies are a favorite form of tokenism used in falsely irenic religious pluralism. Thus, for example, false irenicists will very occasionally and sporadically schedule the celebration of an Eastern Orthodox liturgy (the more thick and smoky the incense the better), Jewish prayer services (yarmulkes, prayer shawls, and chanting in Hebrew by the celebrant are all a must), and the like. Token liturgies are usually greeted with comments from members of the sponsor group such as "interesting," "colorful," "different"—seldom if ever are there attempts by the sponsor group to encounter these liturgies in anything like the religious fullness in which the other tradition experiences them.[49] Rarer still are serious and enduring attempts by the sponsor group to incorporate some of the basic elements or dimensions of these liturgies into its own worship services on an experimental basis. Instruction which treats religious pluralism in a trendy manner or in a token capacity fails to teach learners the basic differences which characterize diverse religious

---

49. Constance J. Tarasar, "Response," *Journal of Ecumenical Studies* 18 (Fall, 1981), pp. 642-643.

orientations. Furthermore, such falsely irenic instruction also prevents learners from expanding their own religious experience through the liberating encounter at a fundamental level with religious traditions which differ significantly from their own.

The third form of false irenicism is that of completely ignoring or totally bypassing the ecclesiasticum over the long term. It is excessive romanticism to believe that the love and goodwill of the participants is all that is ultimately needed for attaining the goals of fruitful religious pluralism. Whether we like it or not, various ecclesiastica are there. Ecclesiastica are a fact of life. Moreover, the nature of the human condition (and, Catholics would add, the direct biblical command of Jesus) requires the existence of an ecclesiasticum, however imperfect and sinful and reactionary this ecclesiasticum might be at times. Efforts at religious pluralism ought never to excommunicate the ecclesiasticum. Now all this is not to say that religious pluralism at every stage must be initiated, worked through, controlled, and formally approved by the eccelsiasticum. The long history of virtually all Christian and non-Christian ecclesiastica shows unambiguously that these official bodies are quite uncomfortable if not actually opposed at the visceral level to religious pluralism of the fundamental and far-reaching sort. Almost always at the beginning of religious pluralistic activity, often in the middle of this kind of activity, and sometimes at the end, it is more productive and indeed more religious to work through one or another part of the ecclesia rather than through the ecclesiasticum to achieve religious pluralism. But at some point the ecclesiasticum must become deeply involved, not in a token way, but in a constructively collaborative manner. One ought to remember that while the ecclesia has historically been more prophetic than the ecclesiasticum, nonetheless every ecclesial activity which has proven to be both Christically authentic and permanently productive sought appropriate timely collaboration with the ecclesiasticum. Given the nature and proclivities of the ecclesiasticum, such collaboration has often brought considerable pain and suffering to the ecclesia in whole or in part. Yet pain and suffering are part and parcel of the prophetic role in the Christian tradition.

Of the many antidotes to false irenicism, one is especially worthy of mention, namely loyalty and love for one's own religious tradition. Such loyalty and love are essential for fruitful religious pluralism, not only because they tend to innoculate participants against false irenicism, but also because they can deepen the spiritual lives of the participants. In activities of a religiously pluralistic sort, spirituality grows not solely from collaborative endeavors with persons of other religious orientations but also from the way in which these collaborative contacts expand the religious life we are already living in our present tradition. Genuine loyalty and true love for our own tradition is never blind or narrow. Rather, this loyalty and love are growth oriented and positively corrective in that loyalty and love empower us to grow spiritually in our own tradition and also to work for an enhancement and even a modification of this tradition as required. This growth, this correction, this enhancement, and this modification necessarily entail change—a change which can only result from open loyalty rather than closed loyalty.

Open loyalty can also help engender internal religious pluralism. In dealing with religious pluralism, scholars as well as activists tend to focus their attention on the acceptance of and the collaboration with diverse religious orientations *outside* their own particular religious institution or denomination. This is external religious pluralism. But another vital, though often neglected, form of religious pluralism is internal, namely the acceptance of and collaboration with diverse religious orientations *inside* one's own religious institution or denomination. Genuine religious pluralism necessitates both internal as well as external pluralism, else it be a sham.[50]

If loyalty and love or our own religious tradition is to be authentic and Christian, then it must be situated within a larger and more powerful context, namely, loyalty to and love for God. *Super ecclesiam et ecclesiasticum Deus est.*[51] Thus true loyalty and love for one's own religious tradition must always be subject to future reinforcements and correctives of God's ongoing revelation. It is well within the realm of possibility that this divine revelation might be such that it leads a person to abandon his or her own religion and convert to another tradition. This possibility is one of the glories—or one of the perils, depending on one's particular viewpoint—of religious pluralism. This possibility is also an opportunity—or a risk, again depending on one's viewpoint—for every person and group engaged in religious pluralism. In assessing the glory/peril and this opportunity/risk, it is well to bear in mind that Christianity is an adventure in our coming unto God. Christianity is not basically a search for a rule of safety.

---

50. In my own experience, I have consistently found that religious ultraliberals tend to vigorously espouse a trendy external religious pluralism while at the same time practicing the most repressive narrow-minded antipluralistic activities toward persons in their own denominations whose religious orientations differ markedly from their own.

51. On this point, and from the explicit perspective of religious instruction, see James Michael Lee, *The Shape of Religious Instruction* (Birmingham, Ala.: Religious Education Press, 1971), pp. 24-27.

THE POTENT ROLE OF RELIGIOUS INSTRUCTION
IN THE WORK OF RELIGIOUS PLURALISM

Religious instruction offers religious pluralism an ideal arena in which to grow and flourish. In its authentic form, religious instruction is a laboratory for religious living in which human beings purposively develop those modes of personal and corporate spirituality best suited to them.[52] Of all sectors of life, religious instruction probably offers the greatest potential for fostering religious pluralism. This fact is due to a combination of four separate but interwoven factors: purpose, objectives, scope, and structure.[53] With respect to purpose, religious instruction by nature is always intentional while other sectors of life are frequently indiscriminate. With respect to objectives, religious instruction by nature is always focused while other sectors of life are frequently blurred somewhat. With respect to scope, religious instruction by nature is always holistic while other sectors of life are frequently segmented.[54]

---

52. This full view of religious instruction perforce includes but also necessarily goes beyond the restrictive confines of religious socialization. Religious socialization is only one dimension of the entire religious instruction enterprise. Consequently any exclusively denominational mode of religious socialization such as catechesis is not religious instruction in its full form. It further follows that any denominational mode of religious instruction such as catechesis whose exclusive aim is that of socialization will find the goal of religious pluralism as distasteful at best or repugnant at worst. A good example of this last-mentioned point can be found in Michael J. Wrenn, "Response," *Journal of Ecumenical Studies* 18 (Fall, 1981), pp. 646-652.

53. Other enterprises or sectors of life often incorporate one or even two of these factors. But only the teaching endeavor contains all four.

54. Holism in this context refers to the deliberate incorporation of all the major domains of human existence into the instructional process so that each domain is given due weight in enactment. These domains include psychomotion, cognition, affect, and lifestyle. Some other religious educationists who, like myself, regard religious instruction as the ideal arena for fostering religious pluralism unfortunately view the scope of religion teaching as exclusively cognitive rather than holistic, a position which can seriously cripple the potential effectiveness of religious instruction as a zone for fostering religious pluralism. See, for example, two highly cognitive formulations by Gabriel Moran, namely his *Design for Religion*, pp. 74, 90-95, and his *Interplay* (Winona, Minn.: St. Mary's Press, 1981), p. 45. *Design for Religion* was written in the period in which Moran believed that theology was the product and process of religious instruction activity. *Interplay* was written in the period when Moran declared that theology was a mere "modest contributor" to religious instruction and that religion teaching had no product content. (Total reversals of position are not uncommon in Moran's writings). Moran's ultra-cognitivist view is echoed by one of his more articulate followers, Kieran Scott in "Three Traditions of Religious Education," *Religious Education* 69 (Summer, 1984), pp. 333-339.

With respect to structure, religious instruction by nature is always systematic while other segments of life are frequently haphazard.[55] Persons can and do gain a great deal of religiously pluralistic learnings in other noninstructional areas of life. But the special advantage of the instructional process is that it systematically provides for greater, deeper, easier, and more efficient opportunities for fostering religiously pluralistic learnings than is typically possible in other areas of life.[56]

Any vision or theory[57] or reality is viable only to the extent to which it is derived directly from practice. Therefore, if we are to develop a refined vision and a valid theory of how to do religious pluralism in general and how to teach for religious pluralism specifically, then we must first actively engage in a wide variety of religiously pluralistic practices. Here the crucial role of the religious educator comes into play. In their daily teaching activities, the religious educators are on the front line with respect to religious pluralism. In all probability the best and the most expansive work in religious pluralism is done in the religious instruction sector.[58] It does not basically matter that much of the ecclesiasticum and the ecclesia fails to consider religious instruction as important in the life of the church.[59] What does matter is that religious

---

55. Systematic in this context does not mean tightly structured. Rather, systematic means that there is a structure which is deliberatively adapted to the exigencies of all four molar interactive variables which are present in every teaching act, namely teacher, learner, subject-matter content, and environment. For a discussion of this point, see James Michael Lee, *The Flow of Religious Instruction* (Birmingham, Ala.: Religious Education Press, 1973), pp. 208, 230-250.

56. Education, of course, is wider and therefore not identical to instruction. Education can be both intentional or nonintentional, focused or nonfocused, structured or unstructured, systematic or haphazard. Instruction, on the other hand, is by its very nature always intentional, focused, structured, and systematic. Instructional activity can take place in both formal settings such as school or church liturgy, or in informal settings such as the home.

57. Vision and theory differ from one another. Vision is a forward-looking and often prophetic long-range view of how a reality should be if it is to attain its full potential. Theory is a statement or group of statements organically integrating interrelated concepts, facts, and laws in such a fashion as to offer a comprehensive and systematic view of reality by specifying relations among variables. Theory is much more formal in nature and structure than vision. If vision is to become fruitful and self-corrective, it must be transformed into theory.

58. For a forthright and amply illustrated example of this point, see Francis D. Kelly, "Ecumenical Issues Within Christian Education Today," *Journal of Ecumenical Studies* 18 (Fall, 1981), pp. 578-579.

59. I side with Francis Kelly and disagree with Stephen Schmidt on this point for reasons which are given in the next two sentences in the text. See Schmidt, "Response," in ibid, pp. 592-593.

instruction does in fact affect more lives at a fundamental level than either the ecclesiasticum or virtually any other sector of the church's ministry. And what does matter is that religious educators are in fact on the front line in developing and evolving and forging new ways of doing religious pluralism in an educationally productive manner. The enmeshment of religious educators with the nitty-gritty activities of religious pluralism generates and corrects both a vision and a theory of religious pluralism in two ways. First, in their efforts to teach learners in and for religious pluralism, religious educators must forge for themselves their own individual vision and theory of religious pluralism. All religious educators have a vision and a theory, however inchoate, prior to and in accompaniment with their actual teaching activity. Second, the process and product results of pedagogical practice in and for religious pluralism afford religious educationists, theologians, religious sociologists, ecclesiastical officials, and others a vast resource of data out of which broader and more elegant theories can be erected both for religious pluralism *in se* and for teaching religious pluralism.

Religious Instruction as Prophetic

To be prophetic is to hasten the future, to bring the God of what will be into the world of what is now. To be prophetic is to be on the front line always. Because religious instruction by its very nature is on the front line of ecclesial activity, it is called to be prophetic. Neither theology nor the ecclesiasticum are regularly if ever on the front line of the ecclesia.[60] Theology and the ecclesiasticum tend to be reactive; religious instruction is inherently proactive. Unless religious instruction is imbued in all its practical and theoretical facets with the incisive dimension, it will not only lose its greatness but will also lose its very soul.

With respect to religious pluralism, religious instruction must be prophetic to one's own religion as well as to all other religions. Religious instruction thus brings other religions into the ambit of one's own religion as well as bringing all religions into fecund and change-oriented interaction with one another. Frequently the first-mentioned of these

---

60. Theology attempts to derive one kind of meaning from what has already taken place on the front line. The ecclesiasticum tries to manage what has already taken place on the front line and what will take place on the front line. Usually theological understanding fails to fully capture the dynamism and the concreteness of the front line in its restrictive nets of cognition, past-oriented reflection, and necessarily one-dimensional understanding. Almost always the ecclesiasticum fails to harness with optimum fruitfulness the creative energy and the breakthrough character of the front line because it tries to put the vigor and the future thrust of the front line into caged structures from the past.

tasks is more difficult and more laden with opposition than the second.

Because it is on the front line, religious instruction activity need not wait until either official ecclesiastical statements or theologians announce that one or another religiously pluralistic pedagogical activity is ecclesiastically or theologically "correct." A proactive stance by religious instruction activity constitutes neither crass disobedience of the ecclesiasticum nor wanton disregard of theology. Rather, religious instruction activity necessarily adopts a proactive stance because it consciously or unconsciously recognizes the inbuilt tendency of both the ecclesiasticum and theology to be inherently reactive. The ecclesiasticum as well as theology must carefully examine, sift, and weigh all the evidence available to it. Judgmental activities of this sort can only be done after the religious instruction activity has taken place.[61]

With regard to both the ecclesiasticum and theology, the concrete here-and-now pedagogical activities of religion teachers are always primary and never secondary or derivative in religious instruction for pluralism.[62] Religion teachers on the front line have their own specific solutions, needs, visions, skills, and resources, all of which are typically unavailable to the ecclesiasticum or to theologians. Religious instruction *in concreto* has an authority and an initiative on its own. Its task is a broader one than merely implementing on a small scale the various directives issued by either the worldwide ecclesiasticum or local church authorities.[63] There are instances in which the local ecclesiasticum or theology does in fact constitute the major objective or subjective prob-

---

61. This temporal and often ontic distance between the event and a judgment about this event frequently detracts from the adequacy of the judgment.

62. In its proper form, religious instruction is not a messenger boy for either the ecclesiasticum or theology. The messenger-boy role all but eliminates the ontic integrity of religious instruction as both a distinct field in itself and an authentically prophetic endeavor. On this point, see Lee, *The Shape of Religious Instruction*, pp. 225-226, 246-248.

63. This paragraph represents a close paraphrase of a statement made by a prominent Vatican official on the subject of ecumenical activity and thus, by what would seem justifiable extension, on endeavors of a religiously pluralistic nature. I should emphasize, however, that the Vatican definitely wishes that all individual and group initiatives, though not required to be totally under direct ecclesiastical control, nonetheless should somehow be done at the very outset in tandem with the ecclesiasticum at the local level and then, as appropriate, at successive higher levels. Such collaboration, asserts the Vatican, will forestall possible imbalances created by any group going out on its own, whether that group consists of members of the local ecclesia or even members of the local ecclesiasticum itself. See Thomas F. Stransky and John B. Sheerin, eds., *Doing the Truth in Charity: Statements of Pope Paul VI, Popes John Paul I, John Paul*

lem for fostering religious pluralism. At the objective pole, some local ecclesiastica and some prevailing theologies do in fact hinder serious religious instruction for pluralism. At the subjective pole, quite a few sincere persons, notably youth and young adults, frequently find many ecclesiastica and many theologies to be closed-minded toward other religions and to be spiritually lifeless in what they advocate and live.

In boldly enacting its prophetic role, religious instruction profoundly enriches the entire ecclesia for two important reasons.

First, the exercise of this prophetic role goes a long way in placing the entire ecclesia solidly on a scientific base.[64] Such a base tends to make the ecclesia more open, more effective, more consistent, and more inherently heuristic. Science proceeds along the well-known lines of gathering facts empirically, placing these facts into a context of empirically supported laws, and finally synthesizing these laws into a fruitful theory. Every workable scientific theory, then, is an *a posteriori* explanation. What all this means in terms of the church is that the scientific mode requires that the ecclesiasticum promote rather than quash prophetic endeavors because the process and product empirical data which are derived from prophetic endeavors are absolutely necessary for expanding, correcting, and/or confirming the theories embraced by the ecclesiasticum. Empirical facts are the starting point and baseline; they cannot be bypassed. While the scientific mode does indeed allow the ecclesiasticum to adequately predict the effects of prophetic ministry from its presently held theory, nonetheless, for reasons I just mentioned the selfsame scientific mode demands that new prophetic activities be encouraged and promoted. As Bernard Lonergan observes, the world has passed from a classicist frame of thinking to a scientific frame, a frame in which the *a priori* and mentalist mode of thought has been replaced by the *a posteriori* and empirical mode. Lonergan goes on to assert that the classical mentality is decidedly oriented away from pluralism while the scientific mode is definitely thrusted toward pluralism. "To confine the Catholic Church to a classicist mentality is to keep the Catholic Church out of the modern world and to prolong the already

---

II, and the Secretariat for Promoting Christian Unity, 1964-1980 (New York: Paulist, 1982), p. 92. My own view is that while initial collaboration between religious educators and the ecclesisticum is sometimes helpful to the prophetic efforts of religion teachers in their work for religious pluralism, at other times such collaboration is deleterious to these prophetic efforts and should therefore be deferred until the pedagogically appropriate time.

64. By science here and in the succeeding pages I do not mean a particular *branch* of learning, such as biology, or a collection of these branches, such as natural science. By science here I mean *a way of examining reality.*

too long prolonged crisis within the Church."[65] A major pervasive crisis in the church today is the intrinsic and therefore deep-rooted opposition between the classical mold of the ecclesiasticum on the one hand and the empirical ongoing concrete nitty-gritty prophetic ministries on the other hand: in short, *a priori* versus *a posteriori*, essentialism versus experimentalism, drawingroom mentality versus front-line activity, classical versus empirical.[66]

Second, the enactment by religious instruction of its prophetic role contributes considerably toward helping place the ecclesia on a solid religious base. Such a base tends to make the ecclesia more open to totally living God's revelation in love. Unfortunately many churches, notably the Catholic church, have as their twin base politics (ecclesiasticum) and cognition (theology). But the soul of religion is neither power (ecclesiasticum) nor cognition (theology). The soul of religion is a living faith and hope and love for God and in God as the Lord meets and greets each person existentially in the crucible of life. Spirituality—that is to say our personal and corporate way of living our religion—often breaks the bonds and crosses the boundaries set by the ecclesiasticum and by other cautious custodians of religion. To live a deep spiritual life is to contact, however feebly and indirectly, the raging fire of God's love and infinite existence, a love and an existence which frequently impels the spiritual person to progress beyond the confines of the structures of the ecclesiasticum and the cognitions of theology. Persons living a vigorous spiritual life which is open to God's pluriform revelation are more likely to push forward the frontiers of ecclesial life in general and religious pluralism in particular than persons whose spiritual life is uniform, stale, and closed. One only has to think of the great mystics in the church to appreciate this point. It is quite possible that without a solid, open, revelation-filled base of personal and corporate spirituality our efforts at attaining religious pluralism will end up to

---

65. Lonergan, *Doctrinal Pluralism*, pp. 4-12, quotation on p. 9.

66. One of the hallmarks of the social-science approach to religious instruction is that it is empirical. In contrast, one of the hallmarks of the theological approach to religious instruction is that it is anti-empirical. Indeed, it is precisely the centrality of an empirical base in the social-science approach to religious instruction which was primarily responsible for the profusion of bitter animosity directed at this approach by many advocates of the theological macrotheory of religious instruction, such as Berard Marthaler, during the first scholarly meeting of religious educationists at which the social-science approach was formally presented (Association of Professors and Researchers in Religious Education, Boston, Autumn of 1971). Marthaler's aversion to an empirical foundation for religious instruction also shows itself clearly in "Review," *National Catholic Reporter* 8 (November 19, 1971), p. 8.

be legalistic, perfunctory, and trendy.[67] A major crisis in many of the
Christian churches is caused by the fact that the ecclesiastica of these
churches offer primarily power, official rules, and cognition (theology)
when what the people really want is to be empowered by their churches
to lead richer religious lives.

*If religious instruction all across the board is going to be successful, it
must have as its ultimate twin base the structure of science and the soul
of religion. Such is the constant recurring axis of this chapter and indeed
of all my writings on religious instruction.*

Like the great prophets of the bible, the modern religious educator as
prophet offers specific suggestions for concrete reform rather than spec-
ulations about things in general. In doing so, the religion teacher as
prophet forthrightly challenges and even sometimes upsets the status
quo. In so doing, this person is following in the footsteps of the great
biblical prophets whose words and activities were "onslaughts, scuttling
illusions of false security, challenging evasions, calling faith to account,
questioning prudence and impartiality."[68]

To the ecclesiasticum and probably to most Christians, the time for
significant ecclesial renewal is always in the future. For the prophetic
religious educator, the time for significant ecclesial renewal is always in
the now.

What Heinrich Fries and Karl Rahner write about ecumenism applies with equal force to religious pluralism: "Each historical tradition
and custom contains, besides its good moments, a moment of inertia
which prevents a society, and therefore also a church, from moving
quickly into the future which God has intended for it and requires of it.
We think that all the churches act with too much tactical caution in the
quest for actual unity.[69]

Courage is an especially important quality for all religious educators
to have when exercising their prophetic role in the sector of religious
pluralism, or in any other zone of ecclesial life for that matter. Prophetic
courage is not that kind of courage endorsed by those ecclesiastical
officials who severely blunt the cutting edge of prophetism by immediately attaching to courage such words as cautious, prudent, and moder-

---

67. On this point, see Douglas Steere, "Ecumenism and Spirituality," in
Ecumenism, ed. Leonard Swidler (Pittsburgh, Pa.: Duquesne University Press,
1967), pp. 113-114.

68. Abraham Heschel, *The Prophets*, vol. 1 (New York: Harper & Row, 1962),
p. xiii.

69. Fries and Rahner, *Unity of the Churches*, p. 9.

ate.[70] Prophetic courage is not that kind of courage enunciated by those mainstream religious educationists who maintain that the worth of a religious education activity should be judged by the degree to which it falls within the mainstream of currently favored affirmations about religious instruction rather than by the degree of that activity's intrinsic excellence, by the degree of its prophetic thrust, or by the degree of its cutting-edge qualities.[71] Prophetic courage is not that kind of courage embodied in those ultraliberal religious education professors whose writings advocate sweeping reform in the church but yet whose personal lives display cowardice in standing up to ecclesiastical and other officials whose positions run counter to what these professors profess to believe.[72] Prophetic courage is nicely exemplified in the etymology of the word courage itself. The word courage ultimately derives from the Latin *cor agere*, meaning to act with and from the heart. In the case of prophetic activity, courage is that which is enlightened by the gospel, illumined by the liturgy and other God-synapsed features of ecclesial life,[73] refined by prayer in all its holistic dimensionalities,[74] and existentially attuned to what God is revealing to us in our own lives and in the

---

70. It is obvious that healthy prudence, balanced moderation, and even a certain degree of appropriate caution are necessary in fruitful prophetic activity in today's church. However, to many ecclesiastical officials, the words prudence, moderation, and caution frequently mean total inaction or just very minor inconsequential adjustments in the status quo.

71. One can legitimately inquire whether Jesus, Paul the Apostle, any of the prophets—religious educators all—were in the mainstream, or indeed anywhere near the mainstream, of the prevailing religious views of their respective eras.

72. In this connection, I am reminded of one such ultraliberal religious education professor who became nationally known and who made a considerable amount of money through advocating that religious instruction should be centered around empowering learners to raise their consciousness and courageously throw off the shackles of all ecclesiastical and cultural oppression. When the administrative officials of the church-related university in which this professor was teaching unilaterally withdrew the faculty's invitation to an outside scholar to speak on campus in favor of abortion, the ultraliberal religious education professor did not initiate a faculty statement of protest, did not lead a public demonstration, did not launch in the national or regional media a condemnation of the university administration for its oppressive activity, or the like. Presumably this professor did not wish to jeopardize his own personal position at the university in terms of future promotion in rank and the attainment of healthy salary increases.

73. The authentic expression of this characteristic is *sentire in ecclesia*, not *sentire cum ecclesia*.

74. On holistic prayer, see James Michael Lee, *The Content of Religious Instruction* (Birmingham, Ala.: Religious Education Press, 1985), pp. 672-676.

Zeitgeist as well.[75] Prophetic courage is necessarily an inextricable feature of the religious educator's entire life, personal and professional, present and future. As Hans Küng reminds us, prophetic courage is not a call for a major or minor revolution per se. This kind of call can only encourage political reactionism by the ecclesiasticum directly or through its religious educational or theological agencies. Prophetic courage calls for and embodies not revolution but authentic reform and renewal. The guiding principle must always be the original and abiding message of Jesus Christ himself, the Lord who gave every portion of his life that we all may live, formal Christians and formal non-Christians alike.[76]

Surely the fostering of religious pluralism through religious instruction activity is an integral and indispensable part of the renewal of the whole church.

In fruitfully exercising its prophetic role with respect to religious pluralism, religious instruction must be thoroughly holistic. Thus religious instruction enactment for religious pluralism ought to necessarily involve all the domains of our humanity. Pluralism can never fully arise from fractionated or nonpluralistic instructional enactment. Religious instruction, consequently, should not restrict its activities solely to cognition, such as multireligious discussion groups. Religious instruction activities for religiously pluralistic outcomes must also include persons from different religions engaging in physical activity together (psychomotor domain), participating in appropriate emotional and attitudinal endeavors together (affective domain), and above all living shared aspects of life with one another (lifestyle domain).

The authentic exercise of its prophetic role necessitates that somewhere along the line, as appropriate, religious instruction collaborate with the ecclesiasticum either in itself or in one of its instrumentalities. After all, the ecclesiasticum is a necessary and indispensable dimension of the ecclesia, and a privileged dimension at that. But the collaboration between religious instruction and the ecclesiasticum should be just that, namely a collaboration, a working *together*, a collegial endeavor. The working relationship between religious instruction and the ecclesiasticum should always be a two-way street. Thus collaboration is far wider and more collegial than the same old story of religious instruction submitting itself to the ecclesiasticum for judgment, refinement,

---

75. Hence the saying, "The voice of the times is the voice of God" (*Vox temporis, vox Dei*).

76. Hans Küng, "Preface," in *The Future of Ecumenism*, ed. Hans Küng (New York: Paulist Press, 1969), pp. 3-4.

approval, and broadening. Collaboration simultaneously means that the ecclesiasticum submit itself to the religious instruction enterprise for judgment, refinement, approval, and broadening. Present prophetic activity of the authentic sort is one which links the past and the future. Thus the past should submit itself to the future, and the future should submit itself to the past.

Until the ecclesiasticum really submits itself to the judgment, the influence, and the broadening of the ongoing religious instruction enterprise, it is highly unlikely that it will optimize its activities on behalf of religious pluralism. There is no doubt that the ecclesiasticum of almost every nonfundamentalist Christian denomination favors, in varying degrees, some sort of religious pluralism. But any major ecclesiastical efforts to foster religious pluralism will never attain their potential and indeed will probably fall very short of the goal in the absence of the invigorating impact of the religious instruction enterprise at the very center of the ecclesiasticum.

In their efforts of behalf of religious pluralism, neither worldwide nor local Christian ecclesiastica at their respective top levels seem to have had any significant involvement with religious educators, despite the fact that religious educators are on the front line in religious pluralism. The only persons whom ecclesiastical officials organically involve in forging the theory and practice of religious pluralism are other ecclesiastical officials and theologians (usually "approved" theologians, seldom prophetic theologians). Let me illustrate the point I am making in this paragraph. One of the most important and highly regarded statements ever issued on ecumenism (and thus, by extension, on religious pluralism) was proffered in 1982 by the Faith and Order Commission of the World Council of Churches (the so-called "Lima text"). This statement was drawn up by a group of ecclesiastical bureaucrats and theologians as a result of over a decade of careful consultation with a wide array of theological scholars and church officials from around the world.[77] Not a single functioning religious educator or educationist seems to have been a member of either the group composing the document or the formal consultors to the process. One can only wonder how genuinely filled

---

77. On the authority of the World Council's Central Committee, over a hundred theologians recommended unanimously to transmit an agreed statement on baptism, eucharist, and ministry to the churches for their common study and official response. These biblical and systematic theologians came from more than thirty countries and represented almost all of the major Christian churches, including Roman Catholic, Eastern Orthodox, Oriental Orthodox, Anglican, Lutheran, Methodist, Reformed, United, Disciples, Baptist, Adventist, and Pentecostal.

with a truly expansive spirit can a statement possibly be when the make-up of the authors of the document and the consultors was anything but structurally pluralistic, namely a monolithic manufacture of just two structures within the entire ecclesia, i.e., ecclesiastical officials and theologians. One can also wonder how genuinely oriented to concrete here-and-now pluralistic reality (to say nothing of that portion of plural-istic reality which is on the cutting edge) can a statement possibly be which was drawn up by two groups of individuals who rarely if ever personally experience the really tough, grinding, daily nitty-gritty front line of religious pluralism

The closedness of the World Council of Churches (in its Lima text) to serious significant collaboration with a pluralistic structural representa-tion of the total ecclesia and of groups of persons like religious educators who are on the front line of pluralism is sadly exemplified by one of the most famous recommendations of the document: "As concrete evidence of their ecumenical commitment, the churches are being asked to en-able the widest possible involvement of the whole people of God at all levels of church life in the spiritual process of receiving this text." This sentence reflects the same old sad story of the Christian churches. The ecclesiasticum and those theologians which it approves engage in cogni-tive reflection and then issue a statement which the ecclesia, having had no significant input into the process, is fully expected to "receive." Genuine give-and-take collaboration between the ecclesiasticum on the one hand, and the ecclesia and some of its key groups such as religious educators on the other hand, is implicitly rejected. The ideal relation-ship between the ecclesiasticum and the ecclesia is reflexively assumed to be that of the ecclesiasticum promulgating and the ecclesia receiving. If the ecclesia does not take the ecclesiasticum seriously, it is largely because the ecclesiasticum has rarely if ever taken the ecclesia seriously. If the ecclesiasticum and theologians wish the ecclesia to take religious pluralism seriously, then these two groups should practice authentic pluralism in their own households in terms of their collaborative rela-tionships with the ecclesia in general and with front-line enterprises like religious instruction in particular.

A specific example might help clarify how religious instruction can and must be prophetic to religious pluralism and, by extension, to the whole church. The specific example which I wish to very briefly discuss is that of who should receive the Eucharist.[78] I am selecting this specific example because of the absolute centrality of the Eucharist in the Catho-

---

78. This topic is a very complex one, and I can offer only the briefest outline in the very short space alloted to this topic. My treatment, therefore, will be very simplified, but hopefully not simplistic.

lic church. If religious instruction can be prophetic with regard to the pluralistic issue of who should receive the Eucharist, then surely it can be prophetic to any other area of ecclesial activity.

There are three major positions on the issue of who should receive the Catholic Eucharist.

The first position holds that only persons in a grace-filled union of faith with the Catholic church are permitted to receive the Eucharist. Catholics not in the state of grace, members of other Christian religions, and persons belonging to non-Christian religions or to no religion at all, are excluded from receiving the Eucharist. This view is sometimes called the closed table because it closes access to the Eucharist to everyone except Catholics in good standing with the ecclesiasticum. It is the position held for very many centuries by the highest levels of the official Catholic church. In recent history, this position has been confirmed by the Second Vatican Council's *Decree on Ecumenism*,[79] by the *Ecumenical Decree* issued by the Vatican's Secretariat for the Promotion of Christian Unity,[80] and by the same Secretariat's *Instruction on Admitting other Christians to Eucharistic Communion in the Catholic Church*.[81] The Catholic hierarchy of the United States has also made a similar declaration.[82] The classical theological rationale for this position was stated very well by Innocent III: "The Eucharist expresses existing church unity and produces further church unity." *(Eucharistia significat et efficit unitatem ecclesiae.)* Unity in cognitive doctrine and in faith are thus the necessary preconditions for legitimate reception of the Eucharist. Persons who are not one in Jesus are unable to receive the sacrament worthily because that which is necessary (unity) for worthy reception is lacking. The Eucharist is "the sacrament of unity, namely the holy people united and arranged under their bishops."[83] Further, the Eucharistic celebration is not a private event performed for the sanctification of an individual soul in attendance. Rather, the Eucharist is a corporate event celebrated with and through the entire corporate

---

79. Sacrosanctum Concilium Oecumenicum Vaticanum II, "Unitatis Redinegratio," #8 (p. 98).

80. Secretariatus ad Christianorum Unitatem Fovendam, "Ad Totam Ecclesiam," #a 55-56 (pp. 590-591).

81. Secretariatus ad Christianorum Unitatem Fovendam, "In Quibus Rerum Circumstantiis," *Acta Apostolicae Sedis* 64 (1 Junii 1972), pp. 518-525.

82. Committee for Pastoral Research and Practices, Committee on the Liturgy, National Council of Catholic Bishops, Monthly Update, "Guidelines for Receiving Communion," November 26, 1986.

83. Sacrosanctum Concilium Oecumenicum Vaticanum II, "Sacrosanctum Concilium" (4 Decembris 1963), *Acta Apostolocae Sedis* 56 (15 Februarii 1964), #26 (p. 107). This document, the Constitution on the Sacred Liturgy, is here quoting *De Unitate Catholicae Ecclesiae* of Cyprian of Carthage (?-258).

ecclesia and pertaining directly to the whole body of the Catholic church. As an essentially corporate function, the entire Eucharistic liturgy, including the reception of the sacrament, concretely embodies the unity of the church, a unity in which non-Catholics do not participate.

The second position holds that only persons who are members of one or another of the Christian churches are permitted to receive the Eucharist. Christians not in the state of grace and all non-Christians are excluded from receiving the Eucharist. This view is called the partially closed table because while it opens the Eucharist to all Christians in good standing with their ecclesiastica, it nonetheless closes access to the Eucharist to persons belonging to non-Christian religions or to no religion at all.[84] The theological rationale is that faith in Jesus and belief in the Eucharist[85] constitutes the fundamental requirement for the legitimate reception of the Eucharist. Central to this position is the theological contention that the Eucharistic gift was made by Jesus to all those who believe in him, not just to any one segment of believers, however privileged that segment may claim itself to be or may even actually be. Belief in Jesus, not membership in a particular religious group, is the fundamental precondition for worthy reception of the Lord's living testament. Further, the Catholic church's present doctrine on who can legitimately receive the Eucharist is incomplete since it was forged in the absence of organic participation by the total Christian community of faith, namely, without the active involvement of other Christian denominations each of which authentically embodies in its own special way God's revelation in Jesus. Any decision on who should or should not dine at the Lord's table should be made by the ecclesiastica of all the Christian churches deliberating and deciding in concert.

The third position holds that everyone should be permitted to receive the Eucharist. This includes Catholics, members of other Christian denominations, adherents of non-Christian religions, and even persons who do not profess any religion at all. This view is called the open table because it does not exclude from the Eucharist anyone who wishes to dine at the Lord's banquet.

In its official documents and in the writings of its approved theologians down through the ages, the Catholic ecclesiasticum has consistently proposed two principal functions of the Eucharist, namely

---

84. Two fine advocacies of the partially closed table can be found in James F. White, *Sacraments of God's Self-Giving* (Nashville, Tenn.: Abingdon, 1983) and Wainright, *The Ecumenical Moment*.

85. This belief in the Eucharist is not restricted to the Catholic belief. It is essentially a Christian belief and thus can legitimately differ with the particular Catholic belief about the nature and operation of the Eucharist.

a sign of unity and a source of grace. The first position (closed table) on the reception of the Eucharist emphasizes the unity function, while the second position (partially closed table) lays stress on the Eucharist as a source of grace.

In examining the validity and the fruitfulness of the first two positions on the reception of the Eucharist, I proceeded in the fashion customary in the church—I adduced relevant theological principles. To highlight the signal degree to which religious instruction practice can be prophetic to pluralism and indeed to the entire ecclesia, I would like to jettison this customary procedure and see what happens when religious instruction practice rather than theological reasons are brought to bear in examining the validity and fruitfulness of the third position (open table) on receiving the Eucharist. After religious instruction practice has been used as both the foundation and the point of departure for examining the open table, theological reasons will be brought in to partially explain and test what religious instruction practice has found about the open table. This process reverses the usual procedure in which theological reasons are propounded and then religious instruction practice is forced to lie in the bed of these reasons, however procrustean this bed might be.

Actually the procedure I am adopting here is the commonly accepted one not only in concrete here-and-now life but in all science as well. The fact of the matter is that theory follows practice because theory is nothing more than a series of progressively abstract generalizations which serve to explain and predict and verify practice. Theory, then, arises from practice, is refined and corrected by practice, and in the end is accepted or rejected on the basis of its usefulness to practice. This largely explains why, in the history of the church, theology has often reversed itself significantly on one or another secular practice (e.g., usury) and on one or another religious practice (e.g., fast and abstinence).

We must always bear in mind that it is a grave error to equate theology with the theory of religion. Any adequate theory of religion is perforce much broader than just theology. Theology is only one theory of religion. Theology is no longer queen of the sciences. Indeed, theology is no longer queen of the religious sciences. The psychology of religion, the sociology of religion, and so forth, make contributions to a general theory of religion which are in many ways just as valid and useful, if not more so, than theological theory.[86] A general theory of

---

86. This fact is obvious when it comes to explaining and predicting such religious practices as determining whether First Penance should precede or succeed First Communion.

religion is a composite made up of theology, psychology, sociology, cultural anthropology, and so on. Religionology is this general theory.

Let me now describe a concrete religious instruction practice, after which I will proceed to discuss briefly the religious instruction axis of this practice. After all this is finished, I will discuss some theological rationales which can be offered to support and refine the particular religious instruction practice. In this way theology will serve religious instruction purposes rather than religious instruction serving theological purposes.[87] This is how things should be in the church. In pastoral activity, theology exists for the spiritual welfare of humanity and not vice versa.[88]

A religion class of interested adults meets once a week to explore religious pluralism. The teacher is Catholic. The twenty-five members of the class include Catholics, various kinds of Protestants, two Orthodox, three Jews, two Muslims, a Hindu, a Buddhist, and two persons who are not members of any institutional religion. The purpose of the class is holistic, namely, to learn the cognitive doctrines of various religions, to gain a warm affective feeling for various religions, and to change personal lifestyle in such a manner so as to live in a more religiously pluralistic manner. When several months of learning have passed, the class decides that it would be helpful to attend the liturgies of various religions. After experiences in Orthodox, Protestant, Jewish, and Buddhist houses of worship, the learners all testify that attendance at these worship services seemed to have enhanced their personal spiritual life, improved the quality of their living in a religiously pluralistic manner, and augmented both their cognitive understanding of and affective warmth for the various religions. On the next Sunday the learners are scheduled to attend a Catholic Mass. They ask the religious educator whether or not they can receive the Eucharist. They know what the Eucharist is, have a positive feeling for it, and strongly believe that they can come closer to God in some way by receiving the Eucharist. The religious educator agrees, and does not inform the person

---

87. Theology must serve its own purpose if it is to be true to itself. The purpose of theology is the cognitive explanation of the nature and workings of God. The findings of theology can be applied to other areas of life. However, the actual concrete application of theology to life is no more theology than farming is biology or physiology is medical surgery. Theology never remains itself when its principles are applied to a concrete area of life. In order to be applied, theology must be inserted into another reality which is basically different from theology in theory, purpose, and procedure. Thus religious instruction activity is no more applied theology than farming is applied biology or than medical surgery is applied physiology.

88. This is precisely the central import of the incident in which Jesus cured the man with the withered hand on the Sabbath (Lk 6: 6-11).

giving the Eucharist to communicants that some of the recipients are not Catholic.

The religious instruction axis around which revolved the teacher's recommendation to these non-Catholics to receive the Eucharist is the central twin axis of all religious instruction endeavor, namely to enhance the learner's religious life through an effective instructional act. The reception of the Eucharist is not only a sacramental act; it is also a highly charged instructional act in the fullest sense of instruction.[89] The religious effect of the Eucharist varies according to the disposition of the recipients. The recipients were all well-disposed.

In recommending that these non-Catholics receive the Eucharist, the teacher placed religious instruction norms over theological norms and ecclesiastical norms. The basis for this act on the part of the teacher is that theological norms are not intrinsically valid for religious instruction activity. Theological norms are valid only for theology; they are not inherently valid in other kinds of activities, as for example liturgical celebration, religious instruction, or the like.[90] The overarching religious

---

89. For an elaboration of the religious instruction act from the perspective of teaching, see Lee, *The Flow of Religious Instruction*, pp. 206-248.

90. Theological norms are operative in nontheological activities such as religious instruction, not inherently but only to the degree to which these nontheological activities accept these external norms and ingest these norms into their proper spheres of activity. In the ingestion of theological norms, the other nontheological activities change the nature and authority of the norm from a theological norm to whatever is the norm proper to the nontheological activities. Thus such norms are not theological norms but norms suggested by theology. For example, in those instances where the ecclesiasticum seemingly imposes theological norms on the faithful, the authority underlying these norms is that of the ecclesiasticum, not that of theology. In actual fact, the use of theological norms by the ecclesiasticum means that the norms have been transformed from theological norms to ecclesiastical norms. What once were theological norms are no longer theological norms but are ecclesiastical norms. To be sure, theological norms may legitimately judge religious instruction and the ecclesiasticum, just as religious instruction and the ecclesiasticum may legitimately judge theology. Still my point remains, namely that theological norms are inherently valid only for theology. My thesis is starkly underscored by recalling what happens when theological norms oppose ecclesiastical norms. Immediately the ecclesiasticum moves to correct these "innovative, novel, and dangerous" theological norms, sharply reminding theologians of the supremacy of ecclesiastical norms over theological norms. What the ecclesiasticum is saying at a basic level is that it has norms peculiar to itself, norms which are different from theological norms. If the "innovative, novel, and dangerous" theological norms are truly prophetic, the ecclesiasticum ingests them at a later time. When this occurs, the theological norms no longer remain theological norms but are transformed into ecclesiastical norms which will be used to impose the ecclesiasticum's will on future ecclesial activity, including theological activity.

instruction norm operative in this situation is that of helping persons to come closer to God through religiously pluralistic endeavors. The salvation of souls is the supreme and ever-abiding religious norm of religious instruction. (*Salus animarum suprema lex*.) From a religious instruction perspective, the Lord's Supper is one of the last places in which to practice restrictive ecclesiastical discipline such as exclusion of persons from the Eucharist. If the Eucharist is anything, it is the outstretched arms of Jesus reconciling everyone to union with himself. The Eucharist is the living salvific testament of God's love for all humanity in and through Jesus. From the point of view of religious instruction, it is a desecration of the Eucharist to exclude anyone from its reception.[91] The Eucharist is God's unconditional love poured out for each and every person without exception. To attach any condition or any strings to the reception of the Eucharist goes against the very purpose and axis of religious instruction in general, of the Eucharist as a religious instruction act, and of the Eucharist as the zenith of God's self-giving.

From a religious instruction point of view, the Eucharist is the supreme personal and instructional expression of the love of Jesus for all of us; how can anyone possibly be outside the orbit of Jesus's redeeming and instructional love?[92] The Eucharist is essentially a meal at which its partakers gain spiritual nourishment, fellowship, and solidarity (but not uniformity). To exclude from the Eucharist those non-Catholics who sincerely desire to partake of it is existentially to teach a noxious form of gnosticism which unduly restricts the incalculable religious and instructional benefits of the Eucharist to a select few.

Again from a religious instruction vantage point, the non-Catholics in the example I have given definitely wish to receive the Eucharist. By receiving the Eucharist they are seeking to draw near to Jesus, to know

---

91. The original Lord's Supper, like all biblical events and like the whole bible itself, has redemption and religious instruction as its inextricable dual prime purpose. Further, the Eucharist is essentially though not exclusively a religious instruction act. On the first point, see James Michael Lee, "Religious Education and the Bible: A Religious Educationist's View," in *Biblical Themes in Religious Education,* ed. Joseph S. Marino (Birmingham, Ala.: Religious Education Press, 1983), pp. 3-8.

92. Theology, of course, makes the same affirmation. To assert that the axes, goals, and norms of religious instruction sometimes intersect those of theology is definitely not to aver that the axes, goals, and norms of religious instruction become subject to the control of theology or actually become theology. To assert that the axes, goals, and norms of any reality which touches or which intersects theology can only be theological is to uphold a rather crude version of theological imperialism—something which is done, for example, by Marianne Sawicki in "Review," *National Catholic Reporter* 20 (October 12, 1984), p. 20.

and feel and experience him in a different manner. They are not partaking of the Eucharist because of what theology or the catechism say about the reality of Jesus's presence in the consecrated species or because of any perceived theological connection between the eschatological nature of the sacrament and the crucifixion/resurrection event.[93]

Having described a specific incident of non-Catholics receiving the Eucharist in a Catholic church, and having touched on the religious instruction axis which confirms this action, I now wish to adduce five relevant theological rationales on behalf of the action which the religious educator took. These theological rationales are being offered neither to supplant the religious instruction axis nor to give this axis allegedly "real" authority. Rather, the theological rationales are being offered to provide a helpful though basically unnecessary external support to the legitimate and sufficient internal authority of religious instruction with respect to the religious instructional action of the teacher.[94]

The first theological rationale on behalf of the religious educator's action in recommending that the non-Catholics in question receive the

---

93. In my view, what a European Protestant has written about eucharistic intercommunion among various Christian religions also applies to cases in which non-Christians wish to receive the Eucharist in a Catholic church: "Instead of sneaking off to a eucharistic celebration in a church to which we do not belong, instead of feeling inwardly resentful of a prohibition which we no longer understand, wouldn't it be better to permit a recriprocal eucharistic hospitality?" This argument, of course, is basically a religious instructional one and not a theological one. (Jean-Jacques von Allmen, "The Conditions for an Acceptable Intercommunion," in *The Future of Ecumenism*, p. 7.)

94. I should note that powerful theological rationales can be offered to condemn theologically the religious instruction action of the teacher. This very fact helps to prove the major point I have been making in these last few pages, namely that the norms and axes of a nontheological activity such as religious instruction or pastoral care or ecclesiastical workings are not ultimately determined by theology but by the particular nontheological activity itself. In the course of actualizing itself, the particular nontheological activity, among other things, selects from a welter of often opposing theological options those particular norms and axes it wishes to utilize for its own purposes. The particular nontheological activity then incorporates and reshapes the theological norms and principles according to its own norms and axes. In the process of this incorporation and reshaping, theological norms and axes qua theology cease to exist and, together with a wide variety of elements external and internal to the particular nontheological activity, are existentially mediated into a new reality, namely, the norms and axes of the particular nontheological activity itself. For a treatment on mediatorship of theology vis-á-vis religious instruction, see James Michael Lee, "The Authentic Source of Religious Instruction," in *Religious Education and Theology*, ed. Norma H. Thompson (Birmingham, Ala.: Religious Education Press, 1982), pp. 165-174.

Eucharist centers on the redemption. Virtually all theological views on the Eucharist are necessarily grounded in the salvific life, death, and resurrection of Jesus because the Eucharist is an integral part and indeed the culmination of Jesus's redemptive work. The Eucharist is the whole person of Jesus, flesh and spirit, giving himself to all humanity without any holding back.[95] The Eucharist is a sacrament of redemption vertically and horizontally—vertically in redemptively bringing human beings to God, horizontally in redemptively bringing human beings to other human beings.[96] The Eucharist is itself the supreme present sacrifice for our redemption; it is Jesus actively continuing to redeem us now. The Eucharist is cosmic in scope and influence. If indeed the Eucharist is the redemptive giving of himself by Jesus to all humanity, why then is the overwhelming majority of humanity banned by the ecclesiasticum from the Eucharistic meal? If the Eucharist is redemptive vertically and horizontally, does not the exclusion of most persons from partaking of the Body and Blood of Jesus wantonly short-circuit this verticalness and horizontalness? If the Eucharist is cosmic in its redemptive scope, how can the ecclesiasticum legitimately exclude anyone in the cosmos from partaking in the Lord's Supper? Can the ecclesiasticum rightly put limits on the all-inclusive redemptive activity of Jesus in the Eucharist?

The second theological rationale in support of the religious educator's action in recommending that the non-Catholics in question receive the Eucharist centers on eschatology. Recent research in both historical theology and in liturgical theology conclude that in the New Testament and in the ancient church the Eucharist was definitely regarded as an eschatological event (the meal itself) taking place in an eschatological context (the liturgical celebration) which is situated in a wider ecology (the whole ecclesia).[97] The Eucharist is at once the firstfruit and the advent of the Kingdom.[98] In the eschatological perspective, the Eucharist makes the Last Things (*eschata*) the present things while still preserving the distinction between the Kingdom now here and the Kingdom yet to come. Eschatologically, the Eucharist is the ontic junction of

---

95. Regis A. Duffy, *Real Presence* (San Francisco: Harper & Row, 1982), p. 145.

96. Wainright, *The Ecumenical Moment*, pp. 55-59.

97. Robert L. Browning and Roy A. Reed, *The Sacraments in Religious Education and Liturgy* (Birmingham, Ala.: Religious Education Press, 1985), pp. 168-172.

98. Geoffrey Wainright, *Eucharist and Eschatology* (New York: Oxford University Press, 1971). The Kingdom is a descriptor for the actualization of all that will come from God through Jesus to humanity.

the past, present, and future Kingdom of God. In this view, the Eucharist is simultaneously the actualized Kingdom of God in the present moment and the firm pledge of the Kingdom yet to come (a Kingdom different from but continuous with the actualization of the Kingdom in the present). If the Eucharist is the epitome of the actualized Kingdom in the present to which everyone is invited (Mt. 22:1-10), then how can the ecclesiasticum prevent persons from being welcomed to participate in the living presence of the Kingdom as this Kingdom is being accomplished in the Eucharist meal?

The third theological rationale in support of the religious educator's action centers on the creation and its ongoing continuance through history to the present moment and beyond. Since the world from the very outset is existentially soaked with God in his presence and power, the world is inherently sacramental in nature.[99] It is within this context of the world-as-the-original-sacrament that the Eucharist is properly situated. Thus the Eucharist is the world in present pleroma, the fully-charged sacramental fullness of the world. In Holy Communion, the world as eucharist becomes the world as Eucharist. If all humanity communes with sacrament (world) by living in it, then is the ecclesiasticum justified in propounding a discontinuity so chasmic as to exclude most persons from participating in that meal which is at once the pleroma and the emblem of the world-as-sacrament?

The fourth theological rationale in support of the religious educator's action centers on reconciliation. The Eucharist experience represents the highest available opportunity here on earth for a person to be reconciled to God.[100] Each person is a sinner to a certain extent; some persons are worse sinners than others. It is in the reception of the Eucharist that each person has a genuine chance to become reconciled to God's salvific activity accomplished initially through creation and

---

99. Thus Theodore Runyon maintains that neither the church nor even Jesus is the original sacrament; each of these realities epitomizes in its own way creation as the original and ongoing sacrament. (Theodore Runyon, "The World as the Original Sacrament," *Worship* 54 [November, 1980], pp. 495-511.) See also Matthew Fox, "Meister Eckhart on the Fourfold Path of Creation-Centered Spirituality," in *Western Spirituality: Historical Roots, Ecumenical Routes*, ed. Matthew Fox (Notre Dame, Ind.: Fides/Claretian, 1979), pp. 215-227. Fox states that in Eckhart's view the world is the redeemer; Jesus is the fulfillment and the reminder of this original redemption.

100. Bernard Cooke argues that the Eucharist as the actual flesh and blood of Jesus helps the recipient, who is also composed of flesh and blood, to identify with the reconciliatory thrust of the Eucharist. (Bernard J. Cooke, *Christian Sacraments and Christian Personality* [New York: Holt, Rinehart and Winston, 1965], p. 158.)

then supremely through the incarnation. If a prime task of the ecclesia is to work with Jesus in reconciling the world to God, then how can the ecclesiasticum refuse to operationalize this mission of reconciliation by denying the Eucharist to all those who wish to partake of it?

The fifth theological rationale in support of the religious educator's action centers on the historical Lord's Supper itself and the existential recovery of this historical meal in the present moment. In recent times there has been considerable theological attention given to the present-day Eucharist as an anamnesis of the historical Paschal Meal.[101] (Anamnesis is a Greek word meaning "recalling to mind.") In contemporary Eucharistic theology, anamnesis refers to the celebration of the Eucharist as the living memorial of the historical Last Supper—a memorial act, not in the sense of simply celebrating an event which occurred long ago, but of re-being that original event. From the anamnetic perspective, the Eucharist is the actual, subjective, existential actualization of the original Lord's Supper in all that historical meal's validity and fullness. Because of its anamnetic character, the Eucharist is the ontic reestablishment today of that great historical event of yesteryear. The dynamics of that great historical event are the real-life dynamics of the Eucharist today. The historical Paschal event luminously shows that the living memorial which Jesus established in the Eucharist is nothing less than the actualization of the salvific reality of Jesus. The Eucharist as the always-present testament of the Last Supper sums up in existential fashion the messianic career of Jesus. The cup is the new *diatheke* (covenant) of and in Jesus's blood, an edible covenant through which all humanity is tangibly offered the real possibility of salvation.[102] Because the Eucharist is the quintessence of the salvific convenant made by God in the physically present existence of Jesus, the church attains the highest actuality of its nature when it celebrates the Eucharist.[103] The Eucharist is thus the here-and-now covenant of salvation which God offers us through the transubstantiated bread and wine. Though God offers his covenant of salvation to all who partake of the Eucharist, the recipient need not accept this offer. This fact manifested itself from the very outset of the history of the Eucharist, namely at the historical Lord's Supper itself. Luke's account of the original Paschal Meal clearly indi-

---

101. See, for example, Joachim Jeremias, *The Eucharistic Words of Jesus*, trans. Norman Perrin (Philadelphia: Fortress, 1977).

102. Johannes Betz, "Eucharist: 1.B. Institution of the Eucharist by the Historical Jesus," in *Sacramentum Mundi*, vol. II, ed. Karl Rahner et al. (New York: Herder and Herder, 1968), pp. 257-261.

103. Karl Rahner, *The Church and the Sacraments*, trans. W. J. O'Hara (Montreal: Palm, 1963), p. 84.

cates that Judas ate the consecrated bread and drank from the consecrated cup.[104] Surely Judas seriously violated the Eucharistic covenant,
as did Peter shortly thereafter when he denied Jesus to the servant
girl.[105] The Eucharist is no guarantee against betrayal and other serious
violations of the covenant by the recipient.[106] To the recipients, regardless of their varying dispositions, the Eucharist is the divine flesh-and-
blood covenant in which the Lord personally and lovingly continues his
messianic mission of preparing all who receive him for the parousia. If
the Eucharist as an anamnetic event is the re-being of the historical
Paschal Meal (the culmination of Jesus's terrestrial messianic mission to
saint and sinner, to Jews and Samaritans alike), can the ecclesiasticum
validly exclude anyone from eating the Lord's body and drinking his
blood? If the historical Jesus invited to be partakers of his original
Supper two persons whom he knew would mortally betray him within
twenty-four hours, can the ecclesiasticum legitimately exclude any person from the Eucharistic banquet?

Of interest is that the Vatican itself has opened the door, if only a
crack, to non-Catholic participation in the Catholic Eucharist. Thus *Ad
Totam Ecclesiam* specifically states that for adequate reasons the local
ecclesiasticum can allow a non-Catholic Christian to receive the Eucharist. Such access to the Eucharist is permitted when the non-Catholic
Christian is in danger of death or is in urgent need (as during persecution or incarceration) if this individual has no access to a minister of his
own particular religion and spontaneously requests a Catholic priest to
give him the Eucharist—so long as this individual declares a faith in the
Eucharist in harmony with that of the Catholic church and is rightly
disposed.[107]

The dispensation discussed in the previous paragraph shows that for
its own legitimate purposes the central ecclesiasticum did indeed shape a
theological rationale, if ever so slightly. In granting this dispensation, the
central ecclesiasticum wittingly or unwittingly conceded that of the two

---

104. Luke 22: 14-23. The accounts of the Lord's Supper given in Matthew
and Mark provide no clearcut indication of whether Judas partook of the
consecrated species.

105. Luke 22: 54-62.

106. Carroll Stuhlmueller, "The Gospel According to Luke" in *The Jerome
Biblical Commentary*, vol. II, ed. Joseph A. Fitzmyer and Raymond E. Brown
(Englewood Cliffs, N.J.: Prentice-Hall, 1968), p. 158.

107. Secretariatus ad Christianorum Unitatem Fovendam, "Ad Totam
Ecclesiam," #55 (p. 590). The theological rationale given by the Vatican for this
dispensation is that all sacraments are not only a sign of unity but are also a
source of grace.

classical theological rationales for the Eucharist, the source of grace takes precedence over the sign of unity.[108] But what would happen to the theological rationale for unity if, from the religious instruction perspective, we would construe unity in a different manner than that done in classical theology? Partly because of the particular philosophical base upon which it was erected, and partly because it was fashioned in such a manner as to be ultimately acceptable to the central ecclesiasticum, the unity which the Eucharist signifies is regarded by classical Catholic theology as structural unity. Religious instruction, by its very existential nature, tends to emphasize dynamism rather than structure, effect rather than essence, facilitation rather than legalism. Applied to unity, the religious instruction perspective tends to regard unity not in terms of formal membership in the juridical structure of Catholicism but in terms of a personal life oriented in large or small measure to God. The religious instruction perspective tends to envision unity not in an *a priori* fashion but in an *a posteriori* manner, that is, in terms of the unity which the Eucharist has been shown to produce. The religious instruction perspective tends to see unity not from the eyes of ecclesiastical discipline but from the eyes of how it can help all persons come closer to God. Religious instruction looks at unity not so much in terms of a common bond of cognitive beliefs but rather in terms of a common bond of affective love and a common bond of lifestyle holiness.

This excursion into the issue of whether the Catholic Eucharist should be given to non-Catholics of every sort has shown that religious instruction contains the capability to correct, to broaden, and to push forward the antipluralistic tilt of the ecclesiasticum and its official theology with regard to one central sector of ecclesial life. In the final analysis, the restrictive stance of the ecclesiasticum toward the open table will have to stand trial and be judged before the face of the crucified Christ who died for everyone, both those within the juridical structure and those outside of it. And it is religious instruction, not theology, which brings the actuality of the crucified Christ to human beings.[109] Herein lies the glory and the power of religious instruction as a privileged prophetic endeavor in the church.

---

108. This concession would be in line with the position of Thomas Aquinas who holds that the principal effect of every sacrament is grace. Thomas Aquinas, *Summa Theologica*, III, q. 62.

109. The nature of theology is to reflect on this actuality. The nature of religious instruction is to existentially mediate this actuality. Theology is a cognitive science. Religious instruction is a facilitational activity.

THE APPROPRIATE MACROTHEORY FOR
RELIGIOUSLY PLURALISTIC INSTRUCTION

If any area of human endeavor is to be successful, it must be supported by an overarching macrotheory appropriate to its sphere of activity. Instruction for religious pluralism is a human field of endeavor. Therefore, religiously pluralistic instruction must be supported by an appropriate overarching macrotheory.

Neither tract nor speculation should be confused with theory. A tract is a statement of a person's own subjective passionate persuasion. Thus a tract is valid and useful even though it might at times contain empty slogans, fallacious reasoning, factual errors, and internal contradictions.[110] Speculation is the exclusive use of conceptual, judgmental, and inferential processes in order to ascertain the truth about any matter of concern or interest. Speculation is primarily a form of thinking, and as such is directly opposite to the empiric. Speculation is valid and useful even when it is not tethered to empirical data and even when the speculation represents a major reversal in the position advocated in a prior speculation made by the same person.[111] A theory is a statement or group of statements organically integrating interrelated concepts, facts, and laws in such a fashion as to offer a comprehensive and systematic view of reality by specifying relations among variables. No theory is valid or useful if it contains empty slogans, fallacious reasoning, factual errors, internal contradictions, inconsistencies, or reversals of position which are left intact. All theory flows from empirical data and returns to empirical data to enrich them.

A macrotheory is an overarching and global form of theory into which are inserted theories and subtheories of lesser scope. Throughout the centuries theology functioned as the explicit or implicit macrotheory for religious instruction. In the early 1970s, the first systematic presentation of a countervailing macrotheory of religious instruction made its appearance, namely the social-science approach.[112] Though most of the writing since the early 1970s on the subject of religion teaching has mindlessly ignored the ultimate foundation of this field, some of the more thoughtful writers have directly or indirectly grappled with the fundamental matrix of religion teaching.[113]

---

110. John Westerhoff is an especially good example of a tractarian.
111. Gabriel Moran is a particularly gifted example of a speculationist.
112. Lee, *The Shape of Religious Instruction*.
113. Gabriel Moran claims that the ultimate foundation of religious educa

Elsewhere[114] I have extensively demonstrated why social science constitutes the only viable macrotheory for religious instruction. Social
science alone has the power to adequately explain, predict, and verify
the phenomena comprising those activities involved in religion teaching. Conversely, I have also extensively demonstrated elsewhere why
theology cannot in any meaningful way constitute a viable macrotheory
for religious instruction because it is utterly unable to adequately explain, predict, and verify the phenomena comprising the activities involved in religion teaching. Tacitly taking these demonstrations as a
fundamental matrix, I will now suggest a few of the many reasons why
the social-science macrotheory is necessary for any genuine embracing
of teaching religious pluralism, and conversely why the theological
macrotheory inherently tends to ruin the possibility of any teaching for
real religious pluralism.

The Theological Macrotheory
For a wide variety of reasons the theological macrotheory of religious
instruction tends to impede the full realization of teaching for religious
pluralism.

Particularity. The theological approach to religious instruction tends

---

tion *in toto* is not to be found either in theology or in social science but rather in
what he terms the "political/aesthetic." Unfortunately for us all, Moran does
not discuss this new macrotheory in detail which is just as well for him, since
any explication of this new approach would lead him into a morass of insurmountable difficulties. Politics is recognized by virtually all political scientists as
a branch of social science; hence the roots of Moran's new approach are social-
scientific. Because aesthetic science is very different in fundamental concepts,
methodology, and intent from political science, there is no way that these two
can be juxtaposed as equals in a new unified approach, as Moran does (his use
of the /). The only sensible thing to do in this case is to make the aesthetic the
way in which the political is carried out; in such an instance the aesthetic
deployment of the political remains fundamentally within the realm of social
science. Yet another confounding problem is that Moran has never written
extensively on the fundamental nature and structure of either politics or aesthet-
ics and so it is not possible for us to really know the shape and flow and content
of religious education as political/aesthetic. In his search for a valid and useful
macrotheory for religious education activity either in part or in whole, Moran
would do well to start where all successful searches for an appropriate theoretical base have perforce always begun, namely, with the here-and-now activities of
the field and with reliable empirical data gleaned from these activities. See
Gabriel Moran, "From Obstacle to Modest Contributor: Theology in Religious
Education," in *Religious Education and Theology*, p. 58.

114. See, for example, Lee, *The Shape of Religious Instruction*, pp. 182-224;
also James Michael Lee, "The Authentic Source of Religious Instruction," in
Religious Education and Theology, pp. 100-197.

to lessen, sometimes seriously, genuine religiously pluralistic teaching because even before this macrotheory is operationalized into concrete pedagogical practice the fundamental question must be decided: "Which particular theology will serve as the norm for teaching religious pluralism?" Once this question is decided, then the possibility for full religiously pluralistic instruction is typically lessened. By its very nature, the theological approach to religious instruction must from the outset enflesh one or another theological position.[115] It is manifestly impossible to have a theological macrotheory of religious instruction which does not rest upon one or another particular theological position, to the relative or even at times to the absolute exclusion of other particular theological positions. By its intrinsic nature, the theological approach to religious instruction cannot be value-free with respect to various competing theologies or religions. The necessarily particularistic character of the theological approach to religious instruction means that both the substantive content and the structural content of religious instruction are determined by one or another particular theology. The theological approach to religious instruction necessarily dictates that one or another particular theological stance must be used as an explicit or implicit norm for determining the inclusion and the interpretation of every single substantive content such as, for example, the divinity of Jesus and the infallibility of the pope (cognitive content), the proper forms of Christian love and the proper attitudes (affective content), and various kinds of conduct (lifestyle content). Furthermore, the theological approach necessarily dictates that all teaching procedures (structural content) be rejected, revised, or accepted on the basis of a particular theological position. Thus, for example, Françoise Darcy-Bérubé, a Roman Catholic advocate of the theological approach to religious instruction, flatly asserts that certain teaching procedures used by Billy Graham are intrinsically and objectively unacceptable because they do not agree with her own particular theology.[116] The possibility of instruction for genuine religious pluralism runs the risk of partial and even total evapo-

---

115. A distinction must be drawn between theology on the one hand and the theological approach to religious instruction on the other hand. Theology is the cognitive investigation of God and, by extension, of God's workings in the universe by means of revelation. The theological approach to religious instruction, in contrast, is the use of theology as the primary and normative determinant of all the substantive content and structural content in religion teaching. In this macrotheory, theology is alone capable of adequately explaining, predicting, and verifying religious instruction phenomena.

116. Françoise Darcy-Bérubé, "The Challenge Ahead of Us," in *Foundations of Religious Education*, ed. Padraic O'Hare (New York: Paulist, 1978), p. 118.

ration in the "purifying" cauldron of theological particularism. The real
issue is not whether the particularism inherent in the theological approach to religious instruction will diminish religiously pluralistic teaching. Rather, the issue is how much this particularism which is inbuilt in
the theological approach to religious instruction will vitiate teaching for
and in religious pluralism. For the relatively few religious educators who
apparently hold a theology which embraces full religious pluralism,
there would be relatively little diminishment, though there would necessarily be some.[117] (However, learners who steadfastly refuse to espouse
religious pluralism will probably receive short shrift from these religion
teachers because the particular theology of these educators is that religious pluralism is required of all learners.) For the vast majority of
religious educators who do not embrace full religious pluralism, there
would be significantly more diminishment of the quantity and the quality of the religious pluralism taught in the lesson.

Orthodoxy. The theological approach to religious instruction inherently erodes the possibility of genuine religiously pluralistic teaching
because this macrotheory is intimately tied in with the reality of orthodoxy. Indeed, orthodoxy and theological particularism go hand-in-hand.
The orthodoxy to which I am referring is twofold, namely orthodoxy
within the context of currently accepted theology and the orthodoxy
within the context of the ecclesiasticum. Both orthodoxies are political
in nature and thus inevitably pollute whatever pure scientific theology
might have been originally devised by a theologian. If a new theology
does not fit in with the prevailing theology of an era or of a group, that
new theology is branded as unacceptable or defective (in other words,
unorthodox) by other theologians. Indeed, I personally know of instances in Protestant as well as in Catholic seminaries in which faculty
members holding a theological view which significantly differs from the
prevailing view of the majority of the seminary's theologians are ostra-
cized by this majority. Though certain liberal or radical contemporary
theologians do not like to be regarded as apologists for doctrines endorsed by the ecclesiasticum, in fact that is what most theologians
usually are. If one or another theology is declared to be unorthodox or
faulty by the ecclesiasticum, then this theology tends to be either buried
or revised in such a way as to fit the requirements of the ecclesiasticum.
History supports Gabriel Moran's contention that even in the modern
world theology can never cut itself loose from ecclesiastical orthodoxy

---

117. In this sentence and in the remaining sentences of this paragraph, I am
referring only to religious educators who espouse the theological macrotheory of
religious instruction.

and that theologians as a whole probably would not wish to cut themselves loose from ecclesiastical orthodoxy even if they could.[118] Even feminist theologians, who have proven themselves to be among the most radical and nonorthodox of post-Reformation theologians, are at bottom arguing not for a decoupling of theology from ecclesiastical orthodoxy but rather about which kind of theology should be ecclesiastically orthodox.[119] Almost every consistent and honest advocate of the theological approach to religious instruction has asserted that all religious instruction must be based on what they typically term "adequate theology."[120] Advocates of the theological approach to religious instruction who espouse a conservative or reactionary theology construe "adequate theology" as being that which is in conformity with the ecclesiasticum's official pronouncements.[121] Proponents of the theological approach to religious instruction who adopt a liberal theological stance construe "adequate theology" as being that which is in conformity with the theology generally accepted by the liberal theologians of the era. The orthodox base of "adequate theology" tends to lessen the possibility for instruction for full religious pluralism because by defini-

---

118. Moran, "From Obstacle to Modest Contributor: Theology in Religious Education," in *Religious Education and Theology*, pp. 55-56.

119. For example, one of the highest priorities of feminist theologians has been the development of liturgical and biblical language which reflects their own theological views. The bible and the liturgy represent the fullest forms of the ecclesiasticum's latent and manifest orthodoxy.

120. See, for example, Michael Warren, "All Contributions Cheerfully Accepted," *Living Light* 7 (Winter, 1970), p. 31; Lawrence O. Richards, "Experiencing Reality Together: Toward the Impossible Dream," in *Religious Education and Theology*, pp. 205-210; D. Campbell Wyckoff, "Religious Education as a Discipline," in *Who Are We? The Quest for a Religious Education*, ed. John H. Westerhoff III (Birmingham, Ala.: Religious Education Press, 1978), pp. 172-180; James D. Smart, *The Teaching Ministry of the Church* (Philadelphia: Westminster, 1954), pp. 24-45; Randolph Crump Miller, *The Theory of Christian Education Practice* (Birmingham, Ala.: Religious Education Press, 1980), pp. 153-164; Johannes Hofinger, *Our Message is Christ* (Notre Dame, Ind.: Fides/Claretian, 1974), pp. 1-19; Lois E. LeBar, *Education that is Christian* (Old Tappan, N.J.: Revell, 1958), pp. 19-20. Indeed, most Protestants use the term "Christian education" rather than "religious education" because they contend that only education which is Christian can possibly be education that is religious.

121. Thus conservative Catholic advocates of the theological approach will always test every theological doctrine and every pedagogical procedure used in religious instruction on the basis of whether this doctrine or procedure has been approved or endorsed as orthodox by the ecclesiasticum, especially by the magisterium. See Kenneth Barker, *Religious Education, Catechesis, and Freedom* (Birmingham, Ala.: Religious Education Press, 1981), pp. 199-203.

tion religions other than one's own are not theologically orthodox and are not based on "adequate theology." To be sure, the reality of religious pluralism is itself a serious challenge (or a serious affront, as some conservative and reactionary theologians might say) to orthodox theology and to the theological adequacy which such a theology proposes as normative for religious instruction.

Ecclesiastical Control. The theological approach to religious instruction tends to diminish the full actualization of religiously pluralistic instruction because of the almost unavoidable inclination toward particularity and orthodoxy inherent in this approach. Since this approach claims that theology is the determining factor and the norm for all religious instruction activity, persons and procedures and programs which are not based on "adequate theology" must be either eliminated or significantly overhauled. From the vantage point of most theologies, religious pluralism tends to be an enfleshment of a more or less inadequate theology; hence the ecclesiasticum or other persons in church leadership positions have no alternative but to do all in their power to constantly and relentlessly eliminate all traces of genuine religious pluralism from religious instruction.[122] Regardless of whether the advocates of the theological approach to religious instruction espouse a conservative or a liberal theology, the result is always the same, namely working to insure that the ecclesiasticum or some other institutional power structure ridicule, censor, bar, or banish all religious instruction activities which go counter to their own brand of theological particularism and orthodoxy.[123] In as much as the ecclesiasticum is typically conservative in its theology, those advocates of the theological approach to reli-

---

122. When I headed up the graduate religious instruction program at the University of Notre Dame, the reigning provost was a certain James Tunstead Burtchaell, a priest who was an uncompromising proponent of the theological approach to religious instruction. When in 1974 I advertised nationally for a person to join our faculty regardless of the religious affiliation of that individual, I received a strong formal rebuke from Burtchaell for inviting non-Catholics to apply for this position. Burtchaell, who at the time was regarded as a liberal theologian, wished our program to have a "Catholic identity," an identity which he seemed to perceive as excluding non-Catholic faculty from our program. One week later Burtchaell unilaterally set in motion the process whereby the graduate religious instruction program at Notre Dame was liquidated. While correlation does not equal cause, nonetheless correlation does equal correlation.

123. Thus the feminist theologian Rosemary Radford Ruether writes that full-blooded religious pluralism "will not be conceded as a theological principle by Roman Catholic magisterial Curial theology. The Curia demands not only a consensus, but a consensus that is fundamentally subservient to the defense of the traditional power structure." Having made this damning indictment of

gious instruction who hold a conservative theology tend to work within the system to make sure that all religious instruction reflects their conservative or reactionary brand of theology.[124] Realizing the conservative nature of the ecclesiasticum, liberal advocates of the theological approach to religious instruction either try to gain control of the central ecclesiasticum so that they can make their own liberal theology normative for everyone or endeavor to capture political power in smaller units of the ecclesiasticum or ecclesia in order to banish any and all theologi-

adequate conservative Catholic theology, Ruether in the very next sentence asserts that liberal and radical theologians must establish their own power structure so that they themselves can control what is or what is not "adequate theology." Thus she adds, "Pluralism can be defended only by making sure that this hierarchical power structure is not strong enough to repress successfully the *institutional bases* of conciliar and liberation theology." Rosemary Radford Ruether, "Is a New Consensus Possible?" *Journal of Ecumenical Studies* 17 (Winter, 1980), pp. 65-66, italics mine.

124. Thus, for example, Johannes Hofinger, an impassioned advocate of the theological approach to religious instruction and a man who championed a traditional theology, banned both Gabriel Moran and myself every year from speaking at a major regional Catholic religious education conference sponsored annually by the Southern archdiocese in which he was a high-ranking catechetical official. He saw to it that Moran was banned because, as Hofinger told me personally, "Moran is not a Christian." (During those years Moran was a member of the Brothers of the Christian Schools and so was presumably living a devout Christian life. What Hofinger was really saying was that Moran's theological views differed significantly from official Catholic theology and hence Moran was not a Christian.) Hofinger also arranged for the archdiocese to ban me from ever speaking at this annual regional religious education convention because he said that my views on teaching religion differed significantly from his own theological approach to religious education. (During those years, Hofinger baptized my first two sons, stayed several times for some days at my home and told me that my family life was deeply religious.) For some odd reason which is still as unfathomable to me as it would be to Hofinger were he still alive, Gabriel Moran claims that the Austrian-born Jesuit was a pioneer in introducing "revolutionary, nontraditional" theology into the American religious instruction enterprise. Moran's assertion is not true. Hofinger was unswerving in his belief that the kerygmatic theology which he espoused constituted the most traditional Catholic theology which could be found and that other competing Catholic theologies were revolutionary because they attempted to revolt against the original kerygmatic emphasis which was palpably present both in the New Testament and in the life of the ancient church. See Gabriel Moran, "Philosophies of Religious Education among Roman Catholics," in *Changing Patterns of Religious Education*, ed. Marvin J. Taylor (Nashville: Abingdon, 1984), pp. 43-44; Johannes Hofinger, *The Art of Teaching Christian Doctrine*, 2d ed. (Notre Dame, Ind.: University of Notre Dame Press, 1962), pp. 48; also Johannes Hofinger, "The Catechetical Sputnik," in *Modern Masters of Religious Education*, ed. Marlene Mayr (Birmingham, Ala: Religious Education Press, 1983), pp. 24, 32.

cal or nontheological positions which are not in accord with their own particular theology—in other words, to establish their own orthodoxy.[125] Throughout history, and in virtually every religion worldwide, theology and ecclesiastical control have usually gone hand-in-glove. Almost inevitably theology tends to seek a home and a fulfillment in an ecclesiastical institution of some sort (often to enforce and make orthodox a particular theological stance). The ecclesiasticum, for its part, needs theology as a necessary intellectual authority to justify its exercise of religious (and often nonreligious) power. Genuine full-blooded religious pluralism tends to be regarded as dangerous to an ecclesiastical institution because it undermines the absoluteness or at least the superiority of the institution's religious claims. Most religious educators work in settings directly or indirectly controlled by an ecclesiastical institution. Such control usually serves as a decided limitation on the degree to which religious educators can promote religious pluralism because each ecclesiasticum is typically tied in with one general or specific brand of theology to the relative (or absolute) exclusion of other theologies and religious viewpoints.[126]

Changeability. The theological approach to religious instruction tends to weaken the full actualization of religiously pluralistic instruction because of the considerable changeableness which seems to be part and parcel of the theological approach. Theology is a very shaky foundation upon which to build any kind of religious instruction theory and practice because normative theologies have come and gone over the centuries. Indeed, normative theologies have changed with dizzying rapidity since the end of World War II. Indeed, since the war, an incredibly large number of competing theologies have existed side by side, each claiming to be the best one and the true one. Kerygmatic theology, process theology, developmental theology, liberation theology, feminist theology, evangelical theology—the list of theological contenders for primacy of place seems endless. No sound, or even mildly enduring, religious instruction activity for pluralism can possibly be erected on such an erratic normative base. The official Catholic church had always condemned religious pluralism prior to the papacy of John XXIII

---

125. To appreciate this point, one only has to look at seminary and university programs of religious education controlled by theological liberals who espouse the theological approach to religious instruction. Seldom if ever do these theological liberals invite persons to speak or teach in their programs if such persons disagree with their own particular liberal orthodoxy or with the adequacy of the theological approach to religious instruction.

126. Sara Little accurately describes this state of affairs when she writes that if theological systems and creeds are predetermined by the ecclesiasticum as sub-

(1958-1963), branding it as the grave sin of religious indifferentism. Thanks to John XXIII and the Second Vatican Council, religious pluralism, albeit in very diluted form, became theologically acceptable to the Catholic ecclesiasticum. But what would happen to Catholic religious instruction for pluralism if some pope or council of bishops in the near future would declare that religious pluralism is theologically passé or dangerous? In short, the theological approach to religious instruction does not offer that kind of base which is inherently and constantly amenable to religious pluralism.

Catechesis. Of all varieties of religion teaching, catechesis is the one which most closely approaches the perfect embodiment of the theological approach to religious instruction vis-á-vis pluralism in that catechetical activity represents the acme of particularity, the apogee of orthodoxy, and the zenith of ecclesiastical control. And so it is quite natural that nowhere are the fundamental weaknesses of the theological approach to religious instruction for pluralism more apparent than in catechesis. Catechesis/catechetics is that form of religious education whose foundations, goals, content, personnel, and legitimacy are authoritatively determined by and are politically controlled by the official Roman Catholic ecclesiasticum in accordance with its particular approved theology. As Kieran Scott accurately observes, the nature, scope, intent, and interest of catechesis is "unabashedly confessional." It seeks to socialize the learner into the Roman Catholic church. Catechesis is rightly called "the nursery of the church."[127] It has always been the consistent position of the Catholic ecclesiasticum that catechesis in all its dimensionalities must constantly be subject to vigilant ecclesiastical direction.[128] So central is vigilant ecclesiastial control over all catechetical activity that catechesis ceases to be catechesis when such control is absent. The one indispensable feature of catechesis is that it be subject in all things to the Catholic ecclesiasticum and that it teach only those things which are consonant with formally approved theology. Catechc-

---

ject matter to be learned, then contributions from any area of life, including other religions and theology, necessarily have to be screened to ascertain their appropriateness to the ecclesiasticum's official or at least approved theology. (Sara Little, "Theology and Religious Education," in *Foundations for Christian Education in an Era of Change,* ed. Marvin J. Taylor [Nashville: Abingdon, 1976], p. 32.)

127. Scott, "Three Traditions of Religious Education," p. 323.

128. Paulus VI, "Evangelii Nuntiandi," *Acta Apostolicae Sedis* 68 (31 Januarii 1976), #65 (pp. 55-56); Joannes Paulus II, "Catechesi Tradendae" (16 Octobris 1979), *Acta Apostolicae Sedis* 71 (31 Octobris 1979), #6 (pp. 1281-1282). It should be noted that in "Catechesi Tradendae," John Paul II specifically notes that Paul VI regards catechesis as a phase of evangelization.

sis, therefore, is intrinsically and sharply tilted away from authentic, full-blooded religious pluralism.[129] After all, American Catholic officials have formally condemned the teaching of any kind of theological plural-ism which does not fall within the limited confines of the particular theology formally approved by the ecclesiasticum.[130] Indeed, the Vati-can's Secretariat for the Promotion of Christian Unity has authoritative-ly declared that as long as Christians are not united fully in faith, all catechetical activity must remain under the proper and inalienable con-trol of the Catholic ecclesiasticum.[131] All catechetical material such as textbooks and resources must receive prior ecclesiastical approval (the *imprimatur*), thus pretty much precluding the possibility of full-blooded religious pluralism entering these learning materials. Further, all cate-chists must receive from competent ecclesiastical authorities both the formal approval and the explicit commission to teach.[132] If catechists introduce any kind of full-blooded religious pluralism into the lesson, they run the genuine risk of having their approval and their commission to teach revoked by ecclesiastical officials. Consequently, catechists will typically be careful to refrain from teaching religious pluralism. Because the essence of catechesis is that it is fundamentally a messenger boy for the particular theology and the orthodox viewpoints expressed in offi-

---

129. In the Apostolic Exhortation *Catechesi Tradendae*, John Paul II sidesteps the relationship between religious pluralism and catechesis. He does however deal with ecumenism and catechesis, stating unambiguously that while catechesis cannot remain aloof from the ecumenical spirit of Christian unity, nonetheless those catechetical activities dealing with ecumenism must teach learners that genuine Christian unity can only be achieved in and through the Roman Catholic church. This viewpoint surely is an indicator of John Paul's views on religious pluralism and catechesis. Joannes Paulus II, "Catechesi Tradendae," #a 32-33 (pp. 1304-1305). For a commentary on this text by leading catechetical authorities, see Robert J. Levis and Michael J. Wrenn, eds., *John Paul II: Catechist* (Chicago: Franciscan Herald Press, 1980), pp. 107-109.

130. *A fortiori*, this condemnation extends to religious pluralism. See Depart-ment of Education, United States Catholic Conference, *Sharing the Light of Faith* (Washington, D.C.: The Conference, 1979), #16 (pp. 9-10).

131. Stransky and Sheerin, eds. *Doing the Truth in Charity: Statements of Pope Paul VI, Popes John Paul I, John Paul II, and the Secretariat for Promot-ing Christian Unity*, pp. 97-98. Of especial interest is that while both the Second Vatican Council and the Secretariat for the Promotion of Christian Unity have been quite liberal (by classical Vatican standards) toward ecumenical activity, both bodies are rather strict in the degree to which they allow ecumenism to enter two specific areas of church life, namely, worship and catechesis.

132. Department of Education, United States Catholic Conference, *Sharing the Light of Faith*, #16 (p.10). This key document constitutes the official nation-al Catholic directory of the United States.

cial Catholic pronouncements,[133] formal ecclesiastical documents assume an enormous importance in catechetical work at every level. Thus the central role of all catechists is to insure that every aspect of their teaching is in accord with the ecclesiastical documents. The chief role of catechetical experts such as university professors of catechetics and diocesan catechetical administrators is twofold: to devise the substantive and structural content of catechesis on the basis of what the official documents declare and to vigilantly monitor any and all catechetical activity to make sure that it is indeed faithful to the ecclesiastical documents. The primary and overarching task of catechesis, then, is to deliberatively mold learners into the shape and form indicated in the ecclesiastical documents.[134] My statements about catechesis expressed in this paragraph are not intended to condemn catechesis in itself but rather to show that catechesis tends to severely restrict and indeed probably render impotent the full actualization of real religious pluralism. There are persons within the Catholic ecclesia who wish themselves and/or their offspring to undergo catechesis because they want to be thoroughly indoctrinated by and into the institutional church, at least for a certain period of time. The legitimate rights of these persons must be safeguarded. But the fact remains that catechesis will never include real religious pluralism.

The Social-Science Macrotheory

For a wide variety of reasons, the social-science macrotheory of religious instruction enables religious pluralism to be actualized as fully as possible.

---

133. This messenger-boy status is not unique to catechesis; in fact, it is a central feature which it fully shares with every other kind of theological approach to religious instruction. Because it is essentially a messenger boy for a particular approved orthodox theology, catechesis is intrinsically deprived of any legitimacy as a field of work or study in its own right. Because it is essentially a messenger-boy for a particular theology, catechesis, like all other forms of the theological approach to religious instruction, is rightfully held in low esteem by theologians, church officials, and even by laypersons. See Lee, *The Shape of Religious Instruction*, pp. 225-226, 246-248.

134. Using terminology reminiscent of a royal seal and the wax, Berard Marthaler states that the purpose of catechesis is "to impress its institutionalized meanings and values powerfully and unforgettably on its members." (Berard L. Marthaler, "Socialization as a Model for Catechetics," in *Foundations of Religious Education*, p. 77.) Marthaler has been the leading academic proponent of catechesis in the 1970s and 1980s and devoted his entire catechetical life to making (and wherever possible, to enforcing) formal ecclesiastical documents directly or indirectly pertaining to catechesis.

Value-Freedom. The social-science approach to religious instruction is value-free in the sense that the teaching act in itself is not intrinsically bound up with any one particular set of religious values. In other words, the religious instruction act can facilitate any kind of religious outcome just as readily as another differing type of religious outcome. For example, a Jewish religious educator can and indeed does use many of the same kind of pedagogical procedures to facilitate Jewish-type religious behaviors in learners as a Catholic religious educator employs in facilitating Catholic-type behaviors in his lesson.[135] It is only because the overall social-science *approach* to religious instruction is value-free that the specific concrete religious instruction *act* can embrace all sorts of differing religious product contents.[136] It is absolutely essential that a macrotheory of religious instruction for pluralism be value-free because only in this way can a general approach to religion teaching embrace all forms of religion without exception or prejudice.[137] (The theological approach to religious instruction is inherently value-laden with theological particularity and so is fundamentally and irreversably thrusted against the teaching of full-blooded religious pluralism.)[138] Because the social-science approach to religious instruction is value-free, it and it alone is capable of accomplishing what any adequate macrotheory of religious instruction must necessarily accomplish, namely explaining, predicting, and verifying the effective pedagogical selection and implementation of the entire pluralistic spectrum of complementary or conflicting religious subject matter. Whereas the theological approach to religious instruction necessarily demands a particularistic intrinsic

---

135. For a further explanation of this point, see Lee, *The Shape of Religious Instruction*, p. 207.

136. This sentence is of crucial importance for an understanding of the social-science *approach* as value-free with respect to religious instruction. The *approach or macrotheory* is value-free insofar as it can intrinsically encompass the teaching of the entire gamut of various religious subject-matter contents. In contrast, the here-and-now concrete religious instruction *act* is value-laden because it consists in the concrete facilitation of specific religious outcomes. See Lee, *The Content of Religious Instruction*, p. 42.

137. Support for this point can be found in Peter L. Berger, *Pyramids of Sacrifice* (Garden City, N.Y.: Doubleday Anchor, 1976), pp. 134-137.

138. Some more liberal advocates of the theological approach to religious instruction attempt to escape the antipluralist inevitability by engaging in accommodationism, namely, by allowing other religions to be taught side-by-side. The genuine pluralistic spirit of such accommodationism rises and falls with the religious expansiveness of the individual teacher; it does not flow in any way from the overall theological approach to religious instruction. In accommodationism, then, the religious educator not only bypasses the theological macrotheory of religious instruction, he or she grossly violates it.

theological judgment from beginning to end, the social-science approach as value-free does not entail any such prejudicial theological judgment at any time. The judgment which social science makes about religious subject matter is essentially a social-scientific judgment and so is not inherently prejudicial for or against any particular religious subject matter. Let me illustrate this point by using an example of the pedagogical procedure known as role-playing. In the theological approach, this teaching technique is immediately and in itself judged by theological criteria as to its intrinsic particularistic value.[139] In the social-science approach, no such theological prejudgment is made or can be made as to the intrinsic pedagogical value of role-playing. Thus the social-science approach allows role-playing to be used in any and all religious instruction activities as long as this technique is congruent with the particular substantive content to which it is concretely conjoined in the religious instruction act.[140] There are, of course, basic presuppositions which the social-science approach utilizes, such as the epistemological presupposition that knowledge is somehow valid. But presuppositions of this kind are not theological or religious values formally considered.[141] Because they are accustomed to dealing primarily or even solely with theology, it is often difficult for theologians and advocates of the theological approach to religious instruction to com-

---

139. Thus, for example, Françoise Darcy-Bérubé, an uncompromising advocate of the theological approach to religious instruction, asserts that there are pedagogical techniques which her particularistic theology *prejudges* as being inherently opposed to the Christian vision. She cites some of the teaching techniques of Billy Graham and the Jehovah's Witnesses to buttress her contention that theology can and must prejudge the value of a teaching procedure on the basis of the degree to which that procedure squares with a particular theology's view of humanity. (Darcy-Bérubé, "The Challenge Ahead of Us," p. 118.)

140. The necessity for this congruence flows from the fact that structural content must be generally in accord with the substantive content to which it is conjoined, else the subsumptional mediation of both contents into the religious instruction act be rendered impossible. The necessity of such a congruence in the social-science approach does not in any way flow from a prior theological judgment about the theological validity or acceptability of the structural content. On this point, see Lee, "The Authentic Source of Religious Instruction," in *Religious Education and Theology*, pp. 165-174; Lee, *The Content of Religious Instruction*, pp. 8, 750-752; Lee, *The Flow of Religious Instruction*, pp. 17-19, 21-22, 29-31, 300-301.

141. It should be noted that the operating presuppositions of social science are empirically tested as far as possible to provide support or rejection for them. (One should recall that epistemological presuppositions such as the validity of knowledge are also presuppositions of theology. To be sure, theology operates on more nontheological presuppositions than almost any other area of inquiry operates out of theological presuppositions.) Further, the assertion that social-

prehend how any general macrotheory of reality (such as the social-science approach to religious instruction) can be value-free.[142] It is almost as if these persons are claiming that because theology is theologically value-laden, every other approach to reality must therefore be theologically value-laden also.[143] The crucial point of this paragraph in practical terms is that the value-freedom enjoyed by the social-science approach to religious instruction enables this approach to embrace in a positive fashion the entire range of divergent religious subject-matter contents. Thus the social-science approach to religious instruction opti-

---

science presuppositions might happen to be more or less in line with some particular theology is far different from asserting that theology is the basis of social science or that there are formal theological values inherent in social science. To be in line with is not the same as to be the basis of, else every area of inquiry be reduced to theology (and lest theology, in turn, be reduced to philosophy).

142. It must be emphasized that the value-freedom of the social-science macrotheory is not metaphysically absolute but rather functionally operational. Value-freedom in social science does not mean that the social-science macrotheory in itself is devoid of all values (the metaphysically absolute conception of value-freedom). On the contrary, value-freedom in the social-science macrotheory means that personal or corporate values are either sufficiently filtered out or made to conform to the canons of the macrotheory so that these values do not significantly alter the basic character, procedures, or results of this approach in itself (the functionally operational conception of value-freedom). To claim that every scientific macrotheory is primarily the enfleshment of personal or theological values is to basically vitiate any sort of objectivity or generalizability of science, and to reduce all science to a hopeless relativism. On this point, see Lee, *The Content of Religious Instruction*, pp. xi, 765.

143. Two related points are in order here. *First*, values are sometimes absolute in theology, whereas in social science values are always treated as variables, even though these values might be absolute in themselves (social science lacks the power to judge the absoluteness of values in themselves). This does not mean that social science denies the absoluteness of some or all values; rather it means that social science utilizes (operational) both absolute and nonabsolute values (metaphysical) according to the variable way in which these values occur in dynamic human interaction. It is illicit to attempt to transfer the necessarily absolutist and metaphysical cast of theology into a nontheological realm such as social science. *Second*, theologians and advocates of the theological approach to religious instruction must learn that other areas of inquiry and activity operate on a different methodological axes than theology and that these axes are not inherently inferior to the methodological axes around which theology revolves. Unless and until theologians and advocates of the theological approach to religious instruction abandon the falsely superior attitude which they frequently take toward other sciences, these persons will never understand such concepts as value-freedom and will never be able to enter into collegial dialogue with representatives of other areas of inquiry or life.

mally fosters and renders maximally effective any and all religious instruction for pluralism.

Particularity. The social-science approach to religious instruction inherently enables the possibility of genuine religiously pluralistic teaching to be fully accomplished because there is no inbuilt particularity in this approach with respect to any specific religion or theology. The social-science approach is neutral in terms of any and all particular religions, not in the sense of being unfriendly or inimical to them, but in the sense of being capable of embracing one or all of them in the concrete teaching act. The social-science approach to religious instruction does not inherently imply any particular religion. The social-science approach is not intrinsically tied in with any religion. The social-science approach does not intrinsically attempt to promote or discard any particular religion. On the contrary, the social-science *approach* accepts every religion and every theology on its own terms, and then empowers the effective facilitation of the particular religion or theology in the concrete religious instruction *act*.[144] James Fowler's work on faith development provides a representative example of how the social-science approach can not only embrace but also actively facilitate the enhancement of faith in persons of all sorts of religious stances, from Buddhist to Jewish to Christian. Using a psychological approach (one variety of social science), Fowler demonstrates that faith is a fundamental *form* of human existence into which can be inserted all sorts of specific *substantive contents* (particular religions). Thus, Fowler argues, pedagogical and counseling procedures utilizing faith-development theory have the power to facilitate the enhancement of faith in persons from any religion whatever.[145] The stages of faith which Fowler discovered are universal in that they embrace persons of every particular religious faith and also persons whose faith is not specifically religious.[146]

---

144. It is crucially important to keep in mind the seminal distinction I made in footnote 136 on the essential difference between the social-science *approach* and the social-science *act*.

145. James W. Fowler, *Stages of Faith: The Psychology of Human Development and the Quest for Meaning* (San Francisco: Harper & Row, 1981), pp. 3-15, 98-116.

146. Craig Dykstra expresses this point very well when he states that Fowler's social-scientific faith-development theory "does not raise the questions of *what* beliefs, attitudes, values, and ways of living are to be normative for a community, much less what (or who) the object of one's believing, knowing, trusting, and love is to be. Rather, it is to help us discern the various [formal] *ways in which* such 'contents' of faith are 'structured' and 'processed' by various people in a

Orthodoxy. The social-science approach to religious instruction inherently enables the possibility of genuine religiously pluralistic teaching to be fully realized because there is no inbuilt religious or theological orthodoxy in this approach. No one religious or theological orthodoxy is normative for the social-science approach to religious instruction qua social-science approach. Social science is a completely independent area of inquiry from theology; hence the social-science approach cannot be validly judged in and for itself by theological norms. Theological norms can only validly judge what some activity means for theology. Theological norms cannot validly judge what an activity means to that activity in itself; nor can theology validly judge what that activity means to the overarching approach of which that activity is a part, e.g., the social-science approach. The only norms intrinsic to the social-science approach to religious instruction are social-science norms such as the empirically derived laws of teaching and learning. Such laws are totally independent of any particular religion or theology; these laws operate regardless of the specific religious setting in which religion teaching occurs, and regardless of the religious or theological stance of either teacher or learners.[147] From what has been adduced thus far in this paragraph, it is readily apparent that the whole issue of "adequate theology" lies totally outside the purview and interests of the social-science approach. To be sure, there are those theological imperialists who claim that there is a distinctively Christian way of teaching and learning. But this claim soon breaks down in at least two ways. First, all the available empirical evidence suggests that religion (and theology) are learned in the same basic way that anything else is learned. The laws of learning apply just as much to the acquisition of specifically religious subject-matter as to specifically nonreligious subject-matter. Second, if indeed there were a distinctively Christian way of teaching and learning then there must also be a distinctively different Catholic or Methodist or Presbyterian or Baptist way of teaching and learning—a prima facie ridiculous claim. Because the social-science approach to religious instruction is independent of any religious or theological orthodoxy, it constitutes an especially enriched framework for the full actualization of religious instruction for genuine pluralism.

---

faith community." (Craig Dykstra, "Faith Development and Religious Education," in *Faith Development and Fowler*, ed. Craig Dykstra and Sharon Parks [Birmingham, Ala.: Religious Education Press, 1986], pp. 256-257.)

147. For a further development of the important thesis advanced in this paragraph, see Lee, "The Authentic Source of Religious Instruction," pp. 177-184.

Ecclesiastical Control. The social-science approach to religious instruction inherently enables the possibility of pluralistic teaching to come to fruition because there is no inbuilt ecclesiastical control involved in this approach. Unlike the theological approach to religious instruction which has a decided affinity to be subjected to ecclesiastical control, the social-science approach has no such inbuilt attraction because its nature and operations lie in an intrinsically different zone of activity than the legitimate role of the ecclesiasticum. While the ecclesiasticum can legitimately determine which theology and which set of religious practices is orthodox, it cannot legitimately determine which procedures and which results of social-scientific activity are social-scientifically adequate or orthodox. The ecclesiasticum may banish a particular practitioner of the social-science approach to religious instruction, but it cannot banish the approach in itself. Some of the most important advances in the Christian churches in the twentieth century have come from social scientists who were censured by the ecclesiasticum for proceeding along the lines of social science, lines which went contrary to what the ecclesiasticum judged to be theologically correct and orthodox. For example, as late as 1950 American church officials spoke out against intelligence tests for Catholic school students, while as late as 1964 the Vatican issued a monitum against using psychoanalytic techniques to assess the aptitude of candidates for the priesthood or religious life.[148] The ecclesiasticum condemned both these psychological instruments on the grounds that they interfered with the free operation of the Holy Spirit's grace. By 1970, however, the ecclesiasticum had conceded that the social-scientific tests were helpful to the work of the church and that the theology underlying the condemnation of these tests was not adequate. Whereas advocates of the theological approach to religious instruction would have routinely sought the answer to the correctness of psychological tests in ecclesiastical pronouncements or in the bible (as authoritatively interpreted by the ecclesiasticum), social scientists sought the answer to the correctness of these texts in the degree to which they measured intelligence and the degree to which they revealed the psychological dynamics of a person's religiovocational life.

Changeability. The social-science approach to religious instruction intrinsically enables the possibility of religiously pluralistic instruction to be fully actualized because it is built upon a reasonably permanent base of social-scientific research evidence. Theological fads and emphases come and go, sometimes seemingly with the speed of light. In

---

148. Suprema Sacra Congregatio S. Officii, "Monitum," *Acta Apostolicae Sedis* 55 (22 Septembris 1963), p. 571.

contrast, social-scientific facts and laws of teaching and learning remain firm. Indeed, the relatively solid foundation of social science is open and waiting to facilitate all sorts of new theological subject-matter. In asserting that the social-scientific facts and laws underlying the teaching and learning of religion are relatively fixed, I am not stating that social science does not grow or that social science does not admit of new interpretations, some of them quite significant. What I am asserting is that the fundamental facts and laws of teaching/learning are rarely abridged. Growth in the social science of teaching/learning consciously and deliberatively builds upon empirically established facts and laws rather than an abrogation of them. Even varying interpretations of social science agree on the fundamental facts and laws of teaching/learning; it is just that the interpretations and the uses to which these facts and laws are utilized vary.[149] Far from diminishing the stability of social science, the growth of varying interpretations and uses of empirically established facts and laws of the teaching/learning act enhances this stability because these new varying interpretations make it possible for the facts and laws of teaching/learning to be deployed in a way which fits all sorts of emerging pedagogical exigencies. Let me use the example of the facts and laws of reinforcement to illustrate this point. The research on reinforcement has always been sharply tilted toward facilitating the acquisition of cognitive outcomes. When a religious educationist wishes to develop pedagogical procedures for teaching affective behaviors, such a person will reinterpret the social-scientific facts and laws of reinforcement to include and enhance the facilitation of affective outcomes. Such a reinterpretation does not destroy or seriously mitigate the facts and laws; rather, the reinterpretation widens the understanding and the applicability of these facts and laws. The elasticity-within-stability which characterizes social science actually promotes religious pluralism since both the subject-matter content and the learners' personalities vary enormously because they come from such different religious backgrounds; hence significantly different pedagogical procedures must be devised first to make allowance for these religiously pluralistic differences, and second to enhance religiously pluralistic outcomes in these highly differentiated learners. Effective teaching for religious pluralism demands a wide variety of teaching styles and models of teaching—styles and models which utilize the basic

---

149. Thus, for example, non-Skinnerian social scientists might disagree with the interpretation and uses of the empirically grounded facts and laws of operant conditioning; however, no reputable social scientist would disagree with the empirically verified facts and laws discovered by B.F. Skinner's research on operant conditioning.

facts and laws of the teaching/learning process in different though connected ways.[150] But unless this elasticity of different teaching styles and
models and procedures is grounded in the stability of established social-
scientific facts and laws, the result will be pedagogical chaos and thus
pedagogical ineffectiveness. It is important to note that despite the
impingement of all different kinds of conflicting theologies upon religious instruction from 1960 to the present, the basic pedagogical procedures used to teach religion have remained essentially unchanged. For
example, Thomas Groome's pedagogical method of "shared praxis"
which he claims to be the one and only method[151] genuinely appropriate
for teaching that kind of religion permeated by liberation theology[152] is
nothing more than a form of the centuries-old teaching method of
reflection-reflection.[153]

---

150. On this point, see Bruce R. Joyce, Marsha Weil, and Rhoada Wald, "A
Structure for Pluralism in Teacher Education," in *Flexibility in Teaching*, ed.
Bruce R. Joyce, Clark C. Brown, and Lucy Peck (New York: Longman, 1981),
pp. 119-140.

151. From the strictly pedagogical point of view, Groome's "shared praxis"
method is mortally flawed because it enfleshes the fatal fallacy known as "there
is only one right method of teaching." Differentiated substantive contents, even
within the same general subject area, require differentiated teaching procedures.
Differentiated objectives and goals, even within the same overall purpose, necessitate differentiated teaching procedures. Differentiated learners, even within a
select population, need differentiated teaching procedures.

152. Actually, Groome goes much further than this. He contends that
emancipatory liberation theology is the finest form of theology. Indeed
Groome's writings strongly suggest that he regards this avowed political theology as the only truly adequate form of theology. It is within this context that
Groome proposes one and only one specific method for teaching religion,
namely "shared praxis." Other teaching methods are not even considered and
thus, by inevitable implication, are banished. Groome's pedagogical exclusivism
with regard to his "shared praxis" teaching method definitely renders his whole
approach to religious education decidedly antithetical to the task of teaching in
and for religious pluralism because any teaching for authentic religious pluralism must itself encompass many pluralistic forms of both pedagogical procedure and substantive content. (Thomas H. Groome, *Christian Religious Education* [San Francisco: Harper & Row, 1980], pp. 24 [lines 27-29], 46-49.)

153. Groome's "shared praxis" method is most definitely not an action-
reflection process, as is erroneously claimed. In a genuine action-reflection
method, both the action and the subsequent reflection upon the action take
place during the lesson itself. In Groome's exclusively cognitivist "shared
praxis" method, the action takes place prior to the lesson—in some cases a very
long time before the lesson. The more closely one examines Groome's "shared
praxis" method from the standpoint of either scientific or practical pedagogy,
the more one is drawn into the inescapable conclusion that it was formulated by
a person or persons who seem to know almost nothing about the nature and
structure of the teaching process. (Ibid., pp. 208-211.)

CONCLUSION

The Seven Stages of Religious Pluralism

Looking over the past and the present, it is possible to identify seven discrete stages in which various religions relate to one another. When teaching for full-blooded pluralism, religious educators should first become aware of the stage which is currently operative in the formal or informal setting in which they are teaching and then tailor their instructional efforts in such a fashion as to move up to the next higher stage.

The first or lowest stage of religious pluralism is that in which a particular religion hates, despises, condemns, or opposes other religions at every turn. At this stage, religious instruction for genuine pluralism is impossible because such instruction is regarded as traitorous by the particular religious context in which the religion teaching is done.

The second stage of religious pluralism is that in which a particular religion enters into contact with other religions in order to make converts. At this stage, religious instruction for genuine pluralism is impossible because the validity of pluralism is rejected. However, this stage does have its bright side in that at least some sort of contact is made with other religions. (Contact is always the sine qua non of every path toward genuine religious pluralism.)

The third stage of religious pluralism is that in which a particular religion grudgingly tolerates the existence and proximate presence of other religions (tolerance is, by its nature, always grudging). This stage represents another small step in bringing about religious instruction for pluralism in that the active opposition and condemnation of other religions as manifested in the first stage and implied in the second stage is now replaced with a passive resignation, a resignation which does not preclude active contact with other religions though it does not warmly embrace such contact either.

The fourth stage of religious pluralism is that in which a particular religion enters into conversation with other religions. This stage represents a turning point in the evolution of religious instruction for pluralism in that for the first time there is some kind of positive engagement with other religions. The fourth stage is seriously limited, however, in that it is almost exclusively cognitive and verbal, and thus is lacking the necessary holistic character of full engagement. The fourth stage is also seriously handicapped by the fact that it is typically done by theologians and other intellectuals rather than directly involving religious educators and members of the local ecclesia in the conversations.

The fifth stage of religious pluralism is that in which a particular religion works together with other religions in a wide variety of activities and projects. These common activities are typically nonliturgical in nature. This stage represents a rich opportunity for religious instruction for genuine pluralism because at this stage a truly holistic encounter with other religions takes place, an encounter which adds the all-important affective and lifestyle dimensions to the cognitive element. Furthermore, this fifth stage is especially crucial because for the first time in the progressive evolution of these seven stages, the religious educators in the field as well as grassroots members of the local ecclesia are involved in cooperative engagement with persons from other religions.

The sixth stage of religious pluralism is that of ecumenism. At this stage, a particular religion works toward an organizational and institutional merger with a kindred religion or religions. This ecumenical stage offers rich possibilities to religiously pluralistic instruction because the particular religion is now striving not only to capitalize on the commonalities which it has with another religion or group of religions, but also is interacting with these other religions meaningfully and grace-fully. Furthermore, in the sixth stage, the common activities among the cooperative religions involve joint liturgical celebrations—small and halting in the first phases of this stage, but growing fuller and riper with each successive phase of the ecumenical journey. Unfortunately, however, the ecumenical stage is more often characterized by cognitive verbal discussions among theologians, intellectuals, and church officials, rather than by either actions or fully cooperative activities in the grassroots world of religious instruction and ecclesial life. To counter this debility, religious educators can seize the moment and during this sixth stage involve the learners in holistic ecumenical activities with other religious groups, as pedagogically appropriate.

The seventh stage of religious pluralism is that in which one particular religion works cooperatively with other religions which have not, can not, or should not ecumenically merge with it. Such cooperative activities are as fully holistic and liturgical as possible, with far greater weight being given to religious life and experience than to ecclesiastical doctrine. This final stage of religious pluralism is characterized by the positive, nonregretful awareness that ecumenical merging in many cases is neither possible nor even desirable. In this final stage, the goal of religious instruction, like that of religious pluralism as a whole, is to help persons from other religions to become better in their own religion, to follow their own religion more fully and more purely so that all persons can touch the veil of God as God has revealed himself to them.

The Flow of Instruction for Religious Pluralism

If it is to be both authentic and effective, religiously pluralistic instruction must flow from, in, and for pluralism.

To be fully and truly pluralistic, religious instruction must flow *from* a religiously pluralistic context and commitment. By this I mean that religiously pluralistic instruction is one whose source of energy lies in the rich soil of an ecclesial atmosphere promotive or at least conducive to religious pluralism, and from the teacher's unshakable conviction to foster such pluralism in the lesson as well as in all of life.

To be fully and truly pluralistic, religious instruction must flow *in* a religiously pluralistic milieu. Unless each lesson is thoroughly soaked with religious pluralism, it will be difficult for the goals and objectives of religiously pluralistic instruction to be accomplished. If religious pluralism somehow remains existentially outside the lesson, the desired results will in all probability never be adequately achieved.

To be fully and truly pluralistic, religious instruction must flow *for* religiously pluralistic outcomes. These outcomes do not just happen, nor do they occur automatically. The teacher must consciously and deliberately structure the lesson so that religiously pluralistic outcomes will be directly facilitated.[154] Teaching for religious pluralism is not a magical or an amorphous affair. On the contrary, this kind of teaching, like all other forms of pedagogy, essentially consists of carefully architecting the instructional variables in such a way as to optimize the probability that the desired outcomes will be successfully facilitated. To teach for religious pluralism is to help make religiously pluralistic outcomes occur, rather than leaving the acquisition of these important outcomes to chance.

If it is to be both authentic and effective, religiously pluralistic instruction must flow toward teaching pluralism and away from teaching about pluralism. Teaching about religious pluralism emphasizes pluralism in its objectivity, an objectivity which is confined to the impersonal and extrinsic dimensions of religious pluralism. Teaching about religious pluralism necessarily stresses the cognitive aspect of religious pluralism, such as knowing the essential dogmas of other religions, being cognizant of the history of other religions, recognizing liturgical patterns of other religions, and so forth. In marked contrast to teaching about religious pluralism, teaching religious pluralism emphasizes pluralism in its subjectivity, a subjectivity which holistically embraces all aspects of the learner's life. Teaching religious pluralism stresses pluralism in its subjectivity, a subjectivity which revolves around the personal and intrinsic dimension of religious pluralism. This subjectivity does not minimize the necessary impersonal and objective aspect of religious

---

154. For an elaboration of this point, see Lee, *The Flow of Religious Instruction*, pp. 230-251.

pluralism; rather this subjectivity incorporates the impersonal and the objective into an overall context of the human and lived experience of the individual. Teaching religious pluralism places great store on the personal involvement of the learner in religiously pluralistic activities. Teaching religious pluralism means that the learners not only know about other religions but, far more importantly, feel for and with and in these other religions (affective domain). Teaching religious pluralism also means that learners live the pluralistic dimension of religion in their own personal lives as far as possible (lifestyle domain). Teaching religious pluralism is existential sharing, reconciling, and deepening—sharing the existence peculiar to each religion, reconciling all religions and their adherents to one another, deepening all religions and their acherents with the enriching waters of other religious traditions and modes of life.

If it is to be both authentic and effective, religiously pluralistic teaching must flow away from catechesis and/or Christian education to religious instruction, from particularity to pluriformity, from faith to charity. To be fully and truly pluralistic, religion teaching must abandon its narrow concentration on exclusive socialization into Catholicism (catechesis) or exclusive socialization into Protestantism (Christian education).[155] To be genuinely pluralistic, religion teachers must abandon

---

155. Socialization is that interactive process whereby persons learn the rules and patterns of conduct of a given society so that these individuals will be able to function adequately in that society by thinking, feeling, and acting in accordance with societal regulations and expectations. The classic overview of socialization remains David A. Goslin, ed. *Handbook of Socialization* (Chicago: Rand McNally, 1969). For a sociological perspective of socialization see Frederick Elkin and Gerald Handel, *The Child and Society*, 4th ed. (New York: Random House, 1984), pp. 3-9. For a cultural-anthropological perspective of socialization, see Thomas Rhys Williams, *Introduction to Socialization* (St. Louis: Mosby, 1972), pp. 1-5. For a feminist perspective on socialization, see Nancy Romer, *The Sex-Role Cycle: Socialization from Infancy to Old Age* (Old Westbury, N.Y.: Feminist Press, 1981), pp. xv-xxii. Considerable misunderstanding on socialization exists among religious educationists. Such gross misunderstandings are probably due to the fact that quite a few religious educationists do not seem to be conversant with the enormous amount of theoretical and practical research on socialization. For example, in the 1979 Toronto meeting of the Association of Professors and Researchers in Religious Education, John Westerhoff publicly proclaimed that socialization and liberation are basically the same process with the same intent. Actually the exact opposite is true, as can be readily appreciated by even the most cursory examination of the socialization literature. For his part, Thomas Groome posits socialization to be opposed to education. In point of fact, socialization is one general kind of education. Education is a value-free approach to facilitating learning in that it can take on the concrete form of a wide variety of complementary or contrary ways of

religious exclusivity and come to embrace that broad pluralism which is part-and-parcel of both the term and the reality of religious instruction. Religious instruction as term and as reality not only incorporates catechesis and Christian education but also has the inherent breadth to encompass the whole range of religiously pluralistic outcomes. Catechesis and Christian education, by their very exclusivist natures, make genuine religiously pluralistic teaching very difficult and probably impossible. To be fully and truly pluralistic, religion teaching must abandon its exclusive stress on particularity and move toward pluriformity. Religious particularism not only thwarts religious pluralism; it slowly asphyxiates the religious life of persons caught in its airless enclosure. God and his ongoing revelation are palpably pluriform. This pluriformity must pervade the work of all religious instruction and most especially religious instruction for pluralism. To be fully and truly pluralistic, religion teaching must forsake its unitary emphasis on faith and move to charity. History has shown that faith tends to divide. For all its power and fruit, faith has historically divided person from person, religion from religion. Faith has also historically separated individuals from a wider pluriformity in vision and life, encasing these persons within the particularities of their own religious confines. History has also shown that charity tends to unite. Where there is charity, there tends to be little or no division among persons, religions, or nations. Charity binds and heals. Charity is necessarily pluriform and universal, extending to each person and group regardless of circumstances. Charity subsumes faith and transforms it with the oil and life of love.

If it is to be both authentic and effective, religiously pluralistic instruction must flow away from theology and toward religious experience. The best that theology can ever do for religious pluralism is to

---

facilitation, including pedagogical procedures for socialization, for liberation, and so forth. See Groome, *Christian Religious Education*, pp. 126-127. (Groome also errs in making education identical to the schooling process when, on p. 127, he calls education "an agency." Education is an overall process and therefore cannot be identified with any particular agency, such as schooling.) For a fine treatment decrying the deleterious effects wreaked on education by misguided attempts to make it dichotomous with socialization, see J. W. Getzels, "Socialization and Education: A Note on Discontinuities," in Hope Jensen Leichter, *The Family as Educator* (New York: Teachers College Press, 1974), pp. 44-51. Tellingly, Berard L. Marthaler understands both the metier and intent of socialization very well. With good reason he views catechesis as essentially a process of socializing learners into the regulations and conduct-pattern of the Catholic church as the church is officially interpreted by formal ecclesiastical documents. (Marthaler, "Socialization as Model for Catechetics," pp. 64-92.)

investigate it from the cognitive perspective.[156] Precisely because it is cognitive, theology can never experience religious pluralism as a lived religious way of existence; only religious experience can do this. Theology is cognitive, and therefore is always *about* religious pluralism; theology is not and cannot be religious pluralism in vivo. Consequently, to teach the theology of religious pluralism is not to teach religious pluralism, but rather to teach *about* religious pluralism. To facilitate the experience of religious pluralism is to teach religious pluralism truly. Even in the cognitive realm, theology is limited because theology constitutes only one kind of intellectual examination of religious pluralism. Because theology is only one kind of intellectual investigation, its cognitive grasp of religious pluralism is necessarily incomplete and to that extent defective. We should not forget that the most genuine and most fecund theological dogmas are those which have been inferred from the religious experiences occuring in scripture and in the church.[157] Religious experience is prior and primary not only to theology but to all of religious pluralism. History, especially since the end of the Second Vatican Council (1965) has shown that discussions among theologians of various religions have more often than not led to nothing more than either continued theological discussions or to "convergence agreements" on one or another point of cognitive dogma. It is only religious experience which, for Christian churches, can authenticate at the human level the pluriform oneness of Jesus. It is only religious experience which, for persons and organizations of all religions, can authenticate at the human level the essential unity of every individual and institution as participants in God's pluriform revelation.

What is most needed in religious instruction for pluralism is not

---

156. Even as a cognitive way of investigating phenomena including religious pluralism, theology's potency is severely limited. It is always a source of amazement to me that some theologians and all advocates of the theological approach to religious instruction grossly overrate theology as an intellectual activity. It should be underscored that even as a cognitive endeavor, theology ranks rather low. As Paul Avis remarks, "Theology is not knowledge as we understand knowledge, but, as the Christian tradition has long known, a form of learned ignorance (*docta ignorantia*). While this conclusion can be established on metaphysical, biblical, or mystical grounds, we are likely to be particularly impressed today by the evidence supplied by the facts of division among Christians." (Avis, *Ecumenical Theology and the Elusiveness of Doctrine*, p. 3.)

157. Since the cognitive dogmas of individual Christian churches were inferred from less than the combined religious experiences of persons in other Christian churches and in non-Christian communities, they are necessarily incomplete and to this extent defective. On this point, see Congar, *Diversity and Communion*, pp. 168-177.

shared theologies but shared religious experiences.

So often the great mystics of every religion penetrate to the essence of things with refreshing simplicity and depth. In teaching religious pluralism, religious educators would do very well to heed the words of the anonymous author of what is possibly the greatest piece of English mystical literature, *The Cloud of Unknowing*: "For though we, through the grace of God, can know fully about all other matters, and think about them—yes, even the very works of God himself—yet of God himself can no man think. Therefore I will leave to one side everything I can think, and choose for my love that thing which I cannot think. Why? Because he may well be loved, but not thought. By love he can be caught and held, but by thinking never. . . . Thinking must be put down and covered with a cloud of forgetting. . . . Strike that thick cloud of unknowing with the sharp dart of longing love."[158]

Religious experience and love—these are the twin pillars upon which any authentic teaching for religious pluralism must be built.

---

158. Anonymous, *The Cloud of Unknowing*, trans. Clifton Wolters (Baltimore: Penguin, 1961), pp. 59-60. Ira Progoff observes that this anonymous author was a tough-minded rather than a tender-minded individual who most probably was not an ivory-tower person but rather one familiar with the frailties and exigencies of concrete human existence. (Ira Progoff, "Introductory Commentary," in Anonymous *The Cloud of Unknowing*, trans. Ira Progoff [New York: Dell Laurel, 1983], pp. 20-21.)

4

Holy People in a Holy Creation

David Ng

A statement about religious education in a religiously pluralistic world must begin with the author's identification of himself or herself. In my case I characterize myself as a religious educator belonging to a mainline Protestant Christian denomination, the Presbyterian Church (U.S.A.). I have served in a variety of jobs within the Christian church, including pastor, curriculum editor, seminary professor, and director of the education division of the National Council of the Churches of Christ in the U.S.A., an organization with thirty-one member denominations, something of a pluralism in itself. I am an educated middle-class male, married and with two grown sons and have lived and worked in a rural village and a medium-sized city, but grew up and lived and worked mainly in large urban areas where there was much diversity of language and culture. I myself straddle language and culture, as an Asian-American born in San Francisco of parents born in China. I have experienced pluralism on its bright and promising side as well as its dark side. I have enjoyed the acceptance of friends, neighbors, colleagues, and church members and also have had directed at me the taunts and jeers and even the spit of those who do not accept and certainly do not love persons who are different from them. My views of pluralism may reflect those of mainline Protestant Christianity; perhaps in the end they reflect only the views of David Ng and this is a statement about pluralism.

Current Expressions of Pluralism

It can be said that pluralism has existed from the beginning of recorded history, or if you choose, from the beginning of time, as soon as there
was more than one particle of matter on earth. Story, legend, myth, and
history tell of differences between people. People are of different color,
language, culture, and beliefs. A great consciousness of pluralism exists
today, particularly a recognition that the former ideal of a benign melting pot is being replaced by an ideal of a mosaic, a unity of peoples in
which the individual parts do not lose shapes and identities but do blend
into a whole greater than the sum of its parts.

Although the world is still racked with the turmoil of racial prejudice,
still violently and oppressively expressed, the ideal of people living together in racial harmony has been practiced sufficiently successfully for
the world to know that it is possible. The possibility comes with an
acceptance of the right of people of a particular race to affirm the
characteristics of that race while living in the mix of multiracial society
which allows no particular race to claim superiority. Similarly ethnic,
cultural, national, and historical backgrounds can be affirmed and the
possibility of a multisociety—multiracial, multicultural, multilingual,
multiethnic, and so on—can be seen. Not that this positive view of
pluralism in society has come easily, for we have witnessed and partici-
pated in our lifetime in the struggles that blacks, or women, or youth, or
other minorities and less-powerful groups have endured to reach a place
where hope is real. Much of the tension today is tightened by the
realization that significant gains in racial or ethnic or other forms of
human harmony are nearly possible. The struggle goes forward.

Migration has much to do with the recent ferment regarding pluralism. As people have left their traditional home regions and for the most
part have moved into cities, this urbanization has made polyglot society
a reality and a positive view of pluralism a necessity. A resident of the
metropolis, such as I, will find life enriched as I learn not only to accept
but to embrace the many languages, foods, customs, styles, values, and
histories of the great pluralism which is New York City. The probable
alternative is war.

One would think that the relentless development of technological
wonders, particularly sophisticated means for mass communication,
would foster a blending or dilution of languages and cultures and a
movement toward some sort of unity of peoples. There is much of that,
and unpleasant reminders of that can be seen and heard when a traveler
comes upon boom box radios in Edinburgh or Tokyo or Marrakesh. For
all the distressing signs of a mass society and groupthink, there are still
the many or plural signs of a pervading pluralism. One would think that

there is something about the human spirit which defies being melted in a single pot.

There is also a rise in consciousness about pluralism in religion. From my perch in a highrise building housing a number of Protestant Christian national agencies, I can see that the denominations, or "communions" as some of them wish to be known, have not talked about church unity as a unity of church structure, at least not in the last quarter of a century. The dreams of a single church of Jesus Christ, however it would have been structured, have become dreams of church unity in which a pluralism of practice, belief, and structure is united in acceptance of differences and in cooperation of efforts. The ultimate goal of real and complete unity is still expressed by many but is tempered by expressions such as "but not in my lifetime," or, *"deo volente."*

From my perch in a denomination's national education office I can also see very clearly that within any single Protestant denomination there is more pluralism than can be listed. Within the newly formed Presbyterian Church (U.S.A.), for example, there is held in tension (often in great tension) the ordered and disordered caucuses, committees, groups, and collections of persons of distinct theological, social, racial, cultural, sexual, and political identity. The Presbyterian Church, like its counterparts, professes unity but is greatly challenged to find ways to practice it in a pluralistic society and pluralistic church.

Like most of its counterparts, the Presbyterian Church (U.S.A.) is a national church with international connections. As it relates to religious partners worldwide it finds itself confronted by other faiths and even by "non-faiths." The religious superiority claimed by the Christian church a century ago has evolved into a recognition of the validity of other faiths and religious practices. Religious educators now work at helping the learners in their religious group to know about and to understand the beliefs and practices of another religious group, not in order to do a better job of proselytizing, but genuinely to learn and benefit from the other group. Christians, even Presbyterians, are learning about prayer and meditation from Buddhists; about God, nature, and earth from Polynesian theists; and about family social ethics from Chinese Confucianists. To be sure, vociferous segments of Protestantism still call for the evangelizing of the heathen and may even suspect that "God" does not hear the prayers of a Jew. Not everything is perfect or even moving in the same direction. But for some of us our view of religious pluralism allows for or rationalizes even that.

The American philosopher, Josiah Royce, predicted eighty years ago that the American melting pot would become "an insipid stew." Within the framework of the American ideal of individualism Royce properly decried the homogeneity which would develop from a giant state which had the tools of mass communication and education and the coopera- tion of giant industry—mass production—which would lead people to "read the same daily news, to share the same general ideas, to submit to the same overmastering social forces, to live in the same external fash- ion, to discourage individuality, and to approach a dead level of harassed mediocrity."[1]

Royce would have preferred instead an enlightened provincialism with regional dialects, ethnic differences, and distinct customs. Interest- ingly, Royce found the image of the Christian church as described by Paul, wherein many members belonged to one body under one head, to be a useful description of his ideal pluralistic society.[2] So the ideal which was posed in biblical times continues to beckon us today. As early as the turn of the century an enlightened philosopher, among perhaps others, perceived that there is value in pluralism and danger in a denial of it. But most persons who acknowledged pluralism had an assimilationist attitude toward it. One of the problems with pluralism has been that those who have had the power to deal with it have chosen to deal with it from their powerful perspective, to the disadvantage of the weak or less- powerful.

Charles R. Foster of Scarritt Graduate School is a religious educator who advises a multicultural resource center and its governing board at the school of religious education. Foster has identified five typical reac- tions of the church, that is, by the powerful in the church, toward those of racial, ethnic, or cultural minority in the church. At a board meeting he spoke of these five reactions. One reaction is cultural annihilation or subjugation. In society this is expressed in a caste system, or apartheid, or slavery—and these expressions are not without church parallels or support, even today. The minority or less-powerful group is not allowed "in," and is ignored or held in contempt. A second form of reaction is cultural alienation, which requires the less-powerful and minority groups to exist in separation. The existence of historical black denomi- nations and of black judicatories within some denominations attests to the remnants of this mentality. Cultural substitution is a third reaction. The supposedly superior group allows others to be with them if these others, whatever culture or tradition they may possess, substitute the

---

1. Josiah Royce, "Provincialism Based Upon a Study of Early Conditions in California," *Putnam's Magazine* 7 (1907), p. 223, quoted in Charles Rice, "The Preacher as Storyteller," *Union Seminary Quarterly Review* 31:3 (Spring, 1976), pp. 184-185.
2. Rice, "The Preacher as Storyteller," p. 185.

culture, values, and beliefs of the powerful. Similar is the popular reaction of cultural assimilation. If the American ideal has been the melting pot, the church has been the kettle for such assimilation to occur, with the blessings of a warm theology. In the name of unity and harmony, persons of racial, ethnic, cultural, and national minority, and women as well, have been warmly invited to be assimilated into the Western, male-dominant, middle-class, individualistic, and imperialistic Protestant churches. WASP is the term we all know, and some have come to despise. In cultural assimilation there is a degree of tolerance for diversity, especially in the light of the prevailing valuation of individualism. But this diversity (or even eccentricity) is acceptable only when it does not challenge the status quo. In some church circles there is movement toward cultural accommodation, as can be seen in various forms of quota systems. A seemingly altruistic attitude of enabling the minority or weak to come in is ultimately felt as paternalistic, since the majority or powerful still dictate the terms.[3]

Fear is still the motor which drives many persons who feel out of control on the cloverleafs and multiple-lane freeways of a pluralistic society. Even in a university setting, where tradition suggests the freeflow of ideas and different views, the reaction to pluralism can be fear. Bernard Cooke of the University of Calgary, commenting on the state of theological reflection in North America today, recognizes the coexistence of differing philosophical and cultural approaches to understanding human experience and the emergence of legitimate systems— black theology and feminist theology being two examples—but Cooke finds many colleagues not open to these different understandings and systems because they are frightening. To listen to another's story, experience, mode of science or philosophy is to admit that one's own way may not be *the* way. It is to have one's identity, perhaps carefully built, questioned. It is to suggest the possible need for change.[4]

In some predominantly Protestant circles, which can be called conservative (let the reader fill in the radicalizing adjectives!) the fear factor is quite concrete and even has an identified enemy: "secular humanism."[5] The threat of change from persons and forces which are different has led some people to warn that the sacred truths and values of Christianity (as

---

3. Presentation by Charles R. Foster, summarized in Minutes of the Advisory Board of the Multi-Cultural Resources Center, Scarritt Graduate School, May 12, 1986, p. 2.

4. Bernard Cooke, "The Current State of Theological Reflection," *Bulletin of The Council on the Study of Religion* 10:2 (April, 1979), pp. 40-41.

5. Virginia Ramey Mollenkott, "Toward a Biblical Basis for Pluralism," *Report from the Capital* 37:7 (July-August, 1982), pp. 4-5.

they understand it) are being threatened by insidious attacks from those who would undermine our faith in God, the Holy (and infallible) Bible, the sacredness of human (and even unborn) life, and democracy, which is our God-given political system. In North America there are large numbers of Christians who do not tolerate pluralism and have given it the pejorative name of "secular humanism," a name almost as vile as "communist."

Meanwhile those who represent pluralism, those like myself who happen to be Chinese-American or some other minority, struggle to make silk from the sow's ear of pluralism. Marginalized and oppressed, we assert our right to be an interwoven part of the whole, and we claim that our distinctiveness adds color and value to the whole. For us pluralism is not just an idea; it is our only hope.

Seeing the Positive in Pluralism

Driven by the personal needs for integrity of being and acceptance in community, and at the risk of rationalizing, persons of minority or less-powerful status in the churches have spun positive fabrics of pluralism—coats of many colors. For me a powerful event or symbol is the Lord's Supper (Eucharist, Holy Communion, and so on; there is no single name for this act of worship in our pluralistic church). I understand I am invited to sup at the Table by the Lord Jesus, the one who loves me, accepts me, and redeems me to a new, creative identity. Jesus has done the same for other persons. I come to the Table at Jesus' beckoning and so do the others. We do not come first out of mutual respect or love for each other but by the invitation of Jesus. It is this relationship with Jesus which mediates a commonality and community for all who come to the Table. When each person comes to the Table he or she finds that one's individuality is respected—we do not have to change histories, or racial backgrounds, or cultures, to come. Indeed, what we bring—our individual histories, and so on—become the gifts we contribute to the others. For me the Lord's Supper symbolizes the unity and diversity of the church integrated into coherence.

The ideal of the community of the Table has not been reached and this brings up the need for justice. Personal and social acts of justice are encouraged and achieved in the name of the pluralistic ideal of the wholeness and harmony, the well-being or shalom which is God's holy communion of all peoples.

Charles Foster, along with others, sees this pluralism in the stories of Babel and Pentecost. Contrary to popular perceptions of Babel as a chaotic cacophony of competitive visions of the good life, so disharmonious as to prevent a cooperative construction of that common life,

Foster sees Babel as a sign of God's love for us. Babel reminds us that we are God's creation, we are human, and we are diverse.[6] To stretch the point, God does a job of religious education in allowing us to discover these truths experientially! To extend that learning we might add that God works in cultures other than our own. The experiences and insights of other cultures can be gifts to us. Pentecost makes the same point. We are challenged to be open to God's activity among people of many cultures.[7]

Major policy bodies in Protestant denominations are supporting positive understandings of religious pluralism, as can be seen in a "Resolution Concerning Multi-Cultural Christian Education," adopted in 1985 by the Christian Board of Publications of the Christian Church/ Disciples of Christ:

RESOLUTION CONCERNING MULTI-CULTURAL CHRISTIAN EDUCATION

WHEREAS, the human family is a multicultural, multiethnic people created in the image of God—forming a pluralistic world through which to proclaim and demonstrate the divine will; and

WHEREAS, the acceptance of Jesus Christ and the proclamation and teaching of the vision of the Rule of God is given and entrusted to all people; and

WHEREAS, on Pentecost the Church was established of "every nation under heaven," and the Holy Spirit empowered every group to hear the gospel in its own language and culture; and

WHEREAS, the Christian Church (Disciples of Christ) embraces members of many ethnic groups in its church family; and

WHEREAS, the Division of Homeland Ministries has formed a network of multiethnic leaders for the purpose of enabling the church to be enriched and strengthened as a family; and

WHEREAS, the Christian Board of Publication follows multicultural and multiethnic guidelines in the development of curriculum materials; and

WHEREAS, multicultural Christian Education is based upon a fundamental belief that all people are valued and respected regardless of

---

6. Charles R. Foster, "From Babel to Pentecost: Christian Education in a World of Many Cultures," *The Baptist Leader* (April, 1987).

7. Christian Board of Publication, Division of Homeland Ministries, Christian Church/Disciples of Christ, No. 8526, "Resolution Concerning Multi-Cultural Christian Education," August 2-7, 1985.

age, language, race, sex, economic class, religion, physical or mental ability, and can strengthen the ministry of the church in

1) enabling persons to discover and affirm their own identity within their cultural context, and thus better understand the relationship of the Christian faith and tradition to their own lives and experience;

2) enabling persons to understand, appreciate, and respond to the identities and gifts of cultural and ethnic groups;

3) enabling persons to understand and appropriate both the particular and universal dimensions of Christian teaching;

4) enabling the whole church to be a witness to the world through a community in which all people live and work together in friendship, interdependence and harmony;

THEREFORE BE IT RESOLVED, that the General Assembly of the Christian Church (Disciples of Christ) meeting in Des Moines, Iowa, August 2-7, 1985,

1) affirm a multicultural educational ministry that reflects the nature, life and mission of the church;

2) call for the inclusion of multicultural content and approaches in all present and future program and curriculum as well as supplementary multicultural resources;

3) encourages all congregations to make use of multicultural program, resources and leadership in their educational ministries.

CHRISTIAN BOARD OF PUBLICATION
DIVISION OF HOMELAND MINISTRIES

The Tasks of Religious Education in a Pluralistic Society

Among the many tasks of religious education are certain major ones. The adherents or faithful members in a particular religion should be enabled to identify themselves and explain their experiences in the light of their chosen religious system. They need to learn a theology which explains life—in relation to the transcendent, in the case of Christianity. They need to know how and why they worship. They need to learn common values and practices. Knowing all of this gives particular meaning to life for these adherents and enables them to be able to explain themselves to others. In today's pluralistic context it can be added that religious education can enable adherents of one religion to recognize, acknowledge, and listen to the explanations of those who follow another religious system.

In the religiously pluralistic society of today religious education has some demanding tasks. These tasks start with identifying theological concerns and include organizing the content and creating appropriate methods.

The theology of a religion will express what the believers understand to be their identity, as individuals and as a community. The purposes of life and the mission of the community are also expressed in theological terms. For many North American Protestant Christians (in a pluralistic society it is virtually impossible to have an absolutely clearly defined identity!) several theological categories are significant. There is a theology of creation which describes our world in global rather than provincial terms. A good God created the whole, good world. This world includes a diversity of people who are to live in relationship; indeed, in harmony and peace. To describe the creator God as a trinity within a unity is a human attempt to acknowledge diversity and relationship even in the transcendent. For Christians the Incarnation is a central belief which gives meaning to human life. Human life—particular human life—is good. Each of us has a unique identity which we can affirm. We live in a certain place and experience a particular history. And as soon as we affirm the uniqueness and goodness of an individual, we affirm the existence of pluralism.

Many images inform the Christian community of believers. Already mentioned are those of Babel and Pentecost, which are currently understood as positive images of the diversity of humankind, a diversity which is pleasing to God and which God has not seen fit to change. The church, which could be seen as a forerunner of God's intentions for *communitas,* is led by an image of the one body. This body has one head and many members. The members are coordinated in their activities by the head but have a rich and necessary diversity of function. The hand serves its purposes and does not try to be an eye; the ear serves the whole body through its functions and does not covet nor denigrate the functions of the foot. The possibilities are endless—and pluralistic.

Another powerful image which leads the Christian church is that of Shalom. Creation has a wholeness, well-being, harmony, and justice which is characterized by the lamb lying beside the lion. The ideal is a peaceable realm. While much argument remains over who can come into this peaceable realm and when the realm is to be realized, the central image of Shalom remains prominent. Religious education serves the church by depicting this peaceable realm, calling people into it, and teaching how it may come about. Witness, mission, service, and social justice are topics for teaching in fulfillment of this peaceable realm.

It may be a big claim to hope that the theological perspectives and images sketched above are major parts of the content of Christian religious education. An even greater hope is that the teaching of these perspectives establish the foundations for Christians to have an ecumenical attitude. Seeing God, world, self, and community in certain ways can help a community of believers to be more accepting of persons of diverse racial, ethnic, cultural, and national backgrounds, even of diverse religious backgrounds. The biblical claim that we love because God first loved us makes good sense in this context. Essentially what is claimed here is that pluralism is the will and creation of God. This is how it is, and this is what we are to teach.

How is religious pluralism, or the acceptance of a world and of religious systems which are pluralistic, to be taught? Positively and lovingly, as implied above. A half-dozen words come to mind to give clues and cues for religious educators who wish to teach constructively and effectively in our pluralistic era.

Religious education must be contextual. This is a lesson from the powerful theologies of the day. Liberation theology and feminist theology, for example, take into account with utmost seriousness the life situations of the learners. One who is enslaved eagerly learns about slavery and liberation and is motivated to act on that learning. Women who have been held in lowly estate or have had their personal lives restricted and their potential thwarted have a great stake in learning how the bible, theology, ethics, sociology, psychology, political theory—anything—can help them gain freedom and self-respect. My own interest in ecumenism, pluralism, community, and justice derive from my context. I and my Asian-American brothers and sisters come upon our interest in the church as a community where justice and love prevail because our experiences and contexts drive us to these concepts and call us to make realities of them.

Helping the people of the Protestant church (I cannot speak for the other sections of the church) to see and identify the pluralistic context of their lives is a necessarily educational task. This task is relatively easy for those whose contexts are in some way oppressive. The unfortunate truth is that so many Protestants are self-satisfied and see no need for change. Or they may fear change for the realignment of status and power that will be inevitable. The visions of Shalom somehow must be made not only concrete but real in the sense of having been experienced. The Protestant churches need to experience worship, community, ministry, and every other form of church life in tangible ways which enable them to say that it is good for brothers and sisters to sit at table together. I have never bitten a Caucasian—except affectionately—and it may be helpful for Caucasians to know and experience how loving I can be. We all need opportunities to be in settings and contexts which bring out the best in us.

Contextualization is of a serious nature. Learning how to identify one's situation, to analyze it, criticize it, and to find, in the bible and other resources, the vision that will model for us a better context, is serious, constructive religious education. If we are open to the benefits of religious pluralism, we can learn about learning contextually and doing theology contextually from our Latin American brothers and sisters who do this sort of education effectively in base communities, people's churches, villages, *favelas* (shantytowns), and even in brigades. For example, bible study in a base community takes into account an indigenous cultural point of reference. The learners try to respond to the needs and concerns of their society through a study and analysis of the social, political, economic, and cultural reality which surrounds them. For them contextualization means starting with reality and studying in order to be able to act effectively in their real context, usually a pluralistic context. North American students of the methods of Paulo Freire are carrying some insights into our churches and seminaries, as are religious educators whose methods include steps for helping learners name their situation and engage in a praxis of story, vision, and action.

Religious education must be ecumenical. At the very least, the learning community ought to consist of a variety of participants engaged in democratic, participatory styles of learning. Leading and following, teaching and learning, can be shared. Different visions and viewpoints can be sought. Especially in this day the religious sensitivities and viewpoints of others need to be appreciated. In global terms Christianity may never have been the dominant religion, and its claims to truth and wisdom need to be placed alongside the valuable truths and wisdom of other faiths and of non-faith. For example, Western scientific method, and Western attitudes about the physical world, have brought our world to far places, even into space. Yet many black holes and other gaps remain, some gaps caused by Western methodology which tends to dichotomize and alienate the physical from the spiritual. Other religions, such as that of Islam, may have tremendous gaps of their own, but they do not struggle the same way as do Christians over the separation of spirit and matter, or science and religion. To be ecumenical in learning is to be willing to seek after truths not contained in the boxes of one's own religion, or denomination, or congregation.

Ecumenical learning does imply certain objectives. It implies community, a broad sense of unity, and movement toward the just and whole community which Christians and Jews call Shalom. It also implies that no one group or ideology is allowed to dominate or to oppress.

Religious education, by being ecumenical, is also participatory. Learning needs to be set up so that concepts are learned not only by thinking about the ideas to be learned. As much as possible, learning can be by participation in activities and then in reflection on these activities to foster the assimilation of what is to be learned. This educational approach is important for adults and imperative for children. Adults are capable of thinking abstractly, in effect capable of learning by thinking about an idea or concept. Yet many adults prefer not to do so. They prefer to think concretely. When they participate actively in learning, engaging persons with diverse opinions and practices, their learning can be enhanced. For Christians to read about Jews is possible, and learning does take place. For many adults learning can be enhanced by visiting a Jewish synagogue, conversing with Jews, looking at their art, sharing meals with Jews, and engaging in other participatory methods.

The value of concrete learning for children is obvious. Less obvious is the value of such learning for youth, who supposedly are able, in Piaget's terms, to use formal operations to think abstractly. Such is the theory. In practice, to cite just one example, most young adolescents still use concrete operations or at best transitional operations when they think. Perhaps a third of them use formal operations by the time they are age fourteen. Public school educator Margaret Trautman made this point in telling fashion when she analyzed the confirmation curriculum of the Presbyterian Church (U.S.A.) and found that the material was "way over the heads of the kids." She urged that the next set of resources be clearly identified for middle and older adolescents since the confirmation process had to do with abstractions such as the church, its global mission, personal commitment, and other theological concepts. Even at that, Trautman urged the use of experiential, participatory learning activities which began with concrete operations and familiar concepts.[8] This is good advice regarding the teaching of pluralism too: make it participatory, and make it concrete.

In regard to pluralism, religious education must be democratic. The role of the teacher ought not to imply moral superiority or in any way exacerbate a pluralistic situation and make it into an alienating experience. The opposite ought to be sought. When learners also help teach, and the teaching role is shared democratically, a unifying experience is possible. Learning can come about from comparisons of and appreciation of differences. An adult forum in which Sikhs, Christians, and Muslims democratically teach each other and learn from each other is better than one in which judgments are made by a single expert teacher

---

8. Margaret C. Trautman, "Theoretical Analysis of the Cognitive Demands of the Concept 'Church,' " Doctoral dissertation submitted to the Graduate Faculty in the School of Education, University of Pittsburgh, 1984.

which imply that one way is superior to another or one way must be believed rather than another.

Democratic learning suggests that religious education emphasize human rather than material resources. Both are needed, but topics such as pluralism, which have to do with human characteristics and differences, are better understood through human agency. This is particularly true among certain groups such as Asian-Americans. Storytelling, the sharing of experiences and insights, the explanation of customs and rituals, and many other topics are learned effectively when people teach them to each other. Granted, one would have a hard time teaching about the tea ceremony without the *realia* of tea, wisk, cups, and pot. Such materials are a necessary part of the learning experience. A person is still required to demonstrate, to explain, to inspire. In the pluralistic North American context, Asian-Americans are not necessarily well-served by printed resources when so many languages are used by the learners. In such pluralisms, communication needs to be personal but also to transcend language. Some of us may need a reminder that not everyone reads—certainly not everyone reads English. The need is for a teacher—a person—more than for a book.

Religious education must be open-ended. No one has all the answers in a pluralistic society. In a pluralistic society there cannot be one answer. These little truths are not easily accepted. Each of us has wished for the grail-like single answer, and whole religious communities have claimed the one, single, clear answer. Our fear of the unknown, of change, of differences must be overcome, and our religious education must open us to new conclusions or temporary conclusions or even no conclusions.

Religious education is heuristic. There is a pluralism of possibilities, and we do not know what we will discover. The general destination is in sight, for we seek a whole or holy creation where holy communities embrace and nurture holy persons. We live and move and have our being in a rich complexity of persons, systems, and communities. To learn about all of this is to taste the pleasure of the pluralism which is God's world.

5

Religious Pluralism and Religious Education
A Black Protestant Perspective

Grant S. Shockley

Several separate but fortuitously interrelated socio-cultural-political landmark events occurred in the latter part of the eighteenth and twentieth centuries that have significantly influenced the shape and direction of Protestant interreligious relationships in the United States. The religion clauses of the First Amendment to the Constitution established a national policy of religious freedom (1791). The birth of the United Nations witnessed the emergence of a new consciousness of the world community as "one" and a *de facto* status of equality for national religions. The awakening of the Afro-Asian nations and their formation of a community of interest at Bandung (1955) sparked the resurgence of older and newer religions in the East. The Black Revolution of the 1960s accompanied by unrelenting demands for racial equality and social justice generated a black theology for the liberation of the oppressed. This development resurfaced "the irrepressible conflict" between "color and conscience" in white Christian America.

Much of the resistance to openness to other religions and resistance to interracial association was rooted in a white Protestant power-dominance formation which from time immemorial has imaged black people as innately inferior in every respect. Second, white Protestants rarely found it possible to divorce feelings of racial superiority from the superiority of the religion they professed and the people they missionized. Third, white Protestants, insensitive to the need for racial justice or indeed social revelance, if it implied equality, categorically precluded open-ended, objective, or even rational discussions of such issues.

Given this situation, the purposes of this chapter are: the exploration of the principles, revelance, and implications of religious and cultural pluralism for Protestant theology, black theology and religious education in Protestant churches, generally, and in black churches, particularly. The following thesis is being advanced as a theoretical frame of reference for the educational task of Protestant and black churches, respectively; increasing religious and cultural diversity in the national and world communities requires that Protestants—for present and future optimum impact and effectiveness—adopt a pluralist approach in relation to other religious belief-systems and especially in reference to black theology. Such a stance would view other religious belief-systems and black theology as equal partners with unique historical and cultural backgrounds, equally valid claims in "naming" ultimate reality, equally effective and equally valid "paths to salvation." In educational terms this approach further suggests a religious education theory that balances "the need to foster roots which will give a person 'a positional identity,' " with one that also inculcates a common commitment to an open, rational, critical approach."[1] More specifically, religious education in relation to the black religious experience should be contextual and educational.

In keeping with the above introductory statements the chapter will discuss two basic issues in the form of the following questions: What is the significance of pluralism for religion, theology, and religious education in Protestantism as it faces a religiously, culturally, and racially diverse society, and what is the significance of pluralism for the black experience, black theology, and religious education in the black church, community, nation, and world?

DIVERSITY, PLURALISM, AND THE NEW PARADIGM

It might be helpful at the outset of this discussion of religious pluralism to look at the term pluralism and observe how it has evolved in usage. Since its introduction in philosophical language about 1720 by Christian Wolff it has had several meanings.[2] Originally, it seems to have referred to philosophers who were not "egoists" or those who

---

1. M. C. Felderhof, ed., *Religious Education in a Pluralistic Society* (London: Hodder and Stoughton, 1985), p. 2.

2. Stanley Ehrlich and Graham Wooten, eds., *Three Faces of Pluralism* (Westmead: Gower, 1980), pp. 2-7.

viewed this world entirely from an "ego" perspective. Later, it was apparently used to distinguish Wolff's ontological ideas from those of the monists and dualists. Still later pluralism meant a doctrine espousing the diversity of existence. During and since the time of Immanuel Kant (1724-1804) the term has connoted (in Wolffian tradition) a positive view of diversity. With William James (1842-1910), the term became an established doctrine in philosophy expressing the general notion that reality is "multifarious." Currently, it is a philosophical theory about the nature of reality which states that truth ultimately has more than one valid construction and that human thinking can approach those constructions in quite different ways. Referred to as the most important philosophical finding of the twentieth century, pluralism has the potential for literally revolutionizing entire fields of knowledge, conceptual frameworks, ways of knowing, and ways of doing.[3] In 1915 Horace Kallen in a brilliant article, "Democracy vs the Melting Pot," applied the philosophical concept of pluralism to the existence of ethnic diversity in a democratic society. In doing this he found the "melting pot" concept prevalent at that time to be inadequate and oppressive. He preferred America to be a "democracy of nationalities" in which diverse racial and ethnic groups would and should be encouraged to participate fully in the total society as equal Americans and still cultivate their ethnic differences. His basic belief on this whole matter was that "democrary involves not the elimination of differences but the perfection and conservation of differences."[4]

Based on the evolution of meaning in the term pluralism, defining religious pluralism is a twofold task. First, religious pluralism must be distinguished from religious diversity, the reality and presence of a variety of types and forms of religious expressions. This is minimal religious pluralism. The essence of religious pluralism is not *realia* but relationships. What is the relation of the content of the various faiths in a community? What is their common history, if any? What are their status and power relations? How do they relate to each other? What are some common human efforts that can be planned and worked on jointly? The second definitional task is analytical. What does the pluralist thesis mean when applied to religion? Quite plainly if "the truth admits of more than one valid formulation" and there are more ways than one to approach it, can there be only one, final, absolute religion

---

3. Walter Watson, *The Architectonics of Meaning: Foundations of Neo-Pluralism* (Albany: State University Press of New York, 1955), p. ix.

4. Horace Kallen, quoted in Stephen Steinberg, *The Ethnic Myth: Race, Ethnicity, and Class in America* (New York: Atheneum, 1981), p. 253.

for everyone or are there different conceptions of the absolute for different people at different times in history? Pluralist John Hick would say, "Thus the great religious traditions are to be regarded as alternative soteriological spaces within which, or ways along which men and women find salvation/liberation/fulfillment."[5]

The pluralist thesis or new paradigm necessitates a reappraisal of at least three fundamental assumptions that are central and normative in Protestant religious thinking: the nature and role of the absolute vs the relative; the universal vs the particular; and the exclusive vs the inclusive. Are the terms "absolute," "universal," and "exclusive" irreconcilable with the pluralist thesis?

In response to these critical questions several things need to be said. First, pluralism is not a new metaphysic: It does not proclaim a new ultimate reality. Pluralism is a method of analysis to aid in critical evaluating, focusing, and objectifying. Absolutes, universals, and exclusive revelations are valid in themselves, and they are valid for those who believe in them. They are elements of the larger truth or the whole of truth which by definition is unknowable by a single individual. The pluralist would suggest further that there are elements of the truth in every statement of it. The most productive way to arrive at the largest truth is to intercommunicate the truth that one holds with truths that others hold. The result of such a "dialogue" could be an enlargement of the truth held by each engaged in such a dialogue. Something of the same approach can be used in dealing with the universal-particular issue. There are universal meanings and there are particular ones. For the pluralist the universal is perceived in the particularities of time, culture, race, nationality, and language. This does not deny their existence or validity as universals. It is simply a statement that conceptions of the universal are plural rather than singular. Again, exclusive revelations are valid for those who have them or accept them for their own from others. They are not valid as claims to or for others. Finally, it is not true that pluralists deny an ultimate deity or divine substance or undergirding essence. The pluralist would only say that such a claim could be held but that it cannot be spoken of in empirical terms. "Ultimate," "essence," and "divine" are true terms and may be ultimately true about the deity to whom they refer. Rupert Breitling summarizes William James on this point of getting truth all together. Breitling says, "There may ultimately never be an all form at all . . . the substance of reality may never get totally collected . . . a distributive

---

5. John Hick, quoted in Leroy S. Rouner, ed., *Religious Pluralism* (Notre Dame, Ind.: University of Notre Dame Press, 1984), p. 194.

form of reality, the each form, is logically as acceptable and empirically as probable as the all form."[6]

NEW PARADIGM IMPLICATIONS

There are several implications for religion, theology, and Protestant Christianity in the new religious situation of diversity. It is here to stay. Second, in the sense of influence and actual power, Protestantism is now a minority faith in a nation where it was once the majority religion. Learning how to be partners in dialogue with other religions and faiths is going to be difficult and challenging. Protestant Christianity needs to learn how to be open to other religions in ways to which it is quite unaccustomed. John Cobb reminds us that "some kind of Christian absolute appears in all . . . major (Christian) formulations and . . . this inhibits total openness to other traditions and their claims."[7] Protestants need to remind themselves that "all claims to universality have to be related to the fact that no particular religion will be the sole religion of humankind."[8] This new realization, however, is a very positive one. We need other insights from sources our culture does not and cannot supply. We also need new strategies to face the new exigencies of our time. David Tracy suggests that "as before so too here, the search should not be for the one and only way to move forward. Rather in keeping with the pluralistic strategy. . . we can say. . . with Kenneth Burke, use all that can be used."[9]

How then shall Protestantism face the new religious pluralism? Martin Marty suggests four ways.[10] We can take comfort in our long vision of history given to us in Teilhard de Chardin's Omega point concept as a placebo interpretation of eschatology and simply "wish it away." Second, Marty suggests that we "move beyond pluralism" or place our faith in a belief that some scintilating synthesis of all the religions will emerge and resolve the dilemmas of the kind of tough dialogue of living with vital and viable religions would bring. A third possibility suggested by Marty is the development of a common faith whether it is really com-

---

6. Ehrlich and Wooten, eds., *Three Faces of Pluralism,* p. 4.

7. Rouner, *Religious Pluralism,* p. 170.

8. Donald G. Dawe and John B. Carman, eds., *Christian Faith in a Religiously Plural World* (Maryknoll, N.Y.: Orbis, 1978), p. 15.

9. David Tracy, *Plurality and Ambiguity: Hermeneutics, Religion, Hope* (San Francisco: Harper & Row, 1987), p. 72.

10. Martin Marty, "This We Can Believe: A Pluralistic Vision," *Religious Education* 75:1 (January-February, 1980), pp. 37-40.

mon for all or a faith at all. This "solution by definition," such as John Dewey's *A Common Faith* attempted, could be worth the effort but hardly the risk of what David Tracy calls "illusory models of pure autonomy and easy coherence." Marty's fourth approach is to learn how to live creatively with pluralism. This is consonant with the thinking of this chapter.

RELIGIOUS PLURALISM AND CULTURAL DIVERSITY

Religious diversity in the United States is a natural and direct consequence of the religion clauses in the national Constitution. The fact that "Congress shall make no law respecting an establishment of religion, or prohibiting the free exercise thereof"[11] provides the authority and the structure within which persons and institutions may express their religious beliefs and pursue their religious activities freely and interdependently.

This coveted constitutional right, unique even among Western democracies is, however, full of tensions and problems. For example: How separate can the churches and the state be? How is it possible to adjudicate community religious disagreements on the basis of a "principle of separation" in the absence of laws? How can religion be divorced from education in an avowedly religious nation? Even more complex than these problems, however, was the generally unwelcomed but necessary presence of a large population of black slaves who had been denied full human rights but granted the right of baptism in most instances. What was their relationship to the religious diversity in the new states of the Union? It was marginal. They had the very dubious distinction, together with the Native Americans, of being the first color minorities to be excluded from most Christian churches on the basis of skin color. The black church that came into being as a result of this anomalous situation has thus been an embarrassing addendum in white church discussions, generally and until recently (1960) in ecumenical conversations. The question of color minorities, especially blacks, then, must be raised in any discussion of pluralism. After 200 years of church independence would they be interested in anything less than peer partnership in a pluralistic dialogue? With this background it is now our task to briefly trace the development of religious diversity, pluralism, and dialogue in the United States with some reference to impinging issues beyond our national boundaries.

---

11. United States Constitution, Amendment I.

The religious situation in colonial America which eventually developed into what we now term "pluralistic" began under quite different circumstances. It evolved from what Philip Schaff called "a motley sampler of all church history."[12] French Huguenots were in the Carolinas and Episcopalians were in Virginia, the Carolinas, and Georgia. The Dutch Reformed and the Walloons settled in New York. The Scotch and the Scotch-Irish Presbyterians were in New Jersey. Roman Catholics were in Maryland; English Quakers in Pennsylvania; Lutherans, Moravians, Mennonites, Dunkers, and German Reformed were also there. Puritan-Congregationalists were in New England, especially Massachusetts and Connecticut. Baptists were originally in Rhode Island and Methodists were practically everywhere along the East Coast, inland, and westward.

Relations between these churches, sects, and religious factions in these early years were highly contentious. Though having fled from established churches, the Congregationalists established a church in New England. The Dutch Reformed did so in New York. The Church of England was established in the South in Virginia, the Carolinas, and Georgia. Actually, excepting the Baptists in Rhode Island and William Penn's "Holy Experiment" in Pennsylvania, there were few places where genuine and open religious liberty could be found!

Discussion about the establishment of religion in the colonies and its place in the upcoming Constitution are revealing. Basically, they did not want to replicate the established churches of England and Europe; nor was this possible. Apparently what they wanted was religious freedom "in extremis." As they discovered, this was untenable and impractical. A conventional wisdom developed that mutual tolerance was not only the better part of wisdom but the necessary basis for survival.

SECULARIZATION AND PLURALIZATION

The "religion clauses" in the Constitution (1791) erected "a wall of separation" between the churches and the new Federal government. These "clauses" did not disestablish religion. That was something that the states would do. What the "clauses" did, however, was of much greater significance. They fortuitously created the conditions in which secularization rather than sectarianism would eventually become a dominant ethos with which religion would have to contend. The secularization of the then "community" or public schools was reacted to by

---

12. Elwyn A. Smith, ed., *The Religion of the Republic* (Philadelphia: Fortress, 1971), p. 247.

the initiation (or continuance) of church parochial schools. Roman Catholic, Dutch Reformed, Lutheran, Episcopalian denominations, and later the Presbyterians, sponsored day schools to inculcate their respective faiths. A second phase of religious pluralization emerged with the development of state systems of public education in the middle of the nineteenth century. Advocating a philosophy of education which emphasized morality and Americanization, the public schools soon began to develop a "moral and spiritual values" approach to education with adjacent observations and celebrations drawn almost entirely from the Protestant or Christian traditions. Their manifesto, as it was expressed in the 1920s, was stated in the following way: "The teaching of moral and spiritual values in the public schools of the United States must be done without endangering religious freedom and without circumventing the policy of separation of church and state."[13]

Summarily, the response of the nation to the disestablishment of religion and the institution of a free, secular public school system was one of wide acceptance and general acclaim. While some parochial schools did emerge, the public, secular school became secure in the life of the nation.

In the second half of the nineteenth century in the U.S. several other factors and forces came into play that enhanced a burgeoning religious pluralism. The emancipation of four million black ex-slaves, indigenous population growth, the influx of European immigrants and the migration of blacks to the urban centers of the North and West. At the beginning of the twentieth century, then, more than 200 religious groups, quasi-religious groups, sects, "new-age" gods, and hundreds of racial, ethnic, and cultural groups could be identified. What questions did this new pluralistic situation raise? First, it caused some much-needed assessment and reflection on the meaning of this new presence of religions, races, and cultures—or what Samuel Hill called "the existence of or presence of a multiplicity of types, expressions, forms, and traditions."[14] This new convergence of religion, race, and culture had to find a "soul." Unrestricted by law in the free exercise of religion, what are the rules, the guidelines, the limits? Again in Hill's words, can we accept another group's "legal and political right to exist in combination with a denial of their theological validity and legitimacy, or even integrity."[15] More simply, would Americans allow others the right to be quite

13. Educational Policies Commission, Moral and Spiritual Values in the Public Schools (Washington, D.C.: National Education Association, 1951), p. 6.

14. Samuel S. Hill, Jr., "The Strange Career of Religious Pluralism in the South" (Tallahassee, Fla.: The Center for the Study of Southern Culture and Religion, July 1981), p. 18.

15. Ibid., p. 18.

different in their religious opinions and still support their right to promote them? A second set of questions that the new situation of diversity
raises occurs in settings outside the United States. What are the implications for religious pluralism and religious education in the recent resurgence of non-Western religions? Need Americans consider the national-
ist religions in China, the Middle East, Bangladesh, and the Arabic
states? What are the power relations and dynamics between and among
these religious groups, some domiciled in homogeneous culture-settings
and some in rapidly heterogenizing situations?

The whole situation calls for a paradigm shift or "a basic change in
the framework of thinking." The "idea whose time has come" for this is
a pluralist approach, a *modus vivendi* for the ordering of a multifarious
religious, cultural, ethnic, and racial situation. What is the shape and
style of the pluralist approach? Essentially, it is one that seeks an ampler
and more functional understanding of the nature and meaning of religion or theology in its situation of diversity—cultural, ethnic, racial,
linguistic; seeks ways of enabling persons to live together more creatively in and with diversity; and corporately designs ways of achieving
selected common human goals.

The pluralist approach to religion and theology is not without its
price. It will demand much of each partner. Premised on this principle
of dialogue, it requires the radical encounter of whole, equal persons
who covenant in mutual respect to open themselves to an issue or issues
of critical concern, seeking to respond as best they can from within the
integrity of their "position identities," their agreement or their separate-
ness. In the happy event that all of the above challenges are met there is
still David Tracy's timely warning: "If the religions enter into this scene
of conflict, they must be able to resist the illusory models of pure
autonomy and easy coherence. Despite their own sin and ignorance, the
religions at their best always bear extraordinary powers of resistance.
When not domesticated as sacred canopies for the status quo nor basted
by their own self-contradictory grasp at power, the religious live by
resisting."[16]

RELIGIOUS PLURALISM AND RELIGIOUS
EDUCATION: CONTEXTUAL PLURALISM

Delineating and designing a religious education program for living
creatively in a society that is religiously, culturally, socially, and racially

---

16. Tracy, *Plurality and Ambiguity,* pp. 83-84.

highly diverse poses a task of considerable magnitude and formidability. Following a brief statement of where we are, some assumptions and the positing of a "contextual pluralism" thesis, a program design will be offered. Generic in conception, it should be adaptable, with modifications in emphasis, for use in church or other religious education settings.

Thus far in this chapter the pluralistic position "that the truth admits of more than one valid formulation" and there are more ways than one to approach it has been established. Applied to religion, theology, and Protestantism this requires an entirely new approach or paradigm. It has also been observed that as religious diversity in the United States has evolved from an "enforced tolerance" into a situation of concerned inquiry about creative ways to live with diversity, Protestantism has been reminded of its "unfinished business" or genuine inclusion of racial and ethnic minorities. These critical issues, still in the process of resolution, as well as the theological and philosophical ones, now become the building blocks of a proposed educational design.

There are several assumptions upon which the entire design must be based. First, the age of pluralism has come, is here, and will remain an integral aspect of our social environment. The "old age gods" are still with us, the "new age" gods are all around, communes, witchcraft, satan-worship, and an innumerable host of "lesser gods" are on the religious scene and active. The sage advice of Martin Marty is in order: "As long as pluralism is here and you learn to live creatively with it, you can make the best of it." Second, the exigencies of the pluralistic situation that confronts us require a paradigm shift, or "a basic change in the framework of thinking about" pluralism. The Committee on Basic Philosophy and Policies at the 1940 meeting of the Educational Commission of the International Council of Religious Education gave a clear indication of the nature of such a shift when it stated that "the function of religious education is not simply the transmission of an authoritative interpretation of the Christian religion, but the reinterpretation and enrichment of the Christian faith itself in and through an educational process."[17] Currently, the social-science approach to religious education is reviving this point of view. Harold Burgess states the position. Grounded in the teaching-learning process this approach "sustains a value-free relationship to theology, the content of theology being accepted and inserted, as appropriate in the approach." Burgess goes on to say that, "Practices generated . . . from the social-science approach have a high degree of specificity to individual situations (and) flow from the

---

17. Harrison S. Elliott, *Can Religious Education Be Christian* (New York: Macmillan, 1941), p. 61.

deliberative effort of the religion teacher to use environmental factors in the here-and-now learning process."[18] Third, religious education in a pluralistic situation must be clear about why and how it must aid persons in personal religious growth and development. John Gilbert correctly insists that a critical function of religious education is the "validation" of personal religious experience. This validation must be clearly distinguished from assent to or acceptance of "symbolizations" of religious experience such as theological doctrines, or creeds.[19] Fourth, religious pluralism will insist that the identity and integrity of heritage and religion be respected in every instance of dialogue partnership. In reference to black religionists, specifically, this will challenge Protestants and their programs of religious education to reeducate practically their entire community to begin to eradicate this more than 400-year prejudice.

Finally, religious education, if it is to reflect the spirit and essence of pluralism, should be proactive and engaged. Its objectives, content, and methodologies should involve persons in actively shaping their present and future rather than passively reacting to the "quiet dogmas of the past." In speaking of engagement in relation to pluralism the principle of dialogue enters. Religious education would certainly wish to engage persons of all age levels intergenerationally in actual dialogue in local communities, nationally and internationally. From such interchanges new and fresh insights will certainly be forthcoming.

If it is seriously considered, as suggested in the beginning sentence of this chapter, that the essential task of religious education is "delineating and designing a . . . program for living creatively in a society that is religiously, culturally, socially, and racially highly diverse," it should not be surprising that its theoretical foundation finds its philosophic-religious roots in pluralism, its theological base in situational or contextual theology, and its religious education undergirding in a social-cultural approach. The resultant theoretical model to guide the practice to be suggested, then, will be referred to as contextual-pluralist. Its selection was based on its ability to perform the critical tasks of analysis, synthesis, comparison, and criticism that will be needed in exploring objectives, content, and methodologies for the components of the proposed learning-teaching design for: religious pluralism; cultural-racial pluralism, and learning to achieve common human goals.

---

18. Harold W. Burgess, *An Invitation to Religious Education* (Birmingham, Ala.: Religious Education Press, 1975), pp. 15-16.

19. John P. Gilbert, "Theological Pluralism and Religious Education," *Religious Education* 70:6 (November-December, 1975), p. 583-584.

Succinctly, a contextual-pluralist approach to religious education for living in a religiously plural society suggests generally that "if a dialogue within the churches is to be opened the study of religion must be placed into an educational rather than an ecclesiastical context"[20] and that there is no one best way for persons to learn or teach. More specifically it suggests that objectives, content, and methods be selected in relationship to: 1) the needs and opportunities for personal religious growth and development and the understanding of other religions; 2) the needs and opportunities for learning to live together in situations of religious, cultural, and racial diversity, and 3) the needs and opportunities for direct participation in corporately achieving commonly perceived human goals.

Premised on the theoretical statements above and the assumptions mentioned earlier, it is now proposed to outline teaching-learning designs for three immediately critical areas of concern as Protestant education faces the intensification of the need for understanding and relating to religious pluralism. The areas of concern to be considered are: 1) understanding religion and religious pluralism; 2) understanding differences and cultural pluralism, and 3) understanding interdependency and achieving common human goals. In each of these areas of concern statements of objective, potential content, and possible methodologies will be indicated.

RELIGIOUS PLURALISM: OBJECTIVE

Understanding, teaching, and learning about other religions begins with an understanding of one's own religious belief or faith. Sara Little suggests that this entails "commitment, feeling, and conscious involvement of the self" rather than mere assent or passive acceptance.[21] This sense of religious self-awareness develops what K. E. Nipkow refers to as "positional identity" or religious "root experience." Such an experience provides a necessary security-base for an "open, rational, critical approach" in dialogue with other religions since the purpose of such an exchange is not primarily to "confess" or "teach" but rather to hear, clarify, learn, and identify with other religions. In sum, the objective of religious education in relation to other religions is the enhancement of

---

20. Norma H. Thompson, "Current Issues in Religious Education," *Religious Education* 73:6 (November-December, 1978), p. 617.
21. Sara Little, *To Set One's Heart: Belief and Teaching in the Church* (Atlanta: John Knox Press, 1983), p. 67.

personal faith and mutual enrichment of individually held faiths
through actual contact, gaining "relevant knowledge" about them, developing an "informed respect" for them, and becoming involved in
some "praxis" expression of them.

RELIGIOUS PLURALISM: CONTENT/METHOD

Content refers to more than factual information and method implies
more than technique in the process of religious education for pluralistic
thinking in a highly diverse society. Concepts become "content" in
seeking to intercommunicate religious ideas and theological concepts
and approaches are "methods" in searching for suitable bridges between
religious faiths and various cultures.

In the area of personal religious development, Paul Tillich's notion of
education in the church as induction may be useful. The principle in the
concept is that of inquiry. The education elicits concerns and questions
which are "existential" and correlates them with symbols and doctrines
into which they have been inducted. This forms the basis for further
inquiry and correlation. Tillich's concept of correlation becomes a dialectical process in an educational encounter-experience with other religions. In this case the generic human need for spiritual identity that
arises out of the human religious nature referred to by Tillich as "ultimate concern" calls for a dialectical approach to teaching-learning or
one that states the basic position of the religion under discussion and
concerns. One of the most effective methods or techniques to use with
this approach is the dialogue, a setting in which there can be mutual
and creative interchange around experiences, relationships, ideas,
and/or issues with the sole intention of honest communication while
maintaining identity, cultural integrity, and openness to innovation.

CULTURAL PLURALISM: OBJECTIVE

Clearly, one of the most urgent pieces of unfinished business in the
United States today is the genuine inclusion of color minorities, especially black people, in the economic, political, social, and religious life of
the nation. An intentional effort to implement the pluralist concept in
Protestant churches and in Christian churches generally would do much
to exemplify the implicit ideal and practice of the radical "equality
principle" of our early national government and historic churches. Cultural pluralism would insist that the identity and integrity of black

culture (as old as human civilization) would through general education become a required offering of our school systems. With this rationale, the objective of religious education in relation to a momentarily expanding pluralist culture is twofold: 1) the recovery and renewal of the unity of people, cultures, and colors that the church once claimed to be its proud and unique possession, and 2) the projection now of the kind of proactive leadership by the churches united which alone will be able to speak to the centuries ahead.

CULTURAL PLURALISM: CONTENT/METHOD

Powerful images exist in the biblical history of the church to instruct and inspire its ministry of teaching and learning that from the beginning divine intention has sought for all humankind, unity and peace through diversity. Walter Brueggmann's reflections on the term "shalom" are illustrative: "The central vision of world history in the bible is that all of creation is one, every creature in community with every other, living in harmony and security toward the joy and well-being of every other creature."[22] Religious education can do more than it is presently doing to activate this vision. First, those who teach must themselves be committed to its possibility and willing to work for its realization. Second, as Harvey Cox suggests, "We need to expose our children with fewer apologies to the apocalyptic and surrealist elements of the bible and let them play with the symbols as they will."

Recognizing and strengthening cultural pluralism, unity in diversity and diversity in unity, while primarily a public responsibility is also an obligation upon parents and others, all of whom are citizens and many of whom are Christians. As Christians it is expected that they not only support the "private spheres of congregational life" but also assist in "shaping the life of the congregation so that it might serve as an agent of transcendence in the public."[23] Such a role would entail encouraging the exposure of all school-age minority children to their own and other minority heritages. This would be done on the basis of sound education and wise citizenship preparation for pluralistic living. Even more importantly it would strike at the heart of all discrimination and bear an irrefutable public witness to the fact that whatever might divide the

22. Walter Brueggmann, *Living Toward a Vision: Biblical Reflections on Shalom* (New York: United Church Press, 1982), p. 15.

23. Jack L. Seymour, Robert T. O'Gorman, and Charles R. Foster, *Church in the Education of the Public* (Nashville: Abingdon, 1984), p. 142.

world cannot and will not divide the church. Buell Gallagher sums it up in saying that in the church "no one had the right to shut another out of full fellowship because of any sort of difference."[24]

The most significant opportunity (and probably the least used) to learn and practice culture pluralism is the church and specifically Protestant churches. From its inception until the fourth century the church was racially and culturally the most diverse institution of its kind. The "defection" of the African church from Western Christianity in the seventh century due to "the refusal of the church of the empire to accord (them) equality of status, caused Christianity to become, for the first time, a white man's religion."[25] The suggestion here is the recovery of the original inclusiveness of early Christendom and the proposal is the involvement of the entire congregation in doing it. For an example, what could happen if, following John Westerhoff's enculturation model, the congregation in its totality became the center for transmitting and experiencing the redemptive love of God revealed in Christ? Would not then teaching-learning experiences guide persons toward relationships that encourage respect, dialogue, mutual acceptance, and equal sharing and valuing of all human experience?[26]

ACHIEVING COMMON HUMAN GOALS

No single word better characterizes the nature of the international situation or forecasts the shape of international relations than the term interdependence. Mutual dependence, however, does not insure mutual trust, the necessary basis of effective interdependent relations. Only deep understanding, respect, equality of status, and personal security can do that. Arnold Toynbee correctly observed: "Human beings have had six thousand years to become strangers to one another, and now we have hardly any time at all for learning the most difficult art of dwelling together in unity." Pursuant to this, the role of religious education in relation to the insistent reality of interdependence and the yet distant real pluralism of faiths, internationally, is critical. Its task is to equip persons—cognitively, affectively, and behaviorally—to discover, analyze, reflect upon, decide, act out, and celebrate, individually as Christians

---

24. Buell G. Gallagher, *Color and Conscience: The Irrepressible Conflict* (New York: Harper and Brothers, 1946), p. 43.

25. Ibid., p. 52.

26. John H. Westerhoff III, *Will Our Children Have Faith?* (New York: Seabury, 1926), pp. 52-54.

and corporately as the church, some of the universal themes, first principles, and prime values of the Christian faith. A second objective is to clarify, instruct, reconcile, and attempt to resolve specific common human issues that are facing our "global village." Hopefully, this will also witness to unities and harmonies that were never thought to exist through diversities and discontinuities that have and will exist.

Dialogue is best suited to begin to achieve the objectives that have been outlined. As defined by Paul Knitter and as it will be used in this chapter it is "the exchange of experience and understanding between two or more partners with the intention that all partners grow in experience and understanding."[27] Dialogue at this dimension is more than protracted discussion, a mere exchange of opinion. It is a philosophy of education, a way of knowing and doing (praxis), and a theological dialectic, simultaneously. Preeminently, however, it is transformational! Knitter details three presuppositions to dialogue that are germane for its educational use. It must be based on "personal religious experience and firm truth-claims." It must also be based on "the recognition of the possible truth in all religions . . . grounded in the hypothesis of a common ground and a goal for all religions." It must be based on "openness to the possibility of change/conversion."[28] The basic educational design that is being proposed here is an extrapolation of the particularistic language, i.e., religion, in the model and the redeployment of the paradigm in relation to other common human issues "in the concern of all religions to promote the unity of humanity and to offset the danger of world destruction."[29] The other issues recommended for dialogue are: humanization and human rights; environment; peace and justice; population/hunger/poverty; and racial justice. Such a program is based on the growing awareness of an increasing number of religionists and theologians that theology as we know and do it today must now be written from within a world religious perspective.

PLURALISM AND THE BLACK EXPERIENCE: EXCURSIONS IN EXCLUSION

Color prejudice, historically and presently, has excluded black Americans from the ethnic-diversity and ethnic pluralist dialogue and

---

27. Paul F. Knitter, *No Other Name: A Critical Survey of Christian Attitudes Toward the World Religions* (Maryknoll, N.Y.: Orbis, 1985), p. 207.

28. Ibid., pp. 207-211.

29. Ibid., p. 209.

rendered them the most unassimilable racial group in the nation. Black people have been aware of this from time immemorial. And no one has expressed it better than the venerated black bard and scholar, W. E. B. DuBois who in speaking of the isolation of black people from the general society said: "One ever feels his two-ness—an American, a Negro; two souls, two thoughts, two unreconciled strivings; two warring ideals in one dark body, whose dogged strength alone keeps it from being torn asunder."[30] This has been the case as far back as one chooses to go in American history. The Declaration of Independence (1776) in its famed statement about the equality of all men ignored the existence of hundreds of thousands of black human beings who were then slaves. Sanction for the continuance of slavery was written into the heart of the Constitution of the nation (1787). In one sentence, not superseded until the ratification of the 14th Amendment (1868), black people were accounted only as "three-fifths of all other persons." Fugitive slave laws had federal approbation until slavery was abolished in 1865. The United States Supreme Court by its Dred Scott decision said in effect that black people had no rights that white people had to respect. Following the Civil War it was necessary to free blacks from bondage, declare them citizens, and grant them the right to vote. Despite these legal protections in 1896 the Supreme Court decided in the Plessy-Ferguson case that separate treatment for blacks is equal. It would be 1954 before another Supreme Court would say that separate is inherently unequal. There is a fundamental lesson for all in this overview of the treatment of black people, one of the nation's several color-minorities. While blacks have been one of the ethnically diverse groups in what became a "plural" society, they have never been (and are not now) really considered to be equal to other diverse ethnic groups. Their relation to American "pluralism" has always carried a negative valence in combination with nonblack or noncolored ethnic group elements.

Black Americans have not only been denied equality as persons; they have also been denied acceptance as individuals and as an entire racial group. Larger than any other ethnic group in the nation, their status is basically governed by their racial identification. The rationale for this is the tacit practice of a policy of assimilation in reference to racial minorities in this country. The Anglo-Conformity sub-thesis of this theory, originally applicable to immigrants and rife with overtones of nonwhite inferiority, blatantly asserts the superiority of Anglo-Saxon culture and lifestyles and presents this as the nonnegotiable basis for becoming an

---

30. W. E. B. DuBois, *The Souls of Black Folk* (Chicago: O. C. McClurg, 1903), p. 3.

American. The melting-pot sub-thesis, also originally intended to apply to nonblack immigrants, espoused a "blending of cultures" approach to assimilation with an intermarriage component. Cultural pluralism, the third model was a "functional integration of people into the economic and political order of the dominant society while they retain a distinctive cultural and institutional life."[31] In reference to black people all three of these theories, and the concept of assimilation itself, were and are patently dysfunctional. They were designed to accommodate immigrants (and others) to a system with exploitive objectives and aggressively dominant motivations. The very simple reason why they are generally dysfunctional for black people and other color-minorities is the fact that blacks are at best only marginally related to the system!

Black objections to the various patterns of acculturation just discussed come under three general headings: goals, objectives, and strategy. Increasingly black people were asking about receding goals despite more than four decades of focused struggle. Progress had been made in voting rights, housing, education, and public accommodation privileges, but as the goals were approached intransigence, backlash, and a reactionary White House administration caused the goals to recede. The objectives of equality, identity, integrity, self-determination, and empowerment, so right and so clear in the 1960s and 1970s, seemed ambiguous and difficult to achieve in the 1980s. Likewise strategy again became an issue. Must we accommodate to the power system and to the open "tokenism" route or remain in the trenches and fight the good fight of liberation for our brothers and sisters? For better or for worse it seems that the way ahead for blacks in America is the honing of our own skills and the solidification of our own community and the extension of the struggle for liberation all in the context of the "two-ness" of our hyphenated America. In any event, most black people knew that despite any moderate success the assimilation approach may have had in pushing a few blacks ahead, the approach itself was bankrupt and must be replaced by one that is far more just in administering equity, inclusive in outreach, and more pluralist in principle.

PLURALISM AND BLACK CHURCHES

Has religious pluralism affected the black church differently than cultural pluralism affected the black community? Does the fact that

---

31. James A. Geschwender, *Racial Stratification in America* (Dubuque, Iowa: W. C. Brown, 1978), p. 55.

there is a Black Church of black churches comprising almost 20 million black Christians not attest loudly to the fact that it is a separate diversity not yet pluralized? Black religion and the black church in the United States have historically been assigned an inferior status in relation to white religion and white churches. Winthrop Jordan observes: "The Negro's color set him radically apart from Englishmen. It also served as a highly visible label identifying the motives of a distant continent which for ages Christians had known as a land of men radically defective in religion."[32] Not only have black people been considered spiritually inferior to whites but they were unwanted as fellow church members. The cycle of nonacceptance is well known: 1) white conversion of blacks; 2) white rejection of blacks as fellow church members; 3) the rise of separate black services; 4) the development of separate black churches, in protest and out of a sense of deep frustration; 5) continued discriminatory treatment of blacks who remained in white churches. What were the radical dynamics operating in this situation? Briefly, most early American black converts (including Native Americans) were in biracial or triracial churches. As these groups developed into settled congregations requiring primary social contacts, peer relations, and equality of treatment, covert racism became overt and segregation patterns became the standard rule and practice. By World War I (1914-1918) the nadir in the church segregation of blacks from whites had been reached despite protests from blacks and some whites. Racial segregation, long practiced in the nation, had been sanctioned by the churches. Between World Wars I and II and until the United States Supreme Court Brown-Topeka decision outlawing segregation in the public schools (1954), the situation did not really improve. Frank Loescher, in speaking of this period says: "The record of its policies and practices makes it evident that in many respects it (the church) has contributed to the seriousness of the very problem it should be helping to solve."[33]

Not only did the black church have grave reservations about white lack of respect for its religious heritage and equality of personhood, it also had ample reason to question their real interest in engaging the systematic causes of racism during the Civil Rights era. At the peak of the struggle for equal rights in the nation, the churches hardly moved beyond tokenism. In the midst of talks about church unions, mergers,

---

32. Winthrop D. Jordan, *White Over Black: American Attitudes Toward the Negro, 1550-1812* (Baltimore: Penguin Books, 1968), p. 20.
33. Frank S. Loescher, *The Protestant Church and the Negro: A Pattern of Segregation* (New York: Association Press, 1948), p. 27.

and cooperation, blacks and other minorities were "power pawns" rather than self-determining power agents. An examination of white support during the rights movement revealed deceptive attempts to "contain" the struggle and defuse its power. Loyalty gave way to arid legalism. Opportunities were offered without the advantages needed to exploit them: Symbolic status was given in the place of substantial authority. Summarily, there was little evidence or hope, then or now, that the objectives of religous pluralism, viz., peer relationships, self-determination, and empowerment would or could ever be achieved. In other words, white pluralism would mean more white racial supremacy, more and more subtle oppression, more defunct assimilation, less justice but more jails, greater tolerance but less dialogue.

With this experiential background it is not strange that the black church's first question in relation to religious pluralism is not its philosophy, objective, or design but its integrity and intentionality. It must know that this venture into religious pluralism would not involve it in another assimilation game in which it would be denied equality, authentic participation, and decision-making power and become comic characters in a glorified "integration" charade.

RELIGIOUS PLURALISM AND THE BLACK CHURCH: THE NEW PARADIGM IN BLACK

Powerful forces, urgent needs, and persistent leadership in both the black community and in the black churches in the late 1960s generated the demand for a new framework in which to do further problem solving in reference to continuing black marginalization, exclusion, and disempowerment. The quest was for a new black paradigm that would articulate concepts, assumptions, methods, and strategies for the social, religious, economic, and political liberation of black people. This desire for a new direction was even more significant because it was based on black community consensus. The black masses were still hopeful for a response to their dire plight. Former assimilationist advocates for whom integration was a great disenchantment and for whom real equality was still a myth were ready to try something new. Black activists were characteristically impatient to move! Prior to exploring the new black church paradigm, however, a closer look at three sets of events, some pluralistically oriented, are necessary. These event-sets relate to the black church; black theology, and the pluralization of black theology.

THE BLACK CHURCH

The black revolution, beginning in the late 1950s, inspired the radicalization of the black church. An organizing convocation for this purpose, held in the 1960s, committed the black church to the black liberation movement. In 1966 a group of black church leaders issued the now historic "Black Power Statement,"[34] reaffirming solidarity with the black power movement and reprimanding white churches for suggesting that black people should only seek power in passive ways. Somewhat later, another statement was made, "The Urban Mission in a Time of Crisis," making it very clear that the black church would no longer tolerate being "by-passed" by the power deputies of white church structures in their work in black communities. In pluralist style it insisted that a peer relationship must pertain in any negotiations, transaction of ideas or strategies or funding in the black community. Worship and music in the black church was reviewed to insure and encourage their reflection of the style and quality of the diverse black modes of worship.

The black theology movement, one of the few unique American contributions to the field of theology, though beginning in a rudimentary form in the nineteenth century, formally came into existence in 1967. *The Report of the Theological Committee of the National Committee of Black Churchmen* spoke to the need for the contextualization of black theology since this had not been done and obviously would not be done by the white theological community. At this same meeting whites (and others) were taken to task for denigrating black religion. The first publication of the movement was James H. Cone's *Black Theology and Black Power* (Seabury Press, 1969). A second phase in black theological inquiry began in 1970 with the organization of the Society for the Study of Black Religion, a forum for theological dialogue and black theological education professional interests.

The pluralization of black theology began almost with the black theology movement itself and continues to the present. Dialogues, conversations, and/or visits have taken place in Africa, Asia, Latin America, and North America. This probably makes black theology one of the most highly pluralized theologies of recent times. The continental profile is interesting: *Africa;* Ivory Coast (1969): Conference and initiation of Pan-African Skills Project to recruit technically skilled Afro-Americans for work and service in Africa sponsored by the All-Africa Confer-

---

34. *"Black Power": Statement by National Committee of Negro Churchmen* (New York: Commission on Religion and Race, National Council of Churches, 1966).

ence of Churches; Tanzania (1971): The first formal dialogue produced *Black Faith and Black Solidarity* compiled and edited by Priscilla Massie (Friendship Press, N.Y., 1973). The Society for the Study of Black Religion and the All-Africa Conference of Churches Consultation; Ghana (1974): Discussion of John Mbiti's controversial paper, "An African Views American Black Theology" and Bishop Desmond Tutu's rejoinder, "Black Theology/African Theology—Soul Mates or Antagonists; Ghana (1977): Pan-Africa Conference of Third World Theologians in which James H. Cone responded to John Mbiti's paper and moved the dialogue to a Third World context.

Latin America: Switzerland (1973): Symposium: Black Theology and Latin American Liberation Theology; *USA* (1975): Detroit Conference on Theology in the Americas; *Mexico* (1977): Conference: Encounter of Theologians; *Cuba* (1979): Consultation: Evangelization and Politics: A Black Perspective.

Asia: Dialogues have not taken place in Asia on a consultation basis. James Cone has spoken there on several occasions and was well-received. His comment is that the Koreans are quite sensitive to the racial issue in the United States. Japanese Christians were found to be "more concerned with Euro-American theologians of the West than addressing the oppression of Koreans or of the poor generally."[35]

NEW BLACK CHURCH PARADIGM

The new black church paradigm is an exemplar model of the promise and fulfillment of religious pluralism in two ways, theoretically and practically. Theoretically, based on the pluralist philosophy that truth ultimately has more than one valid construction and human thinking can approach these constructions in different ways, black theology challenges the notion that European-American theologizing is the only valid construction. Conversely, it affirms that theologizing can and must be done by black people from a black perspective. Second, asserting with John B. Cobb that "nothing historical is absolute and any tendency to absolutize any feature of Christianity is idolatry,"[36] black theology challenges a historic theological position that disputes the validity of its claims and affirms that it is and ought to be a theology of the oppressed.

---

35. Gayraud S. Wilmore and James H. Cone, *Black Theology: A Documentary History, 1966-1979* (Maryknoll, N.Y.: Orbis, 1979), pp. 445-460.

36. John B. Cobb, "The Meaning of Pluralism for Christian Self-Understanding," in *Religious Pluralism,* p. 173.

Third, granted the pluralist principle that the thought enterprise should seek to incorporate various insights into new, larger, and more functional entities by combining and recombining concepts rather than fabricating reductionist syncretisms, black theology affirms the pluralist principle of free-standing inclusivism rather than elective assimilation.

At the practical level religious pluralism has similar implications. Following the general principle of "plural" validity, black theology rejects the notion that "liberation" is limited to a single context or a simple approach. It affirms the sensibility of exploring any and all potentially relevant means of liberating the oppressed. James Cone, for an example, would probably agree with Walter Watson's statement on this point: "The history of philosophy is now seen less as a museum of curiosities and errors and more as an inventory of archetypal possibilities that supply standards and resources for future inquiries."[37]

With this abbreviated explanation of the theoretical basis of the new black church paradigm, we can now move to a discussion of the principal features of the model it suggests.

Rationale: Black theology and a radicalized black church emerged from the 1970s as critical and timely responses to the black revolution for equality, identity, and self-determination. They also present themselves as viable alternatives to white Christianity and white American theology both of which have historically held black religion to be "defective." Further, black theology and the black church was also a response to either the unwillingness or the inability of white Protestantism to offer more than rhetoric to the challenge of their own theology of inclusiveness. This intransigence mandated the black church to develop a new black church style demonstrating a pluralist as well as a holistic approach to a ministry with the oppressed. This new paradigm presents itself as an autonomous, freestanding system emphasizing:

1. "The renewal and enhancement of the black church in terms of it's liturgical life, its theological interpretation (and), its understanding of its mission. . . ."
2. "The development of the black church, not only as a religious fellowship, but as a community organization . . . which uses its resources . . . to address the problems of . . . the black community."
3. "The projection of a new quality of church life which would equip and strengthen the church as custodian and interpreter of that cultural heritage which is rooted in the peculiar experience of black people . . . and the faith that has sustained them."
4. "The contribution of the black church, out of its experience of

---

37. Watson, *Architectonics of Meaning,* p. ix.

suffering and the yearning for freedom, of that quality of faith, hope, and love which can activate, empower, renew, and unite the whole church of Christ."[38]

RELIGIOUS EDUCATION AND RELIGIOUS PLURALISM: A BLACK ETHNOCULTURAL APPROACH

Black theology, inspired by the black revolution, gave birth to the "new" black church as a particular and equal reality within the "universal" reality of the church as a whole. This "paradigm shift," embodying a new "set of conceptual, methodological, and metaphysical assumptions,"[39] reoriented the black church and gave it a self-authenticating mandate to "do" ministry contextually, i.e., in distinctive and unique ways. This epochal decision was not made precipitously. It was made with the realization that it would alienate some liberal whites and some nonradical blacks. It was basically made, however, because a majority of forward-thinking black church leaders knew, in Gayraud Wilmore's words, that "it may be the last opportunity for the church to break out of its symbolic commitment to the illusory goal of one-way integration and permeate the black community with a positive concept of power and a sense of transcendent vocation that will serve the purposes of justice and freedom in a pluralistic society."[40]

Against this background we are now ready to discuss a black ethnocultural approach to religious education in a pluralistic society. It is being constructed for us in black or predominantly black settings. Hopefully it has some adaptability to other situations. It will be discussed under the titles of its component headings: 1) theory, 2) praxis, and 3) pluralization.

THEORY

A contextual philosophy of education implies the need for several theoretical foundations in understanding the role of religious education in a pluralistic society: cultural, theological, and educational. Since the

---

38. Gayraud S. Wilmore, "The Case for a New Black Church Style," in *The Black Experience in Religion,* ed. C. Eric Lincoln (Gardner City, N.Y.: 1974), pp. 34-44.

39. Ian G. Barbour, *Myths, Models and Paradigms: A Study in Science and Religion* (New York: Harper & Row, 1974), p. 8.

40. K. B. Cully and F. Niles Harper, *Will the Church Lose the City?* (New York: World, 1969).

cultural foundation is the matrix from which the other two emerge it will be discussed first.

CULTURAL FOUNDATIONS

From a black Protestant perspective, existing patterns for racial and cultural pluralism are bankrupt. Assimilation, whether it be absorption, Americanization, or cultural pluralism is no longer a highest desired goal for an increasing number of black people. Racial fusion, generating a "new" population and a "new" society, is not even a remote possibility. Americanism, an oppressive conformity with Anglo-American standards, was and is both reactionary and totally unacceptable. Cultural pluralism or participating in the common core of national life while retaining cultural traditions briefly commended itself to blacks until it was realized that whites never intended to share the "core." Clearly, black people in America face a racial-cultural identity crisis. With integration no longer a realistic expectation in either the church or the general society, what was the answer? Many black people, particularly in the young adult generation are developing their own cultural identity modes. Together with what has been done in the black church, it is possible to identify a "black ethnocultural pluralism"[41] mode (or paradigm) as the basis for ministry in black religious education settings. In brief, it encapsulates a number of concepts whose objectives are: equality of person and equal access to advantage and opportunity; functional integration in the general society in areas of public entitlement; the funding, retention, cultivation, and transmission of black heritage and history in the public schools; elective participation in community life and inclusion at all public policy decision-making levels according to publicly accountable determination.

The implications of this new black style should be clear. Just as Protestantism "bought into" the essentially secular model of assimilation rather than its own authentic model of Christian inclusiveness or "incorporation" it must now seek with its people more Christian ways and means to witness to the unity of the body of Christ on matters of race and class. Protestantism has not ventured beyond the prudent and protected confines of local, state, and national legal decisions, community sensibilities, or superficial human concerns.

---

41. Grant S. Shockley, "Liberation Theology, Black Theology, and Religious Education," in *Foundations for Christian Education in an Era of Change* (Nashville: Abingdon, 1976), pp. 80-95.

In the meanwhile, the mood of the black church has radically changed. Self-affirmation, interdependence, and autonomy are the emergent guidelines for the new ecclesiology that inspires a proudly black people intentionally to engage in community ministries of liberation and the mission of social justice.

THEOLOGICAL FOUNDATIONS

Black theology is the revolutionary-change movement that arose in the black church in the late 1960s in the midst of the struggle of the black community for liberation from white oppression and domination. It was one of the very few innovative departures in the entire history of theological thought in America and the first to challenge its dominance from a racial perspective.

Several factors contributed to its emergence: the failure of North American Christianity generally and Protestantism particularly to transcend their white image; the failure of Protestantism in the United States, almost universally, to address the particularity and uniqueness of the black experience and the unwillingness or inability of white majority churches to fundamentally cope with the exigencies of social, economic, and political oppression in the black community.

The central problem to which black theology had to attend was white racism in church and society. Wilmore succinctly states the case in saying, "Black theology . . . is about the disestablishment of this (racist) ideology, the dismantling of the old order based upon it, the liberation from ideology to reality . . . and the development of an inner-directed, self-determined theological reflection grounded in the praxis of liberation."[42] Convinced finally that white and black religious experience "do not name the same reality,"[43] that generally whites are quite uncomfortable in interracial church fellowships, reluctant to respond relevantly to liberation issues and intransigent about the sharing of real power, James Cone enunciated in the landmark book *Black Theology and Black Power* what has since become the general objective of the task of black theology and the mission of the new black church, namely, "to analyze the black . . . condition in the light of God's revelation in Jesus

---

42. Gayraud S. Wilmore, "The New Concept of Black Theology in the United States" in *Mission Trends No. 4; Liberation Theologies,* ed. Gerald H. Anderson and Thomas F. Stransky (New York: Paulist, 1979), p. 116.

43. John B. Cobb, *Christ in a Pluralistic Age* (Philadelphia: Westminster, 1975), p. 19.

Christ with the purpose of creating a new understanding of black dignity among black people, and providing the necessary soul in that people, to destroy white racism."[44]

In relation to religious education in black churches facing a religiously plural society, several implications may be drawn from black theology:

It has provided the new black church with a new set of "conceptual, methodological, and metaphysical assumptions" upon which a theology for religious education may be built and on which a philosophy of education may rest.

The methodology of contextualization in black theology, a particularistic rather than universalistic approach to thinking about a problem, i.e., from the "inside" rather than "outside" of religious experiences, cultures, institutions, practices, or relationships has implications for other cultures, religious or racial groups.

Black theology's rediscovery of the "indisputable biblical grounds that the liberation of the poor and oppressed is at the heart of the gospel"[45] provided a whole new framework for ministry, mission, and education in the new black church.

The clue to religious education in the black church is likewise a contribution of black theology. "An indigenous, inner-directed, self-determined theological reflection grounded in the praxis of liberation from white domination"[46] has provided a basic direction and thrust to the enterprise.

EDUCATIONAL THEORY

"Theory (educational or otherwise) provides a plausible explanation of the principles underlying a particular practice."[47] Such an explanation describes and projects "how and when . . . practice most efficaciously can be employed."[48] It is now the task of this chapter to develop

---

44. James H. Cone, *Black Theology and Black Power* (New York: Seabury, 1969), p. 117.

45. Wilmore, "The New Concept of Black Theology," p. 117.

46. Ibid., p. 116.

47. Burgess, *Invitation to Religious Education*, p. 3.

48. James Michael Lee, *The Flow of Religious Instruction: A Social Science Approach* (Birmingham, Ala.: Religious Education Press, 1973), p. 26.

such a theory of religious education for a religiously plural society, consonant with a black ethnocultural approach, and grounded in black theology. The elements of educational theory selected for inclusion and discussion divide into four categories: 1) conceptualization; 2) purpose; 3) content; 4) instructional process. The latter category has been adapted from the taxonomy of James Michael Lee.[49]

CONCEPTUALIZATION

Lee describes three concepts articulating a relationship between religious education and religion or theology.[50] A "messenger boy" or transmissive view of the role of religious education is one that narrowly limits its function to rote transmission. With some modification it is still used widely today. A second view is the "translation" view. The role of religious instruction in this approach is the transfer of content from one context to another in such a way that it relates to life meaningfully. A third approach is an "ontological mediatorship" or social-science method. Lee defines this as "a view based on the . . . concept of theology suffusing all areas of religious instruction." Lee continues saying, "Thus . . . theology that comprises an indispensable aspect of the mediational process which is religious instruction take(s) on the hue and texture appropriate to its role in furthering the teaching-learning of religion."[51] This concept, together with its further interpretation that "religious instruction is the active concrete process of existentially mediating theology and concrete reality"[52] is quite compatible with the kind of theory which is needed to undergird a black ethnocultural pluralism paradigm.

In terms of purpose the options presented by Lee are noted: 1) intellectualists who generally equate religious education with intellectual development; 2) moralists who contend that religious education should "teach" virtue, and 3) integralists who regard "the primary purpose of religious instruction as the fusion in one's personal experience of Christianly understanding, action, and love coequally."[53] Again this latter concept has very high transfer value into the black ethnocultural pluralism model with its need to emphasize "enabling the learner to actualize in a harmonious, integrated, developmental, and self-fulfilling

---

49. Ibid., p. 32-38.
50. Ibid., p. 17-19.
51. Ibid., p. 21.
52. Ibid., p. 17.
53. Ibid., p. 11.

way. . . the dimensions which have typically been identified as comprising religious behavior."[54]

Lee's resolution of the content-method issue is also useful in developing an educational theory for a black ethnocultural pluralism design. His insistence on a unified approach to these concepts since they merge "in the actual teaching/learning situation" frees black theology and the black experience to have a really "praxiological" experience. There are several helpful suggestions in specific categories in Lee's instructional process taxonomy toward the model that is being proposed. The social-science approach, an experience-directed style, a discovery strategy, and a problem-solving method all have affinity with the objective of religious education in relation to the black religious experience: "to join theological reflection with those processes which expose the structures which enslave, to develop techniques for freedom, and give structure to those values of the black experience for building community for God's people."[55]

PRAXIS

Praxis is crucial in any contextual program of education. This is especially true in reference to the black ethnocultural model that is the proposal in this chapter. What, then, is praxis? What is its significance to this model? How is it to be implemented?

Paulo Freire, whose use of the term informs this discussion, implies that praxis is action and reflection for the explicit purpose of transforming the world.[56] The logic of this definition is derived from the use of the term "word." For Freire it is (or should be) more than an instrumentality for casual conversation for teacher or student. A true word is both reflection and action or praxis. A word without intentional action becomes verbalism, and action without reflection becomes mere activism. The logic of this reasoning and the social implication is clear. A word used to denounce the evil in the world without a commitment to change that world is empty and false. Freire's statement is, "It becomes an empty word, one which cannot denounce the world, for denunciation is impossible without a commitment to transform, and there

---

54. Ibid.

55. Olivia Pearl Stokes, "Black Theology: A Challenge to Religious Education," in *Religious Education and Theology*, ed. Norma H. Thompson (Birmingham, Ala.: Religious Education Press, 1982), p. 88.

56. Paulo Freire, *Pedagogy of the Oppressed* (New York: Herder and Herder, 1971), p. 75.

is no transformation without action."[57]

The significance of this seminal concept for religious education in the black church is crucially important. The Word of God revealed to persons in the world was not a verbalizing word but a transforming word—Jesus Christ! Similarly, black theology is the announcement that Christ is the liberator of the oppressed. James Cone says, "The work of Christ is essentially a liberating word, directed toward and by the oppressed. . . . Christ in liberating the wretched of the earth also liberates those responsible for the wretchedness . . . Mature freedom is burdensome and risky, procuring anxiety and conflict . . . for the brittle structures they challenge."[58]

How is praxis to be implemented? Freire implies that this is the essence of the educational task. The educational responsibility of the church, in this case the black church, is the articulation of true words. Again in his words, "To exist, humanly, is to name the world, to change it. Once named, the world in its turn reappears to the namers as a problem and requires of them a new naming. Men are not built in silence, but in word, in work, in action-reflection."[59]

Having developed the nature of the educational task of the black church (or any church or people) that desires liberation, a *modus vivendi* must be found. For Freire it is dialogue, an encounter between persons, "mediated by the world, in order to name the world."

Operationally, the implementation of praxis education in the black church entails developing a design for it to occur in content, method, style, strategy, and technique categorized in three ways: 1) through action-reflection dialogues that enable persons in specific ways to *perceive* their own oppressive situation and the oppression that surrounds them; 2) through action-reflection modules that enable persons to *conceptualize* new constructions of the realities that are possible; 3) through action-reflection encounters that enable persons in specific ways to change the order of things toward full humanization ever-mindful of the Freire premise that education either functions as an instrument of liberation or domestication.

PLURALIZATION

Thus far in discussing religious education for living in a religiously and culturally plural society from a black perspective it has been deter-

---

57. Freire, *Pedagogy of the Oppressed*, p. 76.
58. Cone, *Black Theology and Black Power*, p. 42.
59. Freire, *Pedagogy of the Oppressed*, p. 76.

mined that such education should be praxis or transformationist-orient-
ed as well as culturally sensitive to the black experience, theologically
grounded in black theology and educationally designed for relevance. A
further and concluding educational task of the black church will be to
insure that the recommended black ethnocultural approach maintains
its contextual integrity, continues pluralistic dialogue, and remains open
and receptive to the truly inclusive community in the immediate or
more distant future.

INTRARELIGIOUS PLURALISM

David Tracy reminds us that "there is no tradition that does not
eventually have to acknowledge its own plurality and ambiguity."[60] It
would be a mistake, therefore, to offer the impression that there is
unaminity of opinion or complete solidarity around any issue in the
black community. For an example, within the black church and its
community there are at least four constituencies with varying opinions
about the adoption of a revolutionary-praxis church style. The
radicalized espouse it, the unradicalized are uncertainly committed but
"supportive," the traditionalists are not as opposed to the idea as they
are to "change," and the non-church community person is most often
unaware of the issues but very aware of the consequences of poverty,
oppression, and discrimination. The task of the educational ministry of
the black church in this instance is clear. Following a pluralistic model it
must create a dialogue or "the encounter in which (praxis) the united
reflection and action of the dialogue is addressed in the world which
needs to be transformed and humanized."[61] In short, it must itself
maintain the integrity of the pluralism it commended to others rather
than attempting to speak for them, even perhaps, in their own best
interest.

INTERRELIGIOUS PLURALISM

Understanding the essence of pluralism is comprehending its nature
as both universal and particular. With the advent of the new black
church, impressions may have been given that it was uninterested in or

---

60. Tracy, *Plurality and Ambiguity*, p. ix.
61. Freire, *Pedagogy of the Oppressed*, p. 77.

indifferent about conversation with not only white churches but other religions, their origins, beliefs, and practices. These impressions were patently false. The black church in the United States is one of the most open institutions in society. It has never segregated because of race and generally has had harmonious relations with all who have sought and desired them. The emerging black ethnocultural approach to religious education will not be an exception to this tradition. It will encourage rather then preclude conversation or dialogue with other religionists or with those who profess no religion or with those who hold other opposing ideologies. Their criteria for participation will be no more or no less than those required by the pluralist framework, namely, equality of status as persons and as groups and "informed respect" for the heritage of another equally valid form of religious expression. Within these guidelines, religious education in predominantly black churches would need to learn from, intercommunicate, and interrelate with persons of their own faith who hold different perspectives, persons of other faiths and persons with differing political, social, or economic ideologies—African, Asian, Hispanic, or European. Given the *de facto* segregation of blacks in the American society the outreach of this program on a natural basis would be limited. Vicarious and simulated experiences would necessarily become an important aspect of any really comprehensive thrust in this direction.

BEYOND PLURALISM

The truly inclusive community just mentioned is no less than what Cardinal Augustine Bea referred to during Second Vatican Council years as "the great goal which is the full unity of the human family."[62] It is also what Walter Brueggmann meant when he said, "The origin and the destiny of God's people is to be on the road of Shalom, which is to live out of joyous memories and toward greater anticipations."[63] Those memories are our former diversities and the anticipations are the new pluralism whose community of communities includes persons of all races, citizens of all nations, and adherents of all religions or no religion. The shape and form of religion in such a community cannot be predicted but its nature and purpose is already known. It will be "a social order founded on the principle of harmonious interaction, for common ends,

---

62. *Saturday Review*, July 8, 1967, p. 11.

63. Walter Brueggmann, *Living Toward A Vision: Biblical Reflections on Shalom* (New York: United Church Press, 1982), p. 16.

among various communities, each of which possesses both identity and openness."[64]

Religious education toward such a community will require infinitely more than "revelant knowledge," "informed respect," and "common human goals." It will need: a new paradigm, "a whole new world culture as a framework for dealing with the problems ahead,"[65] pluralistically, a new scenario of equality following the demise of old dominations. Harvey Cox states the case plainly: "The dialogue begins when domination ends . . . between men and women . . . blacks and whites . . . Catholics and Protestants . . . Christians and Jews."[66]

A fitting conclusion for this chapter on religious education and religious pluralism is a challenge from a theologian who was also a pluralist of sorts, Reinhold Niebuhr: "The world community, toward which all historical forces seem to be driving us, is mankind's final possibility and impossibility. The task of achieving it must be interpreted from the standpoint of a faith which understands the fragmentary and broken character of all historic achievements and yet has confidence in their meaning because it knows their completion to be in the hands of a Divine Power, whose resources are greater than those of humans, and whose suffering love can overcome the corruptions of human achievements, without negating the significance of our striving."

---

64. John H. Westerhoff III, "Religious Education and Catechesis" in *Religious Education in a Pluralistic Society*, p. 57.

65. Keith Irvine, *The Rise of the Colored Races* (New York: Norton, 1970), p. 603.

66. Harvey Cox, "Pluralism and the Open Society," *Religious Education* 69:2 (March-April, 1974), p. 158.

6

Southern Baptists Dealing with Pluralism

William Clemmons

Southern Baptists are a people made up of diverse strands. They find their heritage in seeking to renew the church, while at the same time recognizing that within its own ranks, and within the church universal, it is many traditions, not one. This has been the perennial problem for Baptists who have been influenced by the European Radical Reformation of Anabaptists, who sought to restore the church to its New Testament vision, and yet more directly were descendents of the English Reformation struggle of the Calvinistic Puritans and Separatists who wanted the Church of England to complete its Reformation.

As Baptists have contended for their particular understandings of church, they also have been in the forefront of the struggle for religious tolerance. It was Roger Williams who in Rhode Island became the model for religious tolerance surrounded by the bigotry of the Congregational established religion. Later in Virginia, Baptist John Leland influenced James Madison to frame the first amendment to the Constitution of the United States disestablishing the state churches in favor of "a free church in a free state."

But Baptists have struggled with religious tolerance as they have held to their primary vision of being a church true to the New Testament conception. They have had to accommodate themselves to the reality of wanting tolerance from others, both religious and secular, while having to plead for tolerance within their own household. Such is part of the current problem among Southern Baptists as they wage an internecine

war about the role of the bible in their churches and denomination with
some taking a literalistic, inerrantist position, even in matters of science
and historical data, while others see the bible as authoritative in matters
of personal and corporate faith and practice.

Thus pluralism for Southern Baptists has been an issue that has been
treated at times with dogmatic exclusion and at other times with enlightened tolerance. At times Southern Baptists have shown a kind of
intolerant rejection of those not like them, and at other times they have
demonstrated the charm of Southern, genteel hospitality.

In this chapter I want to examine how Southern Baptists were born
and nurtured in a homogeneous culture of the South and the difficulties
they have encountered as they have moved to other parts of the nation.
Also, I want to look at the question of whether the relative pluralism
they have tolerated as they were a regional denomination is not now
fragmenting the consensus that has kept the various strands together in
their regional home. Several times during their history Southern Baptists have not tolerated a challenge to the status quo and have rejected
the differences as they emerged. What will happen now?

Lastly, I want to examine the ways in which Christian education has
been affected by these challenges and how these have been dealt with by
those guiding the denomination.

BAPTIST BEGINNINGS

Baptists have shared in the basic understandings of the sixteenth-
century Reformation: "priesthood of all believers, justification by faith,
the authority of the scriptures, and the rejection of the Roman supremacy in spiritual matters."[1] In addition, Baptists share other
understandings with those of the Radical Reformation and the Puritans
and Separatists in the English Reformation such as: a regenerate church
membership based on a personal, experiential encounter with Jesus as
Savior and Lord; believer's baptism by the mode of immersion; congregationalism based upon a covenant of believers; confessionalism rather
than creedalism; eternal security of the believer and the perseverance of
the saints in Christian growth; evangelism and missions as the primary
concern of each individual and the local congregation (living for the

---

1. Brooks Hays and John E. Steely, *The Baptist Way of Life,* 2nd ed. (Macon,
Ga.: Mercer University Press, 1981), p. 3. See also H. Leon McBeth, *The
Baptist Heritage: Four Centuries of Baptist Witness* (Nashville: Broadman,
1987).

world); ethical and moral living as essential (separation from the world); pastors and deacons are functions not offices since the essential leadership in the congregation is in the hands of the laity; baptism and the Lord's Supper are the only two ordinances and are primarily symbols; the necessary interdependence and cooperation between congregations in larger bodies called local associations, state conventions, and a national convention; separation of church and state; and a recognition of the universal church.[2]

Baptists also struggle to keep alive many of these historic understandings of what it means to be church, for being a Baptist means recognizing a pluralism of faith stances within a constellation of confessional statements. It is this tension between Baptist theologians and the constituency of the local congregations (the *magisterium* is ultimately located more in the people and pastors of the local congregations than in the elected leaders of the denomination, which makes for an interesting ecclesiology)[3] that at times causes denominational leaders to lose the struggle in maintaining historic Baptist understandings or modifying erroneous ones.

Baptist belief and polity, historically, has been very pluralistic within a certain range of possibilities. This has been because of the individualism inherent in the doctrine of the priesthood of all believers which has traditionally meant that one could read the bible and interpret it for oneself. That coupled with a strong understanding of the church being local, gave rise to varied interpretations and practices which have been tolerated within a narrow range of options.[4]

Baptists began in England in the early years of the seventeenth century out of a group of Puritans who wanted more Reformation than the leadership of the Church of England was willing to allow. As such they were dissenters and persecuted, having to flee to Holland to begin their first congregations. Even then Baptists, who were deeply indebted to John Calvin for much of their theology and practice, were divided on their theories of the atonement. Some wanted to allow that Christ died for all persons, a general atonement, while others, following Calvin, said that he died only for the elect, a particular view of salvation.

Thus, General (atonement theory) Baptists and Particular (atonement

---

2. See James Leo Garrett Jr., ed., *The Concept of the Believer's Church* (Scottdale, Pa.: Herald Press, 1969), p. 322.

3. Nathan Larry Baker, "Baptist Polity and Para-Church Organizations," *Baptist History and Heritage* 14:3 (July, 1979), p. 67.

4. For a discussion of these two principles see Winthrop S. Hudson, *Baptists in Transition: Individualism and Christian Responsibility* (Valley Forge, Pa.: Judson, 1979).

theory) Baptists began their separate ways. Congregationalism coupled with individualism, and with no episcopal or hierarchical authority to restrain the excesses when differences of viewpoint arose and disagreements could not be solved, resulted in new congregations being born. Other denominations have often misunderstood the operation of these two principles among Southern Baptists, which admittedly can be a weakness when these two characteristics permit individualism and independency to be exalted at the expense of corporateness and interdependency.

But James Sullivan, former executive of the publishing house for Southern Baptist Christian education materials, has written about congregationalism as the basic ingredient for a denomination:

> One of the universal concepts of Baptist people is that local churches in the New Testament were autonomous, self-governing, and self-determining. . . . For all practical purposes, Baptists must think of local churches as the building blocks of a denomination. They are the units out of which denominations are to be built in the Baptist concept, or there can be no Baptist denomination. Each church owns its own property, calls its own pastor, makes its own decisions and lives with them, observes the Lord's Supper, baptizes believers into the membership by standards that it considers the church mandates, ordains pastors and deacons, and many other things that are considered prerogatives of the local church. At the selfsame time a Baptist church is self-governing it is also interdependent. . . . (But) the question eternally remains, how these soul-free believers in their locally autonomous churches combine their efforts and resources in massive worldwide endeavors and still maintain that soul freedom and local church autonomy so dear to them?[5]

This tension between individualism/congregationalism and interdependency/cooperativeness has been one of the Baptists' ways of accommodating to pluralism and the diversity of ideas while maintaining unity. It is Baptists' gift and strength while also remaining their burden and weakness. When Baptists disagree with each other they too often split and a new local congregation emerges, most often without any ecclesiastical approval. Then the new often becomes the basis for a new level of consensus among the two groups.

General Baptists, with their more Arminian view of salvation, did not

---

5. James L. Sullivan, *Baptist Polity As I See It* (Nashville: Broadman, 1983), pp. 25-26.

grow as rapidly in England as did the more Calvinistic, Particular Baptists who became the foundation for Baptist life in America. The first Baptist church in America was founded in 1638 by Roger Williams in Providence, Rhode Island, and the first Southern Baptist church was organized in 1682 in Charleston, South Carolina. But growth of Baptists in the South was slow in the eighteenth century with only eleven small churches with 300 members by 1740.[6]

When the Great Awakening occurred from about 1726 to about 1750, a great revivalistic fervor swept throughout New England and spilled over into the South bringing with it those Baptists who were even more committed to a personal religious experience and a conviction that congregations should be made up of only those who had had such a personal religious conversion. Calling themselves "Separate" Baptists, as over against the "Regular," or Particular, Calvinistic Baptists, they wanted congregations made up of regenerate church members only and demanded a clear evidence of the conversion experience of their members in daily moral living. They were also nonconfessional, with the bible as the only basis for their beliefs. Their preachers were largely untrained and zealous in their style of preaching. Finally, their members were from the untrained social strata of society.[7]

THE SOUTHERN BAPTIST SYNTHESIS: FOUR TRADITIONS

Southern Baptists grew from the diversity of these two strands of Baptists in the South, the Calvinistic, Particular (later known also as Regular) Baptists, and the more enthusiastic Separate Baptists. The Particular Baptists were located in the large cities with educated pastors, a Calvinistic confession of faith which became the consensus of theology in the South, and an emerging church and denominational structure.[8]

Separate Baptists, the revivalistic, charismatic, independent Baptists, organized their first church in the South in 1755 in North Carolina and

6. Walter B. Shurden, "The Baptist Association: A Historical Introduction," *Associational Bulletin* 17:10 (November/December, 1983), p. 6.

7. Robert G. Torbet, *A History of the Baptists* (Philadelphia: Judson Press, 1950, rev. 1955), p. 241.

8. Walter B. Shurden, "The Southern Baptist Synthesis: Is It Cracking?" 1980-81 Carver-Barnes Lectures, Southeastern Baptist Theological Seminary, November 4-5, 1980, published in *Outlook,* Southeastern Baptist Theological Seminary Bulletin 30:5 (March-April, 1981), p. 5.

from it there grew churches throughout the South. The Separate Baptists moved with the frontier and became the largest group of Baptists in the South and one of the two foundations from which the Southern Baptist Convention emerged. Walter Shurden has characterized the Separate Baptists as "revivalism, experientialism, anti-confessionalism, exaggerated localism, fierce libertarianism, and a commitment to personal evangelism . . . and 'semipentecostals.' "[9]

Regular and Separate Baptists began to unite in the late 1700s and early 1800s and from their union there emerged the foundation of a new denomination in the South. Baptists North and South, who had united into a single denomination in 1814, called the Triennial Convention, split in 1845 over the issue of slavery and a growing sectionalism. Baptists in the South formed the Southern Baptist Convention, a denomination "Southern" in flavor and with a particular contribution to American Christianity. With the organization of the new Southern Baptist denomination a third strand was woven into the forging of what is today the Southern Baptist Convention, says Shurden.

The Southern Baptist Convention, organized in Augusta, Georgia, in 1845, created a "more connectional, more centralized and more cooperative [denomination] than any heretofore known among Baptists."[10] It advocated an aversion to all creeds except the bible, and was to be united around foreign and domestic missions which was to be accomplished through a cooperation of all the local congregations. Though this new denominational consciousness was regional, it was also a cooperative congregationalism in polity.

The fourth strand of Southern Baptists is found in what Shurden calls the "Tennessee Tradition." During much of the nineteeth century Baptists had to fight for their unique identity with the followers of Alexander Campbell, who advocated a restoration of the New Testament church and a baptism for the remission of sins. In the struggle that ensued Southern Baptists lost many churches to the Campbellism movement (today's Disciples of Christ and Churches of Christ). The most vigorous Southern Baptist debater was J. R. Graves, who in the process of defending the emerging Southern Baptist denomination gave it a distinct ecclesiological identity, but with some erroneous interpretations. He led Baptists to believe that they had an unbroken line of succession from the apostolic church and that all other denominations were institutions made by men. He also told them that the local Baptist church was autonomous and the only valid expression of church, leav-

---

9. Ibid., p. 7.
10. Ibid.

ing denominational structures always as suspect. These, along with other peculiar understandings, created an ecclesiastical system that was narrow and uncooperative and that has been only slowly and painfully repudiated in later years, even at the cost of the forced resignation of one of the presidents of its oldest seminary in 1899. Landmarkism, as the Graves' interpretation was called, gave Baptists an ecclesiology in a struggle for denominational identity, but it did so at the peril of its soul.

These four strands, says Shurden, make up the synthesis that is the Southern Baptist Convention, a diversity that today is being challenged by a breakup of the consensus that held it together from within and a homogeneous culture that sustained it from without. I would now like to examine the twentieth century and the pluralistic challenges that have begun to strain the nineteenth-century synthesis and the ensuing implications for Christian education.

PLURALISM'S CHALLENGE TO SOUTHERN BAPTISTS

When the twentieth century opened Southern Baptists could be characterized as rural, agricultural, racially in two separate groups of blacks and whites, uneducated, and in a homogeneous culture that was referred to as "Southern." Geographically, Southern Baptists were found in the traditional states of the old Confederacy.

The first half of the twentiety century could then be described as a time of consensus and solidification of the emergent denomination which at the opening of this century was only fifty-five years old. It was struggling to survive in the aftermath of the bloodiest war of American history and the years of deprivation caused by enforced Reconstruction. Yet the denomination established its first publishing house, the Baptist Sunday School Board (1891/1896), created an executive committee (1917) to run the denomination between annual national meetings (called conventions), adopted a confession of faith (1925), and created a national funding program called the Cooperative Program (1925) for its mission boards, seminaries, and other enterprises.

These new elements of an emerging denomination provided the necessary stability and order for a group of fiercely independent congregations to pull together into a cooperative fellowship. Yet each time the consensus was tested and a new basis of cooperation emerged, some congregations withdrew. Those who had opposed the establishment of mission boards in the mid-1800s through their hyper-Calvinistic reasoning that God had either elected persons to salvation or damnation, opposed Sunday schools, bible societies, evangelistic agencies, and final-

ly came to be known as the Primitive Baptists. Those who refused to
join the Regular and Separate Baptists' merger about the same time still
can be found throughout the Southeast. And, as a narrower expression
of Baptists' life found in the Landmark movement gave way to a
broader consensus, the Landmark element broke away to form its own
denomination.

Then, during the early decades of this century as scientific positivism
clashed with faith, a new wave of dissent swept religious life in the
nation, especially the northeast and midwest sections. Opposition to
"modernism," linked with liberal theology, caused groups of Baptists to
dissent and form new Baptist fundamentalist denominations. Liberal
theology with its optimism about human betterment and unending
social progress was rejected for a more literalistic, propositional faith. In
the South it took the form, after the Scopes Trial, of opposing the
teaching of evolutionary theory. In Baptist colleges and in the denomination as a whole it became the *cause célèbre* for a belief structure that
was beginning to encounter strain. As a result Southern Baptists adopted their first Confession of Faith in 1925.[11] Also, a small group of
fundamentalists in the denomination, though not as large as experienced by the Northern denominations who were suffering the same
strain, broke away to form a fundamentalist Southern Baptist denomination.[12]

Individualism and congregationalism had again expressed itself in the
splintering and emergence of new congregations and denominations
that wished to voice their diversity in a different manner. The weakness
of congregationalism has often been the failure of many of these splinter
groups to participate in the larger church. But the departure of small
groups of fundamentalists in the early part of this century left Southern
Baptists in a period of relative calm well into the 1960s when a new
storm broke that had been brewing for some time.

The calm that prevailed to about the mid-1960s was characterized by
an unending numerical growth in all areas of congregational and denominational life.[13] A campaign to increase the number of churches and
to add a million more persons in 1954 to its already 5,759,128 enrolled
in Sunday school gave a last spurt to a growth curve that had been

---

11. William L. Lumpkin, *Baptist Confessions of Faith* (Philadelphia: Judson
Press, 1959), pp. 390ff.

12. Walter B. Shurden, *Not A Silent People: Controversies That Have Shaped
Southern Baptists* (Nashville: Broadman, 1972), pp. 83 ff.

13. B. Thomas Halbrooks, "Growing Pains: The Impact of Expansion on
Southern Baptists Since 1942," *Baptist History and Heritage* 17:3 (July, 1982),
p. 44.

unending throughout much of the century. Sunday school growth, however, had begun to flatten out by 1954, and a growth campaign called, "A Million More in '54," though it did not add a million new members in bible study during that year, did add 597,361 new persons to Southern Baptist Sunday schools.

But after that 1954 increase, the Sunday school growth curve continued to flatten out for the next decade, and in 1964 Southern Baptists experienced, along with other mainline denominations, the first numerical declines in their Christian education organizations since they had created them in the late nineteenth and early twentieth centuries. It was a shattering blow to their psyche and the feeling that God had indeed given them the secrets of the "science of Sunday school growth."

From a high enrollment in Sunday school in 1964 of 7,671,165 persons to a low in 1971 of 7,141,453, the Sunday schools of Southern Baptists lost more persons in their Sunday schools than some denominations had in total enrollment. In addition, the percentage of church members enrolled in Sunday school, which had been at an all-time high of 78 percent in 1955, continued to decline with only 54.4 percent of church members enrolled in bible study in 1985, an indication that Sunday schools are increasingly a smaller and smaller part of the lives of Southern Baptists, a denomination that had indeed built its life and the lives of its churches on growing, large, all-age Sunday schools.[14] Another indicator of this decline is found in the fact that in 1954 there were 29,279 Sunday schools, 32,963 in 1964, and 35,692 in 1984. However, as the total number of Sunday schools has increased, the total enrollment in them struggles to remain the same, a further evidence that Southern Baptists are enrolling fewer persons in their individual Sunday schools.

A new Sunday school growth campaign, "8.5 Million Enrolled by 1985" only produced 7,960,796 enrolled by 1985, but it did enable the overall Sunday school enrollment to exceed its all-time-high enrollment of 1964 for the first time in two decades, an increase largely due to an increase in new congregations in the SBC. However, it did not achieve the projected enrollment, so a new Sunday school enrollment campaign called "Challenge 10/90," seeking to enroll 10 million by 1990, was begun. But the preliminary results of the first year of the new push for Sunday school growth indicate that the Sunday school enrollments for 1986 lost 16,823, 0.2 percent of the total enrollment for the previous

---

14. William P. Clemmons, "The Contributions of the Sunday School to Southern Baptist Churches," *Baptist History and Heritage* 18:1 (January, 1983), p. 39.

year. So it seems that it is not at all certain that the denomination has overcome the problems that its Christian education organizations seem to reflect in their statistical downturns.

The same thing can be said of the other three Christian education organizations: Church Training, built as an all-age approach to the youth organization, Christian Endeavor, in the late nineteenth century, fell from a 1963 high enrollment of 2,748,553 to a low of 1,752,026 in 1979 (1,954,345 in 1986). Woman's Missionary Union, the all-age missions education organization for women and girls, went from a high enrollment of 1,512,840 in 1963 to a low of 1,086,785 in 1979 (1,179,913 enrolled for 1986). Finally, the Brotherhood, the all-age missions education organization for men and boys, went from a high enrollment of 634,063 in 1963 to a low of 422,527 in 1970 (569,204 for 1986).

The only exception to the statistical downturn for Southern Baptists has been in the areas of church membership and gifts to the churches and denomination. These grew during the same period of time from 10,193,052 church members in 1963 to 14,486,403 church members in 1985 (though 29 percent of these, or 4.2 million persons, are considered "nonresident members," meaning that they cannot be found!). Also, during this same period of time gifts to all causes rose from $591,587,981 in 1964 to $3.8 billion in 1985, of which $611 million, or 16 percent was given for denominational mission causes. All of this has occurred during a time in which Southern Baptists increased the number of their churches from 33,126 in 1963 to 36,979 in 1985 and their presence from the thirteen states of the old Confederacy to all fifty states of the present union.

Southern Baptist churches are not large churches. Though there were 2,736 congregations in 1983 with 1000 members or more (6 percent), and they had within them 4,910,240 church members (53 percent), the average Southern Baptist congregation had 232 church members, 115 enrolled in Sunday School, 61 enrolled in Church Training, 32 enrolled in WMU, and 22 enrolled in Brotherhood. Sixty percent of all SBC churches had 300 church members or less, though 67 percent of all church members were located in churches of 400 members or above. This makes for an interesting way of looking at church life in the SBC.

If numerical downturn was the first indication that Southern Baptists were encountering the turbulent waters of a pluralistic society, then the cultural upheavals of the 1960s and 1970s, with the backlash of political conservatism and religious fundamentalism, have been the other indicators. What William O'Neil characterized as a "nation coming apart" in the 1960s[15] impacted the South also. But it also produced an intense backlash in politics and religion. William Hull, a Southern Baptist pastor and former dean of the School of Theology at The Southern Baptist Theological Seminary in Louisville, Kentucky, has described the intense conservatism of the South. It is the home of 75 percent of Southern Baptists, where they are the dominant denomination, " 'the Catholic Church of the South' in the sense of fostering an indigenous 'Baptist culture' there."[16]

The Gallup Poll of the fall of 1979, just prior to the Carter-Reagan presidential election, Hull points out, showed 52 percent of the voters in the South identifying themselves as "slightly right" to "far right," politically versus 47 percent for the nation.[17] Another survey found liberal Protestantism "almost totally missing in the Southeast and Southwest." Hull concludes that the area served by Southern Baptists is one of the most conservative areas in Protestantism.[18] Thus, the Reagan sweeps of the South in the presidential elections of 1980 and 1984 could have been predicted. It was a reaction to the pluralism of the previous two decades. Likewise, the congressional and gubernatorial races of 1982 and 1986 have shown an increase in the number of Republican officeholders in those positions, as the leaders of that political party provided conservative candidates for the electorate. In most places the South is now a two-party system as the Democratic Party, the traditional party of the South, has been criticized for its liberal stands against traditional values.

Theological turbulence became the third indicator of Southern Baptists encountering pluralism. The first incident happened in the opening years of the 1960s when a professor at the denomination's Midwestern Baptist Theological Seminary in Kansas City, Missouri, wrote a book on Genesis which was published by the denomination's publishing house. Ralph Elliott, the author of the book, simply said that "in the first eleven chapters of Genesis . . . we are dealing with theological fact, not day-by-day physical history."[19]

---

15. William L. O'Neil, *Coming Apart: An Informal History of America in the 1960's* (Chicago: Quadrangle Books, 1971).

16. William E. Hull, "Pluralism in the Southern Baptist Convention," *The Review and Expositor* 79:1 (Winter, 1982), p. 128.

17. Ibid., p. 133.

18. Ibid.

19. Shurden, *Not A Silent People,* pp. 104-105. In 1986 at the same seminary Temp Sparkman, professor of religious education, was accused and cleared of a charge of heresy relating to a book he wrote on the Christian nurture of children and youth.

What erupted was a decision by the denomination in its annual meeting in 1962 to affirm biblical infallibility in the areas of "historical accuracy and doctrinal integrity," and requested "the Trustees and administrative officers of our institutions and other agencies to take such steps as shall be necessary to remedy at once those situations where such views now threaten our historic position."[20] The denominational publishing house withdrew from sale the book by Elliott and the seminary fired him when he refused to promise not to republish it elsewhere.

Eight years later the interpretation of Genesis arose again in the 1970 annual meeting of the Southern Baptist Convention when it voted to withdraw the first volume of the new Broadman Commentary because of its use of the same historical-critical approach to the commentary of Genesis that Elliott had used.[21]

The Elliott controversy in 1962 resulted in a rewriting of the 1925 Baptist Confession of Faith and its adoption in 1963. But now it was beginning to look more and more like a creed, for after the 1970 decision to remove and rewrite the first volume of the Broadman Commentary, all the employees of the denominational publishing house, the Baptist Sunday School Board, were required to sign it. Also, the publishing house, which is responsible for the majority of the Christian education materials used in the denomination (the two missions education organizations, Women's Missionary Union and Baptist Brotherhood Commission also produce Christian education materials), as well as providing a book and bible sales through its Broadman press and Baptist Book Stores, including a wide variety of church supplies, began to print the following statement on all religious education materials: "The 1963 statement of 'The Baptist Faith and Message' is the doctrinal guideline for this periodical." In addition, it has employed in the years since "doctrinal readers" to insure conformity to that confession of faith. An *imprimatur?*

During the 1970s and early 1980s, a new group of "fundamentalist conservatives" (the official SBC designation for the theological right in Southern Baptist publications, as over against the "moderate conservatives" who represent the traditional theological position—there

---

20. Ibid., p. 109.
21. The most recent result of the continuing push by the theological right in the Southern Baptist Convention is the vote by the trustees of the Baptist Sunday School Board, February 3-4, 1987, to publish a new bible commentary that reflects the view of biblical inerrantists and will "reflect a strong, scholarly defense of the traditional authorship of the biblical books, the Mosaic authorship of the Pentateuch, and a presentation of an apologetic for Creationism in the introduction to Genesis."

are no liberals!) began their own seminary, two fundamentalist newspapers, and their own foreign missions agency within the Southern Baptist Convention, all financed by private donations. Thus began the new national organization of fundamentalists in opposition to the national denominational bureaucracy. The fundamentalists captured the presidency of the Southern Baptist Convention in 1979 and began a process of using the appointive powers of the office of president of the SBC, a post which had heretofore been largely honorific, to name the committee that appointed in turn the trustees of the various boards, agencies, and six SBC seminaries. As of 1986 the fundamentalist conservatives had about 50 percent of the trustees on all of the agencies of the SBC including the seminaries and the publishing house.

Thus far in the 1980s Southern Baptists have faced the issues of biblical inerrancy and the diversity of interpretation about the bible; the "New Right" agenda as expressed in the Reagan administration (specifically, strong military defense, anti-abortion, pro-life stance; the removal of rights for the minorities and the poor; a strong pro-business stand enabling the affluent to be more affluent in spite of the ethical standards of achieving those goals; prayer in public schools; and reduction of the federal budget at the expense of minorities and the poor);[22] the results of the forty year expansion into the fifty states of the United States; and the increasing secularization of American society.

PLURALISM'S EFFECTS ON CHRISTIAN EDUCATION IN THE SBC

Southern Baptists have faced for the past thirty years a series of challenges both from a society that has been changing around it and from a wider participation in that society as Southern Baptist work has spread throughout the nation. The rising pluralism in the society as a whole has produced a variety of responses within the denomination. These can be seen in the large number of resolutions that have been passed at its annual meeting each year upholding traditional values and against what was felt by many Southern Baptists to be a departure from those viewpoints. But it is from within that Southern Baptists seem now to be facing their greatest challenge, one which has begun to produce

---

22. See Samuel S. Hill and Dennis E. Owen, *The New Religious Political Right in America* (Nashville: Abingdon, 1982) and "Patterson Links Social Agenda to SBC Hiring, Says Texas Newspaper," *SBC Today* 4:6 (October, 1986), p. 13.

the most profound effects on Christian education in Southern Baptist churches today.

Racial Pluralism. The first crisis that Southern Baptists faced nearly 150 years ago was the crisis of two races, one black and one Anglo-Saxon white, living in the same thirteen states. "In 1880, the South had only 442,066 foreign-born persons out of a population of sixteen and one half million persons. This increased only to 800,771 foreign-born persons out of nearly thirty-eight million persons by 1930."[23] In fact, New Hampshire received in the decade 1899-1910 more European immigrants than were totally received in six Southern states, Connecticut more than all the South combined and New Jersey twice as many.[24]

But, how the two dominant races would get along and whether Southern Baptists would speak out on the issue of racism became the struggle for integrity that finally boiled over after the 1954 Supreme Court decision outlawing the "separate but equal" segregated public schools. Most Southern Baptists resisted the decision and many set up "white flight schools," called Christian Academies, to avoid going to school with blacks. However, when Martin Luther King Jr. began the Civil Rights struggles of the 1960s, it awoke many Southern Baptists to the rightness of the cause of racial justice.

Again it has been the publishing house that has been most vulnerable as Southern Baptists sought to work with solving the racial struggles that have been part of the tragic legacy of the South. In the early days of the Civil Rights struggle, as the Baptist Sunday School Board began dealing with the issue of racism, Sunday school quarterlies and other Christian education materials were rejected by some of the more vocally abusive racists among Southern Baptists in the Deep South and they returned all of their Christian education literature to the personal home of the executive director of the publishing house in Nashville, Tennessee.

After the assassination of Dr. King and the burning of the cities of the nation in 1968, again the publishing house sought to be responsive to the explosive situation in the nation and brought out in record time "We Hold These Truths," a Church Training adult study piece, in an attempt to give guidance to the churches and church members in working with racism.

But the pressure began to mount against the denominational publishing house. In 1971, after printing a Sunday school quarterly for youth

---

23. William Preston Clemmons, "The Development of A Sunday School Strategy In the Southern Baptist Convention, 1896-1926" (Ed.D. Dissertation, The Southern Baptist Theological Seminary, 1971), p. 164.

24. Ibid.

which used a photograph of two white girls and one black male talking in a school corridor, the director of the division of the publishing house responsible for all Christian educational materials ordered that the entire printing be destroyed and redone before it could be shipped to the churches. When the story appeared in the press, the inside workings of a denominational publishing house under siege was seen. Could those responsible for the publication of Christian education materials survive as they sought to educate a constituency about the biblical values and meanings even when they were at odds with the culture?

The denominational publishing house, the Baptist Sunday School Board, is vulnerable to partisan pressures because of the way it is funded. It does not receive any subsidy from the general offering of the denomination, the Cooperative Program. It is totally dependent on sales from its publications for its survival. At different times it has found itself at odds with its constituency when it tried to move beyond the societal values held by the members and leaders of the churches. Too often it has found that it is not free to buck the tide of cultural meanings and values, even when those held meanings and values have clashed with the biblical witness. And this has been the weakness, time and time again, when a Christian education program is dependent upon a publishing house which is totally reliant on the profits from sales for its survival.

Today, many would say that racism in the South is no nearer to a solution with regard to the black/white issue among Southern Baptists than it was thirty years ago. Southern Baptists still suffer the legacy of having pushed out maybe as many as 400,000 blacks from the balconies of their churches after the Civil War. Yet, today there are 1,100 black Baptist congregations affiliated with the SBC, mainly dually aligned churches in the new areas of Southern Baptist work in the North and West. Add to that number 1,110 Asian churches and 2,730 Hispanic churches, and one begins to get the idea that Southern Baptists (even the name of the denomination no longer fits and proposals have been made from time to time to change the name of the denomination to United Baptist Convention or Cooperative Baptist Churches of America) have a new step that must be made to include visible non-Anglos in denominational leadership.

However, the denominational publishing house is providing selective Christian education materials in French, Spanish, and several Asian languages. It employs persons to work with Hispanic and Asian Baptist churches, and has the largest staff of any publishing house in the nation engaged in Christian education work with black Baptist congregations. The Baptist Sunday School Board has allocated over a million dollars a year for this work and is producing over 100 publications in this area of its work. Even some of the Anglo publications are beginning to have a multi-ethnic character to them in their illustrations and advertisements. Thus, racial pluralism is becoming an emerging frontier for Southern Baptists. But, given their past, it still remains to be seen whether Southern Baptists can be racially inclusive.

Cultural Pluralism. The culture of the South was fairly well homogeneous until World War II. In spite of the two races, one black and the other primarily Anglo-Saxon white, the two races shared a similar way of approaching life. What was true in one area of the South was by and large true in another area. It was a region characterized by its rural, agrarian, poor, and meagerly educated masses. There was a slowness to life and speech which came not only from the intense heat of the summer and the resultant slower pace of life, but from the stoic despair of not being able to do much about one's circumstances in life. The South, as a result of its labor-intensive agriculture, the devastation of the Civil War, and in its aftermath the humbling effects of Reconstruction, did not share in the prosperity and wealth of the rest of the United States, especially as found in its industrial Northeast and Midwest, until World War II.

World War II, however, dislocated hundreds of thousands of Southerners both because of military service and because of the migrations of thousands to the industrial sectors of the nation to work in the plants and industries devoted to producing the war materials. The veterans who returned to the South after the war benefited by attending college and university for the first time, most often the first family members to ever participate in higher education. And they gained by better employment in industries that had begun to recruit workers and managers for expanding businesses in the other parts of the nation during the booming 1950s.

A second consequence of World War II was the presence of thousands of Southern Baptists who stayed on in the industrial centers of the North and the arrival of the newly recruited college and university graduates who wanted churches like they had left at home in the South. Many saw their efforts at establishing new Southern Baptist congregations in the Northeast, Midwest, and the far West of California as a way of evangelizing those liberal, cold, social-gospel churches which they felt were not bible-believing, God-fearing and where a personal experience with Jesus Christ was not central.

From 1950 on, Southern Baptists entered many of the states of the Northeast and Midwest (the date in parenthesis indicates the date they became a Southern Baptist state convention): Ohio (1954), Indiana

(1958), northern Illinois (southern Illinois had become Southern Baptist as they broke away from the Northern Baptist Convention in 1910, during the fundamentalist/modernist crisis), Michigan (1957), Pennsylvania/New Jersey (1970), New York (1969), and New England (1983). Southern Baptists had entered many of the far Western states in the 1940s as Southern Baptists had gone there for work. And the rest of the nation was added in the 1970s with three being added in the early years of the 1980s.

In many of these places Southern Baptists came face to face with their Northern Baptist cousins from whom they had broken away in 1845. And they faced competing with them for persons and churches for the first time since a comity agreement between the two bodies in 1894 had stipulated that there would be only one Baptist convention in each state according to the dominant Baptist group in that state.

But in 1940, Southern Baptists, because of the growing pressure of former Southern Baptists living in the far western, northern, and mid-western states, officially removed any territorial limits to its convention and authorized its Home Mission Board and other agencies of the Convention to serve all the people of the United States.[25] Southern Baptists began a forty-year expansion, including not only the expatriates from the South, but new persons in the states in which they now found themselves. Today, strong Southern Baptist state conventions are found all over the nation, just as they are found in the Deep South.

Not only did this expansion result in more churches and a growing membership, but it also meant restructuring the identity of Southern Baptists and the incorporation of the meanings and values encountered in cultural pluralism different from the cultural homogenity of the rural, agrarian South. The new mix has not always been successful or happy. Many of the new converts in the new states into which Southern Baptists expanded were among those persons unhappy with the mainline denominations present there and had become church drop-outs. Many times their unhappiness with the mainline churches influenced their attitudes toward the new denomination they were coming into. The independent individualism so prized by Southern Baptists had always existed within a balancing act of corporate denominational loyalty which was not always appreciated by the newly attracted Southern Baptists. And too often those Southern Baptists who came from the South established churches that were little more than "down home clubs" of Southern nostalgia, which yielded to frequent trips "back

---

25. Leon McBeth, "Expansion of the Southern Baptist Convention to 1951," *Baptist History and Heritage* 17:3 (July, 1982), p. 34.

home," and an eventual permanent return to the South when possible.

Simultaneously the numerical decline from 1964 to 1984 of the Christian education program, Church Training, where doctrinal issues were studied, church polity was taught, and Baptist history and heritage were examined, occurred over the same twenty years in which half of the new Southern Baptist church members were added to church roles. Thus, most of these new church members have not known the historical Baptist positions, and many, if not most of these persons, have come into Southern Baptist life from the new areas of the nation into which Southern Baptists have entered in the last forty years.

Theological Pluralism. Nowhere has the impact of pluralism been felt more in the SBC than in the area of theological thought. Southern Baptists have historically been very conservative in their theological stances. But the same forces that have prompted David Tracy to write of a "new pluralism in theology"[26] and Lonnie Kliever to speak of a "shattered spectrum,"[27] have also affected Southern Baptists. With theologians receiving better training and participating in the larger ecumenical dialogues, and an increasing number of theologically trained ministers (Southern Baptists have six of the largest graduate theological seminaries in the Association of Theological Schools with more than 12,000 full-time theological students enrolled), it was inevitable that the clash should happen. Most often the clash has occurred in attacks on what was being taught in the seminaries or what was being advocated in the Christian education publications.

Southern Baptists are a people of the bible. Many of their disagreements over the years have centered around differing perceptions of the bible. Without a hierarchy to be the official *magisterium,* the bible becomes central to an understanding of one's personal walk with God as well as being a guide for corporate church life. Thus, a large adult bible-study program is essential to the continuing well-being of the individual, the local congregation, and the denomination. Consequently, the recent argument about the authority of the bible is a pertinent subject for Baptist life.

The traditionalists have lamented the erosion of the authority of the bible as historical-critical approaches have been applied to its study. Their lament is that an approach that questions the historicity and facticity of the bible has in fact undercut the authority of the bible. They have, therefore, in a defense of the bible, advocated a position of biblical

---

26. David Tracy, *Blessed Rage For Order* (New York: Seabury, 1978).

27. Lonnie D. Kliever, *The Shattered Spectrum* (Atlanta: John Knox Press, 1981).

inerrancy in the original Greek and Hebrew manuscripts (which are not available!). And they have extended this inerrancy to cover matters of science, history, geography, and religion. They have often advocated literalism as the basic style of biblical interpretation and a treatment of every part of the bible as being of equal weight in their search for principles and truths upon which to build a propositional theology to which persons are asked to give assent.[28]

Other persons, with this same concern about biblical authority, have asserted that the bible is "God's uniquely inspired, trustworthy Word."[29] They feel that the bible is trustworthy in matters of personal and corporate faith and practice. They contend that this trustworthiness will not rise or fall on the finding of one scientific or historical error in the worldview of the writers and editors of the Old and New Testaments. They point out that only a set of propositions that rise and fall in relation to the errors in those propositions needs an inerrant bible. Pilgrim people, instead, need a record of God's call to faith and the record of their faithfulness. For them, the bible is most important in the formation of lives rather than simply giving assent to propositional truths.

As an example of this problem about the issue of pluralistic approaches to the bible, Southern Baptists' most basic source of authority, a committee appointed by the denomination to investigate the causes of the recent problems in the SBC and to propose a process for reconciliation, concluded the following in early 1986:

> The Peace Committee has completed a preliminary investigation of the theological situation in our SBC seminaries. We have found significant theological diversity within our seminaries reflective of the theological diversity within our wider constituency. These divergencies are found among those who claim to hold a high view of Scripture and to teach in accordance with and not contrary to the *Baptist Faith and Message* [the confessional] statement of 1963. Examples of diversity include the following, which are intended to be illustrative but not exhaustive: (1) Some accept and affirm the direct creation and historicity of Adam and Eve while others view them instead as representative of the human race in its creation and fall. (2) Some understand the historicity of every event in Scripture as reported by the original source while others hold that the historicity can be clari-

---

28. Fisher Humphreys, "Biblical Inerrancy: A Guide For the Perplexed," *SBC Today* (February, 1987), pp. 6-7.
29. Ibid.

fied and revised by the finding of modern historical scholarship. (3) Some hold to the stated authorship of every book in the Bible while others hold that in some cases such attribution may not refer to the final author or may be pseudonymous. (4) Some hold that every miracle in the Bible is intended to be taken as an historical event while others hold that some miracles are intended to be taken as parabolic. The Peace Committee is working earnestly to find ways to build bridges between those holding divergent views and work together in harmony to accomplish our common mission."[30]

After a year of discussion, when it seemed that the seminaries would come under more severe attack, the presidents of the six SBC seminaries agreed to a statement in which they said that, "The 66 books of the Bible are not errant in any area of reality."[31] The statement has become the basis for the Peace Committee asking all of the seminaries and the administrators of the agencies to require all employees to agree to that statement and to insure compliance to it.

Though Baptists hold to the doctrinal understanding of the priesthood of all believers, sometimes referred to as "soul competency," by which is meant "the competency of the soul in religion," that doctrinal position has been severely strained as it has been placed alongside doctrinal conformity, especially as the issue of biblical inerrancy has gained ground. Christian education materials have been most vulnerable to this struggle as the denominational publishing house has attempted to serve all the churches of the denomination.

At the annual meeting of the SBC in Kansas City in June of 1984, the SBC affirmed a resolution (a sentiment of the messengers meeting at the annual meeting but not binding on the local churches) that since sin came into the world through women and Paul commended women to be submissive to men in all things, though women should be encouraged to continue to work in the life of the church, they be excluded from ordination.[32]

The next year the trustees of the Baptist Sunday School Board adopted guidelines for dealing with the ordination of women in their Christian education literature. The guidelines emphasized " 'ordination of deacons and ministers is a matter completely under the authority of the

---

30. "SBC Diversity Found By Peace Committee, Will Build Bridges," *SBC Today* 4:1 (April, 1986), p. 2.

31. Dan Martin, "Six Seminary Presidents Make Reconciliation Try," *Baptist Press,* October 24, 1986, p. 4.

32. Susan K. Taylor, "Women Blamed For World's Sin," *SBC Today* 2:4 (July, 1984), pp. 1-2.

local congregation,' and the board will 'continue to affirm and encourage the biblical and historic contribution of women to the cause of Christ' . . . [however] the 'issue will be dealt with factually and fairly with neither point of view being ignored or disparaged.' "[33]

The solution was simply to reflect both views without taking a stand either way. This did not satisfy either theological viewpoint, for the theologically right said, " 'The Southern Baptist Convention is our market for this literature, and Southern Baptists are overwhelmingly against the ordination of women,' . . . [and added] 'tolerance of women's ordination would lead to tolerance of homosexuality'."[34]

Another issue related to this same concern that has affected the Christian education literature of Southern Baptists has been the issue of the treatment of the doctrine of last things. A rising premillennialism, which held the viewpoint that the Great Tribulation was imminent and that all Christians, the church, would be raptured out of those difficulties *before* the tribulation, after which Jesus would return for a thousand years' reign, this became the dominant position of the theological right. This particular viewpoint dovetailed nicely with the other literalistic, inerrantist view of scripture and a propositional theology. It found its greatest support in dispensationalism and in the notes of the *Scofield Reference Bible.*

Again, because other millennial views were held among Southern Baptists and it coupled with how the church would relate to the world (maybe this is the real issue since most pretribulation premillennialists felt that the world was so bad that God was going to take them out of it, and consequently felt that their support for a pro-military stand was justified), another theological issue had to be faced by the denominational publishing house. Again, the decision was to present all views, though biblical scholars and theologians had written clearly about the errors of the dispensational view.[35]

A third example of the effects of pluralism on The Baptist Sunday School Board is found in the theological stances in the descriptions of the Sunday school curriculum series and the use of scripture translations in those series. Southern Baptists have been one of the earliest continuous users of the Uniform Curriculum Series. Representatives from their publishing house have in recent decades served as chairman of the ecumenical Committee on the Uniform Series of the Division of

---

33. "BSSB: Shun Ordination?" *SBC Today* (March, 1985), p. 1.

34. Ibid.

35. See Dale Moody, *The Word of Truth* (Grand Rapids, Mich.: Eerdmans, 1981), pp. 548 ff.

Education and Ministry of the National Council of Churches that continues to guide the work of the Uniform Series. And in 1966 Southern Baptists, having worked on the Cooperative Curriculum Project of the National Council of Churches, and having been heavily influenced by its work,[36] brought out a new curriculum series, the Life and Work Curriculum. Billed as an "alternative curriculum," it was to be a bible study "which leads the pupil to understand better the *life* and *work* of a church. The increased understanding of what a church is and is to do should result in appropriate *action* by the pupil as a member of the church."[37] The Convention Uniform Series was to continue to focus on the content of the bible in six year cycles of study.

In 1970 the Sunday school series was augmented by yet a third study series called the Forefront Series, in what was described as a "cafeteria approach" to Christian education curriculum. It was an attempt to "segment the market," in marketing terminology in which various audiences could be identified and materials would be provided to them. This was an approach to pluralism, for a statement at that time spoke of curriculum series characteristics that would "more adequately meet the needs of the churches." The new Forefront Series was to be "an innovative, bible-based curriculum for adults, strongly oriented to contemporary issues using innovative methods and design." It was to present the "generally accepted Southern Baptist theological positions with considerable factual presentation of varying views for study and discussion." Contemporary issues would be the primary starting point for the development of the curriculum.[38]

Unfortunately the Forefront Series ceased to exist in the stormy mid-1970s and shortly after, in 1978, a fourth curriculum series, designed for the more fundamentalist segment of the SBC, the Bible Book Series, a study of each book of the bible, was introduced.

In the most recent issue of the *Church Curriculum Base Design: 1984 Update,* the official guide for curriculum development in the SBC, the following statements are made about the three Sunday School Curriculum Series: *Bible Book Series:* "Interpretations generally accepted among Southern Baptists are presented. In dealing with passages on which there is no general agreement among Southern Baptists, more

---

36. See Howard P. Colson and Raymond M. Rigdon, *Understanding Your Church's Curriculum* (Nashville: Broadman, 1969, rev. 1981).

37. From a promotional flyer of 1966.

38. "Church Literature Selection Guide," Nashville: Baptist Sunday School Board, n.d. (about 1970).

than one possible interpretation is given." Also, "interpretations not generally accepted by Southern Baptists are omitted . . . [and] critical problems of date and authorship or content will not be dealt with." For the *Convention Uniform Series:* It "may 'rarely' present views other than those accepted among Southern Baptists to help learners know such views exist." For the *Life and Work Series:* It "presents a variety of interpretations of difficult passages factually and fairly."[39]

Similarly, in an attempt to provide a variety of bible translations for its literature, the theological right has protested anything but the King James Version, which many fundamentalists believe to be the most inerrant. Several times the Baptist Sunday School Board has attempted to introduce modern translations into its curriculum materials, even side by side with the KJV, but to have objections raised by a minority on the theologically right. The official policy about bible translations is that only the KJV will be used in the Bible Book Series and the Convention Uniform Series. In the Life and Work Series a variety of "contemporary translations" may be used but the Revised Standard Version is the primary scripture translation printed in the curriculum pieces.

CONCLUSION

Unity in the midst of diversity has always been the hallmark of Southern Baptists. But in recent decades the fabric of consensus has been tearing and with it the programs of Christian education. As the former executive of the Baptist Sunday School Board has written:

> The difficulty in maintaining the principle of unity in diversity is that there are certain people who find it difficult to cooperate with those who do not hold views identical to their own. A few times in my memory, when emotions were high, the Convention would take extreme positions only to discover that it had created problems more intense than the ones which existed before. . . . When everyone sees everything alike, and few or no objective discussions are heard, invalid decisions are more frequently made. . . . It is when feelings are intense, people take themselves too seriously, no diversity is allowed, and humor is considered out of order that we get ourselves into

---

39. *Church Curriculum Base Design: 1984 Update* (Nashville: Baptist Sunday School Board, 1974, rev. 1980, 1984), Part VII, "Intraprogram Coordination and Design," 1.05.1, p. 7.

trouble. While a few tense moments are inevitable when major controversial issues are up for discussion, it must be kept in mind that there is no place for any degree of intolerance or impatience.[40]

And, the current executive of the Baptist Sunday School Board in a book outlining the future possibilities for Southern Baptists has said:

While I am deeply aware of the greatness of our people and of our potential for greater service to God and others, I am not blind to our present needs, concerns, and differences. A lifetime of living within this fellowship and years of working, relating, reading, and listening have opened my eyes to the needs for renewal within the denomination. Theologians and sociologists have written of our age as a postdenominational era. Persons of widely differing theological stances have claimed that denominations are no longer useful or vital to the work of the church. I don't believe it! But I do believe that we must listen to one another about the perceived ills within the denominational body.[41]

Such is the continuing struggle for Southern Baptists and the ways in which that struggle has impacted Christian education. The issue that is critical for Southern Baptists has to do with the rebuilding of a viable consensus in which the various stands that make up the denomination can coexist. Some believe that the diversity is too great, and there are apparent signs of groups on either end of the continuum breaking away. Others are hopeful that the great diversity can have enough time to see the seemingly irreconcilable differences merge into a new position. One such voice is William Hull who says, "Somehow Southern Baptists need to retain all of the values of particularity which stand them in such good stead today and at the same time develop the versatility to adapt to a future when unity may be prized more than diversity."[42] Only time will tell what will be the ultimate outcome. Meanwhile, the process of Christian education struggles with its task amid the storms.

---

40. Sullivan, *Baptist Polity As I See It,* pp. 203-204.
41. Lloyd Elder, *Blueprints: Ten Challenges for a Great People* (Nashville: Broadman, 1984), pp. 32-33.
42. Hull, "Pluralism in the Southern Baptist Convention," p. 139.

7

The Minority Problem:
Educating for Identity and Openness

Constance J. Tarasar

RELIGIOUS PLURALISM: SOME PERSPECTIVES

Religious pluralism, and the problems it raises, confronts us every day through the media. Mass communications have indeed shrunk our world to that of a "global village" in which events and peoples thousands of miles removed from us enter our living rooms daily and shake our consciousness. Depending upon their origin they stir up in us feelings of anger, pride, envy, hatred, compassion, suspicion, aggressiveness, shame, and, only occasionally, joy.

Looking at the political events that provoke these emotional responses, we see that many carry religious connotations. Religious groups or persons are themselves involved in political struggles—as aggressors, pacifiers, conciliators, critics, or victims. In relatively peaceful contexts, persons and groups of different religious allegiances coexist either in moderate uneasiness or in blissful ignorance of one another. In other situations, religious groups or persons have, for all practical purposes, tried to divorce themselves from the societies in which they live, preferring to work out their spiritual destinies as islands in a turbulent ocean. Regardless of the situations in which we find ourselves, one thing is clear: Religion is not separate from nor can it escape the events that shape this world, and, conversely, the world is not separate from nor can it escape the presence of religion. It is also clear as we observe these events that we cannot speak of "religion" today in an exclusive way, denoting a particular religion such as Christianity; the events and conflicts in our "global village" force us to accept a plurality of religious realities.

Religious Pluralism—Some Parameters

What do we mean by "religious pluralism"? Gerhard Lenski[1] defines religious pluralism as a situation "in which organized religious groups with *incompatible* [my emphasis] beliefs and practices are obliged to coexist within the framework of the same community or the same society," and he includes in his definition of religions both theistic and nontheistic faiths, including Marxism and secularism. The concept of plurality in this definition is based on the coexistence of different religious realities with different ontological bases. Thus, we would contrast—as different realities—Christianity from Buddhism, Islam, Hinduism, and Judaism, though there may exist points of agreement, and, in the case of Judaism and Christianity, a shared history.[2]

Within the Christian tradition, however, the problem is a bit more complex, and, especially in this ecumenical age, even risky, for it is possible to make a distinction between pluralism and diversity. A diversity of forms can exist within the same religious framework. Many Christians, therefore, would claim merely a diversity of form between the different branches of Christendom. Others, however (particularly the Orthodox), perceive substantive differences, not only between Christians and Jews, but also between Christian confessions or communions. The problems faced by Orthodox Christians in the ecumenical movement often can be attributed to theological positions based upon substantive differences concerning the nature of God and his relationship to human persons.[3]

---

1. Gerhard Lenski, "Religious Pluralism in Theoretical Perspective," in *Religious Pluralism and Social Structure,* International Yearbook for the Sociology of Religion, Vol. I, 25-26 (Westdeutscher Verlag Koln und Opladen, 1965).

2. For an exploration of common elements, see Nicholas Arseniev, *Revelation of Life Eternal* (Crestwood, N.Y.: St. Vladimir's Seminary Press, 1982), and the study guide *My Neighbour's Faith—and Mine: Theological Discoveries through Interfaith Dialogue* (Geneva: World Council of Churches, 1986).

3. For example, on the question of the essence and energies of God, as expressed by Gregory Palamas and other Fathers of the Church, see Vladimir Lossky, *The Mystical Theology of the Eastern Church* (Crestwood, N.Y.: St. Vladimir's Seminary Press, 1976) and *The Vision of God* (Crestwood, N.Y.: St. Vladimir's Seminary Press, 1983); or John Meyendorff, *A Study of Gregory Palamas* (Crestwood, N.Y.: St. Vladimir's Seminary Press, 1964) and *Byzantine Theology: Historical Trends and Doctrinal Themes* (New York: Fordham University Press, 1979).

From an Orthodox Christian perspective, therefore, the question of religious pluralism includes not only questions of the relationship of Christianity to other world religions, but also questions of how Orthodox Christians relate to other Christians. This shall be my frame of reference as I speak about religious education and religious pluralism.

A Biblical Vision

From the Christian perspective, the challenge of pluralism has its foundation in the earliest chapters of the bible. The world created by God was one world, the human society one society—called to live in communion with him. The stories of the separation of human persons and societies from God and from one another illustrate in many ways that pride, ambition, and self-glorification are at the root of this separation, a separation that was not intended by God when he created the world.[4]

The biblical story of Babel represents the negative pluralism that resulted. Its corrective in the New Testament is the Pentecost story which gives a positive direction and content to the pluralistic situation in which we live. The Orthodox liturgy of Pentecost makes a vivid contrast between these two events:

> When the Most High came down and confused the
>   tongues, He divided the nations;
> but when He distributed the tongues of fire,
>   He called all to unity.
> Therefore, with one voice, we glorify the
>   all-holy Spirit!
>
> *(Kontakion of Pentecost)*

The Pentecost event, as expressed in this verse, issues a strong *call to unity* as the *raison d'être* of Christian witness and mission. The promise of God is given "to you and to your children and *to all that are far off,* everyone whom the Lord our God calls to him*" (Acts 2:39). But this call implies repentance, baptism in the name of Jesus Christ for the forgiveness of sins, and reception of the gift of the Holy Spirit (Acts 2:38); in other words, in terms of the response of those called, it implies acceptance of the church.

How, then, do we understand this call in the context of religious pluralism? What do we mean by the unity to which we are called? If, as

---

4. See Genesis 1-4, 6, 8-9, 11-12:3 for examples, as well as Arseniev, *Revelation of Life Eternal,* and *My Neighbour's Faith—and Mine,* for non-Christian examples.

Christians, we understand unity to be unity in God through Jesus Christ in the Holy Spirit ("that they may all be one; even as thou, Father, art in me and I in thee, that they also may be in us."—John 17:21), then that unity is manifested concretely in the church, and it is to God through his church that all are called.

How do we consider others who have made a commitment to God, or to some divine presence, who are outside the Christian faith, or the church as we understand it? Are those who have heard a divine call to faith outside the Christian gospel to be consigned to the "outer darkness," considered cut off from the love and mercy of God, excluded from salvation and the joy and peace of God's Kingdom? The answers to these questions concern not only religious education, but, even more especially, Christian witness and mission.

The challenge of religious pluralism also goes far beyond a lowest common denominator "brotherhood of man" theory—which can exist even without God. In addressing religious pluralism, we are concerned (with some exceptions) with those peoples and groups who believe in One God, or in a god or divine presence that is universal, that is concerned for or related to the created world and all humanity. We are speaking about other kinds of religious "believers," and unless we have categorically dismissed any possibility of perceiving even a limited knowledge of Truth outside the Christian community, we must come face-to-face with the spiritual realities posed by the existence of other religions.

Religious Education and Religious Pluralism

Religious education has generally ignored the problem of religious pluralism. Traditionally, the goal of religious education has been to catechize persons for the building up of the religious group, to build up their knowledge and practice of the faith. For Christians, this has meant the building up of the church, the Body of Christ. It implies integration into a community of faith, knowledge, and practice of the faith, leading ultimately to communion with God and life eternal in his Kingdom.

For Orthodox Christians, as well as for persons of other religious groups, *Truth* is at the center of religious faith, for religion is concerned with ultimate reality. The vision of that ultimate reality upon which faith is based provides us with a *worldview* that serves to guide us in particular lifestyle toward that ultimate reality. A religious faith, consequently, is *wholistic;* it concerns the totality of our lives.

At first glance, then, religious pluralism seems to be incompatible with religious education. If the communication of the Truth—about God, the world, human persons, and salvation—within the context of the faith community is the task of religious education, how can the communication of other "truths" that are *incompatible* with *the Truth* be part of this task? Is it possible to teach "religious pluralism" without surrendering to relativism? What are the particular problems that religious pluralism poses for religious education? What should be taught about other faith groups and why is it important?

THE AMERICAN SITUATION

Pluralism in the American context poses different problems than it does, for example, in Asia, the Middle East, or other areas where Christians are in the minority. Religiously, America is predominantly Christian (and, we should also add, secular). Yet, within this Christian context, we find a plurality of Christian beliefs and practices; we also find every other major religious group represented in the country. What is important is not the presence of religious plurality, as protected by our laws, but how Americans react to it.

Americans, generally, are ambivalent toward pluralism. On the one hand, we take pride in our plurality or diversity, seeing in it the proof of our freedom and tolerance of all groups. Yet, having dismissed long ago the "melting pot" theory as a myth, it nevertheless still permeates our consciousness as a dream unfulfilled. We are caught between the richness of diversity and the relative safety of sameness. We are intrigued by differences, yet we minimize them, even pretending that they don't exist. Will Herberg dealt with this ambivalence when he developed the concept of the "common faith" of Americans, based less on theological than social distinctions. Describing Protestantism, Catholicism, and Judaism in America as three great branches or divisions of "American religion," he stated that Americans perceive them as "three diverse representations of the same 'spiritual values,' the 'spiritual values' American democracy is presumed to stand for (the fatherhood of God and brotherhood of man, the dignity of the individual human being, and so on). That is at bottom why no one is expected to change his religion as he becomes American."[5]

Americans seem particularly embarrassed by pronounced differences or conflicts between groups, whether they stem from racial, religious, or economic differences. We want to think of ourselves as "one happy family" until, that is, someone who is a little too different wants to move

---

5. Will Herberg, *Protestant, Catholic, Jew* (New York: Doubleday Anchor Books, 1960), pp. 38-39.

next door. Our first attempt then is to try to solve the problem indirectly, through real estate agents, zoning laws, or anything that will avoid a face-to-face confrontation with the real problem or real persons. As Herberg points out, not every religion is felt to be really American, even though all have freedom and protection under the Constitution. "The Buddhism of Chinese and Japanese immigrants, for example, is definitely felt to be something foreign in a way that Lutheranism, or even Catholicism, never was"; thus, another alternative was that those who were too different changed their status, becoming something more acceptable, "dropping their non-American faith and becoming a Catholic or a Protestant, usually the latter."[6]

In religious matters, we try to dismiss differences by subtly imposing conformity or by seeking superficial unanimity through a relativistic approach. Our religious sensibilities say "it is not good for persons to be different," and it is almost un-American or un-Christian to insist upon the maintenance of our differences. As Michael Novak reflected upon his early public school education, he perceived that "to be modern is decidedly not to be medieval; to be reasonable is not to be dogmatic; to be free is clearly not to live under ecclesiastical authority; to be scientific is not to attend ancient rituals, cherish traditional symbols, indulge in mythic practices" and concluded: "It is hard to grow up Catholic in America without becoming defensive, perhaps a little paranoid, feeling forced to divide the world between 'us' and 'them.' "[7]

Thomas Hopko echoes a similar theme when he says: "References to religious doctrines and practices in America are virtually never references to what is true or false, to what is right or wrong, to what is meaningful or senseless. They are almost without exception in terms of what is modern or backward, civilized or barbarian, democratic or totalitarian, American or 'old country.' " He adds, however, that the content of the "common faith" of Americans today, "is the doctrine that a person may believe and do whatever he or she wishes as long as this belief and action does not conflict with the rights of others to do the same."[8] Thus, "the norms of traditional church disciplines are *felt* to be oppressive and binding, demeaning of individual dignity and liberty. They restrict individual rights, are invasions of personal privacy, viola-

---

6. Ibid., p. 44, n.26.

7. Michael Novak, *The Rise of the Unmeltable Ethnics* (New York: Macmillan, 1973), pp. 65-66.

8. Thomas Hopko, *All the Fulness of God: Essays on Orthodoxy, Ecumenism and Modern Society* (Crestwood, N.Y.: St. Vladimir's Seminary Press, 1982), p. 152.

tions of moral conscience, and reek of old-fashioned dogmatism and bigotry; that is, they are unbecoming for free citizens of modern democratic states in which everyone is equal and free and is obliged to follow his or her own conscience in private affairs." But Hopko adds that the irony of this view "is that this position itself has become as dogmatic and closed-minded as any specific religious dogmatism has ever been."[9]

Hopko describes two tendencies in religious orientation among Americans today: individualistic relativism or crusading sectarianism. The first is a position accepted by the majority in which "there must be 'conversations' and 'sharing' in which people describe what they believe and do with no implication that others ought to see things the same way and act accordingly." The second, tolerated by the minority, is "high-pressure, hard-sell apologetical evangelism aimed at beating the other in polemical encounter and winning the other to one's side through spiritual conversion." For Americans today, he says, "religion must be either relativistic or sectarian. Any other way is not even understood as possibly existing."[10]

From the perspective of religious pluralism, both relativism and sectarianism are "risk-free," for they can coexist without engaging in real dialogue. The tendency to relativism includes minimalism, indifference, and reductionism in matters of faith and belief—allowing that it is all right to let everyone "do their own thing," believe what they want, as long as (on the basis of some minimal common denominator) we can work together. Such an approach has no concern for other beliefs because beliefs are not really important. In some respects, the relativist is even saying that the person or faith group is not important, for the *quality* of relationships is outweighed by the *quantity* (an attitude often found in ecumenical circles, i.e., the more groups we can count in our overall representation, the more "successful" we are). Sectarianism is the tendency to become rigid, severe, isolationist, fanatical, or even triumphalistic in what one feels or believes to be the "only" way. Often majority groups or relativists impose on others these kinds of sectarian mentalities, especially when they refuse to recognize or respect legitimate differences. Both tendencies, however, lack the authenticity or "catholicity" which makes possible true "wholeness" of persons-in-relationship. The relativist and sectarian positions both exclude "all chance for human community of any value and depth."[11]

Is this the kind of pluralism we want—a pluralism based upon indif-

---

9. Ibid., pp. 155-156.
10. Ibid., p. 156.
11. Ibid., p. 157.

ference rather than love and commitment to truth? From Hopko's perspective "the task of all those who care for the dignity and value of humankind in the modern world and especially in America—whether or not they are believers in God, but most certainly if they are—is to defend the principle that men must challenge one another in spirit and in truth so that they might discover together that which is spiritually and morally genuine and be united with one another in the fruits of their discovery."[12]

THE TASK OF RELIGIOUS EDUCATION

How, then, do we approach the challenge of religious pluralism in our society? What do we teach in our churches and religious institutions? How do we look at other faith groups as well as at ourselves?

The starting point for the Christian may be the words of St. Paul: "Whatever is true, whatever is honorable, whatever is just, whatever is pure, whatever is lovely, whatever is gracious, if there is any excellence, if there is anything worthy of praise, think about these things" (Phil. 4:8). The search for truth and goodness should take us everywhere, even to the persons and philosophies that appear to be in opposition to our own. Our first step must be positive, in that it opens up all possibilities; and negative, in that it discards all false presuppositions and prejudices. To accept even the *possibility* that there could be goodness in others or truth in their beliefs is a bold step that is a prerequisite to all other steps. It implies an attitude of respect, an acceptance of our common humanity, and a recognition of our own finitude.

But this first step, however noble, may not be possible if we do not believe in our own self-worth. The biblical injunction to "love your neighbor as yourself" (Lev. 19:18; Mt. 19:19; 22:39) conveys an important principle—that unless we love ourselves, we are unable to love our neighbor. This brings us to the problem of identity, knowing who we are and feeling secure in that discovery. As Novak says, "it is in possessing our own particularity that we come to feel at home with ourselves and are best able to enter into communion with others, freely giving and receiving of each other."[13] Identity is dependent upon many factors: love, trust, respect or recognition, and, ultimately, freedom. It is both personal and communal.[14] To deny someone the respect or validity of

---

12. Ibid., p. 158.
13. Novak, *The Rise of the Unmeltable Ethnics,* p. xxix.
14. See Erik Erikson, *Identity: Youth and Crisis* (New York: Norton, 1968).

their communal identity is to undermine also their personal identity.

This brings us, however, to a major problem that exists in most, if not all, pluralistic situations: the question of minority status. Minority status, be it religious, political, racial, or economic, seriously affects the attitudes of persons concerning their self-identity and their openness to others. It is this factor within the subject of religious pluralism that I would like to explore from the standpoint of religious education.

Majority and Minority Status

It is one thing to look at other faiths and churches as members of a majority group and quite another from the standpoint of membership in a minority group within a religiously pluralistic situation. As members of majorities, we often delude ourselves into thinking that the feelings and beliefs we express are those of the general population. Minor differences of opinion and situations can exist, of course, if they do not disrupt the status quo. As long as they remain "in their place," minorities, we feel, even enrich us, provide us with the possibility to broaden our experiences—tempt us perhaps to try something a bit exotic—and testify by their very existence that people are "free to believe or be" who they are.

The perceptions of a minority group, however, are often quite different. In situations of such "peaceful coexistence," the majority group is often viewed as self-righteously paternalistic. Differences of belief are merely tolerated, without allowing the possibility that they may express Truth. Differences in practice that are "attractive"—liturgy or icons, perhaps, or gospel music—are often superficially adopted much as an interesting plaything or *objet d'art,* or indulged in as a form of mystical or charismatic experience. Those that are objectionable, such as views against abortion or women's ordination, are deemed irrelevant, narrow, or unenlightened in today's society. Rarely is anything in the minority group's system of belief or practice considered by the majority to be of intrinsic value to their own beliefs or practices.

The response of minority group members is varied. Some respond to expressions of paternalism or "interest in the exotic" with satisfaction or excitement that someone has finally noted their existence. But that excitement is generally short-lived and turns to disappointment or feelings of rejection as soon as the "interest" turns elsewhere or its superficiality is revealed. Others react with anger or resentment at being treated with indifference or "used" for meaningless or selfish pursuits. Some make a special effort to be "recognized" by the majority, to legitimize their existence, while other vocal elements try to prove their superiority in spite of their small numbers. Still others do whatever they can to minimize or hide their differences in an effort to blend in and become part of the majority group. In nearly every case, minority group status has served to diminish or obliterate personal and communal identity.

There can be also positive responses or advantages to minority status in a pluralistic situation. As a member of a minority, one is forced to search for self-understanding and identity, if only to explain to oneself and to others "Who am I?" "Why am I different?" "How do I feel about this difference?" "Is it necessary to my life?" (Unlike physical differences such as color or physical impairments, faith or religious difference is voluntary.) Minority persons cannot be indifferent; they cannot take for granted who they are or what they believe, but must make an effort to know themselves in order to make a commitment to their beliefs and participate to the fullest extent possible as a minority in the world. This kind of understanding of ourselves and our faith is critical to religious commitment and spiritual development.

Shaping Self-Identity

The identity of a person is rooted in the history of a people. The story of a people tells us where we come from, what we believe, how we speak, how we are to live our lives, and how we have survived as a people through the ages. As Michael Oleksa points out in his analysis of the Alaskan Yupik and Inupiak Eskimos, to identify oneself by the very name of the tribe is to be a member of "the People" and to know the language of the People—in other words, to be a real "human being," *anthropos*—a person ("-pik" or "-piak" means "genuine" or "real"). Not to speak Yupik, therefore, is tantamount to saying, "No, sorry, I don't speak *human*," and indicates that I am not really a person, one of "the People."[15]

Consequently, to feel secure as a minority group member, one must feel a certain pride as a member of a People (e.g., the "Black Pride" movement helped to give such an identity to blacks in America). To do so, it is important to truly know—experience, as well as learn from books—the story of "my people." How and why do we believe what we do and act the way we do? What riches of tradition do we have to contribute to society as a whole? What does this story mean for my life today? Developing a self-identity (and through it, a worldview) means to reflect upon my life, my convictions, my history, my hopes, and my dreams. In discovering my self-identity and group identity, I acquire an

---

15. Michael Oleksa, "The Confluence of Church and Culture," in *Perspectives on Orthodox Education,* Constance J. Tarasar (Syosset, N.Y.: DRE-Orthodox Church in America, 1983), pp. 8-9.

understanding of the past and a vision of the future, and am enabled to know how to act in the present. Discovering that I am truly "a person" and a member of "a people," I can say with confidence that "I *am* somebody," not "nobody." This frees me then to look at others to see who they *really* are and to come to a genuine understanding of their story, their convictions, and their life today. Although everyone at some point in life must come to this kind of self-understanding, members of minority groups are usually confronted with their "difference" and forced to go through the process earlier in life.

The Search for Commonness

Fortunately, especially in a pluralistic society, few persons desire to be totally different or removed from other human beings. Even believing in our own story and accepting our own commitments, we do not find it pleasant always to be in opposition to others, or to stand alone in our beliefs. As human beings, we desire contact and relationships with others. We search for things that can establish links between us, and we begin by looking for areas of commonness. Without sacrificing the things which we value and which provide the foundation for our self-understanding and identity, we seek those same values or even threads of similarity in others, so that relationships might be established.

In this effort, we become involved in a constant process of discernment that requires questioning, reflection, adjustment or accommodation, joy or disappointment, as well as struggles to confirm or renew our own faith commitment. The basic thrust of the ecumenical movement is related to this search for what we have in common, what we value and make our commitment to, and how, in spite of our differences, we can still work and witness together. This same search also leads us, however, to recognize more clearly where the "commonness" ends—the points at which, because of our beliefs and values, we must state our differences and be willing to accept the consequences. This, too, is part of the process of spiritual growth, and often it requires a special courage to "speak the truth in love."

The task of the religious educator is to encourage both the development of self-identity and the search for commonness. The educator must help students to discover the stories of other peoples, to appreciate their differences and contributions, their difficulties and needs, and to cultivate the basis for openness and dialogue.

Learning to Appreciate the "Other"

Developing an appreciation of the convictions and practices of others cannot be done only through "book learning." More than *knowledge about* the other, we need *knowledge of* those who are different from us. We need to try to experience, to whatever extent possible, their tradition—their vision of life and way of life. This is difficult, regardless of whether we are part of a majority or a minority group.

First of all, we cannot put ourselves completely in the place of the others. Their story is not our story, their experience has not been our experience, their perceptions have not been conditioned in the same way ours have been. Just as we cannot truly appreciate what it is to be poor, homeless, black . . . if we are not or have not been poor, homeless, black . . . , we cannot truly experience *from within* what it means to be Jewish, Eastern Orthodox, Hindu, Buddhist, or Muslim. Nevertheless, this should not prevent us from visiting a place of worship, asking questions about different practices and beliefs, observing patterns and customs of life, and trying to understand the feelings of others as they attempt to tell us what their faith means to them. Such an exchange, however, requires *humility* on both sides, as well as genuine *respect.* On the one hand, it requires us to put aside all feelings of paternalism or superiority, as well as to do some "homework" in advance. On the other, it requires patience and self-control in dealing with superficiality, ignorance, and wrong interpretations.

It is always easier to dismiss or condemn others for their beliefs or actions than to take time to listen and consider why they believe or act differently. It takes a real effort to stop and assess our own emotions when we react to those differences. Before attacking or judging, we need to ask ourselves: Why am I upset by this practice, or belief? What is it that truly offends me or threatens me? Is there some experience in my past, or in the past of the other person or group, that prejudices me? Can I accept and respect a genuine difference of belief or opinion—i.e., can we "agree to disagree"? If we can try to objectify our responses somewhat, then we may be able to enter into a true dialogue.

One of the pitfalls in trying to interpret and accept how others believe or practice their faith is the tendency to put them into easily defined categories that *we* can deal with, but which do not truly represent their reality. For example, we stereotype them as "liturgical" in opposition to "biblical," "traditional" as opposed to "modern" or "relevant," "hierarchical" as opposed to "democratic," and so on. We describe them in ways they would not describe themselves, and we become irritated when they are not willing to accept our categories. How often, for example, have the Orthodox been asked whether they are more "protestant" or "roman catholic"? When they respond that they are neither, the question is generally repeated again, as if it had not been heard correctly the first time! When I am asked what church I belong to and answer

"Orthodox Church in America," the response is inevitably, "Is that Greek or Russian?" To answer that it is neither, but that it is the Orthodox Church for those who live *in America* is again unacceptable; how could an Orthodox Church—which is usually identified by some ethnic label, and, moreover, is "Eastern" (usually meaning "ancient, oriental, colorful" and thus "not relevant" to American or Western society) exist as a nonforeign entity in our country? To explain further that most of our parishes include a good percentage of converts, and not only through marriage, often elicits confusion or denial. The labels have to fit the image *we* have created for one another; it makes no difference that the real "ingredients" do not match.

Dialogue cannot proceed unless we are willing to accept the fact that there are other ways of approaching and speaking about faith. We need also to realize that the same words may mean quite different things in the context of different faith traditions. This is one of the most critical problems in ecumenical dialogue today. As we try to help persons move toward mutual understanding and respect, it is useful to have them attempt to recapitulate or rephrase each others' statements or positions in order to know if their words have been understood correctly. To know that the other person truly understands what I am saying helps me to identify more accurately the real points of conflict; it also helps me to respect an honest disagreement. I know at least that my point has been heard correctly, that our effort to come to terms is not being frustrated or deviated by misunderstanding or indifference. Once I know that I am being valued and heard for who I am, that the intention is positive, then we can begin to enter into true dialogue.

True Dialogue in a Pluralistic Context

True dialogue, according to Thomas Hopko, "is the way of free and open debate and even conflict in religious, spiritual, and moral matters without prejudices or pressures of any sort, either psychological or social (not to speak of legal or physical), with the purpose of coming to one mind and one heart about the deepest and ultimate issues of human life and destiny."[16]

What is implied here is that dialogue is an essential element of religious life in a religiously plural context. To live to some degree in community with others requires dialogue, not isolation. "In the realms of morality, spirituality, and religion," Hopko states, "men must seek together to discover what is true, good, and workable for all. This cannot be done without conflict of ideas, experiences, and methods of

---

16. Hopko, *All the Fulness of God,* p. 157.

spiritual and moral activity and life. It cannot be done without the conviction that what is good, true, and valuable for one is so for the other and the common possession of all."[17] To act, he says, as if human persons were isolated individuals cut off from one another in self-enclosed units of thought and behavior is to violate reality itself.

The basis of such dialogue is *mutual trust* and *openness.* Trust and openness require risk-taking. In order to promote trust, I must take the risk of exposing what is near and dear to me—my hopes and fears, my strengths and weaknesses, my beliefs and attitudes. I must allow my deepest feelings and convictions to be open, and thus vulnerable, to others if I wish to have them measured and tested for their value and truth. This is the risk of living in a pluralisitic context. We cannot pretend to know and live by the truth if we are not willing to expose that truth for all to see and hear, to question and judge against "truths" that others hold dear.

How do we begin to break through mistrust? How can we cultivate the openness that is a vital component for true dialogue? One approach that has been helpful is common action, particularly action in response to a felt need. When disasters strike, people of quite varied ideologies and convictions may be observed working together in harmony. It often, unfortunately, takes a disaster for us to realize our common humanity and our ability to find unity in compassion and love for those who are in desperate need. We need to discover or create more opportunities to work and learn together, side-by-side; we need to keep alive the ecumenical work camps, the neighborhood or community projects, and any effort that breaks through barriers and enables us to meet and cooperate on a common task. Though there are some who try to oppose faith and works, establishing one or the other as a priority for unity, the ecumenical experience has shown that they belong together. Common work can foster better relationships and prepare the ground for dialogue. But dialogue itself is needed for the deepening of those relationships as we continue together the search for unity.

Relationships of trust and openness can be extremely fragile; dialogue has its pitfalls as well as its rewards. As Hopka notes: "Because of the unqualified freedom necessary for this process to go on, there exists the possibility for deviation and division, a 'missing of the mark,' a falling away and a falling apart, alienation, estrangement, disunity, decomposition. . . . It is precisely for this reason that mutual challenge and conflict are necessary with mutual questioning and criticism as well as mutual instruction, inspiration and support." But Christians, he says, are

---

17. Ibid., p. 158.

obliged to foster and defend this process, for "whatever the failures and crimes of Christians in history, the traditional Christian understanding of human beings and life is that man's task and destiny lies in a never-ending process of growth and development into an ever-more-perfect interpersonal community, which is at the same time an ever-more-perfect diversity and pluralism of spiritual insight, experience and action."[18]

In this light, a final requirement for true dialogue is *repentance.* Dialogue directed to the search for Truth, conducted in a spirit of humility and honesty, ultimately results in the necessity of repentance. The final risk in true dialogue is the recognition that we are responsible for sin, for distorting the truth, for ignoring it or refusing to accept it, or for trying to possess it as our exclusive property. Dialogue requires that we recognize the possibility that we may be wrong, that the truth may lie elsewhere, that we may have to change, or that others also share in the same truth that we hold. Not only do we have to recognize the possibility, but act upon the reality when it is revealed—hence, repentance *(metanoia),* and its corollary, forgiveness. Educating for true dialogue means that we must educate for repentance and forgiveness.

The Ecumenical Commitment

The ecumenical movement has created a pattern for dialogue, as well as for common work. It has not had any spectacular successes—no major faith groups have found their way to unity yet—but, like the "little engine that could," it keeps progressing slowly ahead and has been responsible for many church mergers within faith groups. The World Council of Churches' recent statement on *Baptism, Eucharist, Ministry,*[19] is a major step forward in the dialogue process. The establishment of the program of "Dialogues with Living Faiths and Ideologies" is an attempt at achieving a better understanding among the groups that constitute our religiously pluralistic world.

Although most major churches are ecumenically involved at the international and national or regional levels, their constituencies, for the most part, are not. In some cases, the church at the local level is even opposed to the involvement of its leaders in ecumenical study and action. There is a double educational task implied here. On the one hand, there is a great need for better communication and information *within* churches about their ecumenical participation and role in a

18. Ibid., p. 159.
19. See *Faith and Order Paper No. 111* (Geneva: World Council of Churches, 1982).

religiously pluralistic world. On the other hand, there is the need to begin the process of preparing all church members for engagement and participation in ecumenical and religiously pluralistic dialogue and action *outside* their own faith communities.

Religious education should assume a major responsibility in preparing persons and groups for such engagement and dialogue. Unfortunately today, religious education at times still reinforces our stereotypes and prejudices rather than opening up new understandings and attitudes about other groups. The reasons for this are often unintentional, resulting simply from lack of accurate information about other belief systems. There is a need for networking in the development of curricular materials, a system that would enable curriculum developers to locate writers, speakers, and other resources from within the faith groups that are to be studied; much misinformation is conveyed because the development of curricular materials often takes place without the input of those whose beliefs and practices are the subject of the study.

Beyond this brief description of the process or method by which persons and groups might engage one another more effectively in our religiously pluralistic world, it can only be stated that there are no guarantees of success. An understanding of our identity and self-worth, the search for areas of commonness, the effort to learn about and appreciate the other, and participation in true dialogue in an atmosphere of trust, openness, and repentance—all this depends ultimately upon our *will,* upon the strength of our true desire and commitment to keep trying. In a religiously pluralistic world, this is the essence of the ecumenical commitment—the *will* to search and to work toward complete and total unity, while speaking the truth in love.

8

Religious Pluralism: A Jewish Perspective

Sherry H. Blumberg
and
Eugene B. Borowitz

INTRODUCTION

Four separate meanings of pluralism impinge on the liberal Jewish educator and demand attention. One, there are many religions in the world which have truth in them. Two, there are several differing interpretations of Judaism, the religion we hold to be most true for ourselves. Three, in our own interpretation of Judaism, Reform, there are numerous views about what properly constitutes our belief and practice. And four, among religious, Jewish and Reform Jewish educators, there are significant differences of opinion with regard to the content and the method of Jewish religious education. We can best discuss these problems, we feel, by first indicating our position with regard to the last issue, educational pluralism. Indeed, by doing so we hope to be able to set an example of the approach we would take to the substantive religious issues.

We do not believe it is possible to speak to the educational (or religious) differences by offering a single theory which will statisfy everyone and resolve the problems inherent in this realm of thought. We believe that to be true because of the inherent logical difficulties with our approach to pluralism and because of the variety of human factors involved in education. As to the first, we believe that religious, in our case liberal Jewish, education is not so open as to include anything one wishes to introduce into it, yet not so closed as not to take account of the staggering variety of factors that impinge on liberal Jewish education. Hence, we wish to marry a content we cannot specify rigorously to a freedom whose limits we cannot easily define. We affirm both these impulses to be basic to our faith and educational practice, though there is considerable clash between them. These inharmonious premises render our approach essentially dialectical and dynamic rather than defined and linear. Were our faith less fluid, we should still be daunted by the numerous ways our colleagues suggest most effectively transmitting it to our people in this society at this time. And as any veteran of educational activity knows, there is no way of achieving a meaningful consensus on many long-disputed educational issues, even were we to agree on the basic purpose of education in general. Here we tend to side with those who take a generally liberal approach to education, finding this view most consistent with our belief; and yet we remain cognizant of the elements of a more conservative educational ideology that often demand our attention.

We propose to speak to the issue of pluralism in religious education from our particular point of view, recognizing that there are other points of view, seeking to be fair to them particularly when we differ with them, specifying our commitments so that readers know where we stand, all the while seeking to be open to truth others have that we may have slighted or not seen. It is this openness which, while making our educational practice seem fluid, also allows for the "living" quality of Reform, liberal Judaism.

This response to educational pluralism exemplifies our approach to pluralism generally. That is, we seek truth wherever we can find it, including that seen by those with whom we disagree. Yet, we affirm our own truth which, for all its difficulties; we seek to make plain to others, thereby respecting their dignity—part of our faith—as well as refining our own belief. The one factor we would add, were space not a consideration, is the responsibility to communicate the views of others fairly and fully as part of teaching one's own, a liberal commitment which leads us to advocate a place for comparative religion, comparative Judaism, and the varieties of liberal Jewish thought as an integral part of a satisfactory liberal Jewish education.

THE PROBLEM:
THE PARTICULAR JEWISH CONTEXT OF OUR VIEWS

At a meeting of the Religious Education Assocation in 1930, J. H. Randall asked: "Can a man entertain all ideas as provisional hypotheses

. . . and at the same time cherish in feeling and action the conviction of the prophet and saint of old? . . . Can he pour out his soul in worship of a force or an ideal he knows may be superseded tomorrow?"[1] Does the idea that in today's pluralistic world many truths exist create in the minds and hearts of human beings this dilemma when it comes to religion and, therefore, religious education. If so, how do we educate to the beauty of the particular truth without denying the others and yet not become dogmatic? This is the essence of the general problem of pluralism. We know that many of the religions will not be superseded tomorrow, that our challenge is to live with them today.

These general problems of pluralism are by now well known and need relatively little further explication. That is not true of the special factors which we, as Jews, bring to this discussion. For historic reasons, modern pluralism is not a relatively recent challenge to our community. Ever since Jews have been permitted into non-Jewish society as equals it has been the premise of our social lives and a major concern in Jewish living. The matter is so important to understanding the Jewish community that it is worthy of some elaboration.

Before the eighteenth century Jews were not allowed to be citizens in many of the lands in which they lived. In some they were confined to certain areas of the city or land, called ghettos. In others they were forced to wear marks that set them apart. Often this led to theological aversion and persecution. Only when nations became pluralistic (which stemmed from eighteenth-century social and political thought) were Jews able to become citizens. Jewish modernity is therefore based on pluralism in society. Jews found that their security and opportunity for social and economic advancement was tied up with the social-political pluralism of a society.

As Jews accepted modernity in increasing numbers since the early nineteenth century, they faced several challenges from within the community and from without. From within, Jews could not always agree on how to modernize and face the new society. A radical change in the authority/discipline of the community created questions of authenticity in the variant patterns of living Jewishly; a split with regard to the authority of Jewish law as Jews entered the world of modern scholarship added to the complexity with which Jews approached modernity. Thus various movements within the Jewish tradition developed which led to a pluralism within the community itself. As mid-twentieth-century democracy with American values such as its philosophy of individualism has spread, the differences in the Jewish community have also grown,

---

1. J. H. Randall quoted in Shelton Smith, *Faith and Nurture* (New York: Scribners Sons, 1941).

and sometimes the differences are dramatically different from each other. For the liberal Jewish community, this has led to a considerable acceptance of these differences within the Reform movement itself. The pluralism within the community manifests itself as a respect for the value of diversity.[2] Liberal Jewish life and thought has extended this openness both within and without the community.

Having become then so thoroughly involved in the general and pluralistic life of America and of Western civilization itself, there have been three pivotal experiences which have led to a greater interest today in the particular. These experiences—the Holocaust, the birth of the state of Israel, and the decline of preeminent faith in Western culture[3]—have led Jewish educators to a new stage. The new stage is how to now stress and incorporate the particular into the plural.

From the previous paragraphs one can understand why Jewish educators generally approach the problem of pluralism from a somewhat different perspective than that of many of their colleagues in the field of religious education. They are often largely concerned with how now to be open to the truths of others; that is, how to see the universal dimensions of religious truth. Most modernized Jews (not all of the community to be sure) appear to have integrated that notion into their lives, that is, at least as far as the legitimacy of Jews to living as equals among others are concerned. Thus they have integrated the idea that all people possess dignity and other religions have some truth and are entitled to some or considerable respect. In this way they have been substantially universalized. Out of our success with universalization has come its dialectic counter-problem: how in the face of our sense of widespread ultimate truth to affirm our own particular version of it, indeed the one that we take to be the most true for us? The problem, "Why, then, be Jewish?" strikes us with particular force because of our sociology and history. How to affirm our unique vision of the world, how to "choose" to live by that vision and pass it on to future generations in the pluralistic culture becomes the challenge.

Being a minority among a majority in most countries of the world is not easy. There are very strong pressures to assimilate, to be like everyone else. Reform Judaism gives the freedom to individuals to choose their level of observance. Choosing to observe customs and traditions or to hold to values which may go counter to the culture in which one lives or which may make one seem to be "peculiar" or "strange," is often

---

2. Eugene B. Borowitz, *Reform in the Process of Change* (New York: Behrman House, 1978), chapter 12.

3. Ibid., pp. 56-75.

difficult. Added to these problems is the continuing presence of anti-Semitism, even in American society. It is hard to forget that the Holocaust, the attempt to eliminate Jews from the world, occurred in an educated country where supposedly there was equality for all people. This fact makes us especially conscious of our particularity. Even the pressures placed on the state of Israel add to the demand that we recognize our identity as Jews and as citizens of other nations.

Thus for us, the particular version of the question of pluralism which we address is not: how cope with the universality of truth? but, that being taken for granted, how do you educate for that fundamental affirmation while recognizing that a higher priority in our times needs to be given to our particular faith/group? That is the special sense in which we need to talk about pluralism.

The particular situation of Jewish educators facing this challenge of pluralism can easily be generalized. It then becomes the more broad-scale philosophic problem: Must pluralism imply relativism as was suggested by J. H. Randall,[4] that one person's truth is as good as another person's? *And* is there any way of asserting one's own truth without thereby denying or denigrating the truth that might be found elsewhere. Or, in sum, does particularism necessitate intolerance? For most liberal Jewish educators, we believe, the values are clear. With wounds still aching, we know there is a cosmic, qualitative difference between Nazis and their victims; thus, for all our openness, we are far from relativistic. However, seeing the human indignities perpetrated by religious intolerance in our own community and elsewhere, we know we are committed pluralists. With our eyes to our own truth and our own survival we approach our particular version of educating for Jewish life in pluralism.

CONTENT: COMPARATIVE RELIGION, JUDAISM AND REFORM JUDAISM

In many religious schools and day schools across the country Comparative Religion is a course of study. Often in the teen years, Jewish children will learn about the major world religions by hearing guest speakers (often ministers and priests), by attending religious services in churches, and by comparing the tenets of the other faith to the Jewish ideas that they have studied up to that point. There are several texts that educators may choose to reinforce or introduce the knowledge, and

---

4. Randall, *Faith and Nurture.*

there are many additional materials available.

In most Liberal or Reform religious schools and day schools, Comparative Judaism is a common course of study. In these courses, Reform, Orthodox, Conservative, and Reconstructionist philosophy, lifestyle, traditions, and prayer are discussed and explored. Students may again have speakers; Rabbis or educators from the other movements and may visit other synagogues and temples in the community. Often exchanges between classes in one religious school and another are arranged. Implicit in this curriculum is the acknowledgement that Jews act and believe differently within their own religious tradition.

Both of these courses help teach an appreciation of others while stressing the value of what is present in the Reform Jewish expression. The books, materials, and courses are all done with such titles as *Our Religion and Our Neighbors, Four Paths to One God.*[5] Often there are active discussions about the need for such courses, even among Reform Jews, but in most schools they continue to be an important part of the curriculum.

With regard to pluralism in our own movement, Reform Judaism, we can approach our task with a certain philosophical advantage. A decade ago our Rabbi's group issued a statement about the nature of Reform Judaism which deals centrally with the problem of diversity of interpretation among us. The document states: "Reform Judaism does more than tolerate diversity: it engenders it." Understanding that our age will continue to present challenges that will be responded to very differently by different individuals, the document includes:

How we shall live with diversity without stifling dissent and without paralyzing our ability to take positive action will test our character and our principles. We stand open to any position thoughtfully and conscientiously advocated in the spirit of Reform Jewish belief. While we may differ in our interpretation and application of the ideas enunciated here, we accept such differences as precious and see them as Judaism's best hope for confronting whatever the future holds for us. Yet in all our diversity we perceive a certain unity, and we shall not allow our differences in some particulars to obscure what binds us together.[6]

---

5. Several books are in current usage including: Gilbert Rosenthal, *Four Paths to One God,* and Schwartzman and Miller, *Our Religion and Our Neighbors* (New York, UAHC).

6. Taken from the third introductory paragraph of "Reform Judaism: A Centenary Perspective," Central Conference of American Rabbis, 1975.

Living with this challenge often proves frustrating and always proves to be exciting. Educating within this framework calls forth the best that is within us.

THE LEARNER, THE TEACHER, THE SCHOOL

Obviously, the balance between differences of opinion and our sense of what we hold in common will vary with the age and, to some extent, with the social circumstances of the learners. These days even very young children grow up with a sense of the variety of people, languages, and lifestyles. If they do not learn it in their neighborhoods they will quickly get it from television—Sesame Street, for example, makes this one of its major themes. And families very quickly have to indicate that different families do things in different ways, sometimes even when people are cousins. The religious school can build on these bases to extend that sense to religion and religious understandings. Perhaps the easiest way of introducing this to the young child is allowing students to give their own interpretations of various stories and symbols. As they become accustomed to their opinions being sought and respected, even as some other ideas are old and honored, they will be learning the mix of individual and group faith which is the heart of our liberal Jewish pluralism. As children grow and become more socially oriented, the content of their comparative understanding can expand, visits being a particularly vivid way of carrying out such instruction (as was mentioned earlier in our description of the comparative religion and comparative Judaism courses).

In the teenage years, self-assertion grows, calling for increasing room for pluralism of opinion, all the while preserving the group cohesion in which it is being fostered. It thus becomes more difficult to maintain the delicate balance between accepting views yet indicating that some are more central to our tradition than others. Fortunately, with each year students also become more "philosophical," able to think abstractly, and concerned about the greater questions of life. Here, too, we encounter the idealism that wishes to reach across all bounds and to embrace all human beings in friendship. At a time when an unhealthy narcissism threatens to engulf us, it is important to our faith to foster such social concern. But with it we must deal with the realities of seeking to expand and intensify human concerns. Most families have difficulty living in love; how much more so do the problems multiply as groups expand and intensify their differences. But at this point we have reached the adult problem of pluralism, one we face all our lives.

Special attention needs to be paid to one individual who is often overlooked in this process; that is, the teacher. Surely as the learners are entitled to their points of view, so is the teacher. At some point in the discussion the teacher, too, needs to be permitted a say. And should that be somewhat different from the point of view espoused by the religious movement, or the local clergy, or the school leadership, it needs to be balanced against what the institution wishes to impart. The obvious difficulty this creates is that, by virtue of position, the teacher's views seem to come with special authority, thus effectively contradicting the prior commitment to plural understandings. To some extent, that needs to be the case. If the teacher has no special knowledge or insight to bring to the class then that teacher should not have been employed to instruct those in need of greater knowledge. The dilemmas of group and individual here again reassert themselves, and there is no rule which can assure teachers that they are respecting students even as they are respecting themselves and their traditions as they seek to teach in this open yet guided way.[7]

As the guide of all these complex processes we call education, the teacher provides instruction in a proper sense of pluralism simply by classroom management. On a deeper level, as the teacher indicates by the "management" how to keep diversity and unity in healthy tension, the learners are subliminally taught how to manage their own lives and how to participate in and guide their society. To be sure, if this is not made explicit at some point, if it does not reenforce fundamental values learned at home, if it does not find echoes in the broader social structure, if it is opposed by the thousand and one other compelling forces which strongly shape our character, then it will not come to fruition. But for schools committed to pluralism as a fundamental value, the teacher's role as exemplar is as critical as any specific curricular content.

Teachers, in turn, will take their cues from the way in which their school demonstrates administratively its own commitment to pluralism yet tradition. Does it, in fact, allow a variety of personality types and points of view to be manifested in its faculty? How does it deal with

---

7. This is a particular dilemma when a liberal religious school will employ teachers who are far more traditional. Whereas there is a desire to have these teachers impart their knowledge and become models, some teachers have used this forum to denigrate the liberal philosophy or practice. It is here that the educators, principals, and Rabbis have a special role to play in establishing the pluralistic aims of the school and communicating them both to teachers and students.

certain sensitive issues about which there is a difference of opinion in the congregation and the movement, e.g., the celebration of Christmas by Jewish families? How does it seek to provide guidance to its teachers for dealing with such issues, and what is its own sense of the limits within which the expression of individual views is tolerated or unwelcome? Does the administration encourage self-evaluation among students and faculty as well as the responsibility to the group and its evaluation of issues and problems? The social context of the school, then, its "culture," is also critically important to such instruction.

One issue of the "culture" of the school can be illustrated by the difference found in the "religious" vs. "ethnic" nature of Judaism. In this setting of critical thought and celebration of diversity, Reform Jewish education may in some situations no longer be religious education. This problem is more often a problem of the split between a religious perception of Judaism and an ethnic view, rather than one which has grown from the pluralism of the society. For many Reform congregations, Jewish education can be historical and cultural with little or no religious content. How can one define a religious educational experience in a spirit of diversity? We choose to define it by suggesting that it contain consideration of the following: 1) that ideas and experiences concerning God be presented and explored in an open fashion; 2) that a reverential attitude be expressed and hopefully developed toward the values and symbols of the religion which has nourished the people without the denigration of other ideas and symbols; and 3) that a seeking for transcendence, for a sense of the past, present, and future, and the extension beyond one's self toward God be offered as one of the aims of the content. In this way it is understood that the teacher will have to be involved in both cognitive (facts, texts, concepts, etc.) and affective (feelings and values) processes of education and model to the students that religious expression in all of its diversity involves the mind, body, spirit, and feelings of a whole human being.

Reference has already been made to the crucial role of the teacher in communicating this approach to pluralism. We believe the teacher as model is the single most important factor in communicating the dynamic approach to life we have been discussing. For a central role in the teacher's ongoing instructional activity—in every aspect of it—is to mediate between the individual learner's needs and those of the group; that is, of the other learners individually and collectively. Hence, respect for others, particularly for the individuality of others, must always be balanced against respect for self as well as for the group's need to move ahead.

CONCLUSIONS (IF THAT IS POSSIBLE)

At a recent Bar Mitzvah[8] the family chose to write its own service. Some of the work was original, and some was pulled from the prayerbook. Two of the prayers they chose demonstrated the comfort of the American Jew with being Jewish in a pluralistic society. The words of one of the readings are:

O God, the Guide and inspiration of all humanity, you have spoken in a thousand tongues for all to hear. In every land and age, we, your children have heard your voice and imagined you in our separate ways. . . . We give thanks for the sages and teachers of all peoples and faiths, who have brought many to a deeper understanding of You and Your will. Gratefully, we recall that among them were the law-givers and prophets, the psalmists and sages of Israel.[9]

The inclusion of these thoughts illustrates part of our argument. The problem of pluralism that the Reform Jewish educator faces is how to structure the educational process to answer the question of "why" be Jewish and "how to make Jewish choices in this modern world."

Judaism is not only a religion; it is also a way of life. Hence Jewish people can become involved in the "how to" of that life without concern for the "why." Good Jewish religious education asks both the "why" and "for what purpose" questions that help one to find meaning in human existence while teaching the varieties of how to live Jewishly.

For the Reform Jew, making informed and serious Jewish choices in this world is in a sense participating in the ongoing process of Revelation. Every generation has added religious insight and knowledge in the process of interpreting the ancient sacred texts for today. Reform Jewish religious education participates in the art of hermeneutics so that modern Jews may interpret and translate the texts for themselves. Helping people become newly sensitive to God through liturgy, ritual, and scholarship, or thru music, art, and social action is a way of participating in the ongoing process of revelation and in insuring the future of this tradition. Living in a pluralistic society has meant that many more

---

8. The ceremony of accepting Jewish religious responsibility for a young Jew at age thirteen. This particular one occurred in Nyack, New York, on the Shabbat before Passover, 1987.

9. Taken from the Central Conference of American Rabbis' Siddur: *Gates of Prayer* and printed in a "Service in Preparation of Passover," Temple Beth Torah, Upper Nyack, New York, April 11, 1987, for the Bar Mitzvah of Keith Firstenberg.

avenues and images are open to awaken the sensitivity, and there are many more possibilities for hermeneutic response.

What this means is an affirmation of both freedom and tradition, a recognition by choice that autonomy has its limits. In *Reform Judaism Today*,[10] Eugene Borowitz suggested that the proper criterion in every choice is, "As one who shares the Jewish people's relationship with God, what constitutes my proper response to God?"

The Jewish religious tradition and Jews have existed throughout the centuries because of the truths that human beings have found in their texts, values, and traditions. Every religion is a way of trying to understand the world and the meaning of life; each religion has attempted to explain the mystery of the world, human nature, and of God. Judaism, with its passionate relationship to One God, and its ability to awaken the adherent to the miraculous in life, to the responsibility we all have for each other, and to the best that is within us has created a religious tradition filled with beauty, variety, and depth—both intellectually and emotionally. As Reform Jewish educators and teachers model the struggle to live Jewish life to its fullest in this pluralistic society, we confront the future with faith and optimism, understanding that the dilemmas that confront us offer challenges in which to grow stronger.

---

10. Eugene B. Borowitz, *Reform Judaism Today, Volume III: How We Live* (New York: Behrman House, 1978), pp. 45-55.

9

Education in Islam

Abdullah Muhammad Khouj

INTRODUCTION

Many people living in this techno-industrial age believe that human beings created truth, that scientific understanding derived from observation of the material world is the most reliable, complete, and applicable source of knowledge, and that the resulting technology and its processes are the determinants of human success and infallibility. They also feel that the path of personal and professional success lies in the use of science as the shaper of human values and as the decisive factor establishing standards of human ethical and moral behavior.

One way to test the validity of this approach to truth or reality is to determine whether the educational materials based on it are adequate to make people aware of their personal needs and requirements for growth. We also need to assess whether this knowledge, derived exclusively from observation of the material world, can be transferred from one generation to another without distortion.

Even though philosophers and educators agree that this system of developing and transforming knowledge needed by a society can be called education, they disagree on the actual definition of education. Some consider education a science, in the sense that its rules are universally valid and can be established in categories subject to measurement. Others see education as an art, in the sense that it is based partly on

222

intuition and reflects the transcendent and immeasurable nature of the individual person.

Education is the transfer of human values in ways that beneficially influence human behavior. This transformation covers a wide range of processes ranging from the very objective (scientific) to the very subjective (personal).

Those who classify education as a science generally view science or measurement of the observable as the primary source of knowledge. Does science actually hold such an important position? If human nature is limited and fallible, how can science, a product of human effort, be the ulitmate source of truth? If persons exclude guidance from the Divine Creator of all reality from their thinking, and claim themselves to be the judge of what is objective, then are not their conclusions necessarily the ultimate in subjectivity? If science is the elixir of humankind, why are we facing numerous daily problems such as interpersonal conflicts, socio-economic crises, and incurable diseases? Although many social scientists have properly applied the scientific method to their respective fields, they have been unable to solve many emotional and social conflicts.

On the other hand, if education is classified as an art, how can we generalize the results of this art? Art is based on personal experience and subjective understanding. Even though most artists are trained in a scientific manner, the application of their art is personal.

Education includes both objective and subjective methods. Objective methods can be valid for specific learning behaviors in certain learning environments, such as the effect of peer competition on academic achievement among students. Subjective methods can be used to understand human values, but objective methods can also be used to promote comprehension of human values so long as the structure of the values is not destroyed.

Objective and subjective methods can both be effective sources of truth or knowledge, especially when they complement each other. But still another source of knowledge is needed to guide these two sources of knowledge. This is the objectivity that is external to humankind because it comes from the Creator, who understands human nature and psychology better than human beings can ever understand themselves.

The meaning and definition of education derived from this source becomes clear when we study the educational system in Islam and show how this system deals with the human being from the cradle to the grave and how it covers all aspects of his life. The elements of this system emphasize certain guidelines to direct the individual's search for knowledge and to bring about the desired behavior.

The educational system of Islam derives from the Qur'an, the Muslim's revealed scripture; the Hadith (Traditions) illustrating its meaning; and scholarly analysis. The Qur'an, the primary source of beneficial knowledge, cannot be compared to a chemistry book or educational manual. It is a divinely revealed guidebook encouraging persons to study and ponder everything around them. The Traditions of the Prophet Muhammad (pbuh),[1] as the practical explanation and application of this Divine Knowledge, demonstrates the Prophet's practice in reinforcing certain behaviors and in deterring undesirable conduct.

A third source of Islamic knowledge is human intellectual effort *(ijtihad),* an effort to develop solutions for those existing problems and concerns that have no clear resolution in the Qur'an or Traditions. *Ijtihad* is divided into *qiyas* (analogy) and *ijma'* (consensus). The whole field of *ijtihad,* based on a profound knowledge of the Qur'an and Traditions, is the Islamic contribution to education in a pluralistic society.[2]

Many people ask whether the Qur'an, which was revealed approximately 1400 years ago, and the Traditions of the Prophet (pbuh) are still applicable to modern life. To answer this question, we have to examine how the basic foundation of Islam influences its whole ideative and educational system.

This essay offers a conceptual framework of education in Islam as presented in the Qur'an and the Traditions of the Prophet Muhammad (pbuh). Although this essay does not address certain philosophical arguments, it does present the educational system of Islam and characterizes the knowledge that is the basic directive for human endeavor. The elements of this system—purpose, objectives, characteristics, and methods—were clearly stated in the Revelation of the Holy Qur'an.

THE PURPOSE OF EDUCATION IN ISLAM

The overall purpose of education in Islam is derived from the ultimate source of reality, Allah, who says in the Qur'an:

Exalt not, for Allah loveth not those who exalt (in riches). But seek, with the (wealth) which Allah has bestowed on thee, the Home of the

---

1. Pbuh is an abbreviation for "peace be upon him," an expression used after either saying or writing the Prophet Muhammad's name.

2. See Fazlur Rahman, *Islam* (Greenwich, Conn.: Holt, Rinehart, and Winston, 1966; New York: Doubleday Anchor Books, 1968); and Said Ramadan, *Islamic Law: Its Scope and Equity* (London: Macmillan, 1961; 2nd ed., 1970).

Hereafter, nor forget thy portion in this world: but do thou good, as Allah has been good to thee, and seek not (occasions for) mischief in the land: For Allah loves not those who do mischief. (28:76-77)

These verses explain the major principles of teaching human beings how to live properly as members of society and how to benefit from this worldly life while living in remembrance of the hereafter.

This purpose has several objectives. Each objective is a spoke on the wheel of belief. The cement holding the different spokes together is belief in Allah. The outer rim of the wheel is the application of this belief in all one's actions.

The first objective is to make human beings aware of their Creator, Allah. When the individuals have this awareness, they can establish a relationship with Allah. Allah states:

Not an apostle did We send before thee without this inspiration sent by Us to him: that there is no god but I; therefore worship and serve Me. (21:25)

This relationship originates in the individual's submission to Allah, which is possible because our knowledge of Allah allows us to know what he has ordered to our benefit. One product of this submission is the unity of belief.

The second objective, a natural result of the first, is to create a balanced and integrated personality by making human behavior congruent with belief. Believing in Allah is not sufficient if not coupled with acts demonstrating and reflecting this belief. A person's acts must reflect his belief. If persons want to have integrated personalities they must submit to Allah. This submission entails one's beliefs; that is, behavior must be congruent with belief, as Allah explains:

But those will prosper who purify themselves, and glorify the name of their Guardian-Lord, and (lift their hearts) in prayer. Nay (behold), ye prefer the life in this world. (87:14-16)

Unity of belief on both a personal and social level brings about an integrated personality, a unified family, and a harmonious society. Since the family and the society are made up of individuals, the harmony of these two units depends on the integration of the human personality. If every family member has a balanced personality, the family unit as a whole can be integrated. Similarly, when all the families espouse the same beliefs and are integrated, the society functions well because it is united in belief. This process of unification, however, is not mechanical, but involves individual free will and conviction. Allah gave the human being the desire to be integrated and unified. The individual achieving this integration feels satisfied and comfortable with his situation.

To teach the individual to accept and deal with reality as a normal part of this temporal life is the third objective of education in Islam. Persons who have submitted to their Creator realize their own mortality. Because they are realistic, they know how to adapt in a positive way to their environment and to make maximum use of their intellectual abilities. Allah explains how individuals can better themselves through intelligent use of the environment:

And Allah has made the earth for you as a carpet (spread out), that ye may go about therein, in spacious roads. (71:19-20)

It was We Who taught him the making of coats of mail for your benefit, to guard you from each other's violence: Will ye then be grateful? (21:80)

The fourth objective is to show individuals how to become emotionally balanced by fulfilling their needs for relatedness, belonging, and rootedness.[3] Allah created the human being with a need for companionship. The human being overcomes insecurity through having healthy interpersonal relationships out of which develop emotional readiness and shared experiences. Allah states:

It is He Who has created man from water: Then has He established relationships of lineage and marriage: for thy Lord has power (over all things). (25:54)

And among His Signs is this, that He created for you mates from among yourselves, that ye may dwell in tranquility with them, and He has put love and mercy between your (hearts): Verily in that are Signs for those who reflect. (30:21)

The fifth objective, a product of the fourth, is to imbue the individual with a belief in both the unity of mankind and the equality of all people. Allah revealed:

And verily this brotherhood of yours is a single brotherhood, and I am your Lord and Cherisher: therefore fear Me (and no other). (23:52)

---

3. Eric Fromm discussed these concepts in his book entitled *Man for Himself* (Greenwich, Conn.: Holt, Rinehart, and Winston, 1947).

So, after having fulfilled their needs for relatedness, belonging, and rootedness, individuals are ready to advance to a higher stage of humankind. Knowing human nature, Allah shows individuals that the unity of humankind is an important prerequisite for the creation of a harmonious and just society reflecting peace and stability. This peaceful and stable state spawns a belief in the equality of all people in the presence of Allah.

The sixth objective, the stage uniting all the various objectives, is to create a society based on the Islamic creed and Islamic legislation. To maintain the other five objectives, Allah ordered Muslims to preserve Islamic principles. By propagating the Islamic creed, they can set up an egalitarian society founded on belief in one God.

The focus of these objectives is to prepare every individual to be a good human being, and not just a good citizen. Good characteristics as defined in secular terms vary from one society to another. A good citizen is restricted by geographical and political boundaries.[4] The characteristics of the good citizen in a nation are to a certain extent dependent upon the ideals of that particular nation. The concept of a "good citizen" in the non-Islamic environment is entirely contingent upon the philosophies of that distinct society. For example, one institution might consider the person who is successful in human relations and business to be a good citizen. Another nation or institution might say that the obedient person is a good citizen. Because individuals are dedicated patriots, even if they are unsuccessful in business, they may be perceived as good citizens.

As stated in the Qur'an, the characteristics of a good person are the same as those of a good Muslim. Therefore the concern of education in Islam is to prepare a "good human being," not merely a "good citizen." Furthermore, the educational system in Islam goes beyond developing personal characteristics. This system tries to pursue the more comprehensive objectives of teaching individuals how to live in harmony with their Creator, their fellowmen, other creatures, and nature. It illustrates the purpose of human existence and the terms of interpersonal relationships and clarifies varying kinds of human relationships. The objectives of this system directly influence the different relationships a human being has during a lifetime.

A. The Human's Relationship with Allah

In Islam the individual is taught that Allah, the center of all existence, is unique and self-sustained. He is the first and the last. Nothing resem-

---

4. Mohammad Qutb, *Minhaj Al-Tarbiah Al-Islamiyyah,* 2nd ed. (Dar Damashq).

bles him. Although everything needs him, he does not need anything. He is the only ONE. For this reason, man must worship Allah and follow the divine message. Allah says:

> I have only created jinns and men that they may worship Me. (51:56)

Humans were created so that they could worship him and establish faith in him; i.e., humans were made to serve, know, and love their Creator. Both faith and worship are based on openness to Allah, and from him will come an openness to everything he has created as well as stability and inner harmony. The closeness to the Creator is determined by the amount of faith a believer has in him. A strong faith emanates from an intimate relationship just as weak faith results in the separation of an individual from Allah and from other people. Allah states:

> Only those are believers who have believed in Allah and His Apostle, and have never since doubted, but have striven with their belonging and their persons in the Cause of Allah: such are the sincere ones. (49:15)

Allah gives human beings ways to become closer to him and through this intimacy to develop integrated and unified personalities. This is evident in the pillars of Islam, which are inestimable tools causing all persons to remember their Creator and thereby to change themselves as a necessary first step toward changing the world.

Allah teaches that this type of intimate relationship should be the exemplum to establish other kinds of relationships. The belief in Allah determines one's progress in these other relationships. Having a close relationship with the Creator enables individuals to understand the purpose of their existence, to know the right path (Allah's Laws) in dealing with others, and to respect all people. In so doing, every interaction individuals have will reflect their "fear" or "love" of Allah.

B. The Human's Relationship with Self

Individuals believing in Allah as the Creator and Sustainer of everything usually respect themselves and others, accept and try to overcome their weaknesses, acknowledge their strengths, and use their positive attributes in a beneficial way. Persons who fear Allah in their hearts are by definition honest persons: they are honest with themselves and with others. The key to being an honest person is acceptance. The honest person accepts the good with the bad, knowing that the ultimate source of both is Allah, and only Allah knows what for each person is truly good.

If some good befalls them, they say, "This is from Allah"; But if evil, they say, "This is from thee" (O Prophet). Say: "All things are from Allah." (4:78)

In trying to be honest, individuals must accept their limited abilities, recognize their shortcomings, and develop their strengths. Once individuals have accomplished this, they can face criticism, welcome the sincere advice of others, examine the validity of this advice, and determine whether it corresponds to the Qur'an and the Prophet's Traditions.

Acceptance also means to have an open mind and to be open with others, accepting what is in agreement with human nature and rejecting what is in conflict with it. In Islam, people must be taught the positive attributes advocated in Islam, including honesty and acceptance of reality. This must be stressed from the beginning of childhood, so that the child can be corrected and taught to be honest.

C. Interpersonal Relationships

In Islam the relationships between two persons should be based on a common brotherhood of faith. This brotherhood is expressed in certain positive attributes, e.g., respect, honesty, modesty, kindness, and patience. Each individual should respect other human beings. He or she should not judge others on the basis of their position and/or socio-economic status.

Allah is the only one who can judge a person for what he or she says. Therefore, one need not burden oneself with accepting viewpoints that contradict Islamic principles. For example, in addressing someone who has a different point of view, Muslims should be neither offensive nor nasty but should instead be open-minded enough to discuss and illustrate their beliefs.

The Muslim should be honest and sincere in his interpersonal relationships. Although judgment is reserved for Allah, an individual can offer constructive criticism when necessary. As the Prophet Muhammad (pbuh) said, human relationships must be based on Islamic principles, as illustrated in the following Tradition:

The believer is a mirror to his brother. (Hadith)

In fact, everyone must try to help others overcome obstacles and harmful habits. The Prophet Muhammad (pbuh) has stated:

"Religion is sincerity." We asked, "To whom?" He said, "To Allah and His Book and His Messenger and to the leaders of the Muslims and to the common folk." (Sahih Muslim)

When giving advice, Muslims should not exaggerate their own importance. Muslims should be kind to others. Kindness, which entails helpfulness, should be granted regardless of ethno-racial background or nationality. All people should overcome their egocentrism by considering the needs and desires of others. The Prophet (pbuh) addressed this topic when he said:

> None of you truly believes till he wants for his brother what he wants for himself. (Muslim)

To acquire such attributes as respect, honesty, modesty, and kindness, an individual needs patience. Throughout the Qur'an Allah tells the believers to have patience—one of the most important characteristics to be found in human nature.

D. The Individual and Society

In addition to its spiritual function, the educational system in Islam promotes certain socio-economic values. Even though individuals have the right to satisfy their own needs, they must not achieve this while injuring others or society. Honesty requires respect for the society in which one lives. The systems of belief and of worship in Islam require that the individual assimilate their underlying principles. As a result of this assimilation, individuals integrate the principles and make them part of their behavior. The person achieving this integration understands that all people, including those from different ethno-racial backgrounds and socio-economic strata, have feelings, thoughts, and emotions.

The pillars of the faith exemplify the socio-economic values of this educational system. When individuals pray, give *zakat* (poor due), fast, or go on the *hajj* (pilgrimage), they learn to respect society and its members.

Zakat is the poor due that the Muslim is obliged to give to support indigent people. When an individual senses that others need help, he or she has the opportunity through the institution of *zakat* to aid these people, without having to make it public. This institution creates a good feeling between the two participants—the benefactor and the recipient. Benefactors overcome their greed and temper their desire to accumulate material goods.

As a result of giving something that they own to people who are neither their relatives nor their friends, the benefactors learn self-control, respect for others, and an appreciation for what Allah has given them. In turn, the poor individuals receiving the assistance are neither denigrated not insulted; their dignity is not taken away from them. They are not forced to feel inferior or passive. From receiving *zakat,* the poor individual can realize that some people do care about their welfare. This reciprocal relationship effects a mutual understanding between the haves and the have-nots and a good feeling between the giver and the receiver.

The result of these processes is a united and just society whose members have a sense of belonging and worth. These members feel that they can play a positive role in the advancement and progress of their society. Consequently, they learn the meaning of human unity. As active members of the society, they can fulfill their needs for belonging in acceptable ways.

E. The Individual and the Environment

Since the relationship between human beings and nature is very important in Islam, it is defined in the Qur'an. In general, the relationship of persons to their environments falls into two categories, the first being the use of the environment for profitable gains. The second category is the contemplation of the cosmos and its components. Allah created plants and animals as a merciful act benefiting humans. They can use plants and animals to satisfy their need for food, clothing, shelter, and visual stimulation. They, however, must treat animals and nature respectfully and try not to mistreat them. They should not kill animals for the sake of sport. They should kill an animal only for food or when it is threatening human life. Even when they lawfully have the right to kill an animal, they must perform this act mercifully. The Prophet Muhammad (pbuh) explained this when he said:

Verily Allah has prescribed proficiency in all things. Thus if you kill, kill well; and if you slaughter, slaughter well. Let each one of you sharpen his blade and let him spare from suffering the animals he slaughters. (Muslim)

The Prophet's perspective is derived from the Qur'anic belief that, because of their senses, mental abilities, and perceptions, humans hold the highest position in the scale of created beings. Those humans not using their minds are placed at the lowest level in this scale, as Allah says:

For the worst of beasts in the sight of Allah are the deaf and dumb—those who understand not. (8:22)

On the other hand, those employing their mental abilities to please Allah, the Omnipotent Creator, are the vicegerents of the earth. By attaining their goals, they benefit from their surroundings and thereby make their lives more comfortable.

It is He Who hath made you (His) agents, inheritors of the earth: He hath raised you in ranks, some above others: that He may try you in the gifts He hath given you: For thy Lord is quick in punishment: yet He is indeed Oft-forgiving, Most Merciful. (6:165)

In summation, these relationships are only useful and healthy if they are founded on beneficial knowledge. Thus individuals must use this type of knowledge in their search for truth and justice.

BENEFICIAL KNOWLEDGE

Humans have the ability to know, to think, to plan, and to predict. The person without proper knowledge can neither function properly nor reach the highest stage of humanity. For this reason, only those striving to gain knowledge will reach this highest stage of existence. This is why Allah made a distinction between those who know and those who do not know. Allah says that the person deserving a reward is the one who has sound and solid evidence.

Say: "Are those equal, those who know and those who do not know? It is those who are endued with understanding that receive admonition." (39:9)

To help the human being achieve this goal, Allah gives guidance and directives on how to use these mental abilities. In many Qur'anic passages, Allah exhorts persons to understand through intellectual investigation the secrets of this universe.

Therefore, divine knowledge can be employed to establish principles and regulations for dealing with the other sources of knowledge and for further research, intellectual advancement, human happiness, and progress. Consequently, the person with divine guidance can regulate the other sources of knowledge and follow the correct path by applying beneficial knowledge. In this way, persons can enlarge their scope of understanding and broaden their awareness, thereby improving themselves and the society in which they live. Allah illustrates the importance of using the senses to seek and apply knowledge. In the Qur'an Allah shows the connection between gaining knowledge and applying knowledge.

Read! In the name of thy Lord and Cherisher, Who created—created man, out of a (mere) clot of congealed blood: Read! And thy Lord is Most Bountiful—He Who taught (the use of) the pen—taught man that which he knew not. (96:1-5)

Allah urges human beings to explore all sources of beneficial knowledge, i.e., those congruent with Islamic principles.

Say: "Behold all that is in the heavens and on earth"; but neither signs nor warners profit those who believe not. (10:101)

This search for knowledge is endless. According to the Prophet (pbuh), there are two people who will always want more: the one coveting money and the one seeking knowledge. The foundation of all knowledge in Islam is divine guidance.

These are verses of the Wise Book—a guide and a mercy to the doers of good. (31:2-3)

Allah tells humans that faith blossoms from knowledge.

And those who believe in Allah and His apostles—they are the sincere (lovers of truth), and the witnesses (who testify), in the eyes of their Lord: They shall have their reward and their light. But those who reject Allah and deny Our Signs—they are the companions of the hell-fire. (57:19)

Thus worship originates from an understanding of the Qur'an and the Traditions of the Prophet (pbuh). Allah loves worship rooted in divine knowledge. The Prophet (pbuh) said:

The example of guidance and knowledge with which Allah has sent me is like abundant rain falling on the earth, some of which was fertile soil that absorbed rain water bringing forth vegetation and grass in abundance. Another portion of it was hard and held the rain water and Allah benefited the people with it and they utilized it for drinks, making their animals drink from it and for irrigation of the land for cultivation. A portion of it was barren which could neither hold water nor bring forth vegetation (then that land could not render any benefits). The first is the example of the person who comprehends Allah's religion and gets benefits (from the knowledge) which Allah has revealed through me, learns, and teaches others. The last example is that of the person who does not take care of it and does not take Allah's guidance revealed through me. (Bukhari)

To benefit from all sources of knowledge, a person needs divine guidance. Insightful people, those having this guidance, can solve their problems and undauntedly deal with everything in their environment. They have patience, are dedicated, espouse strong principles and values, and accept divinely given regulations. They understand that the key to living a constructive life is to please Allah.

But those who had been granted (true) knowledge said: "Alas for you! The reward of Allah (in the Hereafter) is best for those who believe and work righteousness: but this none shall attain, save those who steadfastly persevere (in good)." (28:80)

As mentioned above, useful knowledge comes from the Creator in the form of principles and regulations. These principles and regulations help human beings understand themselves, their purpose of existence, their relationship to others, and their environment. Therefore, beneficial knowledge offers general guidance and is the root of all other sources of information, because it springs from the unity of belief, a sound legislative system, and moral codes. These three foundations of divine knowledge help humans to seek, understand, and apply truth.

Allah identifies the privileges that he has bestowed on knowledgeable people.

Allah will raise up, to (suitable) ranks (and degrees), those of you who believe and who have been granted knowledge. And Allah is well-acquainted with all ye do. (58:11)

We raise to degrees (of wisdom) whom We please: but over all endued with knowledge is One, the All-knowing. (12:76)

Those correctly applying Allah's principles in their professional and personal lives will receive admonition. Scientists or physicians who acquire this kind of knowledge and apply it in their professions will realize their weaknesses in front of their Creator. They will act modestly, rectify their own beliefs, and educate themselves and others.

Muslims, whether scholars or lay persons, should not be arrogant and overly impressed with their own intelligence. Persons asserting that their knowledge is superior cannot accept criticism because they are living in a state of delusion and false security. On the other hand, persons realizing that their knowledge is limited should petition Allah:

"O my Lord! advance me in knowledge." (20:114)

What is the value of the immoral scientist or the worth of the unrighteous physician? How should we view the brilliant mathematician who invents an instrument whose primary function is to destroy other human beings and living creatures? The individual contemplating these questions can see that divine knowledge instructs and guides man and enlightens the human mind.

Thus, according to Islamic principles, any knowledge, whether theoretical or applied, that meets certain criteria can be considered beneficial. Beneficial knowledge should be used to please Allah and therefore should not be employed to satisfy egotistical desires. It should contribute to the understanding and application of Allah's rules and regulations. This knowledge should lead to the search for new ways of realizing Allah's powers and of improving human life.

The Prophet Muhammad (pbuh) said that the search for knowledge is an extremely significant act of worship and that the acquisition of beneficial knowledge is an honorable task.

If Allah wants to benefit a person, He opens his comprehension of religion and, of course, knowledge is attained through learning. Whoever follows a course to attain knowledge, Allah will ease his way into Paradise. (Bukhari)

The Prophet (pbuh) facilitated the acquisition of knowledge for both men and women:

Some women requested the Prophet (pbuh) to fix a day for them as the men were taking all his time. In response he promised them one day for (the transmission of) religious instruction and injunctions. (Bukhari)

Persons having beneficial knowledge can improve their lives and take their rightful places as vicegerents of the earth, a position reflecting the human being's status as the highest of the created beings. Beneficial knowledge can be used to better the human condition. The human being's use of iron to improve life illustrates this point. Throughout human history, people have used iron to make suitable items.

We sent aforetime our apostles with Clear Signs and sent down with them the Book and the balance (of right and wrong), that men may stand forth in justice; and We sent down iron, in which is (material for) mighty war, as well as many benefits for mankind, that Allah may test who it is that will help, unseen, Him and His apostles: For Allah is Full of Strength, Exalted in Might (and able to enforce His Will). (57:25)

In Islam, knowledge is the vehicle humans use to gain status and authority. It gives them a sense of responsibility and makes them realize their rights and duties. The more status individuals have, the more responsible they become.

There is no God but He: that is the witness of Allah, His angels, and those endued with knowledge, standing firm on justice. There is no god but He, the Exalted in Power, the Wise. (3:18)

Implementing this knowledge can be achieved through four basic principles. The first principle is that individuals should reject any information not supported by sound evidence; that is, any knowledge incongruent with divine knowledge is unacceptable. Individuals must seek truth and have the evidence to support every statement. If individuals do this, they are better equipped to accept and apply the second principle, that of truthfulness, to their worldly lives and to the other life.

And they say: "None shall enter Paradise unless he be a Jew or a Christian." Those are their (vain) desires. Say: "Produce your proof if ye are truthful." Nay—whoever submits his whole self to Allah and is a doer of good—he will get reward with his Lord; on such shall be no fear, nor shall they grieve. (2:111-12)

The second principle is truthfulness, of which one component is the rejection of false information. Truthful individuals are honest with themselves and others. Because they have a clear perception of their own worth, they are not afraid to accept their weaknesses and strengths. Since they believe in the worth of human life, they seek justice and spread love and kindness. Their realistic attitude becomes the impetus enabling them to achieve all their potentials. These individuals knowing the truth must reveal it in a kind and honest manner. They are also obliged to make only true comments. When persons make conjectures based on false evidence, they reveal their false imaginations and distorted perceptions of reality. In turn, their beliefs are erroneous because of their false perceptions of reality. Since truthfulness is so important and is derived from the unity of belief, people should use their sound intellect to ascertain whether something is true or false. Allah says:

No son did Allah beget, nor is there any god along with Him: (If there were many gods), behold, each god would have taken away what he had created, and some would have lorded it over others! Glory to Allah! (He is free) from the (sort of) things they attribute to Him! (23:91)

The third principle is to know of the danger of blind imitation. Allah says:

Wert thou to follow the common run of those on earth, they will lead thee away from the Way of Allah. They follow nothing but conjecture: they do nothing but lie. (6:116)

And they say: "What is there but our life in this world? We shall live and die, and nothing but time can destroy us." But of that they have no knowledge: they merely conjecture. And when Our Clear Signs are rehearsed to them, their argument is nothing but this: they say, "Bring (back) our forefathers, if what ye say is true!" (45:24-25)

And pursue not that of which thou hast no knowledge; for every act of hearing or of seeing or of (feeling in) the heart will be inquired into (on the Day of Reckoning). (17:36)

Regardless of their intellectual ability, persons should not blindly accept every piece of information given to them, for blind obedience inhibits growth and development. Those who blindly imitate other human beings are victims of ignorance. Even intelligent persons, accepting fallacious comments, are impeded in their own development. Illiteracy, however, is not ignorance. Ignorant persons, the ones not espousing any moral principles or values, do whatever they desire and refuse to accept responsibility and sound judgment. Their minds are consumed with useless information.

Two negative effects of ignorance are the ruination of the individual and the destruction of society. Allah described those people belonging to the nation of Moses (pbuh) as narrow-minded and controlled by their materialistic desires.

So he went forth among His people in the (pride of his worldly) glitter. Said those whose aim is the life of this world: "Oh! that we had the like of what Qarun has got! For he is truly a lord of mighty good fortune!" (28:79)

If these people had acquired beneficial knowledge, they would have realized that material wealth can be detrimental. True wealth comes from Allah on the Day of Judgment. Worldly possessions are not true symbols of an individual's prosperity, but can be a mirage of false security.

As stated in the Qur'an, those blessed with teaching ability are obliged to instruct and guide other people. As the Prophet (pbuh) explained, scholars, the inheritors of the prophets, must teach proper beliefs and impart beneficial knowledge. Allah states:

Nor should the believers all go forth together: If a contingent from every expedition remained behind, they could devote themselves to studies in religion, and admonish the people when they return to them—that thus they (may learn) to guard themselves (against evil). (9:122)

The Prophet Muhammad (pbuh) felt there should be a reciprocal relationship between scholars and other people. He stated that those who know should teach those who do not.

He who has learned certain knowledge, keeps this knowledge a secret, and does not teach it to others, Allah will put a muzzle on his mouth on the Day of Judgment.

Those in need of knowledge should try to learn from righteous scholars. They should not hesitate to ask questions and to travel to get answers. Even the most honored people, such as Allah's Prophets (pbut), traveled in pursuit of beneficial knowledge.

High above all is Allah, the King, the Truth! Be not in haste with the Qur'an before its revelation to thee is completed, but say, "O my Lord! advance me in knowledge." (20:114)

For example, when the Prophet Moses (pbuh) heard about a knowledgeable man, he visited this wise man in the hope of gaining beneficial knowledge.

Moses said to him: "May I follow thee, on the footing that thou teach me something of the (higher) truth which thou hast been taught?"

(The other said): "Verily thou wilt not be able to have patience with me! And how canst thou have patience about things about which thy understanding is not complete?" Moses said: "Thou wilt find me, if Allah so wills, (truly) patient: nor shall I disobey thee in aught." (18:66-69)

The fourth principle is that persons searching for beneficial information should be open-minded. They should not be myopic and limited to one viewpoint. Their opinions should not be derived from a false source or from a bad experience. Their judgments should not be restricted to one philosophy or a single method of research. Allah says:

Those who listen to the Word, and follow the best (meaning) in it: Those are the ones whom Allah has guided, and those are the ones endued with understanding. (39:18)

Allah ordered Muslims to screen and review all information they receive. Their judgments should not be prejudiced. They must understand and test all information, using divine principles as the ultimate measurement of what is good and useful and what is bad and harmful.

To sum up, guidance from divine knowledge determines which sources of knowledge are useful and which are harmful. By having divine guidance, scholars in all fields can enrich their lives and orient their academic fields of inquiry. Scholars enriched in this way are not motivated by the desire for material wealth or prestigious positions. Their true wish is to maximize their potentials, while recognizing their weaknesses and shortcomings.

Given its importance, beneficial knowledge should be a primary part of any educational curriculum, whether formal or informal. Both children and adults need this guidance. Although Muslims should try to learn from every experience, they must understand that scientific knowledge is only one source of knowledge, not the ultimate key to human understanding. Humans should use beneficial knowledge as their primary source of information on almost every topic and in all their relationships.

CHARACTERISTICS

This whole constellation of various elements—purpose, objectives, and beneficial knowledge—gives the educational system in Islam certain characteristics. Above all it is:

1. Comprehensive and universal
2. Balanced and harmonious
3. Realistic
4. Continual
5. Unique

A. Comprehensiveness and Universality

As demonstrated above, because the educational system in Islam agrees with human nature, it deals with every dimension of human life by placing equal stress on the physical, mental, emotional, social, and spiritual aspects of the human personality. It addresses every stage of human growth, promotes healthy human development, and helps individuals to adapt in a positive manner in their immediate societies. Within this educational system individuals acquire traits that help them conform constructively to societies other than that in which they were raised. In this sense, this system is applicable to all human beings and all societies. It is not limited to any historical period or geographical area.

B. Balance

By being comprehensive, the educational system in Islam develops each aspect of an individual's life in a balanced manner. In Islam, the human personality is a potent inner power that must be developed in a manner that will produce a useful and righteous member of society. Neither passivity nor extreme dominance are beneficial and serviceable to society. For this reason, those educated in this system learn how to reach the golden mean through balancing their spiritual and material needs. They learn that neglecting their material needs to fulfill their spiritual ones or visa versa is detrimental to their welfare. One aspect of the human personality is not realized at the expense of the others. Several Muslim scholars have said: "Act in this life as if you will live forever and do for the Hereafter as if you will die tomorrow."

When individuals satisfy their desires to the point that they discount their other needs, they develop unintegrated personalities and maladjusted behaviors. The end result is an unhappy individual. Many of these unhappy individuals were educated in systems that stressed the importance of materialism over spiritual development. Many educators teaching in these systems imbue their students with the desire for material success and do not care about the means the students use to achieve their goals. Having learned to devalue morality, these students accept unethical means as legitimate ways to attain their goals.

To illustrate, a student might have the moral desire to become a good doctor. In pursuit of this goal, he or she may attend an accredited university whose instructors believe that material success is more important than human life. Consequently, the student becomes selfishly competitive and egocentric. This negligence of ethics and morality may cause the student to gain success by hurting others (whether at the personal or group level). Because of this attitude, nothing, whether material or spiritual, will prevent achievement of the goal of success. This unbalanced individual may want to reject totally his or her spiritual needs in order to satiate the physical and material ends.

Individuals satisfying their spiritual needs while totally neglecting their material ones also will develop personalities conflicting with their own natures. Having this unrealistic attitude, they may become so absorbed in their religion that they neglect their material and physical pleasures. They may regard their own sexual desires as sinful, the result of which is a denial of reality. This denial causes an inner conflict between their bodily satisfaction and their spiritual fulfillment. They may become so passive that they merely exist instead of live. This behavior contrasts with the balanced personality advocated in Islam. Allah says:

> But seek, with the (wealth) which Allah has bestowed on thee, the Home of the Hereafter, nor forget thy portion in this world: but do thou good, as Allah has been good to thee, and seek not (occasions for) mischief in the land: For Allah loves not those who do mischief. (28:77)

C. Realism

In Islam, a balanced personality is a necessary requisite for having a true perception of reality. When individuals are cognizant of their own shortcomings and weaknesses, they understand their reason for existence and accept their lives. Because they distinguish between right and wrong, they constructively deal with reality and do not withdraw from it. For example, they do not use destructive substances to find fake happiness.

They willingly try to learn from those with good qualities (observation learning), choosing to examine themselves before criticizing others. Their judgments are not based on false reality, but are appropriate responses to given circumstances. Aware of both positive and negative external forces, they will not succumb to destructive influences. Individuals having self-awareness can distinguish between erroneous assumptions and true reality.

Only when they have a realistic outlook and self-awareness can individuals readily accept responsibility and hardships. From an Islamic point of view, responsibility is a natural human characteristic. These two Qur'anic verses demonstrate the emphasis placed on responsibility:

Do ye enjoin right conduct on the people, and forget (to practice it) yourselves, and yet ye study the Scripture? Will ye not understand? (2:44).

We did indeed offer the trust to the heavens and the earth and the mountains; but they refused to undertake it, being afraid thereof: But man undertook it—He was indeed unjust and foolish. (33:72)

Trust is a part of responsibility. As evinced in the Qur'an, trust means the ability to use all one's senses, emotions, and cognitive abilities to handle responsibilities. Responsible persons accept all assigned rights and duties, behave in a righteous manner, and respond to stimuli in a virtuous way. They carefully examine themselves and everything in this world. They are not afraid to evaluate their own behavior in light of ideal values. Their behavior and worldview reflect their awareness. Because they have this awareness, they do not transgress the normal boundaries of humanity as explained in the Qur'an. Staying within normal boundaries requires understanding and dealing with others from the perspective of one's own values and moral code. Hence, if persons base their lives on divinely given values, they can select the proper methods and means to satisfy their needs in a way that is congruent with their natures. Instead of becoming entrapped by their problems, balanced individuals try to find the most logical solutions to their difficulties.

In several Qur'anic verses, Allah says that humans have the ability to acquire, increase, and impart knowledge. For example, Allah states:

And He taught Adam the nature of all things; then He placed them before the angels, and said: "Tell Me the nature of these if ye are right." (2:31)

High above all is Allah, the King, the Truth! Be not in haste with the Qur'an before its revelation to thee is completed, but say, "O my Lord! advance me in knowledge." (20:114)

To recap, responsible individuals control their lives and deal with situations in a realistic manner. Poor persons accepting their plight as Allah's will and deciding to work hard to improve their lives is an illustration of such individuals. Instead of daydreaming or using illegal means to acquire material possessions, they make maximum use of their abilities.

D. Continual Guidance

Forgetfulness is a human trait. In Islam, the human being is viewed as a unique being having a distinct nature. Hence, the educational system in Islam provides human beings with a suitable system that agrees with their nature in two ways. First, this system continually educates humans so as to make them receptive to other people's opinions and guidance. Second, this system provides the means for receiving social reinforcement through group influence (socialization). This reinforcement must be rooted in divine guidance, without which human society would be chaotic and destructive.

Concerning personal guidance, Allah gave humans a well-integrated system of worship through which they receive continual guidance throughout their lives. The five pillars of Islam (profession of faith, prayer, fasting, poor due, and pilgrimage) illustrate this continual guidance.

Prayer has many purposes, some of which are: cleanliness, discipline, social integration, unity of belief, and submission to Allah. When individuals pray on a regular basis, they learn to organize their time, to fulfill their spiritual needs, and to eliminate their prejudices. Men, poor and rich, young and old, educated and uneducated, stand in lines to pray together. Similarly women from all different backgrounds pray together in lines. This spatial arrangement reflects the egalitarian nature of Islam.

A healthy relationship among the members of society is established through a continual system of education. *Zakat* is a good example of this harmony. By giving *zakat*, individuals overcome their greed and egocentricity. Because the institution of *zakat* creates an atmosphere that reinforces a healthy relationship among the various members of the society, a communal harmony is created. The giver of this *zakat* does not feel superior, nor does the receiver feel inferior. The haves and the have-nots can develop an intimate and friendly relationship.

During the month of Ramadan, every Muslim should make the commitment to better his or her life by submitting to Allah. The abstainer gets many rewards, such as learning self-control and how to develop positive feelings toward the unfortunate. By fasting, the rich person starts to empathize with the poor and needy and to appreciate what Allah has given.

Muslims who are financially and physically able are required to make a pilgrimage to Makkah once during their lifetime. Two major positive effects of this *hajj* (pilgrimage) are social integration and social unity.

Regarding social reinforcement as one part of continual guidance, the educational system in Islam provides the individual with many ways to fulfill personal needs and social responsibilities. To make individuals sensitive to their obligations, Allah tells the community to remind its members to accept their responsibilities and to apply Islamic principles to their lives. Since guidance is also reciprocal, the individual should tell the community about its mistakes and obligations. Hence, continual guidance as expressed in the educational system in Islam affects the individual as well as the community.

E. Uniqueness

Historically, the educational system in Islam was a new approach to developing human potential and to making maximum use of the human being's abilities. This system is still making a substantial contribution to the intellectual advancement of mankind. As evinced in its characteristics, this system is unique in the breadth of its purpose and goals. Although the person and the society are interrelated, they are also separate units with unique traits. A harmonious connection between these two units is established through applying Islamic principles to organize society. A socio-economic equilibrium, germinating from the social integration advocated in Islam, is struck among the various strata and interest groups existing in the society. With this arrangement, individual and societal needs can be harmonized in such a way that the individual reflects his nature and the society can mirror its nature.

Associated with this equilibrium is the flexible nature of this educational system, which is applicable to every individual and every group of people in any historical period and geographical area, regardless of socio-economic status or ethno-racial background. These characteristics can be implemented through certain methods.

METHODS

The objectives and characteristics of an educational system can be implemented through the methods used by the educators working in that system. These methods are very important tools in applying the principles to an educational system. By examining these methods one can determine whether this system is pertinent to human nature and suitable to the human being's psychological growth and development. Because the educational system in Islam offers a wide variety of methods, both the professional and the lay person can benefit from it. In fact, the wide range of available and acceptable educational methods indicates how comprehensive and flexible this system is.

In Islam there are several kinds of educational methods, some of which are: observational learning (modeling and imitation); learning from advice; learning by way of orientation, which includes knowledge acquired from recreational and leisurely activities and parables; learning by doing and repetition; and learning through reward and punishment. These methods follow a natural progression.

A. Observational Learning

Some psychological theories emphasize that humans learn by observing and imitating others. Theorists such as Bandura, Twain, and Skinner have discussed observational learning in their works. Bandura (1961) theorized that children learn morality from imitating and observing the behavior of others.[5] In general, role models can be either good or bad examples of human behavior, depending on the particular orientation of the role model. In this way, role models in Islam must exhibit good behavior, which comes from an integrated and balanced personality.

To assist humans in their search for truth and inner harmony, Allah sent prophets and messengers as role models to instruct them because these prophets and messengers unified beliefs and integrated personalities. Thus, a broader modeling has been expressed throughout history in the form of prophets and messengers. The Prophet Muhammad (pbuh) served as an ideal example of a righteous person; as Allah says:

He who obeys the Apostle, obeys Allah: But if any turn away, We have not sent thee to watch over their (evil deeds). (4:80)

For this reason, Allah ordered all Muslims to follow the Prophet's teaching.

Just as morality is taught through learning, immorality is conveyed and transmitted through unrighteous role models. These bad role models are dangerous because immorality spreads like wildfire throughout all levels of society.

---

5. Albert Bandura, *Social Learning Theory* (New York: General Learning Press, 1971); and A. Bandura, D. Ross, and S. Ross, "Transmission of Aggression Through Imitation of Aggression Models," *Journal of Abnormal and Social Psychology* 63 (1961), pp. 375-382.

B. Learning Through Advice

Having accepted the premise that humans acquire knowledge from observing and imitating others, we can establish a second learning method: learning through advice. Humans depend on the opinions of significant others to assess their needs and to make major decisions in life. This advice helps them to overcome specific problems and to make sound decisions. Thus correct modeling is very important in such cases where a person seeks guidance and assistance. Every person has limited knowledge in certain areas. For instance, looking for information on malpractice insurance, a doctor goes to an insurance agent. Conversely, when the insurance agent is sick, he or she goes to a doctor for advice and help.

Advice can be divided into two categories: short-term and long-term. Peer pressure (reinforcement) can be considered short-term advice. Because peer influence is usually temporary, this advice needs to be reinforced through repetition. Long-term advice is the most beneficial form of advice because it is more permanent. Allah gave Muslims the Qur'an, a continual source of guidance and direction, and an ideal and ever-present wellspring of reliable advice. Any advice that is respected and accepted as valid can provoke an acceptable response. The advice coming from a righteous model may affect the recipient, especially if the model's acts are congruent with his or her comments. Any advice accepted as valid thus has a greater chance of bringing about the desired result. Put another way, good advice coming from a good advisor has a better chance to effect positive results, because the recipient will take the guidance to heart. Allah says:

Allah doth command you to render back your trusts to those to whom they are due; and when ye judge between man and man, that ye judge with justice: Verily how excellent is the teaching which He giveth you! For Allah is He Who heareth and seeth all things. (4:58)

In the Qur'an Allah explains how advice is utilized and constructive techniques are enforced to modify behavior.

C. Education by Orientation

Orientation means setting an individual's sense of direction in moral concerns. When an individual understands the purpose of his life, he is better able to project and plan how to use whatever exists in his environment. Orientation is a positive fruit of advice, especially if the advice is sound and comes from a sincere person.

Directives can be given through parables and didactic stories, events, or leisurely activities. Allah knows that humans are inclined to listen to the stories of other people's experiences. Many nonfictional and didactic stories are presented in the Qur'an. These stories can be used as valuable tools to educate human beings. In many of these stories, the events that took place in ancient times are ageless examples. Often a moral lesson is attached to the story, e.g., the accounts of Jesus and those of Moses and his people. In this way, the reader can identify with these personalities and consequently adopt moral behavior. As ways of teaching Islamic values and principles, these stories convey to people both the theory and practice of Islam. Each story provides moral advice not only for those who lived during the time the events took place, but for all humans in every historical period. In essence the morals of these stories are timeless.

Humans learn from actual experiences. Allah, who is merciful and compassionate, revealed the Qur'an to correct the misconceptions prevalent in accounts of the previous revelations, to illustrate bad habits and poor behavior, and to reveal the corrective actions necessary to modify destructive behavioral patterns.

In Islam the individual should use leisure time productively. For this reason, Allah requires all Muslims to pray five times each day, to satisfy their personal needs, and to address the need of others. Similarly, free time used for destructive purposes, such as drinking, gambling, backbiting, and gossiping, is prohibited.

D. Education Through Reward and Punishment

When all methods to educate an individual fail, Allah recommends different forms of punishment to enforce constructive behavior modification. As Allah states, one form of punishment is to make individuals aware of the grave consequences of their actions.

Let not their wealth nor their (following in) sons dazzle thee: in reality Allah's Plan is to punish them with these things in this life, and that their souls may perish in their (very) denial of Allah. (9:55)

If individuals refuse to recognize their negative acts, pressure must be applied to force them to modify their behavior.

Were it not for the grace and mercy of Allah on you, in this world and the Hereafter, a grievous penalty would have seized you in that ye rushed glibly into this affair. (24:14)

The ultimate form of punishment other than Allah's punishment, on the Day of Judgment, is based on the law of retribution.

> We ordained therein for them: "A life for a life, an eye for an eye, a nose for a nose, an ear for an ear, a tooth for a tooth, and wounds equal for equal." But if any one remits the retaliation by way of charity, it is an act of atonement for himself. And if any fail to judge by (the light of) what Allah hath revealed, they are (no better than) wrong-doers. (5:48)

In brief, these are some of the educational methods used in Islam. The whole system is derived from Qur'anic principles and the Traditions of the Prophet (pbuh). Since these principles are not rigid and static in time and place, we can extract from them the necessary means for setting up learning theories applicable to all cultures and all societies.

10

Buddhist Education and Religious Pluralism

Young Bong Oh
and Sun Young Park

INTRODUCTION

Religious education, from the Buddhist perspective, is not only a lifelong endeavor, but actually begins while the child is still in the womb. In Buddhist societies, women have traditionally been urged to prepare themselves spiritually for at least one year before becoming pregnant in order to ensure that they will attract a spiritually developed soul when conception takes place. Then, during the time of pregnancy, the mother is encouraged to withdraw from worldly influences, be peaceful, pray and purify herself so that the child growing within her will be exposed only to positive influences. This is called education of the child within the womb. For at least three years after birth, Buddhist parents are advised to protect their child from all negative influences, such as anger, bad language, etc. In some ways this concept shares certain similarities with Horace Bushnell's idea of the family's role in Christian nurture, as the foundation for Christian religious education.[1] However, Christian religious educators do not emphasize the time before birth; this concept

1. Horace Bushnell, *Christian Nurture* (Grand Rapids, Mich.: Baker Book House, 1979).

seems only to be stressed by Eastern religions.

The primary goal of Buddhist education is spiritual awakening and ultimate enlightenment. This goal of enlightenment has both spiritual and sociological implications for the individual and the community because the enlightened being no longer experiences any sense of separation from others. Subject and object cease. Because of this oneness, the enlightened man embodies and practices true compassion and wisdom within society. This state, described as "One-Body-Benevolence," is the essence of the Mahayana Buddhist Boddhisatva idea, whereby the individual works toward his spiritual liberation while guiding and assisting others along the way with whatever help is required, spiritual or social. From the Buddhist point of view, the Boddhisatva is the ideal teacher. This concept of the religious educator assuming social responsibility, as well as spiritual, is similar to Thomas Groome's observation that "religious educators must lead people out from the lived experience of their faith."[2]

Wisdom is the state a person achieves after enlightenment. The concept of wisdom, within Buddhist philosophy, is based on the theory of dependent origination, or interrelative causation, according to which all phenomena in the universe are impermanent from the dimension of time and without self-nature from the dimension of space.[3] According to Buddhist philosophy, the essence of wisdom and compassion are the same, but aspect and function are different. They are like two aspects of the same coin. Wisdom is the subjective aspect of enlightenment and compassion is the objective concept. The concept of compassion initially depends on the theory of equality and oneness since subject and object disappear. When real wisdom is attained, compassion is also attained. The enlightened person completely embodies both wisdom and compassion and with compassion comes the desire to save all sentient beings. This Boddhisatva concept is a basic Mahayana Buddhist principle, which Buddhist education tries to help the student achieve through concentration and study. The way of practicing (meditation, repeating mantra, sutra study, prayer, etc.) leads to the experience of *samadhi* (transcending subject and object, as well as time and space). Therefore, Buddhist education embraces both practice and intellectual study—theory and practice.

From the Buddhist epistemological point of view, only through widsom can we attain freedom from both self-attachment and dharma attachment (attachment to concepts). This emphasis on nonattachment

2. Thomas Groome, *Christian Religious Education* (San Francisco: Harper & Row, 1980), p. 58.
3. From the Buddhist doctrine of the Seal of the Three Laws.

to empirical self (the impermanent nonself, *anatta*), as well as to inanimate objects and concepts, is another basic principle in Buddhist education, which teaches that all truth is contained within self-nature, or mind. The aim of Buddhist education is assistance in the attainment of spiritual, emotional, and intellectual freedom. Indeed, the Hua-Yen *(Avatamsaka)* sutra proclaims that everything is created by mind alone, thereby asserting freedom even from a creator. According to this theory, the universe and psychophysical reality is an eternal continuum. The self is not an entity or complete unit unto itself but rather a stream of energy *(karma)* whose elements are constantly changing. Buddha thus conceived an entirely impersonal universe where there is no First Cause, or Supreme Creator, only an impersonal process whose ultimate nature can only be viewed as in constant flux.[4] This logic forms the foundation of Buddhism's theory of self-creation, perhaps one of its most unique characteristics.

This theory of self-creation plays a very significant role in the structure of Buddhist education because it not only liberates the individual from dependence on outside influences, such as dependence on a supreme being, grace, scriptures, etc., by encouraging direct contact with the true self, or Buddha-nature, but also results in a heightened sense of respect for other beings, as well as their views, because they too possess Buddha-nature. Obviously, this teaching is not only beneficial to the individual, but the mutual respect and tolerance resulting from this attitude are also desirable qualities in a pluralistic society. Actually, the tolerance and respect Buddhists demonstrate toward other religious doctrines is a manifestation not only of the teaching of self-creation but is also reflective of the Buddha's teaching on the Middle Path which stresses that unity or oneness can be found in diversity.

Until very recently, in Korea, China, and Japan there was very little emphasis placed on religious education as a scientific educational activity using principles of psychology and sociology. The reason for this attitude was that, if the teachings of Sakyamuni Buddha are truly lived in our daily lives, formal religious education is not essential. When the Buddha attained enlightenment, he found the answer to mankind's major problems—old age, sickness, suffering, and death. Simply put, the answer to these problems lies in detachment or annihilation of desire.[5] Once desire is destroyed, we have freedom and ultimately enlightenment. Buddha's teaching is merely a prescription for the attainment of enlightenment.

---

4. Raymond Von Over, *Eastern Mysticism* (New York: New American Library, 1977), Vol. 1, pp. 204-205.
5. The Buddhist doctrine of the Four Noble Truths.

The goal of Buddhist education—whether modern or traditional—is to get the student to this liberated state. The technique, or spiritual prescription, combines three different aspects: faith (belief in Buddha-nature, which involves emotional conviction and joy at the possibility of being released from suffering); understanding (knowledge of the Buddhist scriptures, essentially the Four Noble Truths,[6] which is an intellectual approach to the goal); and practice (application of the Eightfold Path,[7] which involves ethical morality). Faith, understanding, and practice form the basis, or process, of religious education in Buddhism and, interestingly, agree with Thomas Groome's observation that "good education must be cognitive, affective, and behavioral."[8] What Groome refers to as "cognitive" is similar to the Buddhist concept of intellectuality; "affective" can be compared to emotions; and "behavioral" is similar to Buddhist ethical morality. Therefore, the essence of religious education must externalize the truth from an intellectual subjective view; externalize beauty from an emotional subjective view; and externalize good from the free will of subjective view. Eventually, these three aspects must be harmonized and become one. This is so because faith becomes understanding and understanding is expressed as practicing. Understanding and practicing are implicit in the act of faith. This harmonizing, which leads to awakening, is the foundation of Buddhist education, of which faith is the most important aspect. In this respect, the Hua-Yen sutra observes:

Faith is the origin of the True Way,
And the essence of all merit.

---

6. Buddha's doctrine was a response to the human anguish he witnessed as a young man. His response began with the Four Noble Truths: 1) The Truth of Suffering—Life is permeated by dissatisfaction *(dukkha)* and suffering; 2) The Truth of the Cause of Suffering—The origin of suffering is in craving or grasping *(tanka);* 3) The Truth of Extinction—The cessation of suffering is possible by eliminating craving and attachment; and 4) The Truth of the Path—The way or method one eliminates these cravings is encompassed by the Noble Eightfold Path.

7. The Noble Eightfold Path, or eight steps toward enlightenment: 1) Right Views (correct understanding regarding the Four Noble Truths and freedom from delusion); 2) Right Thought and Purpose; 3) Right Speech (avoidance of untruths and idle talk); 4) Right Conduct; 5) Right Livelihood; 6) Right Effort (uninterrupted progress on the path to enlightenment and *nirvana);* 7) Right Mindfulness; and 8) Right Concentration (in order to attain the mystical experience of *samadhi*—transcending subject and object as well as time and space).

8. Thomas Groome, *Christian Religious Education* (San Francisco: Harper & Row, 1980), p. 21.

It causes all the roots of goodness to grow;
It extinguishes all doubts.

However, Young-Ming Yen-Shou's (China, 904-975 A.D.) observation must also be reflected upon:

"Faith without understanding increases ignorance;
And understanding without faith increases distortion of view."[9]

Naturally, this harmonizing of faith, understanding, and practicing cannot usually be achieved without a teacher. This leads to consideration of what is generally described as the three essences of Buddhist education—traditionally and in modern times: image of teacher, quality of education, and image of student. Teachers in Buddhist education are extremely important; they have a tremendous responsibility. In addition, it is believed that they cannot teach successfully until they first embody what they are attempting to teach. In other words, the Buddhist teacher must first attain and embody faith before transmitting it to students. However, in spite of this respect for the role of the teacher, Buddhist philosophy also holds that the individual remains the primary teacher because all things have latent Buddha-nature and, therefore, have access to truth within the true Self. This is why Buddhism maintains that the goal of education is enlightenment because, once individuals attain enlightenment and get consciously in touch with their own inner reality, they transcend the need for the scriptures or a human teacher.

For this reason, traditionally there were no organized religious education classes for lay people. The intellectual aspect of Buddhist education took the form of sutra study, either privately or by listening to sermons on the sutras in temples. However, in addition to this intellectual sutra study, people have always been encouraged to seek spiritual advice from enlightened teachers who have attained true understanding. The Zen Master, or awakened teacher, instructs individuals according to their level of spiritual and emotional maturity. It is a step-by-step process. Actually, the process of individual instruction within Buddhist education has certain similarities to the stages of faith theory taught by modern developmental psychologists, like James Fowler.[10]

In the last few years, Buddhists are beginning to have organized

---

9. Tan-hou Kim, *Bojo Bup'on (The Collection of Bojo's Sermons)* (Seoul: Song Kwang Sa, 1975), p. 61.
10. James Fowler, *Stages of Faith* (New York: Harper & Row, 1981).

religious instruction which is incorporating principles of psychology and social science, as well as traditional religious exposure. The traditional exposure is maintained by organizing field trips to monasteries for retreats. Meditational practice is considered an integral part of Buddhist education. The reason for this emphasis, as mentioned previously, is that Buddhist philosophy teaches that all knowledge is contained within the individual; meditation practice unlocks the door to this knowledge. In turn, the awakened person must then teach others to unlock their inner spiritual treasure. In fact, the process of Buddhist education has been summarized into what is called "The Three Studies": 1) moral discipline—keeping the precepts in order to eliminate desire; 2) meditation practice—to eliminate anger; and 3) cultivation of wisdom—to eliminate ignorance. According to the Lotus sutra, the purpose of the Buddha's appearance in the world was to reveal truth; to explain the meaning of truth and to help human beings to understand it; and, ultimately, to lead them into *nirvana*.

The third essence of Buddhist education is the image of the student. In Buddhism the person is very important because Buddha recognized that every sentient being possesses Buddha-nature, or divine nature. Interestingly, this appreciation for the divine nature of all people led the Buddha to reject the Indian caste stystem. Each individual student in Buddhist education is viewed as a future Buddha. It is the responsibility of the teacher to help students by various techniques to find their true nature. The first step is to make the student realize that everything—except mind, or reality—is impermanent. Once impermanence is understood and accepted, it becomes easier to eliminate desire and attachment, which are the greatest obstacles to awakening. The teacher helps students attain this detached state by assisting them to transcend their egos and become self-less through the development of ego-less interrelationships. The objective is to attain a state where this self-less emotional detachment will be possible in all aspects of life because, it must never be forgotten, Buddhist education is a lifelong process involving transformation of the total person, eventually resulting in enlightenment.

Hopefully, these brief observations on Buddhist educational goals, and the underlying philosophy upon which they have evolved, has helped to prepare the reader for the more extensive discussion of these topics which follows. The essence of Buddhist education has been well summarized in the following observation: "Buddhistic education has its core in special epistemology as the form of awakening in educational philosophy. It can be said that the most important problem seems to be systematizing the theory of human being formation which has awakening as its core and developing it to a practical science of pedagogy."[11]

IDEALS OF BUDDHIST EDUCATION

Among the various approaches to the definition of educational efforts, the etymological analysis of language could be an effective one. A clearer view of the nature of educational efforts can be achieved if the meaning of the word education is grasped through its etymological analysis. The word education can be summed up as "the human effort for the ideal realization of his or her inner potentiality with a proper incentive and help from without."[12] This leads to the basic questions of education. What is the ideal of education? Where can we find inner potentiality for its realization? What is the process and method of education as a proper incentive and help for its realization? These basic questions are raised in an effort to cause Buddhism to examine its educational ideals.

The examination of the educational ideals of Buddhism should start with the examination of its purpose. The ultimate purpose of education is the completion of individuals and society. An individual human is not a perfect social being like an ant or bee, nor an isolated being in the perfect sense of the word;[13] the completion of individuals forms the human foundation of the ideal society. To examine the purpose of Buddhist education, we should understand its human and sociological ideals in light of its view of reality.

The Buddhist view of reality, or world, can be summed up in a word: suffering. The world is full of suffering. However, this negative view of the world is not completely negative but also has a positive side which can stimulate and change life into a meaningful and dynamic experience. Buddhism attributes suffering to the fact that the desire of human beings is not consistent with reality. Humans desire eternity, pleasure, reality, and beauty. However, the reality in which they live is full of suffering because of change, age, illness, separation, and hatred. Beings are not real in the true sense because everything is impermanent under

---

11. Sun Young Park, *Bulgyo-ui-gyoyuk-sasang (Buddhistic Philosophy of Education)* (Seoul: Donghwa-chulpan-gongsa, 1981), p. 244.

12. The words examined here are "education," "pedagogy" (English), "Erziehung" (German), "Jiao yu" (Chinese), and "Kareuchida" (Korean).

13. Bertrand Russell, *Human Society in Ethics and Politics* (London: George, Allen & Unwin), pp. 16-17.

the law of interrelative causation. Our world is impure and subject to the five turbidities, or disturbances.[14] Buddhism attributes the cause of suffering to human ignorance, which prevents people from seeing the true nature of the world full of suffering. Human action *(karma)* stemming from this ignorance causes them suffering because it produces a gap between what they do and what they wish. Human action, in the Buddhist sense, covers every aspect of life: outward existence, such as body and language, and internal activity, emotion, thinking, and will. This theory of ignorance-action-suffering forms the basis of the Buddhist view of human existence.

The primary task of human beings is to free themselves from suffering and to build a society where they can live in happiness and fulfillment. This task can be accomplished only by transcending ignorance. The person who transcends ignorance attains true understanding and is called Buddha, the Enlightened One. If ignorance is eliminated, a purified world of happiness and beauty, called the pure land, is attained. The ultimate goal of Buddhism—and of Buddhist education—is personal enlightenment and the establishment of a perfect society, or pure land. What is the nature of enlightenment and this pure land?

When the historical Buddha, Gautama Siddhartha, attained enlightenment and became Buddha under the Bodhi Tree, what was really accomplished? The enlightened Siddhartha fully understood the law of interrelative causation, which an early Buddhist sutra clearly describes:

The law of interrelative causation is made not by me, nor by anybody. It exists in the universe regardless of Buddha's appearance in the world. Buddha perceives this (law) by himself and attains enlightenment, and preaches, develops and demonstrates it for all people.[15]

This law declares the truth that everything is born, exists, and is extinguished within the framework of condition and interrelationship. Therefore, nothing is independent, real, or eternal, as everything is changing; even cosmic conditions and relationships are constantly changing. This theory that nothing is independent, real, and eternal provides the theoretical basis for another Buddhist theory: the theory of non-self, that nothing has identity. This second theory, in truth, gives

---

14. T.366, p. 348A. These five turbidities *(panca-kasaya)* are: 1) times of famine, illness, and war; 2) the prevalence of wrong thought and knowledge; 3) human agony and suffering; 4) lack of morality and sense of guilt; and 5) shortening of human life. (See explanatory note on Tripitika references at the end of this chapter.)

15. T.99, p. 85 B.

birth to the view that everything, including you and me, are one and the same.

A Buddha is an enlightened being who recognizes the truth of inter-dependence, as contained in the law of interrelative causation, and nonpermanence. Without this understanding, people experience much suffering. The Buddhist view that everything is impermanent and inter-dependent inspires a compassionate, ego-less attitude. Although Bud-dhist philosophy stresses interdependence, Buddhism also stresses that enlightenment is attained solely by oneself. Buddhist enlightenment embodies independence. This aspect of Buddhist doctrine is quite unique and different from other religions, which usually stress dependence upon the mercy of a Supreme Being. This Buddhist charac-teristic of independence was stressed by Buddha himself time and again when he advised disciples to "be dependent upon yourself and the law, and nothing else."[16] He even advised that they not blindly follow him, their teacher, but should instead perceive the law, which he had under-stood and preached, by themselves.[17] This Buddhist emphasis on inde-pendence is well expressed in the Chinese Zen admonition "Kill Buddha if you meet him"[18] and the Korean Zen admonition "Frankly speaking, Buddha and teachers are nothing to me."[19] The ideal man in Buddhism should be independent, free from every dogma and authority, even the authority of Buddha.[20] Most Buddhist sects, with a few exceptions like the Pure Land Sect, strive for an independent enlightenment combining wisdom and mercy. The ideal of Buddhist enlightenment is to combine wisdom and mercy with independence.

Obviously, it is very difficult to find this ideal person who in Mahayana Buddhism is not only committed to his or her own perfect enlightenment but is also committed to helping others to attain this goal. This fellow-traveler-cum-guide on the road to enlightenment is called a Boddhisatva in Mahayana Buddhism. A Boddhisatva is one who explores the truth by himself and then teaches it to others while trying himself to be independent and helping others also to be indepen-dent. In others words, Buddha is the ideal man in the ultimate sense, while the Boddhisatva is the ideal man in the real sense. Thus, every

---

16. T.1, p. 15 B, p. 39 A; T.99, p. 8 A, p. 177 A-B.

17. T.1451, p. 259 A-B.

18. T.1985, p. 500 B.

19. Suhsan-daesa, *Sun-ga-guigam,* p. 169.

20. Sun Young Park, *Bulgyo-ui-gyoyuk-sasang (Buddhistic Philosophy of Education)* (Seoul: Donghwa-chulpan-gongsa, 1981), p. 52. This book *(Bud-dhistic Philosophy of Education)* was published in Japanese with the title of *Bukkyo-no-kyoiku-Shiso* (Tokyo: Kokushyo-Kankokai, 1985).

Mahayana Buddhist strives to attain enlightenment and be a Buddha, while at the same time helping and guiding others to attain the same goal.

Buddha is the only educator in the sublime sense in Buddhism. This is clearly illustrated by the fact that Buddha is often referred to as the Teacher or Preacher of Truth.[21] However, the Boddhisatva, a student-cum-teacher, is the ideal teacher in the real sense. It is quite significant that *"kalyana-mitra,"* the sanskrit word meaning a teacher in Buddhism also means an honest and virtuous friend. Thus, we can clearly see that, in Buddhism, the teacher-student relationship is not the relationship of the leader and the led, but rather of a partnership, where a teacher is leading fellow-travelers.

The next goal of Buddhist education is the building of the pure land. What kind of society is this pure land, the Buddhist ideal society? According to Buddhist scripture, there are many kinds of pure land, among them, Sukhavati, "the Land of Perfect Bliss" is most famous. According to the *Boolsul-muryangsoo-kyung,* this pure land was built by a priest (Bhikku), called Dharma-Kosa, who practiced the life of a Boddhisatva for a very, very long time.[22] When he began his spiritual quest, Dharma-Kosa took forty-eight vows aimed at the perfection of humans and land and determined not to become a Buddha until those forty-eight vows were fulfilled. With this firm determination, he finally succeeded in building the Land of Perfect Bliss, and became Amita Buddha. The *Boolsul-muryangsoo-kyung* describes this land[23] and these vows[24] as:

1) a land of abundance and natural beauty with a pleasant environment providing conditions for learning the truth;

2) a land with the Buddha and numerous Boddhisatvas and good people who stimulate the spiritual development of the inhabitants, who will eventually attain enlightenment;

3) a land whose people are very mentally and physically healthy and strong and possess and wield extraordinary abilities; and

4) a land of freedom and equality because all these values are shared by all.

The building of the pure land is, as mentioned in the story of Dharma-Kosa, achieved by the life of a Boddhisatva. Its relevance to Buddhist education will be more thoroughly discussed later.

---

21. Sun Young Park, *Bulgyo-ui-gyouk-sasang,* pp. 187-238.
22. T.360, pp. 266 C-70 C.
23. T.366, pp. 346 C-47 B.
24. T.360, pp. 267 C-69 B.

Inner Possibility for the Realization of these Ideals

The intentional act of education can have meaning only when it has the possibility of achieving realization of its ideals. When we say that the ultimate ideals of Buddhist education are enlightenment and the building of the pure land, these ideals can be fulfilled only when individuals have the inner potentialities to attain them. The nucleus of Buddhist education is, as has been mentioned previously, the concept of enlightenment. Buddhism's ideal person is a manifestation of the enlightenment experience. Enlightenment also becomes the Boddhisatva's channel for the construction of the pure land and human salvation. The question of realization of the ideals of Buddhist education depends upon human nature, whether it has the potentiality for enlightenment. The main concept of Buddhist philosophy is "that all beings have Buddha-nature."[25] This concept of Buddha-nature refers to both enlightenment itself and the potentiality for its attainment on the part of ordinary people who have not yet attained enlightenment; the possibility for enlightenment; or the possibility to become Buddha. From the Buddhist view, every person has the same nature as the Buddha and possesses the possibility for enlightenment and Buddhahood. Buddha is a man who has attained enlightenment, while ordinary persons are incomplete Buddhas yet to attain enlightenment.

In this sense, the Buddhist view of human nature is quite similar to the theory that human nature is good. However, in the strict sense, the Buddhist view is somewhat different from that theory. Two main themes of Buddhism are everything is eternally changing and everything lacks identity. When we say that all beings have Buddha-nature, that nature is not the unchanging identity. Thus, Mahayana Buddhism often refers to nonself as the void, and it interprets Buddha-nature as the concept of the void.[26] The concept of void in Mahayana Buddhism is a positive affirmation based upon the negation of both existence and nonexistence.[27]

When we say Buddha-nature is void, it means that Buddha-nature is grasped as the functional concept in the positive sense overcoming all fixed ideas. Thus, the Buddhist theory that human nature is born good is different from the general theory that holds goodness as the contrasting concept of evil. It is goodness in the absolute sense which can be attained only after the negation of both good and evil, and the negation

---

25. T.374, p. 407 B, p. 522 C, p. 524 C, and p. 525 A-C; T.376, p. 881 B; T.1610, p. 788 C.

26. T.374, p. 523 B; T.1610, pp. 787 C-88 C.

27. Sun Young Park, *Bulgyo-ui-gyoyuk-sasang,* pp. 41-43.

itself. The goodness in the absolute sense can be understood more clearly and properly as the concept of void.

To have a clearer picture of the concept, we need to reexamine the meaning of the word void. In this respect, Fritjof Capra, a physicist at Berkeley who has made a study of physics in relation to Eastern thought, makes a significant observation.

> In spite of using terms like empty and void, the Eastern sages make it clear that they do not mean ordinary emptiness when they talk about Brahman, Sunyata, or Tao, but, on the contrary, a Void which has an infinite creative potential. Thus, the Void of the Eastern mystics can easily be compared to the quantum field of subatomic physics. Like the quantum field, it gives birth to an infinite variety of forms which it sustains and, eventually, reabsorbs.[28]

The concept of Buddha-nature as void is not the concept of the fixed identity but the functional concept of the possibility of incessant creation which can be called the spiritual light overcoming all oppositions. There are three major views of human nature: good, evil, and neutral. They all emphasize the importance of education from their own viewpoints. However, strictly speaking, the theory of goodness falls into the basic argument that education is unnecessary, while that of evil falls into the argument that education is impossible. And the theory that human nature is neutral, which sees human beings as mere creatures of the environment, tends to consider that education is omnipotent and all-powerful. However, the Buddhist view of void leads to the ideal of self-education, which enables individuals to take great strides toward the goal of education through enlightenment upon the negation of all dogmas and egotism.

PROCESS AND METHOD OF BUDDHIST EDUCATION

What is the proper and desirable process and method of Buddhist education for the realization of its goals? As is widely known among Buddhists, Buddha used various concepts and methods based on the age, class, sex, and occupation of the disciples, just like a doctor prescribes various medicines according to the illness and conditions of the

---

28. Fritjof Capra, *The Tao of Physics: An Exploration of the Parallels Between Modern Physics and Eastern Mysticism* (Boulder, Colo.: Shambala Publications, 1975), p. 212.

patients. The enormous volume of Buddhist scriptures is partly due to the richness of its contents from the development of its thoughts, and partly due to the diversity of its method. This attitude of Buddha brought forth various sects in time, which, in turn, developed their own various methods of education. From this we can easily conclude that the Buddhist process and method of education is not fixed but quite resilient. It requires Buddhism to experiment with ever-new approaches to education.

The most representative theories for enlightenment, the goal of the individual in Buddhist education, are the teachings of the Eightfold Path contained in the early sutras and Zen theory in Mahayana Buddhism. The theory of building the pure land is the theory for the life of the Boddhisatva, which aims at individual enlightenment and the purification of society at the same time. The basic research upon these theories has been undertaken with particular attention to the educational task.

The Eightfold Path is both the process for the realization of the ideals and, at the same time, the goal to be achieved in Buddhist education. The Eightfold Path as the process of Buddhist education has different orders of ascendance, according to the various scriptures. According to the *Saje-ron* sutra,[29] the order is: 1) Right Understanding; 2) Right Thoughts; 3) Right Speech; 4) Right Action; 5) Right Livelihood; 6) Right Effort; 7) Right Mindfulness; and 8) Right Concentration.

The *Sungsil-ron* sutra, on the other hand, has a different order, based upon the order of threefold training: the Code, Concentration, and Wisdom.[30] However, most scriptures start with Right Understanding, which shows that the Eightfold Path as the process of education centers around independent enlightenment through right understanding. The effectiveness of self-realization and motivation in modern education has been proven, though a theoretical approach to their development is not yet clear. Against this background, the Eightfold Path is the focal point of Buddhist education, which requires an educational explanation. To this end, the epistemological approach in philosophy and psychological approach in science are necessary.

The theory and method for enlightenment in Zen have developed in various ways. However, the Zen generally known in Mahayana Buddhism in the Far Eastern countries is that of the Zen sect, which is called Josa-suhn. The most unique characteristic of Josa-suhn is its theory that enlightenment can be achieved in a moment through intu-

29. T.1647, p. 398 B.
30. T.1646, p. 251 C.

ition. As has been previously mentioned, Buddhism views human nature as Buddha-nature and holds it to be void. This Buddha-nature as void displays itself fully through enlightenment. Buddha-nature also describes enlightenment itself.

Enlightenment is quite significant from the Buddhist educational view. The existentialists challenged the traditional view of continuous education, showing the possibility of the discontinuous education in which awakening plays an important part.[31] Eduard Spranger holds that the critical task for education is to awaken the educated inwardly,[32] that is to say, to awaken their conscience. This awakening is nothing but the inward leap of human spirit and soul. Josef Derbolav, unlike Eduard Spranger who considered the awakening as one important aspect of education, thinks that enlightenment and education are one and the same.[33] It is one of the most important problems for modern education to solve the conflict between the discontinuous awakening of existentialism and the continuous and gradual process of traditional education.

Buddhist enlightenment is a wholesome experience of void, which is, unlike the understanding of knowledge attained gradually through the process of reflective thinking and discrimination, the momentary leap of spirit through intuition. This momentary leap of spirit or sudden awakening is called *"don-oh."* Don-oh is quite similar to the discontinuous awakening of existentialism. However significant sudden awakening may be, one single awakening cannot eliminate all the problems of human affairs at once because long-cherished customs and habits cannot be changed easily. Thus we need the gradual and continuous practice of correction of our weakness under the guidance of the spiritual light of awakening. This gradual practice over a long time is called *"chom-soo."* It was Chi Nool, a famous monk in Koryo Dynasty, Korea, who in his theory of *don-oh* and *chom-soo,* asserted that momentary awakening should be achieved first, and then, after it, gradual and continuous practice should be undertaken for a long time.[34] According to Chi Nool, *chom-soo* without *don-oh* is nothing but wandering in a spiritual labyrinth, while *don-oh,* unless followed by *chom-soo,* cannot assure the realization of a wholesome character in which spiritual awakening harmonizes with real life.

---

31. Otto Friedrich Boolnow, *Existenzphilosophie und Padagogik: Versuch uber unstetiege Formen der Erziehung* (Stuttgart: W. Kohlhammer Verlag, 1959), pp. 42-59.
32. Ibid., SS. 42-43.
33. Ibid., SS. 58-59.
34. T.2020, pp. 1006 C-1007 C.

Don-oh is leaping and discontinuous while *chom-soo* is gradual and continuous. From the viewpoint of education for humanization, education which is not guided by self-awakening is basically not education but training. However, as was clearly pointed out by John Dewey, man cannot be fully free from the bondage of habits,[35] and it is true that a single momentary awakening alone cannot solve all human problems. We are obliged to integrate both continuous education and discontinuous education, which is one of the most important tasks of modern education. For the solution of this problem, Chi Nool's theory of *don-oh* and *chom-soo* sheds light on its possibility and direction.

What is the practical method for awakening or enlightenment? There are various methods according to the different Buddhist sects and scriptures. It is impossible to examine all of them here. Wonhyo, a famous monk in the Korean Shilla Dynasty, gives us a simple and correct answer to this matter. Wonhyo emphasized *"ji"* and *"kwan"* as the best method for enlightenment.[36] *Ji* is the stoppage of judgment and cognizance, which take the content of subjective recognition for objective existence. *Kwan,* on the other hand, is a kind of intrinsic intuition which penetrates the true nature of existence against the ever-changing phenomena. According to Wonhyo, enlightenment is achieved by the simultaneous practice of the stoppage of judgment and intrinsic intuition. The Right Concentration of the Eightfold Path and the Meditative Concentration of the Six Paramitas (virtue), which will be discussed soon, correspond to *ji* and the Right Understanding of the Eightfold Path and the wisdom of the Six Paramitas correspond to *kwan.*

What is the method of construction of the pure land, the ideal society of Buddhism? As previously discussed, the pure land is built by the life of the Boddhisatva. The life of the Boddhisatva, in a word, is the Six Paramitas. According to the *Daebanya-haramilta-kyung* sutra, the construction of the pure land is achieved by the Boddhisatva who practices the Six Paramitas along with the forty-eight vows relating to the perfection of individuals and purification of the land.[37] Bhikku Dharma-Kosa constructed the Land of Perfect Bliss with his great forty-eight vows through practicing the life of a Boddhisatva for many lives. He practiced and led the life of the Six Paramitas.[38]

---

35. John Dewey, *Human Nature and Conduct: An Introduction to Social Psychology* (New York: Modern Library, 1922, 1957), pp. 14-88.

36. Wonhyo, *Daeseung-kishin-ronsoki-hwebon,* Vol. 1, p. 11.

37. T.220, pp. 1032 A-1044 A.

38. The Six Paramitas: 1) Giving, the act of service for all without any condition; 2) Observance (of the Code), the act of observing the moral codes and good deeds and tolerance; 3) Endurance, the act of enduring the unendurable

Paramita is a Sanskrit word meaning "arriving at the yonder hill"; the yonder hill symbolizes the ideal world of Buddhism where there is no pain, hatred, darkness, and poverty. By practicing these Six Paramitas, a Boddhisatva is able to complete himself and, at the same time, to help and guide others to the ideal world. Through these efforts by the Boddhisatva for himself and others, the ideal world of the pure land is constructed.

Of the Six Paramitas, Giving, Observance, and Endurance are the social activity of services for others, while Efforts, Meditative Concentration, and Wisdom are the inward work for the completion of oneself. Of these, Giving is the most noteworthy. Giving involves three types of acts:

1) the act of providing others with materials and facilities;
2) the act of providing others with truth and knowledge;
3) the act of freeing others from fear.

The first act is a Buddhist social welfare service in the material dimension; the second act, in the educational dimension; and the third, in the religious dimension. The third act is fulfilled by helping others to possess a firm faith through enlightenment.

It is obvious that knowledge or skill, though important, take the secondary, not the primary, place in the process of Buddhist education, whose nucleus is self-enlightenment. Buddhism cherishes the person and his or her enlightenment first, rather that what he or she knows or accomplishes. With wisdom and mercy based upon that enlightenment, people can make the most of their knowledge and skill for the sake of themselves and their fellows.

BUDDHISM AND RELIGIOUS PLURALISM

Paul Tillich said that religion is "the ultimate concern"[39] and Frederich Streng defines religion as "a means toward ultimate transfor-

---

and forgiving those who inflict it; 4) Effort, the act of unfaltering and brave practice of the life of the Boddhisatva; 5) Meditative concentration, the act of maintaining the clear and peaceful mind with the stoppage of all thinking; and 6) Wisdom, the state of mind to see the truth and value of things through intrinsic intuition.

39. Paul Tillich, *Theology of Culture* (New York: Oxford University Press, 1959), pp. 7-8.

mation."[40] Combining these two, religion is defined as "the ultimate concern and means of transformation." Here the word ultimate implies eternal and absolute. Thus, every religion has a tendency to stress eternity and absolutism in its own way, and the more advanced that particular religion is, the more apparent and stronger this tendency is. The strong exclusionism of religions, or religious sects, against each other is mainly due to this tendency. In European history, there have been numerous wars, small and large, fought by religions under the cloak of a holy war. Even today, conflicts and wars are fought for the sake of religious faith and interest. It is a grave irony that what is understood, tolerated, and forgiven by the unreligious is never understood, tolerated, and forgiven by the dogmatic religious who should practice these virtues.

It is evident that today no one single religion alone can lead mankind and dominate the world. As the world is heading toward an open society, it is undesirable in a harmonious society and a peaceful world for every religion to stress the superiority of its own doctrines and faith exclusively.

The democratic society is basically an open and pluralistic society. The pluralism of a democratic society is its richness, which, on the surface, can be mistaken for conflict and confrontation, but, in reality, is actually harmony on a larger scale. If any religion is sufficiently dogmatic to insist that its doctrine is the repository of truth in the world, that religion tends to exert a harmful influence on a democratic society. Obviously, religious education based upon that type of dogma is not education but indoctrination. Such a religion will view the pluralism of democracy as a grave challenge to its authority because, if it hopes to survive in a democratic society, it will be obliged to discard its claims of doctrinal superiority.

Is it possible to have a theory of education that can be applied to all religions and denominations? According to John Dewey, who clearly distinguishes between "religion" and "religious" and emphasizes "religious" as a quality of experience which has nothing to do with "a special body of beliefs and practices having some kind of institutional organization," it is possible because religious means "a common faith," an attitude, experience, or opinion shared by all mankind.[41] However,

---

40. Frederick J. Streng et al., *Ways of Being Religious* (Englewood Cliffs, N.J.: Prentice-Hall, 1973), p. 6.

41. John Dewey, *A Common Faith* (New Haven, Conn.: Yale University Press, 1934).

there are many problems in Dewey's view of religions based upon in-
strumentalism and experimentalism.[42] It is unclear how religious education beyond simple understanding or the education of morality and arts
can be achieved without any relation to a particular religion.

In spite of these problems, Dewey's "common faith" is quite significant as a means for religious education in a democratic society to
overcome dogmatic and exclusive indoctrination, making a greater contribution to society as a whole. Religious education in a democratic
society must be founded upon the premise that every religion has a right
to believe and preach its doctrines, authority, and concepts of eternity,
while acknowledging the same right for other religions. In this way,
religions can maintain their own doctrines and practices, while transcending dogmatic exclusivity, thereby realizing a love and tolerance
that is not limited by sectarianism. This understanding, based upon
love, tolerance, and mutual respect among religions is required in a
democratic society. Religious education in a democratic society should
strive to:

1) Proclaim the dignity and right to exist in society of all religions;

2) While teaching its own religious views, religious education should
emphasize the harmful effects to society of dogmatic sectarian intolerance;

3) Insure respectful coexistence between the various religious denominations in society by utilizing the religious education experience as
a way to acquaint members with other religious views, explaining apparent doctrinal differences as manifestations of different interpretations of the divine truth, which indeed is contained in all religious
doctrine;

4) Acknowledge and seek solutions to mutual problems faced by all
religious groups in a pluralistic society; and

5) Provide the opportunity for shared religious experience.

What contribution can Buddhism offer toward the achievement of
these goals of religious education in a democratic society? It would seem
that the answer lies in the implementation of the principles of *ji* and
kwan (simultaneous practice of the stoppage of judgment and intrinsic
intuition), which were discussed in the section on the Process and Method of Buddhist Education. These principles of *ji* and *kwan* can be
practiced in any religious setting because all true religions encourage the
development of spiritual insight and higher experience. Once spiritual
awakening has been achieved through the practice of *ji* and *kwan*, petty
sectarian dogmatism could be transcended.

---

42. Sun Young Park, *Bulgyo-ui-gyoyuk-sasang,* pp. 65-83.

The Buddhist concept of the Middle Path, one of the foremost princi-ples of Buddhist thought, could make a very positive contribution to religious education in a democratic society which assures individualism and equality. The philosophy of the Middle Path in Buddhism is the rejection of two extremes, such as hedonism and asceticism[43] and real-ism, which views everything as permanent and real, and nihilism, which views nothing as permanent and real.[44] After attaining enlightenment, Buddha preached the Truth of the Middle Path. This Middle means not merely a mathematical middle, but refers also to the balance between extremes in every situation. This Buddhist concept of the Middle Path is well-illustrated in Buddha's teaching that the sound of a harp is most beautiful and harmonious when the tension is at "middle," neither too loose nor too tense.[45] In this sense, middle may be interpreted as right; Buddha preached that the Middle Path is the Eightfold Path.[46]

Buddha's concept of the Middle Path consists essentially in affirma-tion through negation. Buddha's theory of nonself is an example of negation in this sense. All existence is, in its nature, nonself, as it comes into being temporarily by the law of interrelative causation. This nonself is the negation of realism. This nonself is nonself because it has no reality. Thus, all existence is affirmed again in spite of the fact that it exists temporarily interdependently by the law of interrelative causa-tion. In Mahayana Buddhism, nonself is generally called void, which is empty in itself. It was Nagarjuna who developed this thought into a logical concept in his *Sastra of the Middle*.[47] This logic was further developed by the San-lun Sect in China, which was established by a Korean monk, Sung-rang of the Korean Kokuryo Kingdom.[48] In this way, Mahayana logic was developed into one in which negation and affirmation become one and the same. Here, every opposing existence is grasped as "one and, at the same time, different" and "different and one." This is the basic nature of Mahayana logic. It is the logic of void and Middle Path. Hua-yen philosophy in China, the main sect of Mahayana Buddhism, holds that all opposing existence or concept in time and space or in quality and quantity, such as this and that, big and small, past and future, are "one and different from" and "different from and one."[49]

---

43. T.26, pp. 777 C-778 A.
44. T.99, pp. 66 C-67 A.
45. T.99, pp. 62 B-C.
46. T.26, pp. 777 C-778 A; T.1421, p. 104 C.
47. T.1564, pp. 1 A-39 C.
48. T.1824, pp. 5 B-13 A.
49. T.1868, pp. 514 A-518 C.

Uisang, the famous Hua-yen philosopher of the Shilla Kingdom in Korea, described this reasoning on the oneness of opposing existence.

"Whole in individual and individual in whole.
Whole is individual and individual is whole. . . .
Eternity is a moment and a moment is eternity."[50]

This Buddhist logic, based upon the Middle Path logic of affirmation through negation, and of the oneness of negation and affirmation, is quite different from the Theory of Exclusion of the Middle, one of the main concepts of Western logic since Aristotle. According to Aristotle, "X is either A or non-A." In other words, X cannot be A and non-A simultaneously. This theory is based upon the Theory of Sameness and the Theory of Contradiction. However, in the Buddhist logic of the Middle Path, "X is A because it is non-A." The sutras of Prajna (Wisdom) are representative of the Buddhist doctrines based upon this logic of the Middle Path.[51] In Buddhist logic, A and non-A are ultimately "one and different" and "different and one." The reason for this difference between Aristotle's logic and Buddhist logic is because the former based his view of existence on realism, while the latter based its view on the theory of void. It should be noted that the Theory of Exclusion of the Middle in the formal logic of the West since Aristotle is basically the logic of white and black, in other words, logic of extremes, which has been taught systematically at schools up to the present, especially in the areas of mathematics and science, fostering an exclusive and dogmatic way of thinking.

However, the limitation and shortcomings of the Theory of Exclusion of the Middle has become apparent these days. Let's consider the case of the high seas, for example. The oceans belong to no one nation. However, they belong to every nation just because they belong to none. This situation is clearly understood by the Buddhist logic of the Middle Path, but not by the logic of Exclusion of the Middle. Even in physics, the most logical and exact of all natural sciences, the concept of substance has disappeared and there is no distinction between particles of matter and the space of nonmatter in the Theory of Field. In the micro-world of sub-atoms, matter is space and vice versa. A particle exists momentarily in space, but, a moment after, it is resolved into space.[52] This phenomenon cannot be explained by the Theory of Exclusion of the

---

50. T.1887A, p. 711 A.
51. T.235, pp. 748 C-752 C.
52. Capra, *The Tao of Physics*, pp. 207-223.

Middle. It can be fully explained by the Buddhist logic of the Middle Path. It is the position of the Theory of Exclusion of the Middle that causes a religion to insist upon its distinctness and difference from others, which is usually viewed as the only way to ensure its individualism. However, this position makes it difficult, if not impossible, for a religion to love and tolerate others, thereby posing a seemingly insurmountable obstacle to the attainment of a harmonious pluralistic society. The Buddhist view that everything is one because it is different seems to hold the solution. This concept of "one and different" and "different and one" could enable all religions to maintain individuality while at the same time fostering informed understanding and goodwill, thus eliminating dogmatic sectarian exclusivity which has been the cause of so much suffering throughout history. Hopefully, these observations on the basic criteria of Buddhist education, which have been offered in a spirit of universal brotherhood and ecumenism, will provide some assistance in resolving the unfortunate dilemma posed by sectarian exclusivity in a pluralistic democracy.

REFERENCES

T.No. refers to the number in *Taisho-shinshyu-Taizokyo (The New Taisho Edition of the Tripitaka in Chinese)* edited by J. Takakusu and K. Watanabe and published by The Taisho Issai-Kyo Kanko Kwai (Society for the Publication of the Taisho Edition of the Tripitaka), Tokyo (1924-1932). The Vol. No. refers to the volume and number in the above-mentioned *Taisho-Shinshyu-Taizokyo.*

After (Vol. No.) is the name of a sutra with the Korean pronounciation. Chinese characters, used the same way in China, Korea, and Japan have different pronounciations in each respective country. The names of the sutras listed here use the Korean pronounciation.

A, B, and C after pp. refers to the upper, middle, and lower column respectively.

Hereafter, all the display marks from *Taisho-shinshyu-Taizokyo* are indicated accordingly.

T.1(Vol. 1) "Jang-aham-kyung," pp. 1 A-149 C.
T.26(Vol.1) "Jung-aham-kyung," pp. 421 A-809 C.
T.99(Vol. 2) "Jap-aham-kyung," pp. 1 A-373 B.
T.220(Vols. 5-7) "Daebanya-baramilta-kyung," pp. 1 A-1110 B.
T.235(Vol.8) "Keumkang-banyabaramilta-kyung," pp. 748 C-52 C.
T.360(Vol.12) "Boolsul-muryangsoo-kyung," pp. 265 C-79 A.
T.366(Vol.12) "Boolsul-amita-kyung," pp. 346 B-48 B.

T.374(Vol.12) "Daeban-yulban-kyung," pp. 365 A-603 C.

T.376(Vol.12) "Daeban-niwon-kyung," pp. 853 A-99 C.

T.1421(Vol.22) "Samisaekpu-hwasu-obunyul," pp. 1 A-194 B.

T.1451(Vol.24) "Keunbon-sulilcheyubu-binaya-japsa," pp. 207 A-414 B.

T.1564(Vol.30) "Jung-ron," pp. 1 A-39 C.

T.1610(Vol.31) "Boolsung-ron," pp. 787 A-813 A.

T.1646(Vol.32) "Sungsil-ron," pp. 239 A-373 B.

T.1647(Vol.32) "Saja-ron," pp. 375 A-99 C.

T.1824(Vol.42) "Junggwan-ronso," pp. 1 A-169 B.

T.1868(Vol.45) "Hwaeum-ilseung-siphyunmun," pp. 514 A-18 C.

T.1887A(Vol.45) "Hwaeum-ilseung-bupkyedo," pp. 711 A-16 A.

T.1985(Vol.47) "Jinju-imje-hyejosunsa-urok," pp. 495 A-506 C.

T.2020(Vol.48) "Koryoguk-bojosunsa-sooshimgyul," pp. 1005 C-09 B.

11

Hinduism and How It Is Transmitted

Swami Tathagatananda

BACKGROUND OF THE FAITH

Religion is a constituent element of humankind, and as such it is as old as life itself. The word "religion" covers a vast complex of different facts—various types of worship and adoration ranging from primitive mind to advanced mind. Hinduism or Indian thought accepts all modes of worship as valid. Each is trying to worship the same God who is the only source of his or her inspiration. Hinduism is older than any other religion of the world. The dominant feature of Hinduism is her emphasis on the development of spiritual life, which finds fulfillment in seeking God within and without. Hence Hinduism as a religion is both a way of understanding and a scheme for living. It is a way of life with a spiritual outlook. In it conduct counts more than creed. All sects of Hinduism, whatever be the creed, emphasize the need of ethical life as an indispensable condition of spiritual realization. The goal of religion is the union with Divinity which is "the soul of truth, the delight of life, and the bliss of mind, the fullness of peace and eternity."[1]

The essential concepts of Hinduism regarding God, nature, and soul have been traced to the days of the Rig-Veda, the earliest of the four Vedas, the basic Hindu scriptures. Throughout its long, almost unbroken history of over five thousand years, we find Hinduism has produced

1. *Taittiriya Upanishad,* 1, 6.

saints, sages, and mystics who authenticated, amplified, and elucidated spiritual truth in every age including our modern period. Absolute faith based on verification with regard to the fundamentals and amazing flexibility in readjusting the externals have been the lifestyle through which the Hindu faith has survived and flourished through the ages. That is why it is said to be "ever aging but never old." Hinduism regards as its supreme authority the religious experience of the ancient Vedic sages. It has no single founder; the ancient seers acted as various channels for transmitting to humanity the spiritual truths they experienced. For this reason, Hinduism is also known as Vaidika (Vedic) religion and Sanatana Dharma (Eternal Religion). It may be remembered that the words Hindu and India were coined by foreigners.

The eternal impersonal principles experienced by different sages at different periods were collected together in the Vedanta, the end portion of the Vedas, also known as the Upanishads. Hinduism is rooted in Vedanta.

PHILOSOPHY OF HINDUISM

To understand Hinduism one has to be intimate with its philosophy rooted in Vedanta. One of the fundamental convictions of the Hindu mind is that there is an all-pervading and all-transcending spirit which is the basic reality, the origin and substratum of everything animate and inanimate. This Reality projects, manifests, sustains, penetrates, observes, regulates, and ultimately absorbs within Itself the objective world. As waves have no existence apart from the ocean, so the objective world is rooted in God. Just as a clay pot has no existence apart from the clay, similarly manifoldness has no existence apart from God. God is Existence, Knowledge, Bliss, Absolute. God in Hinduism has two aspects, impersonal and personal. In Vedantic tradition the impersonal God is addressed as That or It and the personal God as He, as well as She. Shri Ramakrishna (1836-1886), a great illumined saint, inheriting the spiritual tradition of Vedanta, said: "When I think of the Supreme Being as inactive, neither creating, nor preserving, nor destroying, I call him Brahman or Purusa, the superpersonal God. When I think of him as active, creating, preserving, destroying, I call him *sakti* or *maya* or *prakrti,* the personal God. But the distinction between them does not mean a difference. The personal and the superpersonal are the same Being in the same way as milk and its whiteness, or the diamond and its luster, or the serpent and its undulation are one. It is impossible to conceive of the one without the other. The Divine Mother and

Brahman are one."[2] Says the Svestasvatara Upanishad (4.3): "Thou art woman; thou art man; thou art the youth and also the maiden; thou are the old man tottering with a stick; being born thou standest facing all directions." Hinduism believes that though God is one, He has various manifestations in many gods and goddesses, any one of which may be adored as a form of the supreme God. We have, therefore, various forms through which God is worshiped. In fact, one is impelled to worship him in whichever thing has glory, grace and vigor (Bhagavad Gita 10/41). The Hindu adores the One God in the many gods. He finds One in all and all in One.

The special characteristic of Hinduism is its liberal attitude based on monism, a philosophical system explaining all reality in terms of one central unifying principle. Deeply convinced of the existence of the Supreme Reality, the Hindu mind allows the widest freedom in matters of faith and worship. As many minds, so many faiths.[2a] Vedanta gives the simile that as milk is ever white in spite of the different hues of the cows, all the different paths earnestly accepted by spiritual seekers will lead to the same goal. "Many are the names of God and infinite the forms through which he may be approached. In whatever name and form you worship him through that you will realize him."[3] This echoes the ancient dictum of the Rig-Veda: "Reality is one; sages call it by various names."[4]

God can be partially described and approached in various ways. But Indian thought is conscious of the immensity, the inexhaustibility and the enigmatic character of God, and so the Hindu mind approaches the different conceptions and representations of God with a deep sense of humility. The special feature of Indian tradition is the spirit of accommodation. Due to this nondogmatic attitude, the Hindu mind is reluctant to assign an unalterable or rigidly fixed form or name to God. A unique feature of Indian culture, at once remarkable and sublime, is its elasticity.

From this it follows that Hinduism looks upon the various religions of the world as so many paths to one and the same infinite Reality. Swami Vivekananda (1863-1902), the foremost disciple of Shri Ramakrishna, recited the following hymn at the World Parliament of Religions held in

---

2. Romain Rolland, *The Life of Ramakrishna* (Himalayas, India: Asvaita Ashrama, Mayavati, Almora), pp. 68-69.

2a. *The Gospel of Shri Ramakrishna,* trans. Swami Nikhilananda (New York: Ramakrishna-Vivekananda Center, 1942), pp. 264-265.

3. *Sayings of Shri Ramakrishna* (Madras, India: Shri Ramakrishna Math, Mylapore, 1965), ch. XI, p. 149.

4. *Rig-Veda* 1-146-64.

Chicago in 1893: "As the different streams having their sources in different places all mingle their water in the sea, so O Lord, the different paths which men take through different tendencies, various though they appear, crooked or straight, all lead to thee."[5]

In the same parliament he also declared:

> The Christian is not to become a Christian. But each must assimilate the spirit of the others and yet preserve his individuality and grow according to his own law of growth. If the Parliament of Religions has shown anything to the world it is this: It has proved to the world that holiness, purity, and charity are not the exclusive possessions of any church in the world and that every system has produced men and women of the most exalted character. In the face of this evidence, if anybody dreams of the exclusive survival of his own religion and the destruction of the others, I pity him from the bottom of my heart and point out to him that upon the banner of every religion will soon be written, in spite of resistance: "Help and not Fight," "Assimilation and not Destruction," "Harmony and Peace and not Dissension."[6]

This catholic attitude of Hinduism is strongly supported by her philosophy and religious experiences. The momentous discovery of the vedic seers is that One is behind many and in many fosters the spirit of accommodation. The Indian mind was saved from dogmatism by the discovery of unity in diversity and by the recognition of the importance of systematic spiritual discipline. This viewpoint is apparent throughout the long course of India's history.

Hinduism is not so much a common creed but a common quest. It is not an organized religion; nor does it depend for its support on any particular creed. It accommodates within itself various expressions of basic truth. In the Gita, we see that anyone who follows with true devotion and sincerity any faith or worships any deity ultimately finds refuge in God.

That God is the ultimate reality behind human life and nature, that experience is the soul of religion, that the goal of life is to know God through intuitive experience, and that the goal can be pursued by following different paths—these constitute the most essential features of Hinduism.

These ideals were not confined to religion in the narrow sense of the

---

5. "The Hymn of the Greatness of Shiva," 7 in *Complete Works of Swami Vivekananda,* Memorial Volume I, p. 4, Henceforth *C.W.*
6. Ibid, p. 24.

word. They found eloquent expression in political and state policy. The same spirit of tolerance and universal acceptance is recorded in Asoka's inscription:

> The King Piyadarshi honors all sects, monks and house-holders; . . . for he who does reverence to his own sect while disparaging the sects of others wholly from attachment to his own, with intent to enhance the splendor of his own sect, in reality by such conduct inflicts the severest injury on his own sect.[7]
>
> It is verily concord among religions that is right and proper as persons of other ways of thinking may thereby hear the Dharma and serve its causes.[8]

CONCEPT OF THE INDIVIDUAL

The Indian mind is singularly dominated by one paramount conception: the divinity of life. The ancient discovery of the divine within the human had tremendous impact on the future development of India's culture. Divinity, the essence of the individual, is distinguished from the psycho-physical complex which externally houses it but is not its real nature. Direct experience of this truth is the high prerogative of everyone. The individual is not the body, mind, ego, senses, or intellect; these are only instruments through which one manifests and acts in the world. Divinity, one's true nature, is immortal, pure, eternal, and nondual. "He (man) is a child of immortal Bliss."[9] The divine nature is also the true nature of animals, but they are incapable of thinking about it. It is only human beings with their unique physical and mental systems, aided by the spiritual environment created by themselves in the course of evolution, who are able to experience the truth. Persons are specially equipped for this great adventure. Human life is a union of spirit and nature, a complex of freedom and bondage, purity and impurity, light and darkness. These two opposite elements, joined together by the inscrutable power of God, produce the human body. Divinity is in essence self-conscious, self-illuminating, the knowing subject, the organizer of experience, and therefore the principle of order. The body is

---

7. Asoka, the great Indian emperor of third century, B.C. *Inscriptions of Asoka* (Asoka: Vincent Smith, 1909), p. 171. Quoted in S. Radhakrishnan, *East and West in Religion* (London: Allen and Unwin, 1949), pp. 29-32.

8. N. D. Nikham and Richard McKeon, eds., and trans., *Edicts of Asoka* (Chicago: University of Chicago Press, 1959, 3rd ed.), p. 53.

9. *Svetasvatara Upanishad* 2.5.

animated by the divine essence. Our ignorance of our real self compels us to identify ourselves with our bodies, and so we suffer. As we gradually awaken to our divine nature and its glory, we become restless pilgrims among God's creatures. This philosophical attitude behind the Hindu view of life gives us the inspiration to wage relentless struggle in religious life. The search for the common source of life, continuous reflection to find out the higher self behind the psycho-physical organism, and intense longing to experience ultimate Truth are the motivations behind spiritual struggle.

CONCEPT OF RELIGION

Religion is vital, progressive, and dynamic. It is discipline which, when pursued earnestly, enables us to discover the spiritual dimension of our life. As Swami Vivekananda said, "Religion is the manifestation of the divinity already in man."[10] It is not a creed, dogma, or scholarship but the subjective experience which transforms our life.

Every religion has two aspects, the ethnic or socio-political, and the spiritual or universal. We are born to ethnic religion and most of us die in it by hugging certain creeds or dogmas in the name of religion. When real thirst after genuine spiritual experience comes in our life only then we enter into the higher phase of religion, the phase of pure spiritual adventure. Here religion means the entire scheme of self-improvement geared to the experience of ultimate truth. Disciplines are observed with a view to develop integrity of character, harmony of life, joy in fellowship, and sincere longing for the vision of truth within and without. This higher religious impulse comes from within. When our life is truly awakened to this quest, moral consciousness quickens and we feel spiritual progress in our lives. This is verifiable truth. It culminates in that plenary experience which enriches life, broadens our views, and purifies our vision. We become universal. Our thoughts and actions are in tune with Divinity. Then we truly enjoy life and can radiate peace and joy, says Vivekananda: "This is the real science of religion. As mathematics in every part of the world does not differ, so the mystics do not differ."[11]

The scientific temper of the human mind cannot remain satisfied with superficial, dogma-ridden ethnic religion. Swami Vivekananda, lamenting over this great loss of human resources due to our stagnation

---

10. *C.W.* IV, p. 358.
11. Ibid VI, p. 81.

in ethnic religion, remarked: "My ideal indeed can be put into a few words and that is: to preach unto mankind their divinity and how to make it manifest in every moment of life. . . . Religions of the world have become lifeless mockeries. What the world wants is character. The world is in need of those whose life is one burning love, selfless. That love will make every word tell like a thunderbolt."[12] Again the Swami Vivekananda said: "My master used to say that these names as Hindu, Christian, etc., stand as great bars to all brotherly feelings between man and man. We must break them down first. They have lost all their good powers and now stand only as baneful influences under whose black magic even the best of us behave like demons."[13]

This teaching of the Eternal Religion of India has been expressed succinctly by Swami Vivekananda:

Each soul is potentially divine. The goal is to manifest this Divinity within by controlling nature, external and internal. Do this either by work, or worship, or psychic control, or philosophy—by one, or more, or all of these—and be free. This is the whole of religion. Doctrines, or dogmas, or rituals, or books, or temples, or forms, are but secondary details.[14]

Spiritual life finds its fulfillment in this freedom. This alone will give us the cosmic vision which is the goal of religion.

CARDINAL VIRTUES IN HINDUISM

Expansion of heart being the rhythm of spiritual life, Hinduism asks its followers to cultivate certain godly virtues. Of all the religions of the world it is known that Hinduism—along with two other faiths, Jainism and Buddhism, which have originated from it—attaches maximum importance to nonviolence. This has been taught time and again by the Hindu saints and sages and is related to the vision of unity in diversity. The science of religion calls for the spiritual development of life, and hence the necessity of cultivating truthfulness, spiritual austerity, simplicity, purity, self-control, nonviolence, renunciation, and service is accepted as fundamental by the Indian mind.

---

12. Ibid VII, p. 501.
13. Ibid VI, p. 301.
14. Ibid I, p. 124.

IDEALS OF SPIRITUALITY, RENUNCIATION, AND SERVICE IN INDIAN CULTURE

In the Hindu view philosophy and religion are not contradictory but complementary: Religion is the practical side of philosophy. The Supreme Reality is at once the Absolute of Philosophy and the God of religion. The indivisible Divinity—source of all beatitude—is the Impersonal-Personal God of Vedanta. The Srimad Bhagavatam proclaims this supreme truth in one of its famous verses: "Knowers of this supreme truth declare that it is one and the same nondual pure Consciousness that is spoken of as Brahman or the Impersonal Absolute (by the philosophers), Paramatman or the Supreme Self (by the mystics), and as Bhagavan, or the Personal god (by the devotees)."[15]

Religion, in the true sense of the term, is the spiritualization of human nature. Self-purification through the development of moral and spiritual qualities is the chief profit gained from the proper performance of duties to society. The individual's perfection is a continuous lifelong process in which all stages are of equal importance. Indian culture generally speaks of four human values—*dharma* (morality or righteousness), artha (wealth), kama (legitimate enjoyment), and *moksha* (liberation or spiritual freedom).

Dharma is considered a primary virtue in Indian culture. It sustains individual life as well as society. It is regarded as the highest social value on which is to be based the other two social values of wealth and legitimate pleasures as well as the spiritual value of ultimate freedom.

The Katha Upanishad emphasizes: "He who has not ceased from bad conduct cannot obtain the vision of divinity by mere intelligence."[16]

Indian wisdom holds that all four, harmoniously cultivated, will lead us to achieving our highest end, or spiritual liberation. Wealth and pleasure are not intrinsic goods. They are good only so far as they contribute to righteous living or the life of duty. Indian culture warns against the easy and glamorous way of vice and urges taking the steep and narrow road of virtue. The Indian mind takes due account of the misery and suffering which the world metes out to a bound soul. In fact, it is suffering and bondage that provoke the problems of philosophy and religion. Evils can be transcended only by gaining a foothold in spiritual culture through consistent spiritual practice.

This spiritual orientation of Hinduism is based on her philosophy

---

15. *Shrimad Bhagavatam* 1.ii.11.
16. *Katha Upanishad* 1.2.24.

which aspires after spiritual freedom. As Radhakrishnan rightly observes,

> In many other countries of the world, reflection on the nature of existence is a luxury of life. The serious moments are given to action, while the pursuit of philosophy comes up as a parenthesis. In the West even in the heyday of its youth, as in the times of Plato and Aristotle, it leaned for support on some other study as politics or ethics. . . . In India, philosophy stood on its own legs, and all other studies looked to it for inspiration and support.[17]

India's spiritual outlook molded by Vedanta philosophy has saved India from destruction. It is not that every Indian is spiritual, but the Indian people have always given the highest place in the scheme of good life to spiritual qualities and excellences. Something in the Indian tradition compels a person at some stage of his or her life to understand the evanescent character of human life and achievement. This insight impels them to cling to righteousness and afterward to seek final release from bondage. *"Moksha*—spiritual freedom—is the masterword in Indian philosophy."

A galaxy of great men and women down the long, checkered history of Indian culture stood for the highest aspirations of the Indian mind and this hallowed tradition helps the common people to be reminded of its supreme importance. The greatest men and women of India were messengers of the Spirit, who taught, through their elevated lives, the fundamental unity of all in Divinity. Their universal attitude of love and harmony, peace and enlightenment, renunciation and service deeply imprinted in the minds of the people the dominance of spirit over matter.

Spirituality can never be gained without renunciation. Renunciation is a positive value, a discipline which is pursued for spiritual awakening. Mind is steeped in matter. Unless it is made pure and stable through exposure to spirit, it will not be fit for the higher values of life. Hence the renunciation of lower pleasures for the sake of lasting joy and fulfillment of higher values. The person is divine and not the mortal body and mind. Matter, being compound, is subject to disintegration. But spirit is singular and immortal and hence never vulnerable.

Indian culture exhorts all to nourish the spirit. This vocation alone can enrich our life and bring harmony and peace. For the Hindu,

---

17. *Indian Philosophy,* Vol. I. (London: Allen and Unwin, 1948), p. 22-23.

religion is not so much a matter of external behavior as of improving the quality of life through spiritual practice. A devout Hindu wants to experience the presence of divinity in life and is ready for consistent struggle to gain that end. Hence the acid tests of the individual's religious life are gradual withdrawal from mundane pursuits, cultivation of a new attitude of spiritual consciousness within and without, love for divine life, humane behavior, unselfishness, critical discrimination, and inner detachment. This elevated life will demonstrate the spirit of self-sacrifice for the welfare of others, sincere love and genuine sympathy for suffering humanity irrespective of creed, color, or nationality.

WAYS AND METHODS OF IMPARTING HINDU CULTURE

In India, the saints and sages have been the true teachers of human life as a whole. Intellectual geniuses have been teachers in particular branches of human knowledge and activity. All schools of Indian philosophy have recognized the intuitive experiences of saints as the strongest proof of the spiritual nature of ultimate Truth. The cultural atmosphere of India always paid homage to those illumined souls whose spiritual realizations help people understand the organic unity of life with spirit as its dynamic center. Religion, in the sense of spiritual self-discipline, has therefore been accepted by all classes of intellectuals as the governing principles of life. From the prehistoric Vedic age up to the present time, saints have always been the true leaders of Indian culture.

India has in no age been without saints of the highest order, and hence the ideal of human life, the ideal of true culture and civilization, has never been lowered in India. The light kindled by the Vedic seers has never been extinguished. The center of her cultural life is held fast by the idealism of these saints, living examples of freedom from human weakness. It is from them that people learn to think of one God, one universe, one humanity, one life pervading the varieties of creation. Backed by their high idealism and living example, the common people gain strength to fight against untruth and injustice, against all kinds of evil in man's dealing with man. In this way spiritual transmission and spiritual growth take very positive forms.

FAMILY LIFE

In Indian culture we find the greatest emphasis being laid on the cultivation of knowledge. This is in keeping with the philosophic bent of mind which wants to search for truth. "Truth alone prevails and not untruth" is a well-known saying in Vedanta.[18]

Continuity and growth in social life depend on the persistence of memory. We naturally feel inclined to follow those precepts which are preserved in our culture. Traditional values are very important in our lives. We cannot safely uproot life from its traditional environment; spiritual life depends on a living tradition and the structure contributes to this tradition.

Hinduism is essentially a religion of values. Spiritual values depend on the price paid in the pains and aches of self-sacrifice. In Indian culture, ideas and ideals are rooted in ancient tradition and associated with the holy names of a long line of ideal parents whose lives have entered into our being. Among the various types of human relationships, that between man and woman is the most important. While monastic life and social service are open to women, marriage and motherhood are considered their normal vocation. The institution of marriage is glorified in Hindu tradition. Man and woman ordinarily constitute a fundamental unity. Hence marriage is a spiritual fellowship. The Indian woman is taught to retain her essential feminine character and grace. She gives more, takes less. She assumes the burden of the family. As the mother she is first and foremost the teacher of her children, the custodian of family culture. It is her supreme privilege to raise her children, to transmit spiritual culture to them and to help them grow in all respects.

To a Hindu, God is the Mother of all creation, and as such God is often addressed as Mother. Indian culture asks men to regard all women, except one's wife, as different forms of the Divine Mother, to look upon women with veneration and tenderness. Hindus are asked to look upon mother as Goddess.[19] The mother is more worthy of reverence than father or teacher, according to Hindu scriptures. Says Manu, the Hindu law-giver, "From the point of view of reverence due, a teacher is tenfold to a mere lecturer, a father a hundredfold to a teacher, and a mother a thousandfold to a father."[20] Mothers are the greatest custodians of Hindu culture.[21] Building on the natural self-sacrifice inherent in motherhood, their cultural training encourages them to

---

18. *Mundaka Upanishad* 3.1.6.

19. *Gospel of Shri Ramakrishna,* p. 168.

20. (Code of Manu) *Manu Smrti* 11.145.

21. S. Radhakrishnan and Charles Moore, eds., *Source Book in Indian Philosophy* (Princeton, N.J.: Princeton University Press, 1957), pp. 189-190. Ref. Swami Madhavananda, Romesh Ch. Mazumdar, *Great Women of India* (Calcutta: Advaita Ashrama, 1953).

honor the ideals of chastity, unselfishness, patience, and forbearance with the hope of raising the spiritual consciousness of the people.

It is the atmosphere of peace based on a spiritual view of life that makes a house a real home, a laboratory for the growth of human personality through renunciation and service, sharing, and caring. The Upanishads expounded the idea of man and woman as equal halves of Divinity.[22] This spiritual view of human beings as envisioned by Vedic civilization became the pivot of Indian culture. It made a powerful impact in socio-spiritual life. Ideals of family life and social relationships were tremendously influenced by that vision of life. The position of a woman in any society is a true index of its spiritual and cultural growth.

According to Indian tradition, that family is happy and prosperous where women are happy and contented. For it is the loving wife, the affectionate mother, the woman of spiritual strength who makes the home a tangible paradise on earth.[23] In that peaceful atmosphere man finds great scope to unfold his divine spirit by emulating the examples of elders who embody high qualities of life. Swami Vivekananda says:

She (Sita) is the very type of the true Indian woman, for all the Indian ideals of a perfected woman have grown out of that one life of Sita, and here she stands these thousands of years, commanding the worship of every man, woman, and child, throughout the length and breadth of the land of Aryavarta. . . . Sita has gone into the very vitals of our race. She is there in the blood of every Hindu man and woman; we are all children of Sita.[24]

Following the footprints of Sita, India in every age did produce millions of women who sacrificed their selfish life to help develop a healthy culture through their self-effacement, nobility, patience, forbearance, and great purity of character. How their dignified submission to man's aggressive attitude often resulted in the refinement of men is a great lesson of human history. Most Indian women accepted cheerfully the rigorous obligations of their domestic duties and so enriched family life as a whole. Through their dedication, heroism, loyalty, and chastity they consequently made substantial contributions to the public good.

---

22. *Brhadaranyaka-upanisad,* 1.4.3.
23. Radhakrishnan and Moore, *Source Book in Indian Philosophy;* Book XII, Ch. 142, pp. 189-190, Ref., *Mahabharata,* Bhandarkar Inst. Edition, Book XII, Ch. 142, footnote.
24. *C.W.* III, p. 255-56.

Our cultural history is replete with examples of women who left an immortal legacy by their exalted living. In modern times we find an eloquent expression of these values in the divine life of Holy Mother, Sri Sarada Devi (1853-1920). Entirely rooted in divine consciousness, she radiated peace, joy, and fullness of life to one and all. Her mother-heart regarded all human beings as her children and poured incessant love on them in the form of spontaneous, ungrudging service and spiritual ministration. The fundamental values that constitute the essence of womanliness, the Eternal Feminine, found living expression in her life; rather, they were the very breath of her life. In Sarada Devi, we find the unique synthesis of the highest spiritual experience and the rigorous exacting demands of domestic life. The constant refrain of Indian culture is to see Divinity in all things. The life of Holy Mother is the latest authentic proof of that high idealism. She is a great educator of humanity.

Hinduism does not demand any undue restriction of the freedom of human reason, thought, feeling, or will. Each person is allowed to grow to his or her best according to his or her own native grain and temperament. This is the well-known doctrine of Svadharma (nature of his own) discussed in the Gita.[25]

To the Hindu mind religion is the manifestation of the divinity already in humankind. A spiritual attitude should be brought to every department of practical life. Marriage is sacramental, and family life, imbued with this attitude, affords each member the scope to manifest his or her native divine qualities through mutual service and self-sacrifice. Conjugal love is to be sublimated into devotion to the spiritual welfare of the entire family, helping all to widen and deepen their character and to perform their domestic and social duties as means to spiritual growth and enlightenment.

Motherhood has been glorified in Indian culture since the Vedic age. In his lecture, "Women of India," Swami Vivekananda said,

From motherhood comes tremendous responsibility. There is the basis; start from that. Well, why is mother to be worshiped so much? Because our books teach that it is the prenatal influence that gives the impetus to the child for good or evil. Go to a hundred thousand colleges, read a million books, associate with all the learned men of the world—better off you are when born with the right stamp. . . . Born unhealthful, how many drug stores, swallowed wholesale, will

---

25. *Bhagavad Gita* 3.35.

keep you well all through your life? How many people of good, healthy lives were born of weak parents, were born of sickly, blood-poisoned parents? . . . We come with a tremendous impetus for good or evil. . . .

Thus say our books: direct the prenatal influence. Why should mother be worshiped? Because she made herself pure. She underwent harsh penances sometimes to keep herself as pure as purity can be. . . . When a man comes in physical contact with his wife, the circumstances she controls through what prayers and through what vows! For that which brings forth the child is the holiest symbol of god himself. It is the greatest prayer between man and wife, the prayer that is going to bring into the world another soul fraught with a tremendous power for good or for evil. Is it a joke? Is it a simple nervous satisfaction? Is it a brute enjoyment of the body? Says the Hindu: no, a thousand times, no![26]

Vivekananda further stated: "She (the mother) was a saint to bring me into the world; she kept her body pure, her mind pure, her food pure, her clothes pure, her imagination pure, for years, because I would be born. Because she did that, she deserves worship."[27]

Vivekananda, following the age-old tradition of India, gave due importance to the role of the family in the welfare of the people. Indian wisdom says that good children come of good parents who are morally elevated, physically strong, and mentally stable. The character of the parents creates a deep impact on the mind of the children. In this connection Swami Vivekananda used to tell the story of Queen Madalasa, a great character in our ancient literature. The Queen used to raise her children with a deep spiritual mood. She knew the divine glory deeply embedded in each life. The divine spark, the soul, is the only source of purity, strength, and perfection. While rocking the cradle with her own hands she used to sing out of deep conviction, "Thou art the Pure One, the Stainless, the Sinless, the Mighty One, the Great One. Thou art not touched by the petty things of this world. Thou art the eternal spirit."[28] Because she raised her four sons with the highest idealism, they made a deep mark by their excellent lives. Such anecdotes compel us to acknowledge the great influence a mother has on her children. Our history is replete with such examples.

Even the great monks like Buddha, Shankara, and Shri Chaitanya

---

26. *C.W.* VIII, p. 60-61.
27. Ibid, p. 61.
28. Ibid III, p. 243, Ref. *Great Women of India,* p. 222.

had profound respect for their mothers. In the Mahabharata, we find that during the eighteen-days' battle of Kurukshetra, even the evil-minded Duryodhana, following Indian tradition, would every day invariably approach his mother, Gandhari, for her blessing and every time Gandhari would say, "Where there is righteousness, there is victory."[29] Her valuable advice has become a proverb in India. She never approved of the unrighteous actions of her son. In the face of defeat, he continued to seek his mother's blessing. Gandhari lost all her sons along with others.

In modern times, Ramakrishna, Sarada Devi, Swami Vivekananda, Mahatma Gandhi, and others carried forward this noble tradition. Swami Vivekananda used to say that mother's blessing is a thousand times more important than father's blessing. He was very devoted to his mother throughout his life. Mahatma Gandhi, to assure his mother, took three vows—not to drink, take meat, or go after women—before his departure for England at the age of nineteen.[30] From his autobiography we know how his reverential attitude toward his mother protected him under great provocation. Modern scholarship also attests the power of parental character and love, and of filial devotion. (Cf. "Ways and Power of Love" by P. A. Sorokin.)

The noble character of parents does command the respect of children. This healthy tradition is a great source of spiritual training in India. It has been well said, "Centuries of life make a little history and centuries of history make a little tradition." A culture may be compared to "a torch that is passed on from hand to hand down the generations." It is unfortunate that due to the materialistic attitude of modern life, India is losing her hold on spiritual values.

FOUR STAGES OF LIFE

Human beings are limited physically but their spiritual dimension is vast and unlimited. By inner penetration and meditation they can touch their divine center and attain the consummation of human evolution, becoming perfect and immortal. Hindu wisdom not only speaks about our divine heritage but gives us positive guidance on how to cultivate

---

29. *Mahabharata:* 11.14.8, 11.17.6. Ref. *Great Women of India*, p. 171. Ref. *The Cultural Heritage of India,* Vol. II, p. 606 (Calcutta: The Ramakrishna Mission Institute of Culture).

30. *Mohandas K. Gandhi: An Autobiography* (Boston: Beacon Press, 1957), p. 39.

the spiritual dimension of life. This constitutes the true intelligence of the intelligent. "The destiny of the human race, as of the individual, depends on the direction of its life forces, the light which guides it and the laws that mold it."[31]

Humans are born with an insatiable tendency to enjoy life and therefore they have to evolve their spiritual lives gradually. They have to satisfy their inner compulsion by seeking excellences in various fields of life according to their capacities. The master urge to seek fulfillment in divine life controls other aspirations militating against the flowering of the personality. Accordingly, Hindu tradition has drawn up a grand scheme of life which enables us to develop a balanced personality.

There are four stages in life: the period of studentship, the family life, a stage of withdrawal from family and retirement into solitary life, and the life of renunciation. Each stage has its own discipline geared to develop spiritual consciousness. In the first period the students lead a celibate life and keep themselves busy in learning and developing their moral character. This is a period of character building. A few well-qualified students may directly enter into the fourth stage.

In the second stage of family life more scope is available to develop our hidden potentialities. Marriage is regarded as a holy union which is very helpful to strengthen our character, broaden our vision, enrich our lives, and spiritualize our emotions. Manu, the Hindu law-giver, is of the opinion that family life is very important, as it gives support to the other three stages. For most people, married life is essential for the healthy growth of spiritual life by allowing scope for legitimate enjoyment and for fulfilling human aspirations in many ways. About the third stage Manu says: "When the house-holder sees wrinkles (in his skin), greyness (in his hair), and the son of his son, let him retire to the forest (detached from family-life)."[32]

The whole life of each person should be a steady progression toward complete renunciation of egoistic life. This gradual withdrawal is recommended for healthy inner strength. Every sincere and earnest candidate for spiritual freedom will find vast scope in each stage for growing toward the goal. The entire life is nothing but a steady journey, with courage and fortitude, to reach illumination. This culmination comes only to a pure mind.

The monk who has willingly taken the vow of poverty and chastity is considered to be the ideal man. Women also are eligible for this vocation, and many women since the Vedic age attained greatness in this life.

---

31. S. Radhakrishnan, *Eastern Religion and Western Thought* (Oxford: Oxford University Press, 1940), p. 2.
32. *Manu Smrti*, VI.2.

The life of absolute renunciation affords an opportunity to wage an undivided struggle to make oneself completely free from ignorance—the source of all misery. The ideal monk is a free soul having no human weakness. Centered securely in his real self, he looks upon everything as a manifestation of Divinity. He is concerned with the welfare and service of humanity. Through his perfected living, he leaves an impact on the collective mind. Divine consciousness transforms our secular activities into a spiritual offering and thereby demonstrates the beauty of spirit and its absolute supremacy. When the soul is released from bondage, communion with the divine within becomes an achieved certainty.

Referring to the unique wisdom of this Hindu planning of life, Paul Deussen wrote: "The whole life should be passed in a series of gradually intensifying ascetic stages, through which a man, more and more purified from all earthly attachments, should become fitted for his 'home' *(astam),* as the other world is designated as early as Rig Veda. The entire history of mankind does not produce much that approaches in grandeur to this thought."[33]

TEACHER-STUDENT RELATIONSHIP

Education, especially spiritual education, demands an intimate, happy, and cordial relationship between the teacher and the taught. In religious life, it is a joint adventure in quest of the divine. Both of them are to be morally elevated, for the student should be fit to receive and the teacher should be capable of imparting spiritual values. In such a noble enterprise, there should not be any hatred or ill-feeling in their minds. Spiritual education in Indian tradition is the awakening of one soul by another soul. Without a high degree of moral excellence and firm conviction of the truth of what he is imparting, the teacher will not be able to inspire the student. Mahatma Gandhi, who qualified himself as a good teacher through spiritual development at Tolstoy Farm, in South Africa, wrote in his autobiography: "It is possible for a teacher . . . to affect the spirit of the pupils by his way of living. It would be idle for me if I were a liar, to teach boys to tell the truth. A cowardly teacher would never succeed in making his boys valiant, and a stranger to self-restraint could never teach his pupils the value of self-restraint. I saw, therefore, that I must be an eternal object-lesson to the boys and girls living with me."[34]

---

33. Paul Deussen: *The Philosophy of the Upanishads* (New York: Dover Publications, 1966), p. 367.

34. *Gandhi: An Autobiography,* p. 339.

The moral character of a teacher along with a loving nature will be a real source of inspiration to the student. The student should respect the teacher and cultivate faith, dynamic humility, and veneration toward him or her. To be really benefited by spiritual idealism, the student should practice self-control, love for truth, and other qualities of head and heart. Because India knew the secret of happy living, students were asked to manifest the divinity within in various situations of life. The difficulty is not so much in the enunciation of principles but in the daily application of those principles to human life and human conscience.

In the Taittiriya-Upanishad we get a glimpse of character-building teaching given to departing students about to begin married life. These unforgettable exhortations do not ignore the practical aspects of life and ask us to experience the divine through the course of life. In this convocation address the teacher says to his students:

> Speak the truth. Practice dharma. Do not neglect the study of the Vedas. Having brought to the teacher the gift desired by him [enter the householder's life and see that] the line of progeny is not cut off. Do not swerve from the truth. Do not swerve from dharma. Do not neglect [personal] welfare [health and longevity]. . . . Do not neglect your duties to the gods and the ancestors. Treat your mother as God. Treat your father as God. Treat your teacher as God. Whatever deeds are faultless, these are to be performed—not others. Whatever good works have been performed by us, these should be performed by you—not others. . . . Now, if there arises in your mind any doubt concerning any act, or any doubt concerning any conduct, you should conduct yourself in such matters as brahmanas would conduct themselves—brahmanas who are competent to judge, who [of their own accord] are devoted [to good deeds] and are not urged [to their performance] by others, and who are not too severe, but are lovers of dharma. . . . This is the rule. This is the teaching. This is the secret wisdom of the Vedas. This is the command. This you should observe. This alone should be observed."[35]

THE INFLUENCE OF THE EPICS ON INDIAN LIFE

A nation lives by the idealism that shapes its destiny. The soul of a race can be known by a sympathetic study of its heritage of visions and

---

35. *Taittiriya Upanishad,* 1.XI.1-4. Quoted from: *Indian Mind,* p. 245, ed. Charles Moore (East-West Center Press, University of Hawaii Press).

aspirations, its inner inclinations, and its constant endeavors to achieve its noblest goals. We must acknowledge the inevitability of human shortcomings which are responsible for its failures. Still, an authentic study of a nation demands the understanding of its ideals and the ways and means it chooses to actualize those ideals. Therefore the soul of Hinduism has to be known through the idealism cherished in the collective Hindu consciousness.

The Vedas, the Upanishads, the epics, the Gita, the Bhagavata, and other scriptures are highly respected by the Hindus in general, irrespective of the particular sects they belong to.

In Hinduism God is not an extra-cosmic spectator of the world-process. God is immanent as well as transcendent. The immanence of God permeates every bit of matter. God guides the cosmos (Gita 9/10). It is the function of God to protect the world, to keep it going on lines of righteousness. God assumes human form in times of spiritual crisis and guides the people to move higher in their spiritual evolution (Gita 4/7-8). The divine incarnations by their holy lives, activities, and teachings have had a far-reaching effect on human life. They leave behind rich examples of holiness which become the subject matter of meditation and the inspiration for holy living for the generations to come.

The Hindu mind is prone to accept something when it has a stamp of authority of a God-man. Thus the Ramayana, the Mahabharata, and the Bhagavata which depict the spiritual glory of Rama and Krishna have inspired countless people down the ages. They are ever fresh. The Ramayana and the Mahabharata are two great epics illustrating the ideal characters of Rama and Krishna who are regarded by the Hindus as divine incarnations. Old truths get fresh representations through such God-men and thus help people to have faith in the truths exemplified by them. The Ramayana contains 24,000 couplets in Sanskrit. It was composed from about 400 B.C. to 200 A.D. The Mahabharata, containing 100,000 verses in Sanskrit, was composed at about the same period. The Bhagavad Gita, the Divine Song of the Lord, occurs in the Mahabharata.

For over two thousand years these two great epics have formed the strongest single factor that has sustained and held together Indian cultural life. Their deep and pervasive influence is felt in religion, morality, literature, and other arts. "In fact, the Ramayana and the Mahabharata," declared Swami Vivekananda, "are the two encyclopedias of ancient Aryan life and wisdom, portraying the ideal civilization which humanity has yet to aspire after."[36] Abstract truth is very difficult

---

36. *C.W.* VI, p. 101.

to comprehend. Epics and other scriptures are very helpful in understanding the real import of spiritual truth, for that truth is exemplified in the great lives. The books are replete with inspiring stories of wisdom. "In these two masterpieces we are brought closer to the atmosphere and ideals and customs of ancient Hindu life than by a hundred volumes of commentary on the Upanishads. . . . Hindu men and women became real to us."[37]

In spite of illiteracy the Indian masses gained insight about religious life from the epics and Puranas, through the media of sculpture, painting, dance, drama, music, religious discourse, recitations, and temple festivals. In this way popular religious instruction was conveyed in a manner which both entertained and uplifted the people.

In the quiet hours of evening, when work is finished, men, women, and children meet together in villages throughout the land and listen eagerly to recitations from them by specially trained storytellers. Thus are brought to the humblest cottage the essential moral lessons and the great spiritual truths of an immemorial tradition. The beneficent effect upon the vast masses of the Indian population can scarcely be exaggerated. By virtue of it one may say that even the lowest Indian peasant or laborer, though illiterate, is still in a deep sense cultivated. Though he may be ignorant in all else, he is spiritually informed. These common entertainments always draw huge crowds.[38]

Many individuals recite a portion from the epics daily as a discipline which will give them spiritual merit. The Hindus find in them "a deep well of strength." In various ways these epics have spread to every part of India and beyond. They form the basis of popular narratives which were turned into ballads recited by wandering minstrels.

About the impact of the Ramayana we quote the remarks of Western scholars. The historian Vincent Smith, in his book, *Akbar, the Great Moghal,* says: "Yet that Hindu was the greatest man of his age in India and greater even than Akbar himself, inasmuch as the conquest of the hearts and minds of millions of men and women affected by the poet was an achievement infinitely more lasting and important than any or

37. *The Wisdom of Asia,* ed. Lin Yutang (London: First Edition, 1949), p. 125.

38. Swami Prabhavananda, *The Spiritual Heritage of India* (London: Allen and Unwin, 1962), p. 80.

all the victories gained in war by the monarch."[39] Tulsidas (1532-1623) is the name of the Hindu saint for whom such preeminence is claimed. George Grieson, an important Western scholar of Hindi, thought that Tulsidas was the best man of his century in India. About the impact of his great book, also known as the *Tulsidas Ramayana,* Grieson wrote: "I have never met a person who has read it in the original and who was not impressed by it as the work of a great genius." And he added: "I give much less than the usual estimate when I say that fully ninety millions of people base their theories of moral and religious conduct upon his writing. If we take the influence exercised by him at the present time, he is one of three or four writers of Asia . . . over the whole of the Gangetic Valley his great work is better known than the Bible is in England."[40]

The Ramayana glorifies the domestic relations which form the nucleus of the entire structure of family life. The chastity of Sita, the perfect wife; the sacrifice of Rama, his filial piety, his love for truth, and his ideal character in every respect of life; the heroism and brotherly affection of Lakshmana; and the great spirit of renunciation of Bharata have entered into the bones and marrow of the Hindus.

The Mahabharata contains episodes covering the entire gamut of life. All shades of life are fully depicted and hence agnostics, mystics, common people, and philosophers are drawn to its variety, immensity, and beauty. The reader or listener is deeply impressed, and the moral values get themselves imprinted in the hearts of the people. The main story relates to the victory of righteousness over unrighteousness. The Mahabharata's story of Harishchandra (who sacrificed everything for Truth) inspired Mahatma Gandhi. In his autobiography he said:

> This play—"Harishchandra"—captured my heart. I could never be tired of seeing it. But how often should I be permitted to go? It haunted me and I must have acted "Harishchandra" to myself times without number. "Why should not all be truthful like Harishchandra?" was the question I asked myself day and night. To follow truth and to go through all the ordeals Harishchandra went through was the one ideal it inspired in me. I literally believed in the story of Harishchandra. The thought of it all often made me weep. My common sense tells me today that Harishchandra could not have been a historical character.[41]

---

39. Quoted by S. N. Sharma, Bombay, India 1954.

40. "Tulsidas, Poet and Religious Reformer," *Journal of Royal Asiatic Society* (1903).

41. *Gandhi: An Autobiography,* pp. 7-8.

If one reads and contemplates these stories and characters, the spiritual law that righteousness is sure to triumph in the end is deeply imprinted in one's mind. Meditation on the lives of the divine incarnation being a great source of spiritual development, both the epics are valuable to humankind.

GREAT MODERN EXAMPLARS

Since the Vedic age, throughout the following centuries India gave birth to innumerable illumined saints and sages who articulated the universal message of her religion, the message of peace, goodwill, and the spirit of accommodation. This great heritage found eloquent expression in Shri Ramakrishna (1836-86) and Swami Vivekananda (1863-1902). In them India's ancient vision of universality found modern expression. Their message is of special interest because they are the creators of a new age, the age of synthesis of yoga, knowledge, devotion, and work.

Romain Rolland wrote of Shri Ramakrishna, "The man whose image I here evoke was the consummation of two thousand years of the spiritual life of three hundred million people."[42] Ramakrishna's life encompassed everything and rejected nothing. Theists, agnostics, and atheists had full access in his loving embrace. His life was the meeting ground of all religions, all paths, and all sects. In his comprehensive scheme of life everyone can find something to inspire him or her to lead the spiritual life. He worshiped God as Divine Mother, accepted a woman teacher, and made his wife his first student. Again, he was never dogmatic and never claimed any superiority for himself.

Shri Ramakrishna, a great scientist in the domain of religion, practiced all the disciplines of Hinduism. Like a scientist he made experiments with religion and found that religious truth is verifiable. He also practiced the disciplines of Islam and Christianity and through them found different faces of the same God. His amazing singleness of mind, sincerity of purpose, and passionate love for the divine demolished all superficial obstacles of dogmas, creeds, and beliefs. Thus he taught: "As many minds, so many paths to the ultimate Reality."[43]

He discovered the true import of universal religion which is not a new faith or a new mode of living but the ultimate truth of all religions, the

42. Rolland, *The Life of Ramakrishna*, p. 14.
43. *The Gospel of Shri Ramakrishna*, p. 572.

experience of divine joy. He respected the uniqueness of each path and asked people to love the followers of all religions without disowning one's own faith. Elucidating this principle through a parable, he says that as a married woman serves her in-laws with love, without affecting her intimacy with her husband in the least, so our love and respect for other paths will not diminish our loyalty to our own faith. Spiritual experience "alone" can help us to have real peaceful coexistence. He also asked people to learn from other traditions to make up for the deficiencies of one's own faith, as no religion is perfect and hence there is great scope for learning from others to enrich one's spiritual as well as social life. Hinduism can be highly profited by emulating the noble and practical examples of equality from Islam and philanthropy from Christianity.

The Hindu doctrines of unity in variety, respect for other religions, and the central importance of mystical experience can be immensely helpful to others. His personal experience of the unity of Godhead did help many in different faiths, including Hindus themselves, to have a deep and abiding faith in God.

Ramakrishna's experience of universal religion encourages votaries of all religions to live together in peaceful coexistence without any dissension. He said:

I have practiced all religions—Hinduism, Islam, Christianity—and I have also followed the paths of the different Hindu sects. I have found that it is the same God toward whom all are directing their steps, though along different paths. You must try all beliefs and traverse all different ways once. Wherever I look, I see men quarreling in the name of religion—Hindus, Mohammedans, Brahmos, Vaishnavas, and the rest. But they never reflect that he who is called Krishna is also called Siva and bears the name of the Primal Energy, Jesus and Allah as well—the same Rama with a thousand names. A lake has several ghats. At one the Hindus take water in pitchers and call it "jal"; at another the Mussalmans take water in leather bags and call it "pani." At a third the Christians call it "water." Can we imagine that it is not "jal" but only "pani" or "water"? How ridiculous! The substance is one under different names, and everyone is seeking the same substance; only climate, temperament, and name create differences. Let each man follow his own path. If he sincerely and ardently wishes to know God, peace be unto him! He will surely realize him.[44]

44. Ibid, p. 35.

The democratic and humanistic temper of the age, demanding the inherent rights of liberty, equality, and fraternity for all persons, is immensely fulfilled in Shri Ramakrishna's vision of truth embracing God, man, and the universe. He said: "I clearly see that He Himself has become everything; that He Himself has become the universe and all living beings."[45]

To Shri Ramakrishna the entire universe is saturated with divine consciousness, but there is greater manifestation of God in humans than other created beings. As such to serve humanity in this spirit is to serve God himself. Ethnic religion brings artificial differences between one individual and another due to their dogmatic attachment to the superficial aspects of religion. Shri Ramakrishna wanted people to be friendly on the basis of their divine heritage. The solidarity of humanity can be achieved by recognizing the divine essence in people.

Swami Vivekananda was an apostle of strength. The secret of his strength was his deep faith in the God within, and he wanted all men and women to cultivate that eternal tower of strength lying dormant in them. In his view, whatever makes us strong is religion and whatever weakens us is irreligion. Everybody should be taught from childhood to have faith in one's own intrinsic divinity. "Men are taught from childhood that they are weak and sinners. Teach them that they are glorious children of immortality, even those who are weakest in manifestation. Let positive, strong, helpful thoughts enter into their brains from very childhood. Lay yourselves open to those thoughts, and not weakening and paralyzing ones. Say to your own mind, 'I am He, I am He' (pure, free, immortal spirit)."[46]

"No books, no scriptures, no science can ever imagine the glory of the Self that appears as man, the most glorious God that ever was, the only God that ever existed, exists, or ever will exist."[47]

Swami Vivekananda was an illumined soul of high stature. He realized Truth behind manifoldness and he inherited the rich tradition of Hinduism reauthenticated by Shri Ramakrishna. So by this training and realization, he could articulate the broad-minded acceptance of all paths as valid in the search for One behind many and One in many. He said,

Our watchword will be acceptance, and not exclusion. Not only toleration, for so-called toleration is often blasphemy, and I do not

45. Ibid.
46. *C. W.* II, p. 87.
47. Ibid II, p. 250.

believe in it. I believe in acceptance. Why should I tolerate? Toleration means that I think that you are wrong and I am just allowing you to live. Is it not a blasphemy to think that you and I are allowing others to live. I accept all religions that were in the past, and worship with them all; I worship God with every one of them, in whatever form they worship Him. I shall go to the mosque of the Mohammedam; I shall enter the Christian's church and kneel before the crucifix; I shall enter the Buddhistic temple, where I shall take refuge in Buddha and in his Law. I shall go into the forest and sit down in meditation with the Hindu, who is trying to see the Light which enlightens the heart of every one.

Not only shall I do all these, but I shall keep my heart open for all that may come in the future. Is God's book finished? Or is it still a continuous revelation going on? It is a marvelous book—these spiritual revelations of the world. The Bible, the Vedas, the Koran, and all other sacred books are but so many pages, and an infinite number of pages remain yet to be unfolded. I would leave it open for all of them. We stand in the present, but open ourselves to the infinite future. We take in all that has been in the past, enjoy the light of the present, and open every window of the heart for all that will come in the future. Salutation to all the prophets of the past, to all the great ones of the present, and to all that are to come in the future![48]

This idea of loving tolerance and active acceptance has an impressive ancestry and a significant continuity in Hindu tradition. It is due to philosophy as well as religious tradition. The source of this acceptance lies in what Radhakrishnan and Moore call the "synthetic vision" of Indian culture in their magnificent *Source Book in Indian Philosophy.*

Again, the synthetic spirit of Indian wisdom which experiences Unity in variety will be immensely beneficial for those who are wedded to the vision of "one world." "To this purpose the contribution of Indian philosophy with its age-long spiritual emphasis is inestimable and indispensable," say the authors mentioned above.[49]

Modern people are unhappy in spite of material plenty and the phenomenal success of science and technology. They are restless, rootless, depersonalized, and depressed. Uncertainty, meaninglessness, and insecurity plague them. Vedanta has a practical message for modern men and women. It never asks anyone to develop blind faith or accept

---

48. Radhakrishnan and Moore, *Source Book in Indian Philosophy,* p. XXIII-XXIV.
49. Ibid, p. XXIX.

any dogma. Vedanta asks everyone to return to one's real Self, and thereby develop self-esteem and self-reliance. This return journey from lower self to higher self, from human weakness to divine essence, from finite to infinite, from ephemeral to eternal, will open a new vista of hope. This change of perspective will give humanity a new lease on life. This renunciation of the superficial, the transitory, for the sake of what is deep and abiding is the real beginning of religious life.

Modern men and women are alienated from living religious tradition. The Ramakrishna-Vivekananda Movement is singularly devoted to making human beings happy by drawing their attention to their own native divinity. "Faith, faith, faith in ourselves; faith, faith in God—this is the secret of greatness. If you have faith in all the three hundred and thirty millions of your mythological gods, and in all the gods which foreigners have now and again introduced into your midst, and still have no faith in yourselves, there is no salvation for you. Have faith in yourselves, and stand up on that faith and be strong; that is what we need."[50]

"Teach yourselves, teach everyone his real nature, call upon the sleeping soul and see how it awakes. Power will come, glory will come, goodness will come, purity will come, and everything that is excellent will come when this sleeping soul is roused to self-conscious activity."[51]

"Ye are the Children of God, the sharers of immortal bliss, holy and perfect beings. Ye divinities on earth—sinners! It is a sin to call a man so; it is a standing libel on human nature."[52]

Paul Deussen, the German orientalist, spoke about this momentous vision of Vedanta:

> If we strip this thought of the various forms . . . under which it appears in the Vedanta text, and fix our attention upon it solely in its philosophical simplicity as the identity of God and Soul, the Brahman and the Atman, it will be found to possess a significance reaching far beyond the Upanishads, their time and country; nay, we claim for it an inestimable value for the whole race of mankind. . . . It was here that for the first time the original thinkers of the Upanishads, to their immortal honor . . . recognized our Atman, our inmost individual being, as the Brahman, the inmost being of universal nature and of all her phenomena.[53]

---

50. *C.W.* III, p. 190.
51. Ibid III, p. 193.
52. *C.W.* I, p. 11.
53. Paul Deussen, *The Philosophy of the Upanishads* (1906 Edition), pp. 39-40, reprinted by Dover Publications, New York, 1966.

Swami Vivekananda's clarion call to mankind to realize the oneness of existence—of God, man, and nature—through living spiritual idealism is the "new religion of the age." It has no church, no book, no founder, no creed, and no priest. Do it yourself. Be and make. The Atman is your own divine self. Be not a stranger to your own potentiality. De-hypnotize yourself.

This new religion only wants sincerity, purity, and one-pointed earnestness to experience eternal bliss even while living in this body. The deep cry of Vivekananda's life, the song of his soul, is to bring the fresh water of spiritual experience to us all. He lit a beacon of hope for erring humanity.

In Mahatma Gandhi (1869-1948), Hinduism found another great exponent of its basic principles of Truth, nonviolence, and selfless service. His whole life in the political field was saturated with the religious spirit, with profound faith in God and in the basic goodness of the people, a faith which he inherited from the spirit of religion. He neither entered into a temple nor worshiped any deity. No image or symbol was used by him during his prayers. He never used patriotic songs in his prayers, either. He was a believer in the Formless God, but he never discouraged others from following other paths. His nonconformism was never superficial. He respected the spirit of religion in all earnestness, but not the letter of it.

In his life the world witnessed a fascinating drama of unremitting endeavor to attain perfection in life. His life was a long and continuing struggle in which he added bit by bit and piece by piece to the stature of his personality. Like a devout Hindu his ultimate spiritual goal was *moksha* or freedom. He said, "I have no desire for the perishable kingdom of earth. I am striving for the Kingdom of Heaven, which is spiritual deliverance."[54]

When we study the splendid mosaic of Gandhi's thoughts and deeds what strikes us most is his steadfast reliance on Truth and its benevolent power. Truth was the foundation of and the background to his religious life. His intrepid spirit made bold experiments to practice Truth in all areas of life. His application of the concept of righteousness to political struggles and national problems made him one of the greatest interpreters of Hindu *dharma*. The purity of his methods were never vitiated by the desire for quick results or by hunger for success at any cost. His imagination was totally free from crookedness of any kind. He was an untiring and relentless exponent of moral force. This moral force was to him not something vague and indeterminate, but an immediate

54. *Mahatma Gandhi: 100 Years*, ed. S. Radhakrishnan (New Delhi: Gandhi Peace Foundation, 1968), p. 14.

and compelling condition. He taught that nonviolence ought to be the law of the human species even as violence, aggression, and assault were the law of the brute and that the dignity of man required his utter obedience to the higher values of the Spirit.

Gandhiji's life was verily a demonstration of the triumph of the human spirit over the overwhelming odds of the unrighteous and the amoral. He made his life a laboratory of the soul in which a rediscovery of the supremacy of spiritual principles was made and proclaimed.

Religion was to him the rudder of the ship of life. He wanted nothing but the spiritual empire of freedom and bliss. His method of gaining it was through selfless work, love, and prayer. He himself said that prayer saved his life, that without it he would have been a madman long before. This was not ordinary prayer, but a deep attitude of seeking guidance from God at every breath of life, the earnest spiritual search to find God in life as we face it from moment to moment. Regarding the tremendous impact on society of this spiritual art of seeking communion with God, Arnold Toynbee says:

Gandhiji had a vast amount of daily business to transact. Under present-day conditions, that is the fate of any leader of any great movement. Yet Gandhiji was never too busy to withdraw temporarily from business affairs for recurrent periods of contemplation. If he had not made this his practice, he would not, I suppose, have been able to go on doing his business, because his spells of contemplation were the source of his inexhaustible spiritual strength. In setting apart those times of contemplation, Gandhiji was being true, not only to himself, but to India. His practice on this point is something that is characteristic of the Indian tradition. . . .

Gandhiji's example shows that it is possible to do arduous practical work without allowing one's spiritual life to be smothered and choked by the cares of the world. More than that, Gandhiji demonstrated that this inspiration is what makes practical activity bear fruit and not work havoc.

This is, I believe, the greatest lesson that India has to teach the present-day world. Western Christendom did recognize and practice the virtue of contemplation to some extent in the Western Middle Ages. Since then we have almost entirely lost this spiritual art, and our loss is serious, because the art of contemplation is really another name for the art of living. So now we turn to India. This spiritual gift, that makes Man human, is still alive in Indian souls.[55]

---

55. V. Raghavan, *The Great Integrators* (New Delhi: Publication Division, Ministry of Information and Broadcasting, Patiala House, 1969).

CONCLUSION

In the first section of this chapter the philosophical background of Hinduism was discussed. The middle section described the various methods by which spiritual culture is imbibed in India. The last section dealt with the modern Hindu renaissance through the lives and teachings of three great exemplars.

To summarize briefly, Hinduism puts its main emphasis on spiritual practice for the sake of direct, intuitive experience of the divine. Ethical disciplines such as truthfulness, non-injury, chastity, and non-covetousness are essential both for the self-purification of the individual seeker and for the development and preservation of a healthy social and cultural environment without which religion cannot flourish. Living exemplars, saints and seers whose exalted living and direct realization of spiritual truth bear living testimony to the relevance and validity of religion, are necessary to keep religion alive and to uplift the society.

Unity in diversity has been the keynote of Hindu thought and life. The Godhead is non-dual, but in the relative world the divine expresses itself through different names and forms and may be approached by various paths. As such, all religions are accepted and respected as valid approaches to the same God. Neither a dull uniformity nor a religious Esperanto is wanted, but rather a sympathetic understanding of the rich diversity of the human mind and human culture. As many minds, so many paths to the ultimate Truth.

In today's world, Indian wisdom is important for our very survival. Its quest for higher values of life, its emphasis on nonviolence, its love for the spiritual over the material, its affirmation and realization of the divinity inherent in man, and its comprehensive, synthetic philosophy of the harmony of religions based on direct, intuitive experience of the One behind the many, of Unity in diversity—all these characteristics breathe a spirit which is universal, positive, and humane. This spirit gives rise to those values of peace, tolerance, and nonaggressiveness which will help to usher in a new climate of friendship and unity for mankind. The modern relevance of the Indian spirit has been appreciated by many Western thinkers. We conclude with quotations from two of them.

Will Durant writes in *Our Oriental Heritage:* "Perhaps in return for conquest, arrogance, and spoliation, India will teach us the tolerance and gentleness of the mature mind, the quiet content of the unacquisitive soul, the calm of the understanding spirit, and a unifying, pacifying love for all living beings."[56]

---

56. Will Durant, *The Story of Civilization,* Vol. I, *Our Oriental Heritage* (New York: Simon and Schuster, 1935), p. 33.

Highlighting the need for the accommodative spirit of Hinduism, Toynbee says:

At this supremely dangerous moment in human history, the only way of salvation for mankind is an Indian way. The Emperor Asoka's and the Mahatma Gandhi's principle of nonviolence and Sri Ramakrishna's testimony to the harmony of religions: here we have the attitude and the spirit that can make it possible for the human race to grow together into a single family—and, in the Atomic Age, this is the only alternative to destroying ourselves.

In the Atomic Age the whole human race has a utilitarian motive for following this Indian way. No utilitarian motive could be stronger or more respectable in itself. The survival of the human race is at stake. Yet even the strongest and most respectable utilitarian motive is only a secondary reason for taking Ramakrishna's and Gandhi's and Asoka's teaching to heart and acting on it. The primary reason is that this teaching is right—and is right because it flows from a true vision of spiritual reality.[57]

---

57. Arnold J. Toynbee, in foreword to Swami Ghanananda, *Shri Ramakrishna and His Unique Message* (London: Ramakrishna-Vedanta Centre, 3rd ed., 1970), pp. viii-ix.

12

Future Directions

Norma H. Thompson

"Existence on the frontier, in the boundary situation, is full of tension and movement," said Paul Tillich.[1] "It is in truth not standing still, but rather a crossing and return, a repetition of return and crossing, a back-and-forth—the aim of which is to create a third area beyond the bounded territories, an area where one can stand for a time without being enclosed in something tightly bounded." The concept of the frontier with its boundary line seems a fitting metaphor for the position of religious education at the present time with respect to religious pluralism. We are on the "frontier"; we are "in the boundary situation"; and it is "full of tension and movement." We are creating a "third area beyond the bounded territories," but it is only a beginning, and we do not want to close ourselves in but to move on to new frontiers. Perhaps this movement beyond the bounded territories is similar to Moran's meaning when he describes religious education as "transforming" Jewish, Christian, Muslim, Hindu, and other education.[2]

As inadequate as our efforts are to cross and recross the boundaries delineating one religion from another, we occasionally feel the exhilaration of appreciating and understanding the meanings, the values, and

---

1. Paul Tillich, "Frontiers," in *The Future of Religions,* ed. Jerald C. Brauer (New York: Harper & Row, 1966), p. 53.
2. See Gabriel Moran, *Religious Education Development: Images for the Future* (Minneapolis: Winston, 1983), p. 12.

the ideas of another religious group. We feel at peace, and the tension drops away. Of course, our understanding is fragmentary, and tomorrow we may think we have not understood at all. But a frontier has been crossed, and we can never be the same again. Yet we cannot stop there, on the frontier. Tillich states further: "Frontier is not only to be crossed; it is also something which must be brought to fruition." Given the fact that in this book we have begun to cross and recross the frontier, the question now is how do we bring it to fruition?

When we examine the chapters written by persons of different religions, we are aware that the approaches taken by these authors are not the same. In fact, even the discussion of the meaning of religious pluralism shows differences, as do the usages for the term, religious education. Most of the writers assume a variety of religions in a society and are concerned about the relations among these religious groups. Most writers, too, assume that religious education goes beyond Jewish education, Christian education, Muslim education, Buddhist education, Hindu education, and all the other specific educational activities of religious groups, though they may or may not see these efforts as parts of a greater unity.

The approaches found here to examining religious pluralism and religious education include viewing the situation from the perspective of minorities (racial or religious) within a majority of the same faith; charting the history of pluralism within one denomination; educating in a particular religious group (Buddhist, Muslim, and Hindu), and showing how the approaches to religious pluralism are found within the teachings of that group; and working through a model for education regarding pluralism—the social-science model of James Michael Lee, a model for black churches described by Grant Shockley, a Reform Jewish model set forth by Sherry Blumberg and Eugene Borowitz, and clues for religious education in a pluralistic society by David Ng.

Some writers have spoken explicitly to the questions posed regarding the effect of religious pluralism on theory and practice in religious education—on purposes, context, methodology, and content—and others have woven their attitudes on these matters into an integrated picture of education in a particular group. It was not my intention that all writers speak to the same issues, but rather that they should share their own concerns from the perspectives of their own situations. Although it is not possible for members of religious groups to wait until they have dealt with the pluralism within their groups before reaching out to persons of other religious persuasions, still for some of us the tensions and problems of religious pluralism within one denomination or religious group weigh heavily upon us as religious educators. The divisions in the Southern Baptist Convention as exhibited in newspaper accounts of state meetings are sufficient to warrant Clemmons' effort to work through the history and current situation within that convention in search of some answers which may not only help to solve the problems of that denomination but also point toward some approaches to living with other religions. For Jews, as for most of our religious groups, the divisions within have brought us to the realization that we cannot speak for those who take different stands, but only for ourselves. Blumberg and Borowitz face clearly the fact that they are speaking from a Reform Jewish point of view and that Orthodox or Conservative Jews might work in a different fashion. The fact that ethnic, national, and racial experiences make a difference in how we face the issues of religious pluralism is evident in Shockley's examination of the black church within Protestantism in the United States, and Tarasar's minority report on the Orthodox Church in America shows how minorities are often so involved with maintaining their own distinctive identity within the larger majority culture that it is difficult for them to cross the borders on the frontier and relate to other religions. Khouj's treatment of Muslim education, Tathagatananda's presentation of Hindu education, and Oh and Park's development of Buddhist education remind us that we are only at the threshold of communication between these "Eastern religions" on religious education theory and practice and the "Western religions" which have been involved in discussing these issues since at least the turn of the century. While educational terminology and categories are common among Buddhist and Muslim educators, efforts to communicate with religious educators of other faiths are just beginning. Finally, while considerable effort has gone into developing theory in religious education over the past few decades, or to creating models, few such theoretical works have attempted systematically to deal with the element of religious pluralism. Thus, the efforts of Blumberg and Borowitz to develop a theory for Reform Jewish education, of Shockley to think through the theoretical problems of black Christian education, and of Lee to explore the religious pluralism dimensions of his social science theory provide some models with which religious educators can deal as they struggle with the issues.

DIALOGUE AND METHODOLOGY

Although the introductory chapter did not develop the subject of methodology in religious education in relation to pluralism in religion, it seems important to highlight the role that dialogue (now sometimes trialogue) has played and continues to play in this theoretical aspect. The *Living Room Dialogues* which opened up conversations between Roman Catholics and Protestants at the time of Vatican II are an excellent example. We hear less about dialogue between Roman Catholics and Protestants these days, but all over the U.S.A. there are dialogic groups of Jews and Christians seeking to learn from each other and to discuss the issues which separate them. The newly opened Center for Jewish-Christian Studies and Relations at General Theological Seminary in New York City holds joint seminars for students from the Episcopal seminary where it is located and Hebrew Union College in New York, where students may discuss problems and issues with each other—theological, scriptural, and social. These seminars are only a beginning in the effort to integrate educational and social experiences for students and members of the community.

Dialogue may take many forms, but common to all forms is the desire to "relate" to persons of another religious group. The document on dialogue and mission of the Vatican Secretariat for Non-Christians formulates this approach very clearly when it states that "before all else, dialogue is a manner of acting, an attitude and a spirit which guides one's conduct. It implies concern, respect, and hospitality toward the other. It leaves room for the other person's identity, his modes of expression, and his values."[3] In this sense, then, dialogue is the attitude which must prevail in every relationship, not just when members of two groups are gathered together for some sort of "program." It is the spirit which must prevail if people are to achieve full humanness.[4]

In this broad sense dialogue covers any of the experiences which cross the frontiers that may be included in our religious educational efforts, but it seems that the churches and synagogues (since the actual dialogue meetings have been primarily between Christians and Jews) have concentrated on drawing members of the two groups together for discussion, examination of resolutions and documents, and sometimes some educational programs within the churches and synagogues themselves, or in the community. Usually these groups consist largely of clergy, with a sprinkling of laypersons in some cases, and the leadership is ordinarily clergy. One Muslim-Jewish-Christian dialogue group in the New York metropolitan area includes some clergy, but it also has lawyers, heads of

---

3. See the Secretariat for Non-Christians, "The Attitude of the Church Toward the Followers of Other Religions, Reflections and Orientations on Dialogue and Mission," No. 29.

4. See JED (Joint Educational Development), Task Force on Guidelines to Alleviate Stereotyping, "Liberating Words, Images, and Actions: Basic Statement of Intention."

religious agencies, persons in state and local government, and the like. Still, this is a very erudite group, and its impact on the ordinary lay person in any of these religions is not clear. Another dialogue group, Jewish-Christian, includes lay persons, but it is a select group capable of operating at a very high level and again not representative of education among the ordinary parish and temple laity. Such experiences are enlightening and provide growth; they are probably extremely important as beginning efforts; but we must move into educational efforts that reach the lay people in the local congregations if we are to achieve significant results in educating for religious pluralism. Creative minds will need to work at developing other types of experiences which work through the issues and problems in relations and bring about some understanding and respect for other religious forms and concepts, "a sense of individual dignity, capacity, and worth" of all people, "interpersonal relations of trust, freedom, and love," and "a society that enhances freedom, justice, and peace."[5] Although it is possible to see that some of these experiences involve visitation to houses of worship of other religions; participation to whatever extent seems appropriate in liturgical services of others; working together on projects for the community or for other groups; learning together in classes, seminars, club groups, and other combinations; and joining in social action experiences together, the creativity needed in this area is only beginning to surface. Those pathways for the most dynamic experiences to achieve these goals are not yet apparent, and it is too easy to pick up on methods and techniques which are already current in the society.

APPROACHES TO RELIGIOUS PLURALISM

Martin Marty names several approaches to religious pluralism,[6] the first of which is to wish it away. This is the approach that prevails in most of our communities. We see persons of other faiths and nationalities, but we do not think of ourselves as having any responsibility to reach out to them, to understand them, to involve them in cooperative efforts to work together for peace and justice. We just go on as if religious pluralism did not exist. Marty says we may do this eschatologically; that is, we wish it away "by saying we know that at the outcome of history the secret of its oneness will be there, and those of us

---

5. Ibid.

6. Martin Marty, "This We Can Believe: A Pluralistic Vision," *Religious Education* 75:1 (January-February, 1980), pp. 38-40.

who have diverged in the middle of history will converge in the end,"[7] and he cites Teilhard de Chardin's view of the Omega Point as the "most familiar expression of this vision."

A second approach is to "move beyond pluralism through a synthetic vision." By this he means that we in a sense step outside history in order to get a vision that simplifies life. Arnold Toynbee put on such spectacles "in his belief that the Jewish, Christian, and other religions could merge with scientific faith into a kind of new synthesis." The problem with this approach, as Marty points out, is that none of the groups involved in the synthesis are ever satisified with it, but he notes that Peter Berger "has written extensively on how natural and important it is for us to come under such a sacred canopy, to live inside a sacred cosmos in which not everything is up for grabs every day."[8]

A third strategy for dealing with religious pluralism is "to take action to overcome it." This approach usually involves coercion. It may be harsh coercion, as in the "Maoist years in China or the era of the Gang of Four." These years "are seen by most Sinologists as times for profession of a single, forced religious faith." Or it may be soft coercion, and here Marty uses John Dewey and *A Common Faith* as one example. He describes it as "a very militant book in which Dewey said that *the* religious agencies, *the* religious organizations, cannot provide the coherence that society needs and that his 'common faith' which overarches them all and takes away from them their particularity, their angularity, their misfit character, must become aggressive and articulate."

Finally, Marty says religious pluralism may be approached by learning to live creatively with it; that the first three strategies are not going to work, though people will keep coming back to them. We must come to accept the fact that pluralism is here to stay, and he turns to John Courtney Murray's statement in *We Hold These Truths*. Murray believed that there could not be more than one God, and there could not be more than one truth. So "he started by saying 'religious pluralism is against the will of God,' a metaphysical statement you do not all have to agree with. But his next idea is a clear one: religious pluralism may be against the will of God, but it is the human condition." Following Murray's argument, Marty writes:

> Whatever creedal commitment we make about the final oneness of reality . . . we have to know that whether as a result of the Fall, of

---

7. Ibid., p. 38.
8. See Peter Berger, *The Sacred Canopy* (Garden City, N.Y.: Doubleday, 1967).

ignorance, of cantankerousness, of adventure, of imagination, of innovation, inside history we are participants in a condition that will keep us pluralists—most of all if we remain free. And so Murray ended by saying that religious pluralism will not marvelously cease to trouble the human city.[9]

Marty concludes his discussion of strategies for dealing with religious pluralism by saying that "as long as pluralism is here and you learn to live creatively with it, you can make the best of it."

Perhaps "making the best of it" is all that can be expected in a pluralistic world, but I should rather put the emphasis upon the creativity part of Marty's formula. Creativity assumes there are fresh and exciting things to discover; that the world is an opening one; that something new and positive is possible. Though some religious groups do indeed claim to know the truth, still "the truth" is elusive and humankind is not likely to come to a point where all people hold the same to be true. But a creative and open attitude toward truth, and a respect and appreciation for all human beings, can open the human being to shining insights and to deep relationships which would never otherwise be a part of his or her experience. So, as Marty says, "This is never a comfortable vision" (to live creatively with pluralism), but it is a growing, developing one. It appears to be in accord with Moran's vision of religious development in which he claims that we need a theory of development that can encompass the religious diversity of our day. "Religious education is the name for the needed response in a radically and obviously pluralistic world."[10]

In order to live creatively with religious pluralism, a number of models have been proposed for education. Going beyond the dialogue approach discussed earlier, the most familiar strategy has been the class on world's religions, on history of religion, the Bible as literature, or philosophy of religion, at either the high-school or college level. Readers of this volume are no doubt familiar with such courses, so there is no need to describe them here. A syllabus developed by a Canadian school system states the purpose of such a course:

> "World Religions" introduces students to the fact that the spiritual nature of human beings is identified in virtually every culture in the world and that some form of religious life and expression runs like a thread throughout human history from the earliest days. Much of this

9. Marty, "This We Can Believe," p. 40.
10. Moran, *Religious Education Development,* pp. 12-13.

expression derives from the search for answers to questions about the meaning of life and the mysteries of nature. Religion and religious forms are investigated as one way in which societies have attempted to find answers to these fundamental questions and to interpret and respond to human experience.[11]

In a broader framework than classes Gabriel Moran describes "ecumenical education," but the goal appears to be the same. "The aim of ecumenical education is the same as education itself, namely, the lived truth of a humanized world."[12] He explains the ecumenical as referring to "a way of specifying or concretizing the truth by presenting the religious alternatives that life offers," and states his presumption that "questions of final meaning, symbolism, ritual, and claims for total commitment arise in every life. The intention . . . is not to prescribe that people must accept a religious belief and ritual but that this issue ought to be intelligently dealt with in education."

In discussing the religious educator's role in relation to cultural pluralism, Donald Miller proposes a new approach which focuses more on "form" than on "content." He claims that "the purpose of religious education is identity construction,"[13] so it is applicable to various religious contexts (Christian, Jewish, Muslim, and others). His thesis that the purpose of religious education is identity construction means that the "educative endeavor of the religious community is to nurture in individuals the formation of a unique and distinctive identity, one which faithfully represents the integrity and historical roots of the community of which one is a member." In a pluralistic society individuals choose the religious community with which they associate themselves, but within that community the goals of religious education are usually clear. The efforts of religious educators are aimed at enabling the individuals "to achieve an identity which, because of its attentions to questions of meaning and purpose, gives perspective and unity of life-plan to the multiple activities in which an individual engages."[14] In order to do this, religious educators must help the members of the community "to see the world through new eyes, the prisms through which one peers being the structures and symbols of one's religious tradition." Miller claims

---

11. See the syllabus of Toronto, Canada, *World's Religions.*

12. Gabriel Moran, *Design for Religion* (New York: Herder and Herder, 1971), p. 85.

13. Donald Miller, "Religious Education and Cultural Pluralism," *Religious Education* 74:4 (July-August, 1979), pp. 339-349.

14. Ibid., p. 344.

that within the religious community identity is structured on three levels: 1) Theoretical, "which encompasses the role of reason and the intellect in the life of a community." 2) Practical, "the dimension of worship and personal communion with the divine." 3) Sociological, "the web of interpersonal relations which are often summarized in procedural norms of various types." The formation of identity occurs on all three levels, so it becomes obvious that "religious education embraces the whole experience of religious life within community."[15]

FUTURE DIRECTIONS

Is it possible, after realizing the reality of religious pluralism in today's world and after examining the thinking of religious educators who are representative of various religious groups, to project some directions for the immediate future? Projecting toward the future is always a difficult and risky business, because it is impossible to know what unforeseeable events and problems may arise. Wars, in which the enemies are clearly divided religiously as well as politically, geographically, or economically, lend themselves to growing mistrust and misunderstanding. It is extremely difficult to bring about respect for the religious traditions and beliefs of another religious group in the midst of war with its propagandistic claims. However, the possibility for nuclear annihilation of earth's people may be more effective in establishing a climate for peace, reconciliation, and cooperation than any claims of democracy, socialism, or communism. On the other hand, natural cataclysms often bring people together across ideological lines. In the face of earthquakes, hurricanes, floods, and other disasters people work together for the good of human beings without thought of religious divisions. So it is impossible to foresee the tenor of the world ideological climate or what forces may hasten pluralism in various parts of the world, or hinder it in others. Nevertheless, as futurists attempt to do, some tentative suggestions for the direction of religious education in the immediate future in the Western world can be made, with recognition that events may intervene which will negate these suggestions.

First, for professional religious educators greater knowledge about education in other religions is imperative. The chapters in this book dealing with education in Islam, Buddhist education, and Hindu education are a beginning attempt to provide some of this knowledge for Jewish and Christian educators. More interchange is needed, and jour-

---

15. Ibid., p. 349.

nals like *Religious Education, Living Light, Jewish Education,* and magazines put out by denominations, religious agencies, and curriculum publishers are likely places for this interchange to take place. No doubt there are journals and magazines for educators in Islam, Buddhism, Hinduism, and other religions with which Jewish and Christian educators should become acquainted. Such interchange could draw the educators in these religions into a sharing of ideas on the development of theory and practice in religious education unprecedented in the history of the world. *The Journal of Ecumenical Studies* is one medium which shares across religious lines, but primarily it has served only Christians and Jews and has not served the needs of religious educators. Perhaps this should change, and religious educators of all religions might find this journal a helpful outlet for exchange of ideas.

A second direction is related to research. The studies of Olson, Fisher, Strober, and others on prejudice in curriculum materials have initiated a process which must be continued and expanded. With the awakening consciousness of religious prejudice and discrimination which has been taking place in the past twenty years, one wonders what is the present situation in curriculum materials and in other religious publications? Is there further change in the way Jews and Judaism are presented in Roman Catholic curriculum materials since Fisher's studies? What has happened to Protestant materials since 1972 when Strober did his study of Judaism in denominational materials? How are Muslims depicted in both Roman Catholic and Protestant curricula? How are Protestants, Roman Catholics, and Muslims described in Jewish materials—Reform, Conservative, Orthodox, and Reconstructionist? Are Buddhism, Hinduism, Taoism, Confucianism, and smaller groups handled at all in Protestant, Roman Catholic, Muslim, and Jewish materials? To look at the other side of the picture, do the materials published by Hindu, Buddhist, and other groups say anything about other religions in the community? If so, what attitudes are to be found there? Are there materials in English which can be shared with English-speaking religious educators? How are such minority religions as Christian Science, Mormon (Church of Jesus Christ of Latter Day Saints), Holiness groups, Unification Church, and many others handled? How do these groups speak of other religious groups? Is there recognition of racial minorities? Ethnic minorities? It is obvious that a great deal of research is needed before the problems can be identified and before the attitudes being fostered by curriculum materials become evident. Research is also needed on other publications which reach lay persons in parishes and congregations. Can such research be financed? Will religious educators be concerned enough to work at this pressing task?

Third, the work of educating for religious pluralism must be seen as a whole. At the present time it appears that the major educational effort in this area is allocated to colleges and universities, with structured courses in the backgrounds of religion. Theological seminaries, also, are expected to include courses on world religions, philosophy of religion, psychology of religion, sociology of religion, and the like, but local congregations are usually not regarded as educating for religious pluralism except perhaps the clergyperson is involved in dialogue, adult classes may include courses or lectures on various religions, and some denominational materials do include some lessons or units on other religions for children or youth. Usually these take the form of visits to a synagogue or having a rabbi come to a Christian class or group meeting. Denominations are thought to give leadership with resolutions and statements by prominent leaders, and sometimes to debate issues in assemblies or district meetings.

So much controversy exists about the role of the public school in relation to religion in the United States that only a few states have committed themselves to teaching about religion, though the British have experimented a great deal with teaching about religion in the schools and seem to be making some strides in the direction of greater understanding and respect among the students.

Very little attention has been paid to the home as perhaps the most influential institution in forming the attitudes of children and youth toward religious pluralism, and yet one of the major tenets of education, psychology, and sociology emphasizes the importance of the early years in a person's development. So perhaps one of the most urgent tasks for the future of religious education is to sort out the roles of each of these institutions in educating for religious pluralism.

Fourth, religious educators must be more involved in the dialogues and studies which are taking place. Since the clergy, denominational leaders, and heads of religious agencies appear to be the persons most often involved in dialogues between two religious groups, the unusual and exciting experience of these people cannot be adequately shared with the members of local parishes and congregations. This results in two educational efforts running parallel and not meshing into a unified program. If the clergy see themselves as the primary educators, then a unitary effort can be made, drawing other educational leaders (ministers, teachers, youth and adult group leaders, and the like) into a total program that continues dialogue at various levels and involves members of different groups, searches their own curriculum materials and resources for prejudicial statements or handling of scriptural materials, examines the language and ritual of the liturgy in relation to persons of other religions, arranges for interchanges and cooperative projects with other groups in the community, and in many other creative ways fosters religious pluralism. But rarely does this happen; so it appears that those persons—clergy and lay—whose primary responsibility is the educational work of the synagogue, church, temple, or mosque must become more involved in dialogical relationships in which their own consciousness is raised, so that they, in turn, can bring the adults, young people, and children to a new awareness of the religious situation in the community and of the wider concerns of the many religions in the world.

Fifth, an outgrowth of greater involvement in dialogue is the need for religious educators to think beyond dialogue as "the" method of education for religious pluralism and to find new and creative techniques. As in all other teaching, many approaches are possible—different times, places, types of experience, and techniques—so, too, in teaching for religious pluralism we have only begun to explore effective methods for providing thought-provoking and rich emotional experiences for our parishioners, which should lead to creativity on their parts and the development of many forms of education. It is impossible to project what those experiences may be, but it is evident that we have not started to make adequate use of world events, or local community events, or dig into the religious components of those events for purposes of understanding and developing relationships. There are films, television documentaries, video and audio cassettes, and other audio and visual forms rich with materials showing the human experiences of persons in different religions, as well as a great deal of knowledge about these groups. It is not at all easy for parishes and congregations to sort out the great amount of such resources, find the ones most suitable for their purposes, learn to judge them for quality, and arrange to have them at the proper time and place. This problem will never be solved, I think, until religious groups in a community band together to provide a media center where such resources can be collected and maintained. This may be done in connection with a college or university within the area, or by denominational offices cooperating for this purpose. It can rarely be done adequately by one religious group without violating the spirit of religious pluralism.

Probably nothing goes more deeply into the feelings and emotions of persons than a visit to another religious group during its service of worship, or liturgy. There is debate as to how fully a devotee of one religion can participate in the worship of another group, but however this controversy is resolved, the impact even of observing the worship experience of others is a deeply moving experience, and usually it raises many questions in the minds of the observers. However, the follow-up of such experiences is quite important for the education of the individual. How do one's questions get answered? What misunderstandings may be retained if such questions go unanswered? Do these experiences lead to other contacts?

Sixth, the chapters in this book presenting views of minority groups within a majority religion pose many questions regarding the role of religious education in both the minority and majority groups to bring about acceptance of and treatment of each other as equals. It often appears that members of a religious majority can relate to persons of completely different faiths more easily than to those of minorities within their own tradition. The tensions which have existed for nearly a century between more conservative and more liberal Protestants, for example, seem no nearer to solutions now than in the past and, as Grant Shockley rightly points out, the failure of white Protestants to accept black Protestants as equals is only further compounded by the theological spread from conservative to liberal within both groups. Further, the nearly complete lack of communication between Protestants and the Christian groups which Protestantism has spawned over the period of its history in the U.S.A. is a travesty on the spirit of Christianity. I am speaking of such groups as Christian Science, the Church of Jesus Christ of Latter-Day Saints (Mormons), the Unification Church, Jehovah's Witnesses, and other religions whose theological and social concepts are distinctive enough to set them apart from the main body of Protestantism. What does religious pluralism have to say about all of these religions and their relation to the larger Christian groups in a democratic society, as well as to the more exotic religions from other parts of the world?

Seventh, the description of education in Buddhism, Hinduism, and Islam all stress that the teachings regarding religious pluralism are inherent in the principles of the religion; that if the members of their religious communities live according to the concepts and ideals of the religion, then the ability to live with persons of other religious persuasions in a pluralistic society would be automatically cared for. These writers all insist that such mode of living is the educator's major concern. This belief holds, I think, for most of the religions of the world, which raises the question as to what attention should be given to overt education regarding other religions and what should be given to making clear the way of life implicit in one's own tradition. Is Donald Miller's assertion that the purpose of religious education is identity construction within one's own religious community a viable option for all religious education? The history of religion and religious education has not given much reason to hope that the teaching of one's own tradition without specific efforts to acquaint members of the religious community with other traditions will resolve the problems of religious pluralism.

CONCLUSION

In 1968, Kendig Cully concluded his work, *Does the Church Know How to Teach? An Ecumenical Inquiry,* by calling attention to the fact that the nonprofessional will hold an increasingly important place in ecumenical relationships as time goes on. He made the observation: "To date only a relatively small proportion of the memberships of Catholic and Protestant churches have been involved in authentic encounters with their counterparts. As ecumenical dialogue-action spreads more widely among the people, the church will have to face even more earnestly than it has done to date: Do we know how to teach?"[16] How much have things changed in the parishes and congregations (even the Roman Catholic and Protestant churches, which Cully was discussing) in these past twenty years? Will we ever learn "how to teach"?

---

16. Kendig B. Cully, ed., *Does the Church Know How to Teach? An Ecumenical Inquiry* (London: Macmillan, 1968), p. 351.

Contributors in Order of Presentation

NORMA H. THOMPSON, Professor Emerita, New York University, New York City

GABRIEL MORAN, Professor and Director, Program in Religious Education, New York University, New York City

JAMES MICHAEL LEE, Professor of Education, University of Alabama, Birmingham. Publisher, Religious Education Press

DAVID NG, Associate for Communication and Support, Presbyterian Church (USA)

GRANT S. SHOCKLEY, Professor of Christian Education and Director of Black Affairs, The Divinity School of Duke University, Durham, North Carolina

WILLIAM CLEMMONS, Professor of Christian Education, Southeastern Baptist Theological Seminary, Wake Forest, North Carolina

CONSTANCE TARASAR, Managing Editor, *The Orthodox Church,* and Lecturer in Religious Education, St. Vladimir's Orthodox Seminary, Yonkers, New York.

SHERRY H. BLUMBERG, Instructor in Education (Rabbinic Faculty), Hebrew Union College, New York City.

EUGENE B. BOROWITZ, Professor of Education and Jewish Religious Thought, Hebrew Union College, New York City

ABDULLAH MUHAMMAD KHOUJ, Director, The Islamic Center, Washington, D.C.

YOUNG BONG OH, Priest, Won Kak Sa Buddhist Temple, Salisbury Mills, New York

SUN YOUNG PARK, Dean for Academic Affairs, Dongguk University, Seoul, Korea

SWAMI TATHAGATHANANDA, Spiritual Leader, The Vedanta Society, New York City; a Senior Monk of the Ramakrishna Order in India

Index of Names

317

Index of Subjects